IRELAND'S ARCTIC SIEGE

The Big Freeze of 1947

KEVIN C. KEARNS ∾

Gill & Macmillan

Gill & Macmillan
Hume Avenue, Park West, Dublin 12
with associated companies throughout the world
www.gillmacmillan.ie

© Kevin C. Kearns 2011
978 07171 4863 9

Index compiled by Helen Litton
Cartography by Design Image
Typography design by Make Communication
Print origination by O'K Graphic Design, Dublin
Printed and bound in the UK by the MPG Books Group

This book is typeset in 11/13.5 pt Minion.

The paper used in this book comes from the wood pulp
of managed forests. For every tree felled, at least one
tree is planted, thereby renewing natural resources.

A CIP catalogue record for this book is available from the
British Library.

5 4

To Ella, my granddaughter
And to Tess, my pal
Their spirits so bright

The Author

Kevin C. Kearns, Ph.D., is a social historian and Professor Emeritus at the University of Northern Colorado. He has made 38 research trips to Ireland, a number of which were funded by the National Geographic Society. Of his ten books on Dublin, five have been bestsellers, most notably *Dublin Tenement Life* which was number one on the *Irish Times* bestseller list for many weeks. He now resides in the coastal village of Camden, Maine.

"*The blizzard took Dublin by surprise, with a 62 mile-an-hour wind behind it ... left drifts of up to five feet. Transport was almost paralysed ... telephone communications reduced to a tangle of torn wires and fallen poles.*"

(*Irish Times*, 3 February 1947)

"*To-day the Irish nation faces a national emergency as grave as any in its history. The people face the possibility of famine ... all because of the worst spell of winter weather in the country's history. This is a fight for survival.*"

(*Irish Independent*, 17 March 1947)

"*What did the Government do ... when people were cut away from help and lives were lost in the snow? They were not roused from their stupor. They sat snugly and smugly in Government Buildings and did nothing. It sounds unbelievable, yet it is true. They did nothing.*"

(*Sunday Independent*, 9 March 1947)

CONTENTS

ACKNOWLEDGMENTS

This book is based on extensive archival research and the gathering of oral history testimony from individuals who lived through the winter of 1946/47. There are, therefore, many persons to whom I am indebted. Simply put, without the Dublin City Library and Archive in Pearse Street my books could never be written. My deepest appreciation is extended to their superb staff, unfailingly professional and helpful, always welcoming and friendly, year after year, with special thanks to Dr Mary Clark, City Archivist, and Dr Máire Kennedy, Divisional Librarian, Special Collections.

My gratitude also goes to Erin O'Mahoney of Met Éireann, who agreeably dug through department files of 1947 for some dusty documents that were of great value in reconstructing the meteorological conditions of the winter months.

To all those whose oral testimonies are included in this book I owe a huge debt, for it is through their vivid recollections that this story truly comes alive. Their words and graphic descriptions give authenticity to events difficult for others to imagine. Appreciation also goes to Liam Cradden, secretary of Guinness Pensioners' Association, and Gerard Lovett, general secretary of the Garda Síochána Retired Members' Association, for assisting me in finding a number of important respondents. And to Gerry Creighton, retired operations manager of Dublin Zoo, who provided information about the impact of the severe weather on the animals. Three persons who possess truly remarkable memories deserve special mention: Tony Ruane, Máirín Johnston, and Una Shaw.

Particular gratitude is extended to Fergal Tobin, publishing director of Gill & Macmillan, and Deirdre Rennison Kunz, managing editor, patient shepherds once again through the exacting editorial process. Over the course of forging seven books together their critical eye, wise counsel and friendship have always been most comforting.

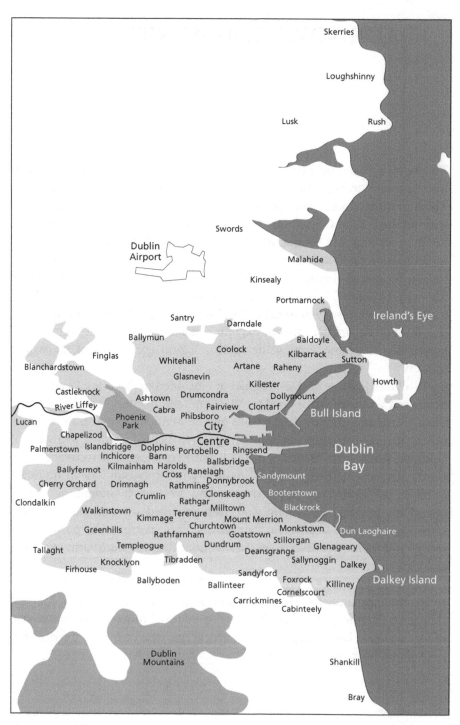

Figure 1: Dublin City Area

Figure 2: Map of Ireland

PROLOGUE

Snow seven feet deep in inland areas . . . at least one 50-foot drift near Glencree. The hamlet of Moneystown at Roundwood has been "lost" in the snow.

(*Irish Times*, 26 FEBRUARY 1947)

Unfortunately, it is true that people are to-day perishing from want and cold in this civilised city of ours!

(*Dublin Evening Mail*, 17 MARCH 1947)

People have begun to strip their houses of woodwork to make a fire.

(*Irish Independent*, 10 FEBRUARY 1947)

This story might have come from some Polar Expedition. It is almost unbelievable that such conditions could exist in Ireland.

(*Irish Times*, 13 MARCH 1947)

Unfathomable.

Beyond the living memory of the oldest of the old. Beyond tales passed down from great-great-grandparents. Beyond all human memory. A winter never like it before, or since.

An aberrant, "freakish" Arctic siege with ferocious blizzards that invaded the Emerald Isle and entombed it in snow and ice. Suffering and death. Inexplicable to meteorologists. "In an age of simpler faith," wrote the *Irish Times*, "it would have been said that the wrath of God was directed against Ireland."[1] If contrived by a novelist, it would scarcely be credible. A preposterous story—yet utterly true.

SUMMER AND AUTUMN, 1946

"You'll never get out of this county if you don't smarten up!" his mother told him. So Brian Kelly studiously followed her advice, spent five years in secondary school, and obtained his Leaving Certificate. At the age of twenty, in 1946, he joined the Garda Síochána, leaving behind his family's farm in Co. Donegal. He had bigger plans, for a more lively, adventurous future in bustling Dublin.

Only a few months after proudly putting on his Garda uniform he found himself bending over in a field, working from sunrise till sundown.

Many thousands of others, the likes of shop assistants, office workers, civil servants, factory workers and professionals, had also hardly anticipated spending late summer and autumn doing back-breaking manual work on a farm. But they enthusiastically volunteered. Nature had called them to duty. So had Dev.

The drenching rains of August and early September had inundated Ireland's farmland and threatened the harvest. Only a massive national harvest campaign, supported by hordes of city-dwellers, could save the crops. "De Valera *implored* city people to come out and help save the harvest," Brian Kelly recalls, "and we *did!*" He found himself working shoulder to shoulder with employees of Clery's department store and the Gresham Hotel—a stimulating social mixture, all motivated by practicality and patriotism.

With a favourable break in the weather, by October the "battle for the harvest" was won. But a smaller crop than usual meant food shortages ahead. And the frantic effort to salvage the harvest meant neglecting to cut and collect enough turf for the winter to compensate for diminished supplies of British coal.

On New Year's Eve, as Dubliners congregated exuberantly beneath Christ Church Cathedral, awaiting the toll of the great bells and the robust singing of "Auld Lang Syne," farmers and city-dwellers throughout the country gave thanks for the harvest and hoped for a better agricultural year ahead. And, with fuel supplies precariously low, prayed for a mild winter in the months to come.

JANUARY 1947
January entered timidly. The first twelve days were generally calm, with unseasonably mild temperatures. Sixteen-year-old Joe Kirwan, a bike messenger-boy from the Coombe, hoped the good weather would last. So did Eddie McGrane, a year older, as he and his pals in An Óige liked winter hiking in the Wicklow Mountains.

Around mid-month, weather developments far from Ireland conspired to end their good luck. A "persistent anti-cyclone" centred over northern Russia began shifting towards Scandinavia. At the same time a "very deep depression" about six hundred miles to the west of Ireland, along with "an associated vigorous trough," began moving eastwards, forming an atmospheric configuration that could potentially trigger violent weather, with fierce winds and extremely cold temperatures. Most Irish people, knowing little about "anti-cyclones" and "troughs," paid little heed to such information.

Seán Lemass, Minister for Industry and Commerce, understood the implications all too well. An onset of frigid, stormy winter weather could severely strain the country's limited supplies of fuel and food. On 1 January the *Irish Press* called the country's "supplies position . . . as bad as it was in the worst war years," explaining that, while the "scarcity of food will be acute" during the coming months, the "fuel shortage presents the graver problem."[2]

Four days later Lemass began the rationing of flour and bread, the result of a poor home crop and global wheat shortages.

On 19 January a "cold easterly regime set in," as the pressure distribution was dominated by anticyclones over both Scandinavia and Greenland, at times forming a continuous belt, while depressions followed tracks south of Ireland. The next day a cold north-easterly airflow invaded Ireland and Britain, bringing night frosts and intermittent snowfalls.

It was on the 24th that the "severe cold spell" began, as the incursion of Arctic air brought temperatures down to 5 and 10 degrees of frost—between 28 and 22 degrees Fahrenheit (-2 to $-6°c$). People bundled up, put a few extra lumps of coal or sods of turf on the fire, and waited for the cold snap to end.

There was a strange occurrence in Dublin on the morning of Sunday the 26th, at exactly 10:27. People in their homes and at mass felt a queer, quivering sensation. Children asked puzzled parents what it was. According to the seismograph at the Jesuit house of Rathfarnham Castle outside Dublin it was a "fairly large earthquake," which lasted sporadically until about noon.

Shortly thereafter, at 1:30 p.m., Dublin experienced its first real snowfall of the winter. The *Irish Times* welcomed it poetically as a "portion of heaven's swansdown white." It transformed the city's parks and squares into Christmas-card scenes, as adults strolled about admiringly and children gleefully tossed snowballs. "Wasn't snow wonderful!" everyone exulted.

On the night of Tuesday the 28th "winter tightened its grip," as the *Evening Herald* aptly put it. Meteorologists attributed it to the formation of the "Scandinavian anti-cyclone . . . regarded as a kind of western extension or outpost of the Siberian system."[3] As temperatures fell to 17 degrees ($-8°c$), Dubliners saw ice-floes the "size of hearth rugs" floating down the Liffey and ships in the port penanted with huge icicles. Newspapers published doctors' warnings not to "tempt Providence by going out without plenty of clothing." Shops did a rush trade in heavy coats, scarves, gloves, and boots, for those who could afford them. Ill-clad tenement-dwellers wore what they had.

As Dubliners were struggling through what the newspapers were calling the "Big Freeze," the messianic labour hero "Big Jim" Larkin lay dying in the Meath Hospital. It was the only topic of conversation besides the weather. Before dawn on 30 January the mercury stood at a bone-chilling 9 degrees Fahrenheit ($-13°c$), a colder temperature by several degrees than recorded that day in Antarctica.

The next night, "nature's refrigerator was switched down again," sinking to 7 degrees (−14°c), an "exceptional figure for this country," meteorologists confirmed.[4] With the brutal east wind slashing across the country bringing temperatures "drawn from the heart of Siberia," Irish people were experiencing a true wind-chilled cold that felt well below zero. A deep Arctic freeze.

Some five thousand miles from Ireland, Jerome Namias, a senior meteorologist with the us Weather Bureau, was tracking an expanding "hemispheric-wide aberration" that was producing "most peculiar weather" in parts of Europe.[5] Using the most advanced meteorological instruments in the world, he "watched it grow" as the normal polar air mass pushed far south of its usual domain. Ordinarily the polar region was covered in winter, with a cap of cold air reaching down to latitude 60°N (southern Norway and Leningrad). This winter, he discovered, the "polar air mass was much larger," drawing polar air all the way down to latitude 45°N, well south of Ireland and Britain. Furthermore, he determined that this January the "prevailing Westerlies failed" in their regular role of moderating normally temperate Ireland, leaving it in a vulnerable position to become "frozen and snowbound." Indeed by late January he concluded that Ireland was already "getting Siberian weather."

His greatest concern was with the weather zone where "along with the cold there could be a belt of storms where the east and west winds meet." In these "collision" areas, powerful air masses met and battled for supremacy, with the potential to generate violent weather. Possibly raging blizzards. Throughout February he would watch it with fascination and mounting concern.

FEBRUARY

On Saturday 1 February, Captain S. G. Hickman and his crew of thirty-five on the *Irish Plane*, a 7,250-ton vessel, were on a routine voyage from Swansea to Cork with a cargo of coal. Seas were mildly choppy, nothing unusual.

It was not until 1948 that the Meteorological Service assumed responsibility for the weather forecasts broadcast by Radio Éireann, up to then provided from London; and it was not until 1952 that it began to supply forecasts to the newspapers. Instead the papers often relied on their own "weather experts"—"weather prophets" some preferred to call them, with mild derision. On this weekend they had forecast no storms.

Unknown to those on land and at sea, during the afternoon there began a mighty struggle between two behemoths: warm, moisture-laden clouds and winds from the south-west off the Atlantic, and powerful, invading, frigid east winds from the high-pressure zone to the anti-cyclonic north. In such a confrontation the colliding systems do not intermingle, as the high pressure to the north and east of Britain and Ireland provided a block to the usual movement of depressions. As a consequence, the warm, moist air is forced to rise over the denser cold air, until it can no longer hold its moisture, creating a classic condition for potential violent, blizzardy weather.

Some time around 8 p.m., with winds raging at 60 miles per hour, the *Irish Plane*, fighting mountainous seas, "ran into the hurricane," as one crew member put it. It was driven aground about fifty yards from a steep cliff. Meanwhile in Dublin people were flocking to cinemas, theatres and dancehalls, unconcerned as "a gale steadily rose" and temperatures fell. W. H. Booth and J. O'Brien, *Sunday Independent* van-drivers, were expecting a normal night of deliveries to distant counties.

At 1:30 a.m. on Sunday morning the blizzard began. By 2:30 snow was falling at a rate of more than an inch per hour, sticking thickly to every surface. As "the blizzard raged during the night," in the words of the *Irish Independent*, the snow "plastered against walls and trees as firmly as if it were put on with a trowel."[6] Before long Booth and O'Brien found themselves marooned in a deep snowdrift in Co. Kilkenny. Dubliners awoke on Sunday morning flabbergasted to "find the city bogged in snow," drifts reaching five to six feet deep. Transport was paralysed, and telephone and telegraph communications in a shambles. Much of the ESB's electricity system was knocked out, creating a general condition of "havoc" in the capital.

Life in the countryside was brought to a standstill as heavy snow and high drifts blanketed the landscape, closing roads and confining people to their houses. In Co. Carlow, Jim Nolan had gone to bed on Saturday night with the sound of the wind screaming, "as if it was coming from some big blower in the heavens."[7] When he arose next morning, "I could not believe my eyes—all I could see were the tops of trees covered by huge drifts."

A "surprise blizzard," the *Irish Times* called it.

In an editorial headed "Snow menace" the *Evening Herald* reasoned that a blizzard's "visitation, however crippling, is comparatively rare" in Ireland, emphasising that "in these latitudes we are not equipped for this Arctic weather."[8] Furthermore, "our cities and towns have been treated to a demonstration of their helplessness" in the face of such an onslaught. Warning both Government and public against ill-preparedness, the newspaper asserted: "Our methods of clearing away the menace are almost pre-historic manual labour." Fortunately, it was considered very unlikely that another such blizzard would strike for many years, even decades.

On 8 February newspapers printed alarming news. The headline in the *Evening Herald* read: "Economic Dunkirk facing Britain." With British ports, railways, roads and mines snowed under and frozen shut, the country's coal industry was brought to a halt. The Minister of Fuel and Power announced a ban on coal exports, including exports to Ireland. The Irish Government, industrialists and public were thunderstruck. A CIE spokesman promptly declared that the country's railway system faced a "complete paralysis within a very short time." Dublin Gas Company called it "disastrous," while P. L. McEvoy, president of the Federation of Irish Manufacturers, exploded: "This is the last straw!"

———

With no forecast for bad weather, on the weekend of 8/9 February another fierce storm unexpectedly erupted. By 10 o'clock on Saturday night the eastern and southern seas were roiling, as "a gale was blowing wildly, driving seas high above ships caught out in the open."

The *Ary*, a 642-ton collier, was headed from Port Talbot in Wales to Waterford with coal loaded before the ban. At 10:45 the vessel was listing dangerously, and the captain ordered his seventeen crewmen to take to their two lifeboats. They were left to drift helplessly, with no oars, sails, food, or water, in towering seas and pitch-blackness.

By Sunday morning the country was again besieged by "another all-day blizzard," leaving a wide swath of destruction and mayhem as transport and communication systems were disrupted or destroyed. The midlands, Co. Dublin and the Wicklow Mountains were battered worst, with drifts of eight feet and higher reported. Roundwood, the highest village in Ireland, was cut off by drifts ten to twelve feet high, as was Glencree, where the Irish Red Cross Society and French Sisters of Charity were using the old barrack buildings as a temporary home for some forty-six German and Polish war orphans. They had supplies of food and fuel to last for a month—of normal winter conditions.

The next day Lemass declared to Dáil Éireann that the country was facing a "first-class crisis in domestic fuel . . . Turf is sodden, useless as fuel."[9] With disquieting candour, he summed up by saying that there was "nothing to do about it . . . We can pray for good weather."

Dubliners, now frantic to find any turf, "literally invaded turf depots," reported the *Irish Times*, "as they pushed and shoved their way forward."[10] A black market thrived as profiteers exploited the poorer classes. As scant coal supplies simultaneously dwindled, Dublin Gas Company was forced to slice daily usage from 8½ hours to 5. Housewives gasped. Even the internal heating of the GPO was discontinued, and staff members wrapped up in coats and scarves. In striking contrast, the members of Dáil Éireann, heated by abundant supplies of oil, were warm and snug in their privileged quarters.

Meanwhile newspapers carried word from islands off the south and west coasts that desperate inhabitants were forced to strip wood from their cottages, even burn furniture, to survive the cold. Dubliners found it hard to imagine.

On the 12th one crewman from the ill-fated *Ary* washed ashore in his lifeboat along the Waterford coast—the only survivor. The blizzard had claimed the lives of sixteen of the seventeen seamen.

In the heart of Dublin a number of schools were going unheated or being shut down because of a lack of fuel. Alderman Alfie Byrne was furious, regarding it as scandalous. Irate parents wrote letters to the newspapers, calling conditions "uncivilised." One man asserted: "It's *inhumane*! Why risk their lives with colds and flu?" In his letter to the *Dublin Evening Mail*, A. T. Jordan pithily stated: "I'm sure that the Dáil would soon adjourn under similar circumstances."

———

By the 14th, St Valentine's Day, there was little to feel cheerful about. The bitter cold, blizzards, fuel and food crises had diminished the quality of Irish life. As one citizen expressed it, they were "days of gloom and muddledom *in excelsis*."[11] That evening, as patrons streamed out of the Capitol Cinema in Prince's Street, having just seen *Our Vines Have Tender Grapes*, starring Margaret O'Brien, they were met with yet another depressing reality. The ESB's new ban on all signs and display lighting had just gone into effect. The customary brilliance of O'Connell Street and College Green was dimmed dismally. A pall fell over the city.

That week came the news of the first blizzard deaths on land, those of 65-year-old John Kelly of Glendalough and sixteen-year-old Charles James Healy of Co. Leitrim. Death by exposure during a blizzard was insidious, cruel. Prolonged. Slowly losing life from sub-freezing temperatures, hypothermia, exhaustion, stretching over hours of physical pain and mental torment.

By the third week of February the elderly and poor in particular were suffering, and some perishing, from cold and hunger and sickness. With meagre funds, many were sacrificing food for a few extra sods of wet turf. They were increasingly susceptible to an unbridled "influenza epidemic" sweeping the city, knocking off their feet even tens of thousands of younger, healthier citizens. On the 19th the *Irish Times* published shocking news: "The death rate in Dublin has more than doubled since the beginning of the cold weather ... Undertakers say they were never so busy."[12] Hospitals, undertakers and mortuaries could barely handle the demands upon them. From other parts of the country came similar reports of death rates doubling and trebling. Coffined bodies were being stored, waiting for the ground to thaw for a proper burial, or placed in temporary shallow "snow pits."

Dublin's tenement-dwellers were dying at the highest rate. There were documented cases of people actually starving to death in the heart of the city. One distressed citizen wrote to the *Irish Independent*: "Our Government are allowing the poor of this country to starve . . . Many of them are dying of slow starvation."[13] One miserable, frail old woman confessed that "death would be a merciful release."

As the startling death rates were being publicised, newspapers confirmed that many thousands of Dubliners, not only in the poor city centre but in the suburbs as well, were now forced to strip woodwork from their homes and even burn furniture for heat.

At Dublin Zoo the keepers revealed that "animals are suffering much from the cold," as they worked through the nights trying to keep them warm and alive. Some had already been lost. Tropical birds, reptiles and monkeys were at the greatest risk. Some snakes were "so badly frozen that they had to be thawed out," a tedious process of slowly bathing them in warm water.

———

By now, Dublin's weather "experts" were targets more of scorn than of derision, having failed completely to predict both blizzards. Lives had been lost. On the 20th the *Irish Times* reported that its weather experts definitely saw the winter weather nearing its end. Readers were elated on seeing the headline: "Experts say snow has gone."

Scarcely thirty-six hours later "King Winter returned to battle with renewed vigour . . . in an onslaught which caused general paralysis."[14] A ferocious two-day blizzard ripped across the country, piling up several feet of new snow. On the road from Glencree to the Sally Gap there were now drifts of ten to sixteen feet, as high as a double-deck bus, and Co. Wicklow villages were completely isolated from the outside world.

What distinguished the third blizzard from the previous two was that at one point it evolved into what the *Irish Press* called an "ice blizzard." As temperatures dropped, a sleety snow became crystallised, turning Dublin into a glazed "skating rink." Roads and pathways became treacherous. Vehicles skidded out of control as brakes were rendered useless. Pedestrians and horses fell and were injured. The *Sunday Independent* dubbed it the "night of mishaps," resulting in the "biggest crop of accidents due to snow and frost" in living memory. Ambulance bells rang incessantly, clearing the way for victims with fractured limbs, broken shoulders and backs, and head injuries. Like a war zone, "hospitals presented a typical 'behind the lines' scene," trying to cope.[15]

In the countryside, farmers despairingly saw their sheep and cattle trapped in drifts, dying or dead. In places where the snow was chest-high or shoulder-deep, farmers "did not dare to check on their animals sunk in the snowy morass." Some older residents of Co. Wicklow were saying there would "be no more sheep left alive."

By the time the third blizzard abated, the wicked winter had an official name: "King Winter." The enemy.

———

On the Monday following the blizzard CIE announced that passenger services on the main railway lines were being "brought to a standstill." Furthermore, unless coal supplies became available "very soon" the entire system would have to close down. The crisis was declared "unparalleled in the history of Irish Railways."[16]

People felt frustration and strain because of the weather, along with disenchantment over the inept and passive role of the authorities, who had failed to assist during one crisis after another. During the last week of February there was a dam-burst of criticism, directed at the Government and weather forecasters. Both press and public believed there were many actions the Government could, and should, have taken. "The Army should have been utilised in this serious crisis," charged the *Dublin Evening Mail*, "but the Government is too high and mighty to listen to suggestions from anybody."[17] Fine Gael put forward a motion in the Dáil condemning the unconscionable failure of the Government to respond to the worsening weather and the fuel and food shortages. It would not even provide food kitchens requested for the hungry. The *Irish Independent* contended:

> The Government cannot be blamed for the abnormal weather, or for the collapse of the British coal industry. What the Government must be held responsible for is the utter inactivity shown during the past month.[18]

As for the incompetence and blundering of the weather experts, now viewed as pariahs rather than prophets, the *Dublin Evening Mail* opined that they should be thankful they are "living in a very tolerant country—in some countries they would be put to death as enemies of the people."[19]

About midday on 24 February a cable from Russia had Dublin's "weather experts" buzzing over news that Moscow's temperature had reached 33 degrees (1°c) by 8 a.m., with scattered rain. This created a "meteorological hubbub," which prompted some prognosticators to conclude that the warmer weather in Russia "may at last indicate that Europe's icy spell is ending." The *Irish Independent* blared the good news: "Hopes for a break in cold spell."

That afternoon the *Evening Herald* predicted that Tuesday the 25th would be a dandy day, with "fine weather . . . moderate winds . . . good bright periods." Around the country, spirits rose.

——

In the middle of the night of 24/25 February the storm slammed into Ireland with meteoric impact. Under the cover of darkness it churned across the landscape like some giant locomotive. By 3 a.m. the snow was so dense that "visibility was reduced almost to nil," accumulating inches per hour. A replica of the other blizzards—only far mightier.

Early on Tuesday morning an ESB spokesman revealed that damage to the major trunk lines was so "very much worse" than with the previous blizzards that "conditions beggar description." In like manner, Post Office officials stated that their "*entire* telephone trunk line" was so badly torn asunder that "communications are in chaos." People around the country were cut off from communicating with one another and with the outside world. In the capital, emergency services—hospitals, doctors, fire brigade, ambulances, Garda stations—were unreachable. City life was brought to a halt. Legislators living in the suburbs and outside counties were stranded, with 131 of the combined Dáil and Seanad membership of 198 absent that day.

The countryside was smothered. Three to six feet of new snow atop that already embedded. In parts of the midlands, Connacht and Co. Wicklow drifts of twenty feet were common. When Christy Wynne awoke in Boyle, Co. Roscommon, everything had "disappeared under a huge blanket of snow . . . There were drifts fifteen feet high. The town looked like a lost village in Siberia."[20] The reliable *Irish Times* would verify at least one "50-foot drift near Glencree," and that the "hamlet of Moneystown at Roundwood has been 'lost' in the snow."

Landscapes were wildly and weirdly transformed by the heavy snow and drifting caused by gale-force winds. A "white desert," one person called it; to another it was a "white wilderness." Unknown. Forbidding. Entire animal herds had simply vanished. Some farmers barely recognised their own strangely distorted land. In Co. Sligo, Thomas Crosby found that the freezing temperatures had "solidified the surface, and it was possible to walk over submerged trees."[21] Scenes out of a fantasy world, or science fiction. Amidst the tortured terrain, an unknown number of people were missing and dead.

People were calling the monstrous blizzard the "Big Snow." The *Dublin Evening Mail* identified it as the "white enemy." In after years old-timers would remember it as the "daddy of them all."

——

CIE bore the greatest burden of the blizzard calamity. Provincial buses were stranded in massive snowdrifts on country roads with marooned, frightened passengers. Trains were blocked on their tracks, some derailed. CIE workers were trained to provide a transport service, not to act as rescuers in an Arctic blizzard. Yet that was the role suddenly thrust upon them. As superintendents hurriedly organised rescue squads, they expressed fears that their own men "risked being marooned in 'no man's land' . . . in drifts of snow up to ten feet."[22]

With the terrain disguised by the massive blanket of snow and crystallised ice layers, the rescue crews forged blindly into unknown territory. In the words of one rescuer, the "western world beyond Longford was just a snow-covered mystery—as to the rest of the west north of Galway and south of Sligo, all was silent."[23] Upon entering the snowy wilds of Connacht one member of a CIE convoy, Leslie Luke, exclaimed that he could compare it only to what he "imagined the snow-covered steppes of Siberia to be like." All along the way they heard "fantastic rumours about the size of drifts . . . buses marooned with passengers said to be starving."[24]

While CIE crews operated as "first-responders" in the blizzard's wake, in every county "pick and shovel" gangs of volunteers were being organised. They ranged from a dozen or so men to nearly eight hundred in Co. Wicklow. Newspapers named them the "snow armies," which quickly caught on with the public, who liked the military parlance of armies that "attacked" snowdrifts on the "front lines of the battle." The country was even divided into the "Western Front" and the "Eastern Front." Their "weapons" were rudimentary: shovels, picks, hatchets, ropes, chains, pneumatic drills, planks, and food rations for several days' duty. When CIE squads and snow armies pushed far west into the area of the Twelve Pins and Maumturk Mountains they encountered a new enemy: avalanches, which blocked roads and trapped vehicles.

On their heels followed smaller rescue sorties, seeking to find and relieve people trapped in their own houses, some confined for weeks and now without food or fuel. In Connacht they "stopped at a snowed-up cottage and found the family in a stupor, without food or heat, unable to move."[25] Many houses were snowed up to their roof and chimney peak. In one instance the rescuer "found himself looking down a cottage chimney—the only means of communication left to the inmates"—an apt term for those so imprisoned.

After several days favourable to rescue efforts the weather again deteriorated on 3/4 March. With winds reaching gale force, another blizzard struck. This one smashed the south of the country the hardest, and "Dublin escaped the full force of the blizzard," at least in snowfall. However, only nine miles off Dublin the violent winds drove the *Bolivar,* a Norwegian ship on its first voyage, into the Kish Buoy, where it broke in two. Its crew and passengers, among whom was Admiral Lord Mountevans, one of Britain's most decorated war heroes, were rescued by daring life-saving crews, depriving "King Winter" of more victims.

By the first week of March the inhabitants of Co. Wicklow's highlands were in dire need of food, fuel, and medical assistance; as the *Irish Times* headline read, "Wicklow conditions desperate." There was particular fear for the welfare of residents of Roundwood and the orphans and nuns at Glencree.

With improved weather, 6 March was designated "D-Day" by the rescue authorities for a frontal attack on the snow and ice barriers isolating residents. Two powerful machines had been secured for the operation, one a "trac-tractor," with caterpillar tracks, powered by a diesel engine, the other a converted 12-ton tank conveyor fitted with a large snow-plough.

Meanwhile the Red Cross Society announced that it was making plans for an emergency airlift to "drop food and medicine from planes to those cut off from the outside world." Special containers had been rushed from London, similar to those used by the RAF for parachuting supplies.

After a two-day assault with battalions of men and machines, smashing and gouging their way through towering snowdrifts and glaciated ice barriers, the isolated villagers were liberated. As local crowds cheered their arrival, one elderly resident blurted: "It has been the blackest five weeks in the history of the district." The following morning the Red Cross Society announced that it was cancelling plans for the airlift.

In the week following the great blizzard, rescue crews discovered a number of bodies embedded in the snow, victims of exposure. Cos. Sligo and Mayo suffered "triple deaths." People had died from exposure, drowning, road accidents, sea disasters, influenza, and hunger; the elderly succumbed to multiple causes. Yet there was no central Government agency recording the myriad weather-related deaths nationally. No toll of the dead was being chronicled for history.

––––––

Early March was a period of profound inquiry. After the forty-second consecutive day of Arctic temperatures and five blizzards, public endurance and tolerance were nearly exhausted. In an editorial, the *Irish Press* acknowledged the pervasive gloom and discontent weighing upon the spirits of the people:

> "Now is the winter of our discontent . . ." One is very sure about the discontent—nature is now only a graven image of herself. The days are steely; the things we love are petrified. The east is purple-cold. There is a

skin of snow on the ground; only once in three weeks have we seen the stars.[26]

"King Winter" was now spoken of and written about by public, press and even clergy as evil, sinister, wicked. "The blizzards have been fierce and malevolent," wrote the *Sunday Independent*; "the whole character of the weather is implacable."[27] Newspapers were depicting alarming scenarios about a "new Ice Age" on the way.

People were seeking answers. What was causing it? Man, nature, God, fate? Was there some *meaning* behind it?

Ireland's weather experts remained perplexed, admitting that "there is no parallel for the weather of the past February . . . It was a freakish month. There was no accounting for it." If weather analysts were befuddled, ordinary citizens had their own hypotheses. As the *Dublin Evening Mail* put it, six weeks of horrific weather is "permitting theorists to air their views freely." The topic fuelled conversation in every circle. The most prevalent ideas, with assorted twists, concerned sunspots, atomic bomb radiation, planet misalignment, Gulf Stream disruption—and God's wrath.

Man's wrath was by now directed chiefly against the Government. Apart from a few token gestures, over the six-week crisis period the Government had blatantly neglected to assist needy and suffering citizens, prompting the *Sunday Independent* on 9 March to level a scathing indictment:

> The glorious isolation of the Members of the Government . . . when people were cut away from help and lives were lost in the snow . . . they were not roused from their stupor. What did the Government do? Sat snugly and smugly in Government buildings and did nothing.
>
> It sounds unbelievable, yet it is true. They did nothing.[28]

That night, for the first time in six weeks, the mercury did not fall below 32 degrees (0°c). The next day the "first general thaw set in," accompanied by a moderate *west* wind. On Tuesday 11 March headlines switched from blizzards to the question of spring tillage. Would there even *be* a spring ploughing and sowing? Immediately, a "tillage crisis" was declared. Some 2½ million acres needed to be cultivated in order to feed the country. Tillage was already five to six weeks behind schedule. It seemed an impossible task.

———

As the anti-cyclonic regime from Russia to Greenland finally dissipated and the polar air mass retreated northwards, Ireland's weather gradually returned to normal, bringing warmer temperatures, more sunshine, and continuing thaw. Rain instead of snow. Then—*heavy* rains.

The St Patrick's Day weekend of 15–17 March brought a stunning reversal of weather conditions. Torrential rains driven by winds of 60 to 65 miles per hour lashed the country. Combined with much warmer temperatures, this triggered a colossal "quick thaw" of the country's massive snow-pack. The hurricane-like storm created huge volumes of water as rivers overflowed, inundating farmland under three and four feet of water. "Throughout the four Provinces the land is lying deep in swirling waters," reported one newspaper. "The carcases of sheep and cattle are floating down swollen rivers."[29]

Human bodies were found as well.

Farmers despaired. As one farmer from Lusk, Co. Dublin, plaintively muttered, "the soil is nothing better than slop now." It was hardly possible to envisage tillage, crops, a harvest. Even the dainty shamrock, ruined by the weather, was in short supply on St Patrick's Day, going on the black market for the first time ever. Only one in ten Dubliners could afford shamrock—one of winter's last cruel indignities.

Dublin was swamped. Streets became streams, with shops and houses flooded, people having to scramble up stairs as furniture floated around below. In hilly suburbs like Howth the soil became so saturated and destabilised that landslides occurred and "washed away thousands of tons of cliff face."

On St Patrick's Day the *Irish Independent* declared that the country faced a "national emergency as grave as any in its history . . . The people face famine . . . This is a fight for survival."[30] Newspapers printed apocalyptic warnings of famine, hunger, death. With food rations already tight, and the prospect of a small harvest, or none, people were fearful. The *Dublin Evening Mail* confirmed that "people are to-day perishing from want and cold in this civilised city of ours."

———

Providentially—or so it seemed—the morning following St Patrick's Day "dawned bright and clear . . . with warm sunshine," accompanied by a strong south-west wind that "gave promise of drying the land." Now, wrote the *Irish Times*, it all came down to a "race against time."

A vigorous national "tillage campaign" was launched. Ireland's six thousand tractors were fitted with lamps and ran all day long and throughout the night, with relays of drivers. As days went by, the good weather held. On 22 March the temperature climbed into the 70s, with radiant sunshine and drying winds. Floodwaters receded, and the land dried at a faster rate than expected. By the 24th, tillage was well under way in most counties. People credited St Patrick for "answered prayers." A miracle, many were calling it.

Meanwhile the British authorities announced that, owing to the remarkably improved weather, the "movement of coal generally is now returning to normal." The 28th of March was the eleventh consecutive near-perfect day for the tillage drive. Life seemed to be turning around.

On 3 April the *Irish Independent* conjectured that "the fate of the vital spring crops is now hanging precariously in the balance" and noted that April would be "the last lap in the grim race against time."[31] By the second week of April tillage was declared to be in "full swing." The following week the British coal ban was lifted, and Dublin began receiving 11,000 tons a week.

The second day of May saw the country's last frost occur, nailing King Winter's coffin shut. Shortly thereafter the *Irish Independent* proclaimed: "Once again, the farmers, under Providence, saved the country."[32]

The first day of June arrived with scorching sunshine and a temperature of 84 degrees (29°c). "Flaming June burst forth in all its fullness," exclaimed the *Irish Times*. The summer turned out to be the best in living memory, bar none. Gloriously sunny, hot, and dry. "That was the greatest summer we ever had," vouches Seán Whelan; "it was *fabulous!*" Everyone says the same. It wasn't hyperbole: the meteorological records at the National Botanic Gardens in Glasnevin confirmed "a memorable heat wave in the summer . . . The month of August was the best in 80 years of record keeping . . . record sunshine."

1947. The worst winter in Irish history, followed by the best summer in living memory.

————

On 24 December, as 1947 drew to its close, the *Irish Press* was reflective in its annual Christmas message:

> We in this country have, through the mercy of Providence, escaped the worst disasters of the times—hunger, freezing, real famine.[33]

Not all escaped. Exactly how many people perished during the winter months from direct and indirect weather-related causes will never be known. However, considering the dramatically inflated mortality rates throughout both urban and rural Ireland, along with the considerable number of blizzard deaths, the number is surely in the hundreds. The general population felt a collective sense of survival. "When you look back on it now," says Mary Dunne, "you think, sure, we *were* survivors!"

One year later Gordon Manley, a distinguished member of Britain's Royal Meteorological Society, presented a paper at the society's meeting entitled "Looking Back at Last Winter—February 1947: Its Place in Meteorological

History." It pertained specifically to the unprecedented weather in Britain and Ireland. Following his address he informed his audience that "some time must always elapse before a full account can be compiled of a 'historic' spell of weather." However, on the basis of existing historical meteorological information it was his conclusion that the winter of 1946/47 was "so exceptionally memorable" that it defied comparison with previous terrible winters. What made it unique, he explained, was the *combination* of events and their *prolonged* character: freezing temperatures, accumulation of snow, depth of drifts, wind velocities, violence of blizzards, number of sunless days. Nothing like it had been documented in the scientific annals of meteorology in the modern age.

In 1952 Manley, who remained fascinated with the bizarre winter of 1946/47, drew upon more complete meteorological data to arrive at the astonishing conclusion that "an almost exact working model of the conditions of the Ice Age can be seen in the events" of 1947 in Britain and Ireland:

> We can see why the limit of the ice sheet in one glaciation almost reached the Thames . . . For thousands of years the battle between tropical and Polar air was repeatedly fought over southern England.[34]

As it turned out, newspapers and weather experts who claimed that Ireland was experiencing a "little Ice Age" may not have been far wrong.

Though Manley considered the brutal winter to be "exceptionally memorable," would it be *retained* in human memory as time passed? In the *Irish Press* of 22 March 1947 Ora Kilroe wrote prophetically:

> We'll talk of it while this generation lasts and in the next one too, for by that time it will have become a legend. A legend of destructive ferocity for which even the oldest of the old people can find no equal in their long memories.[35]

But what of generations thereafter?

Over the next half century those who had lived through the experience talked of it frequently at first, especially when another winter was approaching. Often with trepidation. As Carmel Byrne tells it, "it was talked about in later years . . . 'Oh, please God we *won't* get another winter like that in 1947!'" Many survivors were haunted by such a fear, remembering it in almost Biblical terms: the onslaught of Arctic cold, blizzards, freezing, hunger, death, floods, and threat of famine.

As the decades passed it gradually found its place in oral history and folklore, spoken of from time to time in homes and pubs, on farms, within families passed down to children and grandchildren, as Jim Maloney explains:

It was talked about for years and years, in the public houses . . . and any place else. Oh, the old men'd be talking about it. And it went from father to son and so on. Now I have two sons and a daughter and, oh, I've told them about the Big Snow, all right, and how we coped and got on. So it was passed down.

By the end of the century, however, those who had personally experienced that most horrid of winters had either passed away or grown old. Their first-hand stories were fading away. In the twenty-first century, younger generations caught up in the frenetic, high-tech life had little interest in gloomy tales of grandparents about "hard times" and "harsh winters." In 2008, after the passing of two-thirds of a century, survivors expressed concern that their experience would soon be forgotten. Most were now in their late seventies, or eighties and nineties, their oral history fast vanishing.

After sixty-two years, still no book had been written on this epic event in Irish history. An unprecedented catastrophe not chronicled by scholars for future generations. A glaring omission in the country's historical literature.

At eighty years of age, Joe Kirwan has had plenty of time to reflect on the winter of 1946/47. How at the age of sixteen he suffered through it on his messenger bike, falling on icy cobblestones, once nearly losing his legs beneath a tram. In his opinion, a winter beyond the imagination of anyone who hadn't lived through it. With so few survivors remaining to tell the story, he's baffled why no book had been written on so tragic an event: "It should be *written* about, for posterity! But you've got to talk to people who experienced it." And it is important to do so, for, as the *Irish Press* affirms, "there are heroes in this winter saga."[36]

Such a book is best written as a narrative history in which natural events and human experiences are intimately intertwined, allowing survivors to tell, with vivid immediacy and often emotion, of their fears and reactions at critical moments. In this sense it is a historical drama, both suspenseful and inspiring, a tale of human suffering, endurance, death. Authentic courage and heroism. Faith. Ultimate survival. As the *Irish Times* wrote on 13 March 1947, "this story might have come from some Polar Expedition . . . It is almost unbelievable that such conditions could exist in Ireland."[37] Some sixty-three years later, Una Shaw agrees:

I know it sounds like the Dickensian days, but people today can't possibly imagine just how bad it was! How horrifying to be at the mercy of nature.

Chapter 1 ∾

BATTLE FOR THE HARVEST (1946)

Nothing is of greater urgency than to save what remains of the harvest and turf . . . if our people are not to be hungry and cold during the winter. If calamity is not prevented it will bring suffering into every home.

(*Irish Independent,* 6 SEPTEMBER 1947)

My older sister and my father, they volunteered to help the farmers. It was an awful time . . . and if they hadn't saved the harvest there would have been a famine!

(UNA SHAW, 78)

We'd go off in the army lorries down the country to help take in the wheat. Out in the fields, they showed us what to do. We loved it! And coming back we'd have a singsong.

(AGNES DALY, 81)

AUGUST BANK HOLIDAY, 1946

Weather was on everyone's mind. It was the week of the August bank holiday, and most Dubliners had outdoor plans of one sort or another. The gift of good weather ensured a glorious week, while rain would bring gloom and disappointment. Early August was always dicey.

On the morning of Saturday 3 August sixteen-year-old Annie Gahan awoke early in her tenement dwelling in Francis Street in the Liberties. She needed to help her mother, one of Dublin's storied street dealers, to prepare for a day of selling at the Baldoyle Races. "She had a tea tent and sold tea, sandwiches, and cake. I helped her doing it for as long as I can remember." In good weather, throngs descended on the racecourse and spent freely. Those enjoying a lucky day with the horses might press a few pence or even a shilling into her palm. A few coins could get her into the local cinema, this week showing the rousing western *Don't Fence Me In,* starring Roy Rogers, one of her favourites.

As she helped her mother make mounds of sandwiches she peered out the window at the grey, sullen clouds settling over the rooftops. On dismal, soggy days spectators didn't buy as much at her mother's tent. She'd keep her fingers crossed for decent weather.

Foul weather threatened holiday plans for thousands of Dubliners. When a light summer rain began falling at about 10 a.m. many fretted. However, by 11:30 it was apparent that most had decided to proceed with their outings, as hordes of cyclists, hikers and motorists "hoping for the best" were seen heading out of the city. Scores of others were preparing to visit seaside resorts, sports events or Dublin Zoo or to enjoy a picnic in the Phoenix Park.

By noon a steady shower fell along the east coast. Undaunted, people stood in long queues waiting for buses, trams and trains to take them to their holiday destination. With umbrellas popped up and picnic baskets in hand, they were in cheerful spirits. Meanwhile down at the docks the Brazilian ship *Cometa* was unloading hundreds of cases of oranges. During the war years Dubliners rarely saw an orange, a lemon, or a banana. As dealers wheeled their barrows of oranges through the streets the Dublin air was suffused with what one reporter called the sweet "aroma of the golden fruit," enticing those standing in queues or milling about the city centre.

In addition to the hugely popular Baldoyle Races, two other holiday events were the dog show at Monkstown and the Blackrock swimming championships. This year the dog show was attracting record numbers of entries and spectators. The English springer spaniel Tania, proudly owned by C. S. Dorrity, would trot off with the ribbon for the highest honours.

As swimmers were competing for awards at Blackrock, ordinary bathers at Dublin's seaside resorts had to be cautious this year. J. W. Bigger, professor of bacteriology and preventive medicine at Trinity College, had just published his study confirming that parts of Dublin Bay and many coastal areas were "contaminated with sewage to such an extent as to be unsafe for bathing." A problem long in the making. Mothers were advised to keep an eye on their little ones.

By mid-afternoon on Saturday a drenching rain was driving people indoors, and Dublin's cinemas and restaurants were profiting, with capacity crowds all day. Patrons endured long queues to see some excellent films, such as the smash hit *The Bells of St Mary's*, starring Bing Crosby and Ingrid Bergman, showing at the Metropole. The Adelphi was featuring Gene Kelly and Frank Sinatra in *Anchors Aweigh*, while the Grand Central offered more serious fare in *Destination Tokyo*, with Cary Grant and John Garfield. As people stood patiently in cinema queues getting wet, at least they could buy a luscious orange from street dealers for 3 pence.

Throughout the remainder of the weekend and during Dublin Horse

Show week the weather stayed nasty, intermittently misty, drizzly, rainy. As always, crowds adapted to prevailing conditions, visiting a variety of indoor events. The Royal Horticultural Society of Ireland drew admiring crowds with its profusion of exotic, colourful flowers and alluring scents. And "if showers had their effect on the outdoor events," one newspaper wrote, "they helped to swell the crowds in the Industries Fair," where by afternoon "one had to elbow one's way around."[1]

A magnet for young and old alike was the model railways exhibition. This year CIE boasted a special attraction, a model of the largest and most powerful locomotive in Ireland, the *Maeve,* which hauled mail from Dublin to Cork. The model, nearly six feet long and precise in every detail, had been created by a Co. Wicklow amateur over a period of four years. Admirers leaned close to marvel at its intricacy. Those not interested in trains could wander around looking at new inventions, such as the latest in washing-machines, which had women wishing.

On 8 August, "Ladies' Day" at the Horse Show, "inclement weather militated against any [outdoor] display of fashion . . . a day for raincoats rather than finery."[2] Though drizzly conditions drove the fashionable set indoors, smart outfits with "rainbow colours" dazzled admirers. Fancy hats stole the show. Laden with a brimful of flowers and clouds of veiling, some were trimmed with paradise plumes and exotic fruit, looking like a Brazilian carnival. Onlookers smiled. However, it was noted that, by contrast, upper-crust gentlemen appeared less impressive than usual, as they were not sporting their grey toppers as in pre-war days.

At the end of the soggy week the *Irish Independent* declared that the "weather was a spoil-sport." It was mild chastisement. In months to come the weather would be called far worse: a "malignant evil," "wicked," an "enemy," even the "wrath of God."

———

Farmers had more serious concerns about early August rains, as it was a critical time for the coming harvest season. Compulsory tillage regulations introduced during the war years were still operative in 1946, under which farmers were required to cultivate a certain proportion of their holdings. Growing wheat was essential for ensuring the country's supply of flour for bread. Vast acreages of wheat, oats and other grains would soon be ready for autumn harvesting, for which dry, sunny weather was required.

Few farmers were unduly troubled by the early August rainfall, which wasn't that unusual. So long as it didn't persist. However, some of the old-timers who trusted their instincts would later confess that they had a nagging prescience before the 1946 harvest season that the weather would "turn bad."

Some of these premonitions might have been bred by post-war reports from various parts of the world about "peculiar" weather patterns. Spells of weather that were abnormal: too cold, too warm, too wet, too dry, too windy. Unusual tornado, hurricane, typhoon activity. It had meteorologists from as far apart as the United States, Japan and China scratching their heads. Among both scientists and lay people, two hypotheses had a popular appeal. The first was the belief—or at least suspicion—that atomic bomb testing, and dropping, might be causing climate change. The second related to curious sunspot activity, prompting the notion that there might be some connection between the sun and Earth's climatic cycles.

On Friday 9 August newspaper-readers stared in awe at a photograph just released by Associated Press. It was a wide-angle picture of the huge mushroom-shaped cloud arising from an American underwater nuclear blast in Bikini Lagoon in the South Pacific—one of the most historic photographs ever taken. Viewing the unearthly sight, people found it all too easy to imagine massive clouds of radioactive contaminants ascending into the upper atmosphere and being carried by winds clear around the planet. In every country people wondered if such a colossal—and yet scientifically unproven—force could alter nature and weather patterns. The world's farmers in particular believed that meddling with nature could be risky. It might bring tragic consequences for those who lived off the land—and, consequently, for all consumers of food.

Back in 1946, immediately following the war, Dubliners closely followed news of sunspot activity and atomic bomb testing, as articles regularly appeared in the newspapers. In McDaid's pub in Harry Street, a mecca for the city's intelligentsia and literary luminaries, the legendary barman Paddy O'Brien recalls stimulating debates over unleashing atomic power.

During the early months of 1947 the topic would appear more often in Irish newspapers, discussed widely and debated vehemently. Cursed by many.

———

Over the weekend of 10/11 August a strong depression slowly formed to the south of Ireland, moving gradually in a north-easterly direction. By midday on Sunday seamen some distance from land felt the winds picking up, saw skies darken as clouds ominously gathered. A storm was sure to strike.

Throughout Ireland multitudes were enjoying cycling, hiking, camping, picnicking, seaside bathing. In Dublin every golf course was packed, and the bay was filled with boaters. The Phoenix Park and the zoo were filling up by the hour. Many Dubliners had headed for the nearby mountains to cut their own turf for the coming winter.

Late afternoon brought a quickened breeze and a slight drop in temperature. To many it was welcome. By early evening an overcast sky appeared threatening but nothing to suggest anything other than an ordinary August rainstorm, which would quickly pass, leaving the air fresh and cool.

On Sunday night, between 9 and 11 p.m., a strong gale gathered force. The first bursts sent campers dashing to fortify their tents and seamen to furiously secure their vessels for facing a big blow. Shortly after 11 the wind grew angrier, increasing rapidly in velocity from 30 to 35, 40 then 45 miles per hour. Around the city, loose windows began rattling, and debris was blown through the streets. Then, following the howl of the wind, a torrential rainstorm lashed the city and the east coast, while "campers were forced from their tents and hurried into towns to seek accommodation."[3]

Throughout the entire night the storm continued, showing no sign of abating as Dubliners awoke. Veering now south-west to north-east, the winds hit 50 miles per hour between 7 and 10 a.m. on Monday as the "rain descended in torrents."

During the storm the wind was abeam the mail boat as it travelled from Holyhead to Dún Laoghaire, causing it to roll heavily for most of the journey. Those aboard were tossed roughly about, and stomachs churned. When its 1,100 visibly shaken passengers finally set foot on terra firma, observers commented that they "looked very much worse for their trip." In Dún Laoghaire harbour eighteen yachts of varying classes were either awash or capsized. One 32-year resident of Dún Laoghaire remarked that it was the worst storm he had ever experienced in August.

On Monday morning, with the storm still raging, Dubliners had to brave the gale as they made their way to work. "They were soaked as they waited in queues for trams and buses . . . as bus conductors did their best" to squeeze in as many passengers as possible, with an apology for those left behind.[4] Bus-drivers and motorists risked getting stalled as they dared to drive through vast pools of water.

By noon on Monday, after nearly twelve continuous hours of heavy rain, "streets became like miniature rivers as the gullies failed to take the volume of water."[5] Where storm drains clogged, pools formed, larger and larger. In many places residents and pedestrians found themselves stranded on one side of the street, unable to proceed in any direction—without a boat.

By now, water was entering houses and shops, doing considerable damage. As residents frantically sought to protect furniture and valuable belongings, shopkeepers hurriedly tried to move merchandise to higher shelves. In some of the city's lower spots water accumulated to a height of several feet, flooding lower levels of houses and driving inhabitants up the stairs to the first floor, where they yelled out the windows for help. Dublin Fire Brigade and the Gardaí were called to carry out evacuations. Eleven families had to be evacuated at Classon's Bridge in Milltown when the Dodder flooded and water tore through their houses. Accommodation for the homeless victims was provided by the Red Cross Society.

At about 1 p.m. the storm ended, and waters began subsiding. People ventured outside and sloshed through the streets. Shopkeepers propped their doors open as they tried to sweep out the water and muck. Children splashed happily in the ponds. Everyone was talking about the ferocity and duration of the storm, as meteorologists were tallying the totals. When it was all over the amount of rainfall was verified at 2.4 inches—the equivalent of 240 tons to the acre.

———

No-one needed to tell Irish farmers about water volume per acre. All they needed to know they could see with their eyes from the window. City-dwellers may have been drenched, inconvenienced, even made temporary evacuees; farmers, however, had suffered a serious blow. Possibly a lasting blow, some worried.

In the aftermath of the storm, the *Irish Independent* reported, "from the Provinces has come news of homeless families, damaged crops, burst river banks, broken bridges, drowned animals and flooded roads."[6] Much of the countryside had been ravaged by violent wind and sheets of rain, turning fields into swampland. As accounts filtered in it seemed that Leinster and Munster had been the hardest hit. Here, it was said, "torrential rains beat the crops to the ground." As surely as if a hurricane had swept over. Wheat, oats and barley fared worst, and there were many reports of hay, both loose and in stacks, having been simply carried away by floods before the farmers' eyes. In north Co. Dublin much wheat, heavy in the ear, was levelled, while oats and barley were battered nearly flat. All across the land, "farmers expressed grave anxiety for the harvest."[7]

Apart from the extensive damage to crops, turf was shockingly deteriorated. Many boglands and bog roads were completely under water. Laboriously cut turf, awaiting transport to city homes or depots, was sodden, some of it as mushy as a saturated sponge. From the Dublin Mountains came word that "thousands of tons of [cut] turf are believed to be past saving."[8] This was devastating news to those who had cut the turf, mostly poorer Dubliners, who needed it the most. Paddy Casey, a young garda on one of the city's toughest beats around Queen Street, Benburb Street, North King Street, and Dominick Street, had seen how, during the earlier, drier days of the summer, thousands of men, and some women as well, had toiled at cutting their own turf for the coming winter. Men "cycled up to the Dublin Mountains, maybe fifteen miles, and they'd spend the day cutting the turf," observed Casey, "to have a fire for the winter . . . Some poor people wouldn't even have a bicycle to do that." They returned filthy, with aching backs and hands raw and blistered but with confidence that they would have a warm turf fire come winter. Now, it seemed, all their efforts were futile. Weather had ruined their cut sods as well as their security. The full gravity of this loss would be known only in months to come. Pray to God that the winter was a mild one!

After the early August deluge, farmers hoped for sunshine and drying winds. Just the opposite occurred. The second half of the month saw "almost incessant rains." With each passing wet day farmers increasingly "viewed their harvest with gloomy apprehension," and their families suffered along with them.[9] By late in the month much of the wheat crop remained quite unripe, because of the absence of sufficient sunshine. Since the "Grow More Wheat" campaign had been launched fifteen years earlier it was the most unfavourable grain harvest the farmers had faced. Oats were as bad as wheat.

It ended up being the wettest August in two decades, and many farmers openly "resigned themselves to heavy losses."[10] Others, the most optimistic, contended that if September weather was favourable, much of the harvest could still be saved. Few dared to speculate about what might befall them if September proved a continuation of August.

SEPTEMBER

On Sunday 1 September most of the country was again experiencing moderate to heavy rain at frequent intervals, prompting one newspaper to conclude that "hopes for an 'Indian Summer' were dashed." Leaving farmers with nothing to do but peer out their windows with worried expressions.

Farmers in Cos. Cork and Kilkenny were lucky. They could at least forget their weather woes for the day and concentrate attention on Croke Park, where their teams were meeting in the all-Ireland hurling final. It was one of the most anticipated matches in years, followed by hurling enthusiasts all over the country. Despite their worries, spirits were high among residents of the two counties. It was a welcome diversion. To many farmers' wives at their wits' end with their husbands' anxiety it was a blessing, albeit a temporary one.

Early on Sunday morning excited spectators began flowing into Dublin by car, bus, and train. Despite the rain, flooded patches and slippery roads some "hardy folk whom the weather did not deter" were cycling all the way from Co. Kilkenny to see their team in action. By late Sunday morning O'Connell Street was thronged with bellowing supporters of the two teams, flaunting their colours and taunting one another. Dublin's hurling aficionados were no less enthusiastic as they packed pubs, debating which squad would come out on top. Here again weather became a topic. Would the wet, soft condition of the playing-field allow for a fair match? Or might it favour one team over the other?

By match time 64,415 roaring spectators were crammed into Croke Park. They were not to be disappointed by what one sports reporter would describe as a "thrill-packed" hurling contest, marked by "brilliant passages," despite the poor conditions. Cork took an early lead, but the entire crowd was "on tiptoe as deafening cheers punctuated the second half," when Kilkenny gallantly strove to reduce Cork's slim lead to two points.[11] Though Cork prevailed by nine points, everyone left feeling they had witnessed a great hurling final. In the rain, they straggled homewards or towards the pubs.

———

Three days later, on 4 September, ugly weather struck again. Rain fell "heavily and continuously" all across the country. In Dublin, 1.8 inches of rain was recorded at Rathfarnham Castle over a period of twenty-four hours, again causing localised flooding, traffic delays, damage to houses and shops, and evacuations. The countryside was drowning in water. Every county was now reporting heavy losses to crops: cut hay lying unsaved in sodden fields, potatoes blackening, wheat beaten down. More turf saturated, under water, beyond reclamation. "Harvest hopes are rapidly diminishing" in every province, reported the papers. Millers around the country were forced to cease operations, awaiting deliveries of wheat. One prominent miller flatly predicted that "it could become disastrous" if there was not "an immediate improvement" in the weather.[12]

Some farmers were heard muttering that the "harvest was finished." Hearing such dire predictions, the *Irish Independent* despatched a reporter on a 120-mile investigative trip through farm country to determine at first hand whether such Doomsday declarations were valid or exaggerated. Along the way he chatted with farmers, jotted down observations, plodded through fields to examine the soil and the crops:

> Everywhere I went I found the harvest fields about two or three weeks in arrears. Passing through Co. Dublin and Co. Kildare I noticed that about one-third of the grain crop was cut, but none of it had been brought into the barns. It was mostly in stooks and presented a rain-sodden, half-rotten appearance. In many fields it was found impossible to use a mowing machine. In many cases farmers had given up hope of even cutting the crop by scythe and were resigned to leaving it tossed and tumbled in the field.[13]

An altogether desperate situation was his final verdict. His editors weighed the evidence he presented—fields waterlogged, crops beaten down and rotting, machinery unusable—and forged their grim headline for the next day's paper: "Food emergency threatened."

———

Patrick Smith, Minister for Agriculture, in consultation with his staff and county authorities, arrived at the same stark conclusion. Even with a spell of favourable weather the harvest was too far behind schedule and the fields too soft for the crops to be saved by farmers alone using the traditional methods. Assistance was needed, on a large scale. So, on 5 September, for the first time in the country's history, he made a fervent appeal for volunteers to help save the harvest and avert a critical food shortage. Calling it a "harvest crisis of unprecedented seriousness," he explained that, owing to the "disastrous weather" over the previous five weeks, much of the farm work would have to be done by hand.[14] He needed thousands of willing hands to assist lone farmers on their land.

The minister suggested that cities and towns throughout the country should establish centres at which volunteers could enlist. Furthermore, he encouraged employers to release workers, with pay, so they could participate.

While the press lauded the minister's call for action, it asked, "Why was not the Army being loaned, why were not the road workers and Garda being invited to help?"[15] On this question the Government was silent.

The day following the minister's appeal for volunteers the *Irish Independent* published an editorial, headed "No ordinary crisis," in which it emphasised that there existed, in reality, a dual crisis, of both crops and turf. Both must be saved in order to avert disaster in the months ahead:

> Nothing in this country is now of greater urgency than to save what remains of the harvest and turf . . . if our people are not to be hungry and cold during the winter and spring. If we are left short of grain, potatoes and turf the farmer will suffer grievous loss—but the loss will not end there. If calamity is not prevented it will bring suffering into every home.[16]

All were at risk: every man, woman and child in Ireland.

The weekend of 7/8 September saw an enthusiastic response to the minister's plea. Cities and towns quickly set up volunteer centres and arranged for their transport to farms. Owners of cars, vans and lorries offered their vehicles for the cause. Men and women, young and old, marched down to sign up and do their patriotic duty. Enthusiasm was infectious. Newspapers called it a "nation-wide rally to save the harvest." There was a sort of military spirit about the movement. Volunteer vernacular drew on such terms as "fight," "battle," "crusade," to "win a victory." As the national campaign began, people in streets and in shops talked excitedly about how the "battle" was being waged.

While every tractor in the country would be put into use whenever and wherever possible, much of the harvest had to be carried out by manual labour. Reapers armed with scythes cut the crops into swathes, from which it was lifted and tied into sheaves. Newspapers stressed that the "most useful type of volunteer is he who possesses knowledge of farm operations." However, no-one was turned away. Those unfamiliar with the processes were instructed, and most caught on quickly. There was *something* for everyone to do.

In Dublin the central bureau for volunteers was established at Parnell Square, where queues formed early in the morning. Many employers were giving their workers leave to work on farms. Universities, which were just resuming, were considering postponing the term to allow vigorous young students to help out. The GAA and other sports organisations, such as hockey, rugby and soccer clubs, were cancelling contests and rounding up rugged athletes to volunteer *en masse*. At a meeting of the National Federation of Irish Ex-Servicemen at its head office in York Street it was decided to encourage all members to assist farmers. Farmers particularly welcomed ex-soldiers, as they found them to be a "well organised and disciplined force." Even the Catholic Boy Scouts of Ireland at once pledged to do their part.

As ordinary citizens from about twelve to seventy were eagerly offering their services for the harvest campaign, the *Irish Independent* caustically commented: "Not a word so far about what the Government itself proposes to do." The crisis could hardly be more threatening:

> It is very much to be feared that such privation as this country has not known since Black '47 may overwhelm our country in the next eight or nine months.[17]

With even boy scouts responding to the call, in a radio broadcast on the night of 8 September the Taoiseach, Éamon de Valera, finally announced that the Minister for Defence was "releasing suitable men from the army ... so that they may assist in saving crops." He did not identify what he meant by "suitable"; but many soldiers surely had a farming background.

———

During the second week of September the "harvest army," as it was now called, expanded as the campaign gained momentum. In the newspapers, volunteers were being hailed as "patriots" and "heroes." This, of course, spurred volunteerism, and people boasted of "joining up" as if in an actual military force. Without uniforms, they at least had a "badge of honour," it was said.

With all volunteers welcome, the harvest army comprised an extraordinary social mixture, especially for class-stratified Ireland. Young lads in short trousers, giggly adolescent girls, grey-haired hobbling First World War veterans, professionals and labourers. Grannies weren't sent into the fields but could help with the preparation of food. Volunteers were formed into work parties and assigned to a particular farmer and immediately felt a sense of purpose and camaraderie. For younger participants it was something of a lark, a real "adventure." Older volunteers understood that theirs was a historic task.

Seventeen-year-old Agnes Daly was a typical recruit. She jumped at the chance to get away from Clarence Street and join the harvest forces out in the open countryside. She liked excitement. Six years earlier, on 31 May 1941, her house had been only a short distance from the North Strand when the German bombs fell, causing more than forty deaths and mass destruction, havoc, and hysteria. A large piece of tram track flew through the air, barely missing her head. She was seasoned to excitement and drama. So she skipped down to Parnell Street, signed up, and awaited her transport:

> It was great for us. I was in the army lorries going down the country to help take in the wheat. We'd all be allocated to some farmer, just went out in the fields, and they showed us how to put it all in stacks. And you'd spend your day out there. We thought that was a marvellous thing, being brought out. We loved it—being driven along in the army lorries. And it was lovely coming back, when we'd have a sing-song.

For city-dwellers of all ages, especially those confined in an impoverished world of congestion, traffic, tenements, noise, and dirt, being out in the fresh, open, tranquil countryside was invigorating. But it was hard work.

As it turned out, children of school age and boy scouts played a significant role in the harvest effort. Young, fit, and wildly enthusiastic, they worked vigorously, receiving high acclaim. As they were being praised at home they also received an accolade from abroad. It seems that Father Edward Flanagan of Boys' Town in the United States had just returned from a summer visit to Ireland, where he had been impressed by the character of Irish lads. "The boys of Ireland are blessed above all other boys," he said, "because the nation has faith."[18] He asserted that when given "proper direction" in their schools, in church organisations and on the athletic field they would surely grow up to be the "type of men that will make Ireland a great nation."

Some other children would soon be in the news. On 9 September, as harvest volunteers in lorries and other vehicles were heading south out of Dublin, they may have noticed a small convoy of cars and Red Cross ambulances carrying children from the age of about five to thirteen. These forty-five German and Polish war orphans, rescued from bomb shelters just after the war, were being taken on a journey up to Glencree in Co. Wicklow. Here they would stay at the Red Cross hostel during the winter months as they awaited adoption or placement. It was thought that this would be a safe and healthy sanctuary in the rugged highlands for children who had suffered such trauma and loss in their young lives.

If winter brought some nice snowfalls to Wicklow's mountains, the children could delight in making snowmen, throwing snowballs, sledding. A wonderfully tranquil, recuperative setting.

——

On the morning of Monday 9 September, following de Valera's broadcast, there was a surge in volunteers, comprising both individuals and groups. At the Harvest Labour Bureau in Parnell Square more than three hundred helpers were despatched in the first few hours to needy farmers in north Co. Dublin. The Dublin Chamber of Commerce and the Federation of Irish Manufacturers were strongly encouraging their members to participate, while the Student Representative Council at UCD opened a recruiting office for both students and staff.

With "Ireland's New Land Army," as it was dubbed by newspapers, now on the march, no-one wanted to appear unpatriotic. From every county, people of diverse ages, occupations and social and economic rank were joining up. As one reporter observed, it was an uncommonly egalitarian army, embracing "those to whom harvesting hitherto was an unknown occupation." Working in the fields side by side were dockers, draymen, coopers, stonecutters and coalmen with leathery hands as well as soft-palmed barristers, bankers, civil servants, teachers, and organists, all with sleeves rolled up and perspiration flowing down. A socially levelling experience in Ireland—one appreciated more by participants with the passing of years, and reflection.

Among their ranks was twenty-year-old Brian Kelly, a fresh recruit in the Garda Síochána. One of seven children, he knew that his future was not on the land. So he listened to his mother's words of advice. "My mother said to me, 'You'll never get out of this county if you don't smarten up.'" This meant five years of secondary school and getting his Leaving Certificate. "And I joined the force before I was twenty, one of the youngest." He was in the midst of training when de Valera made his broadcast about needing volunteers and releasing some soldiers from the army. When this was expanded to include some gardaí, Kelly and some of his mates were eager to do their part. Within days he was out of the barracks, out of uniform, and in the fields again. His familiarity with farm operations and implements made him a valuable volunteer, and he felt pride in his role:

The harvest was almost gone when de Valera implored city people to come out and help save the harvest. And we *did*. Including *myself*—and all the young-fellas who were in training. We were all released on full pay. Oh, yes, this was a big effort, at the behest of de Valera. And they got a *huge* response . . . civil servants and workers in the big drapers, from Clery's staff, and the Gresham Hotel, I worked with them all."

When volunteers returned home to their districts they had lively stories to tell about country life and the interesting people they had met in the fields.

_____

As the battle for the harvest was being vigorously waged, that for the turf was woefully neglected. Though many boglands were under water or too sodden, others were dry enough to be worked. Especially vital was retrieving the massive amount of turf already cut, awaiting transport to Dublin and other towns before winter set in. However, in many counties turf workers were being diverted to agricultural fields. This neglect was extremely worrisome to those who saw them as nearly equal vital resources that had to be saved at all costs. The *Irish Independent* criticised the policy of crops over turf as myopic and risky, emphasising Ireland's precarious dependence on British coal:

> The provision of fuel is hardly less important than the saving of the food supply. It would be foolish to expect such early expansion of coal imports as would allow an adequate ration for domestic purposes.
>
> We must continue to depend mainly upon turf, so it is vitally necessary to recover as much as possible of the tens of thousands of tons of turf still lying on the bogs.[19]

The paper argued for more, not fewer, workers on the bogs over coming weeks. Words unheeded. Most people saw the winter months ahead as remote, while the threatening food crisis seemed immediate.

Soon after Christmas they would be seeing life through a different prism.

FRIDAY THE 13th AND "D-DAY"

Friday 13 September brought the best possible luck: sunshine, warm temperatures, drying winds. And *hope*.

Weather for the next few days was predicted to be "ideal" for farm work. So, the coming weekend was christened "D-Day in the fight for the harvest." An all-out national effort would be made. Optimism grew as new volunteers steadily signed up. On farms and in towns, people spoke of little but the fine weather that had finally arrived. "Make the most of it!" was the rallying cry heard from Donegal to Kerry.

There was a call for five thousand more volunteers for the perfect weekend of harvesting. On Friday morning at the Parnell Square centre between 8 and 10 a.m. more than a thousand people signed up and were promptly sent off to farms. Another six hundred soldiers were despatched by the army authorities. That afternoon all the Dublin rugby clubs met at their grounds and jointly recruited another five hundred volunteers. The ESB granted leave with pay to employees who signed up; some 164 immediately stepped forward. Stewards of the Turf Club cancelled race meetings at Mullingar and the Curragh to encourage people to head for the farms instead.

Una Shaw's sister and father joined up. From their home in Rutland Street in the heart of the city they walked over to Parnell Square, wrote down their names, went outside, and waited for their lorry. The whole family was proud of their effort:

> They did it for *nothing*. Went out, and they'd work *all* day. And they'd get one meal. And I remember farmers saying that city people worked harder than they did! If they hadn't saved the harvest there could have been a famine.

At day's end volunteers returned home utterly fatigued from the wholesome work. On the land, out in nature. But with back aching and hands blistered. Faces, arms, necks lobster-red. Filled with satisfaction and pride.

"D-Day" weekend of 14/15 September surpassed all expectations. Superb weather prevailed, and optimism seemed suddenly contagious. Some buoyant Co. Dublin farmers were saying that, given a few more days of such weather, it would "suffice for saving about 85 per cent of the wheat crop."[20] An unimaginable speculation only a week before. At Sunday masses priests around the country preached of the power and blessings of prayer, patriotism, volunteerism, helping one's neighbours. Every candle was lit.

But there were those more cautious, and realistic, who warned of over-optimism, noting that the food crisis was far from over. Weather could be cruelly capricious. The *Irish Independent* warned that the battle was not won yet:

> We have now reached the critical period . . . a supreme effort to stave off what still threatens to be the worst calamity the country has experienced for the past one hundred years.[21]

––––––

D-Day weekend was as frenetic for organisers behind the scenes as for volunteers bent over in the fields. Their two greatest challenges were transporting the thousands of helpers and then feeding them. Requiring the same strategies as that of an army. But they had no advance planning opportunity, had few resources, and were almost wholly dependent on the generosity of "volunteers behind the volunteers."

Newspapers published inspirational photographs of men and women engaged in the noble battle to harvest crops and save the nation from starvation. Meanwhile, behind the scenes, missed by the camera's lens, were battalions of other helpers, making mounds of sandwiches, wrapping food for the front-line troops. Nor was there adequate acknowledgement of the hundreds of individuals and business firms that donated cars, vans and lorries for transport, without which no army could be moved. Others offered tyres, petrol, drivers to the cause. Each vehicle as it left Dublin was so tightly packed with farm helpers that the tyres nearly burst. Some did. As they wended their way along roads towards farmland, local people lined their route through towns and villages, waving and cheering them on as heroes. They laughed, waved back, and sang. Feeling, indeed, a bit like real heroes.

The Red Cross Society assumed the primary responsibility for feeding the harvest army. Food was donated by grocers, butchers, shopkeepers, and individuals. Victuallers brought in armfuls of uncooked meat for the Red Cross to cook. Tinned meat, bread, beans, biscuits, cheese and fruit flowed in. Messrs Mills, caterers, offered to supply four hundred sandwiches a day. Messrs Kennedy, bakers, sent five hundred two-pound loaves. Half a hundredweight of jam was received from Messrs Holloway, jam manufacturers. No food merchant wanted to appear un-cooperative—or to be outdone by competitors. These "rations," in military parlance, had to be prepared, transported and distributed by volunteers, who received little attention. The task fell to hundreds of helpers, mostly women and girls. All carried out their duties cheerfully, with a feeling that they were doing their small part in the larger operation.

Long before dawn, lights were on at the Red Cross premises, so that the packets of sandwiches, cheese, biscuits and fruit could be ready for transport. Knowing the recipients would be famished, and appreciative. Several younger women, apparently in their late teens or early twenties, had been slapping sandwiches together for hours, all the while hearing "exciting tales" from the fields, where the "real action" was taking place. Finally, it was reported, they became "so anxious to get out to the farms that they refused to remain behind" any longer.[22] They whisked off their aprons, hurried down to the volunteer centre, and were last seen giddily piling into the back of a lorry headed towards the "front."

Apart from food, medical supplies were also donated by several city firms. Mostly bandages, disinfectant, dressings, headache and body ache tablets. Minor mishaps did inevitably occur, such as cuts, scrapes, bruises, and sprains. As well as insect bites and stings. Red Cross ambulances were on call in case they might be needed for something more serious. Ironically, the most widespread infirmity was a forgotten one: sunburn. Some cases quite severe. After weeks of rain and overcast skies, everyone so eagerly welcomed the sun that they were apparently oblivious of the risks of overindulgence.

———

The main headline of the *Irish Independent* on 16 September told in large type that the tide had turned: "Harvest army is winning battle."

The long spell of incessant rains had been broken, replaced throughout the second half of September by consecutive days of warm temperatures, bright sunshine, and drying winds. A few sporadic showers were not harmful enough to halt the army's forward movement. The harvest was progressing at a faster rate than had been expected even by the most optimistic. This was due not only to the huge number of volunteers and the excellent weather but also to the fact that many men were familiar with all aspects of agriculture and harvesting. On many farms, harvesting operations ran so smoothly and with such haste that at day's end farmers were in some disbelief at what had been accomplished. A "miracle," some were calling it.

Throughout September and into October the harvest army steadily advanced, slowed occasionally by a wet spell but not seriously impeded. Good to excellent weather held out in most of the country. In late October a light snowfall covered the remnants of some uncut corn and effectually terminated harvesting. While the rate of success in saving the crops varied from county to county and from farm to farm, it was generally concluded that "a major proportion of the harvest was saved."[23]

Unfortunately, the same could not be said of the turf. The country's vast turf resources had been neglected in the frantic effort to secure the wheat, oats, potatoes and other crops. During the fine, dry weather of autumn scores of men had been taken from the bogs to work on farms. Leaving a bounty of turf, cut and uncut, which could have been saved. With late October snow and the onset of some rainy weather again, thousands of tons of cut turf in the Dublin Mountains and elsewhere was considered by the authorities "past saving," too sodden or disintegrated, or the roads too marshy and impassable for vehicles. There seems to have been an assumption on the part of the public that, if need be, coal rations could somehow be augmented, or dry turf somehow brought into Dublin from distant counties. Assumptions that would be proved deadly wrong.

DECEMBER

By Christmas, people had put fears of famine behind them. Food and fuel might be short, but they'd make it through the winter just fine. It was time to be joyful. Dublin's main shopping streets were gaily decorated with garlands, wreaths, bells, and ribbons of red, green, gold, and silver. Jammed with adults and children in good cheer, enlivened by earnest carollers and bell-ringers. Along Grafton Street young and old crowded before the large windows of Brown Thomas and Switzer's to get a closer look at the colourful animated scenes showing Santa, his reindeer and elves busy in the workshop.

Along Henry Street, dealers such as Ellen Preston treasured their five-shilling licence to sell there for the month, having had to sleep out in the street the night before to claim their place. "We'd go to sleep or sit there with a few chips and have tea and a bit of a laugh," and the next morning she would put up her board, and "the place was yours" for the entire month. Tired but happy, she sold holly, mistletoe, small toys. A few paces away, Moore Street dealers were equally ebullient, singing Christmas songs aloud.

On Christmas Eve large congregations attended midnight mass. However, the weather did not fit the occasion. As throngs flocked to churches all over the city between 11:30 and midnight, "hopes of a 'white Christmas' were dashed," wrote one paper, as gale warnings went out and rain followed.

Christmas morning mass-goers, including those attending high mass in the Pro-Cathedral presided over by Archbishop John Charles McQuaid, gave thanks to God for having seen them through a stressful year. That evening the Christmas dinner and pudding were especially savoured. On the chilly evening, people tossed a few more lumps of coal or turf on the fire for extra warmth.

––––

Dubliners relished New Year's Eve. While many people attended parties and get-togethers of every sort, the "gayest and brightest," wrote one newspaper, was the "Charladies' Ball" at the Mansion House, where more than eight hundred guests crowded into the ballroom, providing a "lively spectacle in fancy dress costumes of brilliant hue."[24] Elsewhere around the city were "special cabaret and carnival dances," which drew capacity crowds, as strangers in the streets turned to wish each other the compliments of the season. The city was in high spirits.

As midnight approached, people swarmed towards Christ Church Cathedral for the ancient tradition of the ringing of the mighty bells. They gathered in twos, threes and indecipherable little mobs of merrymakers, many in silly hats. Fuelled by drink, ready to sing aloud and shout out their New Year's wishes. Guests from the Shelbourne Hotel and dockers from tenements along the quays showed up to stand shoulder to shoulder. In the midst of the merriment an *Irish Press* reporter scribbled his notes:

> From 10.00 until well after midnight people kept themselves warm with spontaneous and vigorous dancing to the music of accordionists who moved around collecting pennies. Simultaneously, others were singing "Patsy Fagan" in lusty voices, while now and again fireworks were detonated.[25]

At the stroke of midnight the great bells rang out. Everybody linked arms, and all voices joined in "Auld Lang Syne," to the accompaniment of ships' whistles, factory sirens, locomotive whistles, and motor horns, a cacophony of celebratory sounds.

However, apart from the raucous celebrating, for a good many participants there was an underlying reflection about the year that was passing. By any measure it had been a year of considerable disappointment and stress. Hopes for a rapid recovery from wartime hardships were never realised. Then the harvest crisis and food and fuel shortages. Rationing remained a difficult way of life. The *Irish Independent* captured the mood of many:

> A year ago people sighed with relief at the close of a year which brought peace to a war-ravaged world, and joyously welcomed the new year full of hope for the coming of an era of security and prosperity.
>
> On New Year's Eve 1946 they turned their backs on a year of disillusionment that blighted most of their hopes.[26]

As Dubliners partied well past midnight and into the wee hours, most farmers were soundly sleeping. They had survived the harvest crisis. The year had left them spent. On the last night of 1946 they deserved a peaceful slumber, comforted by thoughts of a kinder year ahead. "As winter set in, farmers counted their losses and hoped for a better year to follow."[27]

Chapter 2 ∾

"BIG FREEZE" AND "BIG JIM"

The old year has gone and whatever may have been our lot during the past twelve months, we are turning a new page in our life history with hope. Let us be kind to the strange New Year.

(*Irish Press*, 1 JANUARY 1947)

With 23 degrees of frost last night Dubliners awoke still shivering as the "Big Freeze" continued.

(*Evening Herald*, 30 JANUARY 1947)

It was so cold that you couldn't breathe! You got pain actually from shivering, you'd be tensed up.

(UNA SHAW, 80)

The body of "Big Jim" Larkin was escorted . . . as the motor hearses crunched through the snow, streets lined with people who whispered, "he was a great man."

(*Irish Times*, 1 FEBRUARY 1947)

NEW YEAR'S DAY, 1947

A few minutes past one o'clock, as boisterous revellers were still carousing about Dublin's streets and guests were dancing and drinking champagne at the Charladies' Ball, the first baby of the new year to be born in the city's maternity hospitals was brought into the world. In the Coombe Hospital, Mrs Silke of 3 Nash's Court, off James's Street, gave birth to a baby girl of 8 pounds 4 ounces. When she was being discharged to take her infant daughter home, everyone at the hospital wished them well, reminding Mrs Silke to keep her baby warm this winter.

The morning of New Year's Day was traditionally tranquil, leisurely. Wonderfully lazy. There was nowhere to go, nothing to do. People slept late, shuffled around in slippers, had breakfast and tea while perusing the morning paper. Drowsily, they skimmed and skipped around for news that caught their attention. Those with herculean hangovers from their New Year's Eve bash were in no mood for encountering bad news to start off the new year. Newspapers published some optimistic articles to cheer people up, instil hope, get them off in the right spirit for facing the unknown year ahead.

In its "Happy New Year" greeting to readers the *Irish Press* wrote of a baby born even earlier than Mrs Silke's:

> The year is ours, twelve whole months of it. Let's give it a chance to be a good year. It's only a baby now, and it needs care and sympathy. Let us open our arms to it, for it is new and unsullied, and there are no black marks on its history.[1]

One disquieting news item, however, could hardly be missed, as it was on the front page of all the papers. An announcement from London that the coal shortage was now of the "utmost gravity." In the post-war period, British coal mines were under-productive, in dire need of modernisation, better management, and capital. Mines, coal ports and railways all needed rehabilitation. There was real worry that an unusually cold winter could lead to a reduction in power, transport, and industrial output. It could also mean diminished exports to Ireland, which depended on British coal for running the country—transport, energy, heating, industry. Ireland was already receiving significantly less than before the war. Barely sufficient to get people through even a mild winter.

On 1 January, in an effort to restructure and modernise Britain's anaemic coal industry, the country's mines were taken into the ownership of the nation. British politicians were confident that this scheme would boost productivity. Confidence was high that the bold plan would remedy the country's coal problem. Given time. And favourable weather. Irish people, no less than the British, were fervently hoping the scheme would be successful.

With the dawn of 1947, as Irish people were looking forward, meteorologists and astronomers were already glancing backwards at the year just passed. A year that "hadn't treated us as we would have wished," reflected the *Irish Press*. Weather records for 1946 showed how unkind the year had been. Data compiled at the Jesuit observatory at Rathfarnham Castle verified that it had rained on 296 days, with a total rainfall of 39.14 inches, making it the wettest year since the establishment of the weather station there in 1924. Furthermore, sunshine had been far below average, resulting in an exceptionally dull year. The prolonged wet, overcast conditions had not only taken a heavy toll on crops and turf but had cast a depressive gloom over the land. People were hoping for a sunny, warm, dry year ahead.

Ireland had not been the only country to experience abnormal weather in 1946. From many parts of the globe had come reports of unusually wet, dry, cold, hot, snowy or stormy conditions. Meteorologists, astronomers, other scientists and lay people had their favourite hypotheses. During 1946 astronomers found that a significantly increased number of sunspots provided some "remarkable solar phenomena," visible even to the naked eye.[2] They especially noted the "great sun spot of February, 1946," the largest ever recorded at the Greenwich observatory outside London. Another giant sunspot was recorded in July, a third in November, and two in December. Associated with the July sunspot was one of the greatest solar flares ever witnessed. After about twenty-six hours, when this had reached maximum brilliance, a major magnetic storm erupted. At no time during the year was the sun's disc free of spots, and at times there were as many as ten groups, generally in the highest latitudes.

This was an age when many scientists and others speculated about a causal relationship between sunspots, solar flares and strange weather phenomena. In Ireland there were a good many adherents of this hypothesis. So, when the papers published articles about weather abnormalities and unusual sunspots it fuelled curiosity and discussion about a possible link. Some wondered whether their persistence throughout 1946 might be an omen of more aberrant weather to follow in 1947.

On New Year's Day an article in the *Irish Independent* about the "race" for supremacy in atomic power between several countries drew the attention of those already suspicious, or convinced, that atomic bomb clouds unleashed into the atmosphere were causing climatic disruption. The article reported from the bottom of the world that ships in the us Antarctic Expedition were using new multi-power, high-definition lenses, and two planes from the ship's group had begun photographing the South Polar continent. This made the Soviet Union suspicious. A charge was made in the Red Army newspaper, *Red Star,* that the expedition was "connected with the atom race," that Americans were really searching for uranium to "strengthen their position in the atomic sphere."[3]

Accelerated atomic bomb testing, many believed, could have serious, even catastrophic consequences for the earth's climate, weather and agricultural productivity. Possibly even affecting small farmers on the most remote peninsulas of Co. Donegal.

On the first day of the "unsullied" new year most Irish people were inclined to be optimistic about the year ahead, as weather experts reassured them that "normally January has a spell of either mild, damp weather or cold, dry weather." The moderate Gulf Stream and favourable winds should, as usual, keep Ireland's climate temperate. The hopes were that 1947 would bring a bountiful harvest and the better quality of life that people had expected when the war ended in 1945.

The new year began benignly. Temperatures were moderate, conditions dry and a bit breezy. Quite calm and comfortable for winter. The economy and the supplies situation were more worrisome. On 4 January the Minister for Industry and Commerce, Seán Lemass, announced that the country faced a "grave grain position" and that flour and bread would have to be rationed, beginning on the 18th. Bread was Ireland's most basic food. As John Gallagher (now 78) of the Coombe vouched, "the poor people and the old people *lived* on bread and tea!" The new ration meant a flat rate of 4½ pounds of flour or 6 pounds of bread per person per week, a sharp reduction of a fifth.

Lemass explained that the problem was not due entirely to the bad domestic crop of 1946 but also to the diminished availability of wheat imports from abroad. Ireland's harvest may have been saved, but it was down significantly, in both yield and quality. The home wheat crop only met about half the country's needs. With global shortages, imports could not compensate. Unfortunately, lamented Lemass, the "situation is unavoidable . . . There are no means by which we could avoid bread rationing."[4] And there was no point in grumbling about it.

To exacerbate matters, he added that the rationing of sugar to half a pound weekly per household had to be continued "until further notice." And, under an Emergency Powers Order, domestic soap rations were also to be cut by a third. This was because of limited stocks of the principal soap-making oil and a difficulty in importing more. For people who had expected an improvement in the quality of life when the war ended it was all discouraging.

On Saturday 5 January the new year's calm was disrupted as most coastal and many inland areas were "swept by fierce south-easterly gales." Heavy seas, driven by strong winds, pounded the east and south coasts. Heavy rain caused flooding in places. At least the temperature throughout the country remained a "little over the freezing point."

Three days later another severe gale and rainstorm slashed across the country, drenching Dubliners, soaking farmland and bogs, and endangering ships. One seaman on the mail boat to Dún Laoghaire, carrying 650 passengers, reported that the vessel rolled so heavily that he feared "she would turn turtle." Seamen were particularly wary in stormy weather when visibility was bad, because the British Admiralty had been warning shipping that floating mines from the war years had been spotted off the south coast of Ireland. Beware.

The next few days returned to a state of calm, mild, quite enjoyable weather. Better than usual for Ireland. But weather data coming in from distant countries forewarned of potentially serious long-term problems:

An anti-cyclone centred over North Russia covers most of North and

Central Europe. A very deep depression is situated about 600 miles to the westward of these islands and an associated vigorous trough just off western Ireland will move eastward.[5]

Most people had little if any familiarity with the term "anticyclone," which in meteorological jargon means a system of winds that rotate about a centre of high pressure, clockwise in the northern hemisphere, usually having a diameter of 1,500 to 2,500 miles. Capable of generating forceful air currents in a vast clockwise outward spiral, thus producing powerful prolonged winds up to gale force, carrying Arctic air great distances, and, if colliding with other air masses, generating intense storms.

This particular one had the look of a "persistent anti-cyclone," meaning it could hang around for quite some time. With developing deep depressions simultaneously to the west and south of Ireland it could be a recipe for violent weather ahead. If temperatures dropped, even blizzards. In an age before satellite imaging, meteorologists would do their best to watch the weather's complex evolution. But theirs was an inexact science.

———

With the exception of the two storm outbursts, early January's weather remained favourable for the first eleven days. On the afternoon of Sunday the 12th it suddenly grew blustery. People standing in long queues at Dublin's cinemas buttoned their coats and pushed up collars. In the bleakness of January, the city's picture-houses and theatres always did brisk business. This particular Sunday the Savoy in O'Connell Street was showing a real thriller, *Spellbound,* starring Gregory Peck and Ingrid Bergman. It was drawing huge crowds, as word spread that it was a film not to be missed. Herbie Donnelly, who had begun in 1939 as a pageboy, was the youngest usher on duty. In those days he regarded his uniformed role as "more like the guardsmen outside Buckingham Palace." The Savoy could hold 2,700 patrons, "who dressed up for the occasion." Over his fifty-odd years as usher at Dublin's finest cinemas, including the Theatre Royal, he would meet the likes of Judy Garland, Gene Autry, and James Cagney. But he always had a special affinity for the most ordinary and humble patrons he assisted. He had been well trained to keep the queue orderly, handle large crowds, and manage emergencies. This Sunday, with *Spellbound* showing, he had a packed house and throngs waiting outside. All anticipating an exciting, tense film experience.

As darkness fell, the weather turned angry, with strong winds and heavy rain. Those in the queue tried to huddle close to shop fronts for protection. Then, between 5 and 6 p.m., Dublin was hit by a "gale of unusual severity," with winds of nearly 60 miles per hour, driving the rain horizontally. All along the coast, ships either remained in port or headed there as quickly as possible.

About 6:15 several of the ESB's trunk lines were knocked out of action by the storm, resulting in a sudden black-out throughout Dublin and other parts of the country. Savoy patrons engrossed in *Spellbound* got a fright when the film stopped and the lights went out. Donnelly and his fellow-ushers sprang into action with their torches to begin leading people calmly down the aisles, reassuring the nervous along the way, then showing them out through the doors into O'Connell Street and into the teeth of the gale, which came as another shock. From there they had to be guided by bus or car lights. All across the city the scene was the same, as people were led out of cinemas, theatres and restaurants and into the drenching storm.

Meanwhile the staff of the city's telephone exchanges, which burst alive with callers, were struggling to work by candlelight, as were others in homes and hotels. The black-out would last for six hours.

The *Evening Herald* wrote that the combination of black-out, stormy weather and cancellation of Sunday-night entertainment made Dubliners "disagreeable."

In other parts of the country the wild weather brought different sorts of problems. Out west in Co. Mayo, when the temperature dropped the snow began falling. In several counties spectacular lightning bursts lit up the sky, and thunder cracked. In Westport men sat huddled inside Moran's public house, glad to be dry and safe. Suddenly, a lightning bolt ripped a hole through the roof and knocked plaster off the upstairs fireplace, beside which the publican's terrified mother was sitting. Pubmen below had a "narrow escape," wrote the *Irish Press,* when the "lightning made a sound like a bomb exploding and was heard by all the people in the village."[6] Breaking the large mirrors in the pub, it jolted everyone into perfect soberness. One regular—by name James Joyce—was knocked unconscious. After recovering and being given a gratis pint he rather enjoyed the attention heaped upon him by mates.

Quite a different drama was unfolding at Shannon Airport, where Captain Hilary was having difficulty keeping his aircraft steady as he descended for a landing in the high winds. He was already behind schedule because of unusually strong headwinds. The plane was being buffeted back and forth by tricky gusts and lifted by updrafts, making control challenging. An experienced, unflappable pilot, he slowed the plane, held a tight course, gradually descended, then touched down on the runway. But before the plane had lost its forward speed he was caught in a powerful surge of wind and lifted up again. Instinctively, he thrust it aloft and pulled away from the landing zone, leaving his passengers in wonderment.

He circled, aligned his plane with precision, then came in for another landing. The plane was observed by those on the ground to be "caught again by a gust of wind, made airborne and carried off the runway." For several seemingly interminable seconds it seemed to float just above the ground. By this time, white-knuckled passengers were gripping their seats, straining to see out the windows. "When he finally successfully got it down for the *third* time," the *Irish Press* reported, "it landed on the grass and was bogged down in the sodden ground."[7] Disembarking passengers were visibly relieved that their aerial roller-coaster ride was over.

It was surmised that Captain Hilary might be able to claim the record for most aeroplane landings in such a short span of time.

Following the storm turbulence and chilly weather of the 12th, most of the country enjoyed another "spell of unusual mildness," as Dubliners walked the streets in light coats or jumpers. It would later be said that in mid-January "no-one expected the winter to go down in the annals of harsh weather." Indeed during the days from the 13th to the 18th many people were expressing hopes for a "real touch" of winter, with a nice fall of snow and a few frosty nights to allow for some ice-skating.

————

On 14 January the *Irish Press* published an editorial asserting that Ireland faced a "supplies position . . . about as bad as it was in the worst war years."[8] Calling for the strictest economy in the consumption of bread and fuel, it advised citizens to act "just as if the war had never ended." Warning that the months ahead would grow worse, it stated:

> It is evident that the scarcity of food will be acute . . . [But] for the remainder of the winter the fuel shortage presents the graver problem.[9]

The *Irish Independent* declared that a "fuel crisis" already existed. Not only because "coal is short and imports very low" but also because the "quality has deteriorated" to an appalling level.[10] If coal ran out, domestic turf would *have* to be substituted for it. At present, however, most cut turf was soggy and the boglands waterlogged and inaccessible. Only a spell of very dry weather could save the turf.

With mild weather prevailing, most people were not unduly worried about a fuel shortage. But they dreaded the bread rationing that was due to begin on the 18th. With the global wheat shortage, imports might decline further. In fact it had just been learnt that Ireland was not on the list of countries to which the United States would be supplying a total of 1.2 million tons of wheat and flour. Britain was to get its share, as were other war-torn European countries. Ireland instead would be sent maize, which the Irish Government had found out "had been earmarked in America for human food." This news was taken not only as a disappointment but as an insult:

Authorities in America expect the people of Eire to overcome their bread difficulties by eating maize, or "yellow meal". It is 100 years ago since the Irish people were driven to fall back on "yellow meal" in a substantial way as a diet.[11]

This news prompted Roddy the Rover (Aodh de Blacam) in his regular *Irish Press* column, "Seen, Heard and Noted," to remind readers of the suffering exactly one hundred years earlier:

This year we keep a tragic centenary. "Black '47" will always mark the greatest depth of misery into which the Gael ever sank . . . a whole nation perishing into famine.[12]

———

On 18 January there developed a "pronounced anti-cyclone over Brittany and deep depression over Finland and Greenland." Temperatures remained relatively mild throughout Europe, and there was nothing to suggest that any severe weather was approaching.

Then, on the 19th, a "cold easterly regime set in." The pressure distribution was dominated by anticyclones over southern Scandinavia and Greenland, at times forming a continuous belt, while depressions followed tracks southward of Britain and Ireland. The following day a "major change in the weather occurred" when high pressure migrated to northern Scandinavia, allowing a cold north-easterly airflow to invade Britain and Ireland, bringing night frosts and intermittent showers.

On the 24th "really wintry weather" struck. By 6 a.m. the fall in pressure, with a rise in Finland, resulted in an extremely cold easterly airflow across Ireland. Temperatures began a dramatic plunge, 5 to 10 degrees below the freezing mark.

The sudden change from mild and dry to extremely cold, snowy and windy brought scores of Dubliners down with colds and coughs. By the last week of January medical authorities announced that Dublin was "being swept by a very heavy epidemic of a severe cold of the influenza type."[13] It spread with alarming swiftness. Schools began closing down and businesses losing staff. It was a particularly mean strain of flu, which knocked people off their feet and kept them down for days. Sixteen-year-old Seán Whelan, along with his five brothers and three sisters, who lived in Ballybough in the shadow of Croke Park, were all stricken and debilitated by the flu:

A terrible flu epidemic that winter. I got it myself—it was *dreadful*. I had a dreadful chest pain, cough; my lungs were congested. A terrible headache, and I had perspiration. And I was *frozen*. I was *ice-cold*. Oh, I was dreadfully weak.

Victims were sapped of strength and the stamina needed to fight it off. The epidemic was made all the worse for those afflicted because it struck at the onset of harshly cold weather, coupled with fuel and food shortages. The city's poor, elderly and undernourished were suffering the worst.

On the evening of Saturday the 25th, about the time film-goers were filing out of the Adelphi having seen *Blossoms in the Dust,* starring Greer Garson and Walter Pidgeon, the skies began spitting sleet and hail upon hapless pedestrians. Queuing for buses to get home was cold and messy. As people climbed into bed, the weather worsened. For the next twelve hours, "driven by east wind squalls up the Liffey," the storm made streets slushy. As overnight temperatures dropped below freezing, early Sunday morning mass-goers had to be careful on the slippery surfaces.

At 10:27 a.m. Dubliners at home, in churches and in the streets felt a sudden, strange trembling. Those at mass looked around at one another, to make certain others were feeling the same odd sensation. In many homes small glass and china pieces jingled, jitterbugged and danced right off the shelf or table, smashing on the floor. Lampshades quivered. In old, arthritic tenements cracking was heard. Children asked puzzled parents what it was. According to the seismograph at Rathfarnham Castle it was a "fairly strong earthquake," which lasted sporadically until about noon.

A strange experience for Dubliners: an earthquake, and during a snowfall.

Later that afternoon, between 1:30 and 2, the flakes became denser as it turned into the "first considerable snow storm" of the winter for Dublin and environs. The *Irish Times* welcomed it poetically as "a portion of heaven's swansdown white." Citizens who had been hoping for "real snow" were delighted, strolling through the Georgian squares and St Stephen's Green, gushing over the Christmas-card aura. Children frolicked, throwing snowballs, making snowmen, sliding on footpaths.

Wasn't winter snow wonderful!

Apparently not for everyone. Some more practical Dubliners grumbled that they did not like the snow's effects "on the badly insulated urban dweller." To them, winter cold and snow meant physical discomfort and treacherous conditions. In an editorial on "The first snow" the *Irish Times* assured pessimists that the winter would soon glide into spring:

> Cold weather and bad times both pass, and soon the year will reach the pleasant downward slope which leads into the green valley of spring; and the snows of yesterday will chill only the imagination, and not the feet.[14]

A dose of optimistic reassurance that the first snows of winter were really heralding the arrival of spring, not far behind.

Winter wasn't about to depart quite yet. Throughout Sunday night and into Monday the temperature remained below freezing as the snow continued. After twenty-four hours much of the country had been covered by a "blanket of snow," with the deepest accumulations in the Dublin area and the Wicklow Mountains. The *Irish Press* decided to despatch a reporter and photographer to the mountains to cover the first lovely snowfall of the year, to bring back some interesting first-hand observations. The reporter enthusiastically embraced his assignment:

> We had heard that the snow was over eight inches deep, so we drove up into the high places to see for ourselves. Grinding up Kilgarron Hill we were in the first of the real snow country . . . The Sugar Loaf reared an Alpine head . . . Snow on houses on the Glencree Road looked like Christmas cards.[15]

Accompanying his light, amusing article in the next day's paper were photographs of a boy in a cart, a postman making his rounds, and children in a jolly snowball fight. The general impression was that of winter's snow being wonderful and welcome.

Snow reports from other parts of the country varied. Some areas got barely a dusting, while others received a good coating. The oddest occurrence was reported in Co. Cork. In the Midleton region "a remarkable feature of the snow-storm" was a highly abnormal heavy fall of snow in seaside districts, in some places to a depth of several feet, while not far away there had been only light falls. Older local people couldn't recall such a strange event: "old seafaring men say the vagaries of the storm are an omen of further bad weather."[16]

From distant parts of Europe came other unusual weather stories. The French Riviera was seeing its first snowfall in a hundred years. Residents, in childlike manner, stepped outdoors to feel snowflakes on their faces. In Germany large blocks of ice on the Rhine were forcing barges to put into safe ports. In London frost was affecting the faithful functioning of Big Ben. In the chimes, before striking the hour of 9 p.m., the second phrase was missing— a bad omen to many Londoners. Meanwhile in Ireland radio enthusiasts found their short-wave reception very erratic. "The phenomenon reported is the 'radio echo,' as they heard the same programme a few seconds later" by turning to another point on the scale.[17]

Nature was causing some peculiar things to happen.

———

On the morning of Tuesday the 28th a trough of low pressure associated with a shallow depression over France brought periods of snow, as high pressure persisted to the north-east of Britain. A synoptic situation was forming characterised by extremely low temperatures, with depressions periodically approaching from the south and south-west of Ireland, drawing moisture-laden clouds off the Atlantic, capable of producing heavy snowfall.

Irish people, provincial by nature, were accustomed to thinking of their island as having its own localised atmospheric system, creating distinctively "Irish weather." In late January, however, British and Continental meteorologists were finding quite the opposite: that the abnormally low temperatures invading Britain and Ireland were actually "drawn from the heart of Siberia," part of a broad and complex weather system:

> The Scandinavian anti-cyclone can be regarded as a kind of western extension or outpost of the Siberian system . . . [But] the problem presented by long, cold spells is on a hemispheric, possibly even global, scale, and the Siberian anti-cyclone alone does not provide an adequate explanation of them.[18]

The complexity of such a hemispheric weather anomaly was beyond the comprehension not only of lay people but of Dublin's designated "weather experts" as well. Yet they were expected to predict in daily newspapers what weather was ahead tomorrow, and the next day. And the next.

Throughout Tuesday snow fell along the east coast, accumulating to several inches in Dublin, slickening streets and slowing traffic. In the Wicklow Mountains, around Glencree and Roundwood, the snow was measured in feet. Some miles away in the Irish Sea the fishing boat *Anastasia* bound from Wicklow to Arklow was in mechanical distress amidst a snowstorm with swirling winds. Its engine had broken down while rounding Wicklow Head, and it was now drifting dangerously towards submerged rocks known darkly as "the Wolves." The Wicklow lifeboat responded to a distress message, raced to the rescue, and managed to tow the disabled boat to safety, none too soon.

On Tuesday night "winter tightened its grip," as the *Evening Herald* ominously put it. With a cover of snow on the frozen ground, Dublin's temperature dropped to 15 degrees of frost—17 degrees Fahrenheit (−8°c). Following the night of deep sub-freezing temperatures, Dubliners awoke on Wednesday morning to find themselves in "a frozen blanket . . . locked fast in the icy grip of winter's worst bite."[19] Pedestrians braving the cold on their way to work looked at ice-floes the "size of hearth rugs" floating down the Liffey.

The severe cold was a serious threat to a population not equipped for protecting themselves against it. In the newspapers, doctors were quoted as warning people not to "tempt Providence by going out without plenty of clothing." Shopkeepers were doing a rush trade in heavy coats, gloves, scarves, jumpers, boots—for those who could afford them. Fashionable ladies from Ballsbridge and Howth were seen flaunting luxurious fur coats and fur-lined boots. In sharp contrast, the ill-clad tenement-dwellers were "suffering the most from the Arctic spell."[20] Tenement families were typically large, with six to ten children. With the critical need for rent, fuel and food money, a mother could barely clothe her children decently, much less *warmly* for sub-freezing weather. Footwear was appallingly inadequate, and people stuffed cardboard or cloth into their shoes, good for the first few streets. Many young lads were actually going barefoot in January, risking frostbite.

With the sudden onslaught of dangerously cold temperatures, tenement mothers did their best to find some warmer garments for their children. To obtain the extra shillings they resorted to their only sources: pawnbrokers and moneylenders. Many of the latter were mercenary and unscrupulous. At the pawn offices, of which there were still forty to fifty in Dublin in the late 1940s, they handed over anything they possessed to get a few quid. Thomas Lyng, who began his apprenticeship as a pawnbroker in 1938 at the age of fourteen, still in short trousers, saw their desperation as the winter of 1946/47 set in. Pawnbrokers, most of whom "had hearts," would accept almost anything a tenement mother placed on the counter before them: a well-worn rosary, wedding picture, photo of the Pope, bible, wedding ring, trinkets. Lyng recalls: "Oh, *desperate*. Really hardship cases back then. People in tenements, they were pawning *everything!* We started taking in spectacles, false teeth, bird cages, crutches, walking sticks, scissors, open razors."

If they could come up with a few bob they could head for the city's second-hand markets, most notably the Iveagh Market, Daisy Market, and Cumberland Street, where dealers stood beside mounds of clothing and footwear. As the old saying in Dublin went, and true enough it was, "half the population was clothed in the cast-offs of the other half." At the Daisy Market, Annie Ryan, Margaret O'Connell and Kathleen Reilly saw the place besieged in late January by women desperately seeking warm clothing for their family. The worsening influenza epidemic gave greater urgency to their mission. Kathleen Maguire stood beside her six-foot mountain of clothing as women forced their way forward, "this market *packed* with people . . . mad to root through the heaps of coats, hats, shoes." With so many hardship cases, the big-hearted dealers virtually gave many items away.

Dublin had become a city of people growing frantic to get fuel and clothing as night temperatures dropped ever lower.

———

As Dubliners struggled through the first week of bitter cold, Big Jim Larkin, the messianic labour leader, lay dying in the Meath Hospital in Heytesbury Street. He had been seriously ill for some weeks but was now nearing his end. On the 28th, as he held on to his last hours of life, Father Aloysius, who had administered the last rites to James Connolly in 1916, attended devotedly to him. It is not known whether Larkin still had his vision, but if so his view out the hospital window would have been obscured by heavy frost.

At noon on Wednesday the temperature was between 27 and 25 degrees (−3 to −4°c), the sharp wind making it feel even colder. Along O'Connell Street and Grafton Street people rushed into well-heated shops, such as Clery's, Brown Thomas, and Switzer's, the immediate relief showing on their faces. Outdoors, pedestrians had to cope with what the papers were calling "treacherously ice-bound" surfaces, while hospitals were kept busy with patients suffering bruises and broken bones. The elderly were most at risk; as the *Irish Press* noted, "wary folk brought out that rather unfamiliar weapon in modern years—the walking stick."

Dublin's sea of cyclists were particularly bedevilled by the frigid, slippery conditions. Not intentionally foolhardy, they nonetheless had to get to work and back, crossing icy cobblestones and tram tracks along their way. 27-year-old Dick Curtis worked at Guinness's brewery as a checker, recording the number of barrels brought back each day. Every morning, whatever the weather, he had to cycle to work from the northern suburb of Whitehall. Young and fit, he had a better chance on the slippery streets than most cyclists. But even he had to exercise caution. "You developed survival skills . . . To get a better grip on the icy roads I used to reduce the pressure on the tyres, so they were softer." Nonetheless, "I had quite a number of falls all right."

Many cyclists took terrible tumbles in late January. Women seemed to have the greatest difficulty navigating the dangerous streets. In the early morning of the 29th, 21-year-old Helen Ralphe was on the way to her job when her bike slipped on North Strand Road, becoming entangled in the wheels of an oncoming bus. To the horror of onlookers, she was dragged some distance along the ground. People ran to assist her, and she was rushed to Jervis Street Hospital with injuries to her side, to be told there how lucky she had been. Shortly thereafter Miss S. Thornton of Portland Row was detained in the same hospital after suffering a fractured leg when she too fell from her bicycle. The city's cyclists were fervently hoping that the cold, icy spell would end soon.

On the other hand, some Dubliners welcomed the snow, as they "looked on the white carpet as a gift from the gods."[21] Light-hearted stories in the newspapers offset the bad news about accidents. Three African students at Trinity College, who had never before seen snow, were observed giggling as they threw snowballs at one another. Elsewhere children made snowmen, built snow castles, and slid fearlessly on slippery pavements. Throwing snowballs was the most popular sport, usually at one another, though some bold lads targeted adults. One "miniature battle," reported the *Dublin Evening Mail,* "centred around a bank porter with his shiny tall hat." As daring snowballers peeked around the corner and fired away, the porter at first smiled and held his ground. As the boldness and the barrage increased, the smile disappeared and the hat was removed, immediately ending the challenge and the fun. A wise decision, considering that some tightly packed snowballs could do harm. In one unfortunate case a snowball flung at a passing bus smashed the window and injured a passenger. Meanwhile, in the Phoenix Park, people with toboggans or sleds whizzed down slopes in obvious delight.

Snow could be fun. Or a nuisance. Or plain hazard. In any case, people believed that it wasn't likely to be around for very long.

––––

On the evening of Wednesday 29 January, Archbishop McQuaid drove through the frigid streets towards the Meath Hospital. He had received word that Jim Larkin was fading. He didn't want to wait until morning. The car pulled up before the hospital entrance, cleared of snow and ice. The archbishop stepped out and walked purposefully through the corridor, saying little to those around him. As he entered the dying 72-year-old Larkin's room he quietly exchanged a few words with Father Aloysius. We do not know whether Larkin was aware of his presence.

By the time McQuaid left the hospital the temperature had dropped another degree or two. Throughout the night it would slip downwards a notch at a time. By about 1 a.m. it had already reached the previous night's minimum of 17 degrees (−8°c). Dubliners were sleeping under every item of bedding they possessed. In tenement rooms they slept with their clothes on, commonly two, three or four to a bed or straw mattress, huddling together, sharing the warmth of body heat.

On the 30th "Dubliners awoke to-day shivering as the 'Big Freeze' continued," wrote the *Evening Herald*, "with acute disinclination to get out from under the blankets." No-one wanted to rise and face the day. The piercing cold had become *painful*. Children cried. Grannies sat mute and motionless, a shawl or bedding cocooning them. Mothers tried again and again to coax a bit of heat from wet, smouldering turf.

Anyone who could do so stayed indoors. But many had to brave the Arctic conditions at the crack of dawn or early morning to carry out their necessary duties: milkmen, lamplighters, papermen, postmen, dockers, carters, market dealers. Ill-clothed for facing such risky elements. Indeed, on that day their city was colder than Antarctica.

With the Siberian siege now in its seventh day, Lemass was worried, knowing that people were burning their meagre fuel stock at an alarming rate, trying to survive one day at a time. When coping with the "hurt" of the present cold, little thought was given to conserving fuel for the days ahead. As

January was ending, most people shared two assumptions: firstly, that the Arctic cold snap would surely end soon—and not return; secondly, if it did not, the Government would have an emergency scheme for assisting needy citizens with the provision of fuel.

At mid-morning on Thursday, James Larkin quietly passed away. As the city sluggishly, grudgingly churned to life, word of his death spread. "Big Jim's gone," people said to one another. For a moment it got their minds off their own misery. Many looked backwards, and remembered.

Throughout the day the temperature remained well below the freezing mark. Around the country, schools were running low on fuel, some closing. Only 20 out of the 150 children in Rosslare National School were able to make it. In Co. Laois it was the same. Cavan Circuit Court had to be cancelled, as litigants were unable to travel by road. The Irish Automobile Association was warning drivers not to venture out unless it was absolutely necessary, as roads were treacherous and engines unreliable in such temperatures. The elderly were becoming shut-ins, fearful of falling or freezing if they set foot outside. Funerals were being postponed, as burial was impossible in the frozen ground.

The keepers at Dublin Zoo were in a quandary. Said one: "It's very hard on the animals . . . difficulties in maintaining heating. But hot foods are given them, and other measures have been taken." For the delicate tropical animals it was not simply a matter of providing heat but of maintaining the consistent level that they required. They had recently lost Charlie, the chimpanzee, and several great apes, even a male zebra. Tropical birds and reptiles were at great risk. Bread rationing exacerbated their problem, as it was food for many animals. It was now a round-the-clock battle at the zoo.

———

Bus conductors and drivers were feeling a terrible strain in trying to carry out their duties. Dubliners *en masse* depended on buses to get them to work and home, to town for shopping, medical purposes, entertainment. With many cyclists and motorists now having to rely on them, buses were in greater need than ever. Even the most experienced drivers had fits of frustration—and fear—trying to keep their vehicles from slipping, sliding, spinning out of control on the slippery streets. Certain spots were notoriously treacherous, such as Glasnevin Hill, George's Street, corners along Dame Street. On Emmet Bridge in Harold's Cross bus conductors had to get a dustbin and scatter the contents under the wheels to enable their buses to get over the bridge. Conductors packed their buses beyond normal capacity, having to cast a sympathetic glance at those left behind in the cold queues. The extra weight, of course, made the vehicle more unwieldy for the driver.

On certain routes, drivers found it too risky to try to stop at certain points and passed by the stops, leaving waiting passengers exasperated. Drivers knew that if they halted to collect people they might not be able to gain traction to proceed. At one such high-risk point the driver stopped for passengers, "and then on its upward climb the bus not only failed to start forward again but slid backwards for a distance of about ten to fifteen yards."[22] To the disbelief of passengers, whose heads swung around to see where they were headed. At the end of his stressful day's duty one driver pulled into the garage and told his supervisor of a bad spot in George's Street: "That corner gave me some of the worst moments of my fifteen years of driving." Many drivers were reporting that their health was suffering because of the the tension; the streets had better thaw out soon, or who knows what!

Pedestrians had to fend for themselves. Those who could do so layered themselves with multiple jumpers and coats, wrapped their neck in a scarf pulled up above their chin, hat as far down as possible in an effort to protect ears. The incessant east wind stung their eyes and mouth. People grimaced, dropping their head as they walked yet trying to see where they were going. Most had to walk, some for miles. Fifteen-year-old Mary Dunne had just left St Vincent's Girls' School in North William Street, where she lived, and had taken a job with a tailor, about a twenty-minute walk away. Ordinarily she enjoyed the trek; now, with the biting cold, she dreaded it. She found a way to hide most of her face with a pixie—a knitted hood that covers the neck and fastens under the chin, combining the functions of hat and scarf. Hers was long enough for her to be able to put "half of it up around your mouth, from the wind."

Some people were so buried in tangles of clothing that only their eyes were exposed. It's no wonder that about midday on Thursday pedestrians and motorists along Lower O'Connell Street were dumbstruck by an incongruous sight, caught by a passing reporter:

> Shivering Dubliners in Lower O'Connell Street at 12.30 today were astonished to see a hatless, coatless middle-aged woman in summer attire —white silk blouse, pinafore-style frock. She had a shopping bag and umbrella. In reply to an enquiry the woman said, "The cold? I don't feel it!"[23]

Whether an eccentric, exhibitionist or madwoman, no-one knew. In the 1940s, Dublin had plenty of each.

By now Lemass feared the worst. On the 30th he gave a candid speech at the Accountants' Dinner in the Royal Hibernian Hotel:

> Fuel is our most intractable problem. Supplies of coal are in volume only 40 per cent of pre-war, and much less in calorific value. Probably never

again will we have coal supplies as before the war. Our turf situation, due to abnormal weather conditions, may become critical if we do not experience protracted dry weather.[24]

He then added a cogent observation about people's attitudes. Irish people, he conceded, had endured periods of hardship and scarcity during the war years, but there was "one fundamental difference now." During the war years, "people expected difficulties and were mentally prepared for them—now the public outlook is different." Eighteen months after hostilities had ceased, citizens had good reason to expect that general living standards would have improved, that they would no longer be forced to face shortages of food and fuel.

Their discontent was understandable.

On the night of 30/31 January the cold was more penetrating than the previous night's, with the temperature reaching 7 degrees (−14°C), "an exceptional figure for this country."[25] Painfully cold, both physically and psychologically. With the cruel east wind raging across the bay and up the Liffey, Dubliners were now experiencing a wind-chilled cold that felt far below zero. An authentic Arctic cold. One newspaper attested: "The east wind is the bane of Dublin."

———

By Friday morning, tributes to Larkin were pouring in from all parts of the world. The *Irish Times* wrote that "'Big Jim' was a revolutionary, journalist, orator," who would be chiefly remembered as the heroic labour leader who worked among the unorganised dock workers of Belfast and Dublin early in the century. The 1913 lock-out was marked by the most stirring scenes ever witnessed in Dublin labour disputes. Police baton charges were a feature of every meeting held by workers; on one day alone there were five hundred casualties. Now, thirty-four years later, many of those surviving casualties would walk behind his coffin in the cold and snowy streets.

The *Irish Press* called Larkin's death the "end of an epoch in Irish history," noting that his name had become synonymous with labour unrest, as historians spoke of "Larkinism":

> Larkin, who had the stature of the great demagogue, broadly built with a picturesque mane of silver hair and a voice that sounded trumpet clear, was the greatest labour personality since James Connolly . . . With friend and foe he was the incarnation of the common people.[26]

Prominent personalities at home and abroad heaped praise upon him. Lenin had called him "a man of seething energy . . . of remarkable oratorical talent, a leader who performed miracles among the unskilled workers." Seán O'Casey hailed him as God-sent:

> It is hard to believe that this great man is dead, that this lion of the Irish Labour Movement will roar no more. There was a man sent from God whose name was Jim . . . Jim Larkin is not dead . . . but will always be with us.[27]

George Bernard Shaw was more succinct:

> We all have to go. He did many a good day's work . . . A monument should be erected to his memory.

All through the last day of January people whom Big Jim had touched, both directly and indirectly, trekked the cold, icy streets to churches to offer prayers for their fallen hero.

With nature's refrigerator cranked down to a dangerously low level, doctors and newspapers again warned the public against venturing outdoors unless properly clad. People darted to their destinations. Multitudes of Dubliners who normally dragged themselves to their dreary factory work found for the first time that they were happy to arrive. Many factories were heated by boilers or machinery, as well as body warmth. Sixteen-year-old Rita Gerster was working in Burton's tailoring factory. "You'd be *delighted* to go to work," she says, "because of the heating in the factory, with the irons and all." Arthur Murphy worked in Winstanley's shoe factory in Back Lane, with a big boiler and 150 workers generating plenty of body heat. Some workers would doubtless have slept in their factories if allowed to do so.

Those less fortunate who worked in the city's factories, shops and offices that were inadequately heated, or completely unheated, kept their coats, jumpers, scarves and even hats on during the entire day. Those who worked with typewriters, cash registers and other machines fumbled with numb fingers as best they could. The privileged minority in houses and offices warmed by central heating were greatly envied.

Many Continental countries were also experiencing sub-freezing temperatures. In cities such as Paris and London hordes of citizens found some relief in underground railway stations, where they spent nights *en masse*. Dubliners had no such subterranean sanctuaries. Their primary places for warmth were cinemas, theatres, pubs, and libraries, in the latter creating obvious problems for the staff. In Dublin, the *Irish Press* revealed, every cinema was packed "by people who sought warmth and shelter from the icy air." The city's pubs were so tightly jammed that men had to fight their way to the bar or to the toilets.

Outdoors, ice-floes on the Liffey were growing in size, drifting together and forming frozen platforms. The city's ponds, lakes, canals and rivers were freezing over, tempting to children and skaters. But the ice layer was still far from safe. Workers at Dublin Zoo reported ice on their lake, measured at about 1½ inches thick. Four inches of solid ice was considered the safe minimum for skating. "Stay off the ice!" the public was repeatedly warned. In previous years tragic deaths had occurred from careless playing on ice.

By 31 January, the *Evening Herald* reported, "fallen horses were a common sight on the streets." Dubliners had great affection for horses and were always distressed to see them fall. Eight-year-old Josie Sheehan lived in the Liberties, near the Guinness brewery, and hated seeing the great beasts that hauled beer casks going down hard on icy streets, with an awful bellow and terror-stricken eyes. "There'd be lots of men and straps and ropes, all trying to get the poor unfortunate horse to his feet, and he'd be frothing at the mouth and in an awful state." Local women would rush out with a bin of ash to sprinkle on the ground for grip.

The best protection for horses—though by no means flawless—was to have farriers fit frost nails on their hooves. In late January the city's farriers had never been busier, working eighteen hours a day and still unable to handle all the business queued at the doors of their forges. John Boyne, aged fifteen, was doing his apprenticeship under his father in their forge at the corner of Pearse Street and Macken Street. There were still, he recollects, "about forty or fifty forges around the city." Farriers didn't mind getting only a few hours of sleep, because they had a sense of duty—and earned good money. "It was our best time to earn money, in the frost and snow," Boyne says, "a kind of harvest time for farriers." Up at three or four in the morning, a farrier could work virtually non-stop from dark to dark—"a panicky time for us!" Across town in his forge in Pleasants Lane, off Camden Street, James Harding, born in 1917 and boasting of "striking at the anvil" at the age of twelve, tried to give preference to milkmen, breadmen, and turf men. It was up to the farriers to keep Dublin moving.

———

On the last day of the month the authorities described coal imports from Britain as "abysmally low" and the quality as "steadily deteriorating." British factories were now closing down because of lack of fuel. In Dublin it was rumoured that Irish Coal Importers were trying to place an order with Fire Creek Colliery in Pennsylvania for a meagre emergency ration of nine thousand tons of high-quality coal. But even if the project was successful this would have to be loaded at the port of Baltimore in the third week of February for the three-week voyage—arriving in the middle of March. There was no "quick fix."

Later that morning the Government announced that on 3 February crucial cuts in coal supplies would be made. Citizens were surprised to learn that these cuts, amounting to a reduction of a quarter, would even apply to hospitals, hotels and other institutions and to industries. With the coal crunch becoming more severe by the day, some industrialists and institutions were talking of the possibility of conversion from coal and turf to oil. Though Ireland had a decent supply of oil, such conversion required time and money, as well as overcoming some storage and transport problems.

Citizens were now also having difficulty getting paraffin oil (kerosene), as supplies were running low, largely because of a shortage of tank wagons. Alderman Alfie Byrne revealed that even milk was running short in Dublin, at the rate of about three thousand gallons per day, largely because of lower production. And, because of the weather, vegetables were in short supply in Dublin's markets. Stalls that were normally spilling over were now half empty.

Life seemed to be in a downward spiral.

There were those who used humour to soften the bite of the "Big Freeze." Some journalists endeavoured to use wit as warmth. In his regular *Evening Herald* column, "Argus" wrote:

> I am glad that I have not had to start using the furniture for kindle wood. I find chopping up even kitchen chairs to be exhausting work, and when one gets amongst the upholstery of the period pieces it gets very complicated.[28]

Within a few short weeks, readers would not find such waggish words amusing.

At 7 p.m. on the last day of January members of the Workers' Union of Ireland escorted the body of James Larkin from the Meath Hospital to Thomas Ashe Hall in College Street, head office of the union. "Sharp orders from inside the hospital silenced the murmurings and brought hospital staffs to the windows and doorways," the gates opened, the band began to play, and the hearse and its escort crunched out through the snow. "In a hush broken only by the strains of the 'Dead March' in 'Saul' and hundreds of shoes on snow and slush," wrote the *Irish Times*, "'Big Jim's' body was carried through the streets," while people whispered to one another, "He was a great man."

All along the route people lined the footpaths, leaned out windows, watched thoughtfully. Through Kevin Street and around by Christ Church the procession moved. Then the band stopped, orders rang out for a quick march, the hearse accelerated, and the long queue of homage stepped down Cork Hill. Again the Dead March began, and far along Dame Street wide ribbons of people lined the paths. Traffic waited patiently in Grafton Street and Westmorland Street as the cortege advanced down College Green to Thomas

Ashe Hall. Everyone wanted to get near Larkin:

> The hearse stopped and the crowd surged forward. Civic guards and trade
> unionists linked arms to withstand the pressure of over 2,000 persons.
> Guards forced clearance by putting their elbows into the nearest chests
> and pushing hard.[29]

A gap was cleared as James Larkin Junior and Denis Larkin, his sons, entered
the building while the coffin was carried into the hall. Then the crowd pushed
again. Photographers' bulbs flashed as the coffin was carried up the stairs and
laid on a bench. For the next hour or so select individuals, mostly
representatives of the union, public bodies and political parties, filed past the
coffin. The masses who failed to gain entry on Friday night vowed to be back
first thing on Saturday morning—regardless of weather.

———

January ended on a dismal note of brutal cold, worsening fuel and food
shortages, and a hero's death. The mood was made all the more bleak by the
fact that total sunshine for the month was only 36½ hours—less than half that
of 1946. By the 31st, eight days into the Siberian siege, suffering Irish people
were wondering what was causing such severe, abnormal weather. At the
month's end the *Evening Herald* distilled it into a simple explanation:

> This is the cause of it all—a persistent anti-cyclone centred over Norway
> and Sweden is attracting freezing winds from North Russia.[30]

How long, people wondered, would the anticyclone "persist."

———

One person, some five thousand miles from Ireland, was puzzled by the same
question. However, he understood that there was no simple single cause of
what was a complex and baffling weather phenomenon occurring in January
1947. And not just in Ireland.

Jerome Namias, a senior meteorologist with the US Weather Bureau, used
the latest scientific technology of the time to analyse global weather patterns
and anomalies. He had seen some climatological abnormalities during his
career, but what he was now observing was quite inexplicable. Which is why
it so aroused his fascination.

He and his colleagues were assiduously "plotting variations, from normal
pressure all over the northern hemisphere," detecting a number of strange
deviations from the norm. One development in particular held their
attention: the normal polar air mass was expanding far south beyond its usual

domain. Ordinarily, the polar region was covered in winter with a cap of cold air that reached down to latitude 60°N (south Norway and Leningrad). This year, however, Namias discovered that the "polar air mass was much larger" than usual, bringing the polar east winds down to latitude 45°, south of Britain.[31] This meant that "winter storms which normally plague Iceland were felt as far south as Bermuda."

Furthermore, quite to his surprise, he found that this January the "prevailing Westerlies failed," allowing Arctic east winds from Russia to invade western Europe, leaving Britain and Ireland in a vulnerable position to become "frozen and snowbound." Indeed by the last week of January they were already "getting Siberian weather," as he called it. Other northern European countries were similarly affected: Germany, Poland, the Low Countries, and parts of central Europe. France was divided, with intense cold in the north but relatively mild weather in the south.

Namias was especially interested in a precarious weather zone over Britain and Ireland, where "along with the cold could come a belt of storms where the east and west winds meet."[32] In these "collision" areas, powerful air masses confronted one another and battled for supremacy, with the potential to generate violent weather, possibly raging blizzards. He saw that the combination of the expanding polar air mass, anticyclonic regime to the north, invasion of Russian Arctic winds and passing depressions and low-pressure systems off the Atlantic to the south created a dangerous weather chemistry for Ireland.

At the end of January he determined it to be a "hemispheric-wide aberration," which was already producing the "most peculiar weather."[33] Honestly admitting that he did not know "what made the polar air mass grow so big this winter," he vowed to "watch it grow," analysing its daily evolution in hopes of finding scientific explanations.

He suspected that February and March might be turbulent months.

Chapter 3 ∾

"SURPRISE BLIZZARD"

The storm was howling over the land, the trees crashing and slates flying, windows rattling and dogs trembling.
(*Irish Press*, 4 FEBRUARY 1947)

The blizzard took Dublin by surprise. With a 62 mile-an-hour wind behind it, it left a foot of snow and drifts of up to five feet. Transport was almost paralysed, telephone and telegraph communications were reduced to a tangle of torn wires and fallen poles.
(*Irish Times*, 3 FEBRUARY 1947)

It would cut *you. I remember that* vividly, *it was like needles or pellets going into your face!*
(JOHN GALLAGHER, 77)

The S.S. Irish Plane, *her steering gear broken in mountainous seas on one of the wildest parts of the southern coast . . . ran into the "hurricane" . . . and ran ashore about 50 yards from a cliff.*
(*Dublin Evening Mail*, 2 FEBRUARY 1947)

SATURDAY 1 FEBRUARY

Captain S. G. Hickman and his crew of thirty-five men on the *Irish Plane*, many Dubliners, had just returned from an uneventful voyage to New York. Their 7,250-ton vessel was one of the finest in the fleet of Irish Shipping Ltd, insured for the considerable sum of £150,000. From America they had brought back a cargo of a thousand tons of car parts and typewriters, most destined for Cork. After first unloading some crates in Dublin and taking on some new export items, they headed over to Swansea to take on a supply of coal and were now on their way down to Cork. From there they would sail back to New York with a cargo of whiskey and wool.

On their stopover in Dublin local crew members enjoyed shore leave to visit family and friends. The ship's fireman, Terence Keegan, had only to amble over to Railway Street to his home; John Coyne was from Dorset Street; Charles McDermott lived in Townsend Street, Patrick McCarthy lived in Temple Bar, and John Kavanagh was an Irishtown man. First Officer John Caird was from Dundrum, while Captain Hickman was reunited with his family at their pleasant house in Northumberland Road. Most were seasoned sailors, got on well, performed their jobs proficiently. In emergencies they acted swiftly and effectively. They depended upon one another.

In February seas could be rough, but the trip down to Cork and onwards to America was expected to be routine. Weather forecasters predicted no serious storms.

––––––

On Saturday morning, as the *Irish Plane*, full-bellied with Swansea coal, steamed steadily towards Cork, the Dublin scene was dominated by the masses converging on College Street. Outside Thomas Ashe Hall mourners formed a lengthy queue to pay their last respects to James Larkin. From 10 a.m. till past ten that night the stream of friends and admirers would continue. Sullen, heads down, collars up against the cold wind, they inched forward outside the WUI offices. Strangers were drawn to share personal thoughts with one another. Grannies fingering worn rosary beads and calloused dockers whispered, "He fought for the workers." Heads nodded.

The coffin was laid on a bench roped off in the centre of a cold room hung with black curtains and lit by shrouded lamps and four candles. One after another, mourners shuffled forward and slowly ascended the stairs:

> They stepped nervously into the room, walked quickly around the coffin. Many stopped at the coffin, touched the joined hands holding beads, murmured and went on.[1]

And so it went throughout the day. Filing past the open coffin, people found it strange to see a man of such enormous energy and passion now silent and lifeless. Many retreated down the stairs with tear-stained faces.

As crowds waited in frigid streets to pay homage to a hero, elsewhere in Dublin a trickle of people, mostly women, paid a sad visit of another type. In a dingy room in North Earl Street, "Miss Ima Weight," billed as "the world's fattest woman," was "on view" from 2 p.m. to 10 for an admission fee of 4 pence. It was a spectacle for Dubliners seeking novelty in the boring winter months. "By popular demand," it was claimed, her appearance had been extended. Gawkers had the choice of spending their money on a matinée that weekend or seeing the "freak show," as many unkindly put it. While some visitors exited giggling, others showed sympathy. A good many doubtless feeling ashamed of themselves.

Dublin itself was about to have a memorable visitor.

———

By early Saturday afternoon a herculean battle was under way in the upper atmosphere. Unknown to Captain Hickman and his crew, and to Dubliners going about their usual weekend activities.

In the North Atlantic the Gulf Stream normally carried warm water polewards, bringing with it from the south a steady flow of westerly winds, caressing Ireland. These winds, having traversed vast stretches of warm water, acquired much of that warmth. So long as they continued over their normal course, rain and drizzle fell upon the Emerald Isle; "but if anything happens to stop this air flow the weather can change suddenly and severely."[2]

The warm air from the Atlantic picks up abundant moisture during its long sea passage and is less dense than cold air. If two conflicting air masses—the warm from the west and south and cold from the east—confront one another, they do not intermingle, as the lighter air is forced to rise over the denser cold. In rising it expands, there being less air above to compress it, and reaches a point at which it can no longer hold its moisture. With the invasion of the cold east wind from Russia on 24 January the stage was set for potential—probably inevitable—collisions of warm and cold air fronts on a massive scale.

By about 1:30 on the afternoon of Saturday 1 February the curtain was about to be drawn for the first act.

It began with successive attempts by warmer air masses to move in from the south. But the entrenchment of high pressure to the north and east provided a block to the usual movement of depressions. Thus began the struggle between the two atmospheric behemoths. At first they met head on and lay heavily against one another, like two giant Sumo wrestlers. They pushed, shoved, tested one another's power. A forceful anticyclonic regime with fierce winds and frigid air battling against mild, moist oceanic fronts stubbornly trying to follow their normal northward course. Harbouring no intentional ill against people.

As opposing systems exerted their full strength against one another in the struggle for supremacy, the warm, moist air was steadily forced to rise higher and higher. Simultaneously, the Siberian air was dropping temperatures lower and lower. The low-pressure frontal troughs carrying clouds moisture-laden to capacity tried to surge forward. But the icy blast "drawn from the heart of Siberia," which had been sweeping the Continent for several weeks, was by now accustomed to getting its way.[3] Creating the weather chemistry for a violent outcome. It was an ancient story. As the British meteorologist Gordon Manley succinctly explained, "for thousands of years the battle between tropical and Polar air was repeatedly fought over the British Isles."[4]

Over the course of history creating Ice Ages.

———

On the Saturday afternoon of the first week of February, Captain Hickman and his crew were oblivious of history's destiny. All they knew was that the winds were picking up quite suddenly, the seas growing choppy. Not unusual along Ireland's south coast.

By about 5:30 p.m. the winds had accelerated to nearly 50 miles per hour, the sea forming mountainous waves. Captain Hickman conferred with First Officer Caird about the worsening weather, especially as the ship's steering gear did not seem to be functioning properly. No more than an hour later, with the wind now in excess of 55 miles per hour, Hickman and Caird found themselves fighting to control their vessel. Terence Keegan, who was on watch at the time, saw that they were nearing Daunt's Rock, 5½ miles west-south-west of Ballyshane, near Ballycotton, known notoriously as "one of the wildest parts of the southern coast." By this time the storm clouds were spitting sleet and snow, making Keegan's visibility extremely poor. To the best of his recollection it was somewhere between 7 and 8 p.m., with the wind now raging at nearly 60 miles per hour, "when we ran into the hurricane."

With the ship heaving and lurching, thrashed by seas towering over the deck, the captain and first officer struggled futilely with the damaged steering mechanism. Shortly after 8 o'clock the steering gear completely broke down. As Captain Hickman shouted out orders to heave two heavy anchors overboard to try to keep the ship from drifting dangerously, "all the engineers were working like madmen to try and get us out of trouble," to repair the steering.[5] Barely able to keep their footing or to handle tools, the best they could do was to hastily devise an auxiliary steering gear. But within fifteen minutes it too was disabled. A few minutes later the force of the wind and sea proved too much for the anchors and, "pounded by huge waves which lashed high over her decks, she dragged and drifted."

Now at the mercy of the sea, in pitch-blackness, during what would later be called the "worst gale they had ever experienced," a sickening feeling crept over the crew.

With the 7,000-ton *Irish Plane* being tossed about like a toy boat, Captain Hickman gave the order to fire flares aloft, though realising that under such conditions there was little chance of their being spotted. At the same time wireless messages were being frantically sent, offering at least some hope. The winds were now screaming at more than 60 miles per hour, and the men could barely hear one another speak. Then the electrical system went, and the crew felt the fear of being on a coffin ship.

Some time close to 9:15 p.m. the ship abruptly struck ground at Kelly's Cove, about six miles east of Ballycotton, near Roche's Point, one of the rockiest parts of the jagged south coast. It became wedged between two large rocks about 50 to 70 yards from shore, standing on a perfectly even keel, broadside to a cliff about forty feet above the sea. In the darkness, with the storm at full blast, they knew only that they had run aground.

Meanwhile, at the Ballycotton Life-Saving Station, where at least one of the distress messages had been picked up, the men on duty sprang into action. As they left the comfort and safety of their small turf-heated station to collect their rescue gear they had to lean into the wind and snow to keep their balance. They could only imagine what the crew of the imperilled ship were enduring at that moment. If indeed the ship was still afloat, and the men alive.

As it turned out, the Ballyguleen Life-Saving Station had also received a faint distress message, and its men were also scrambling to respond. What ensued over the next sixty to ninety minutes was "a dramatic dash" as the men "set forth over fields and by roads in the gale," fighting the blizzard all the way, to reach the point on the coast at which they believed the ship most likely to be.[6] A frantic race described by one of the rescuers:

> We tried to get round to them, but were unable to make it—the seas were terrific. Then we went overland and found roads blocked by fallen trees. The rescue took place in a raging storm ... When we finally got to the cliff top the vessel was barely discernible in the blinding storm.[7]

As this was going on the Red Cross contingent from Ballycotton and Cloyne, along with gardaí, were making their way towards the cliffs with the same life-and-death urgency.

———

As the shipwreck drama was being played out on Saturday night, in Dublin crowds were attending the cinemas, theatres, dancehalls, filling pubs and mobbing their favourite fish-and-chip shops. Early in the evening it was windy and sleety. Gradually, the temperature dropped and snow began. By the time the night-owls were heading home the winds had whipped up to 35–40 miles per hour. Hats flew off and tumbled along the pavement in O'Connell Street. As people anxiously awaited the last bus home, coats were buttoned to the top and collars turned up.

W. H. Booth and J. O'Brien, *Sunday Independent* van-drivers, were unconcerned. Nasty weather never deterred them. They had a job to do. Veterans of the paper delivery business, they knew how much the Sunday morning newspapers meant to people around the country. They were proud and dutiful in their role. Over the years on the road they had handled all sorts of rainy, foggy, windy, snowy weather. This night there had been no storm forecasts. It was probably a minor squall that would pass over soon. They would depart as usual, drive through the night hours, and have the papers delivered in distant counties by dawn for early readers.

——————

The first rescuers reached the cliffs above the stricken ship some time between 10 and 10:45 p.m., straining to see the vessel wedged upright on its keel. But being battered unmercifully by huge waves. Standing atop the cliff, they had to be careful not to be sucked over themselves by sudden, unpredictable backwinds. Finding their megaphones useless, they depended on torches and lamps to try to communicate with the ship's crew. They were surprised to find that Captain Hickman and his officers were at first determined to "hold on as long as possible," declining their offers of rescue. They were hoping the storm would subside soon and they could use lifeboats. They'd wait it out—for a while longer.

Less than an hour later Captain Hickman had a change of heart. In a sea gone wild, with the ship growing less stable in its rocky niche, they finally "had no option but to accept assistance and leave the ship."[8] Without delay. Shortly before midnight the captain reluctantly gave his order to "abandon ship." Minutes later an *Irish Independent* reporter who had got word of the drama arrived on the scene in the company of a life-saving team:

> An eerie scene presented itself when I arrived at the bleak headland about midnight on Saturday. The fierce gale continued to rage with heavy squalls, and the only illumination was supplied by the lamps of the life-saving service and a lamp on the bridge of the ship. The order had just been given and the rocket service, manned by sturdy volunteers, had succeeded in securing a line to the ship.[9]

With the ship unreachable, the only means of rescuing the crew was a breeches-buoy, a one-man seat supported by ropes fired by a rocket from the shore. When the rocket-powered lines crossed the bow they were quickly but carefully secured to the mainmast by the most skilled seamen. Once firmly affixed, the apparatus had to be tested for safety, to make certain it could hold a man's weight and carry him across the roaring chasm. A guinea-pig was needed. The cook, P. J. McCarthy, was chosen. Whether by captain's order or volunteering we do not know.

With his crewmates standing in tensed silence, McCarthy was strapped in tightly, then swung over a roiling sea in hurricane-force winds at midnight. His figure faded away within seconds into the blackness. About half a minute later, rescuers on top of the cliff spotted his form emerging with their torches, and he was drawn, yard by yard, closer. Grabbed by men on each side, he was jerked forward onto terra firma and quickly released. Without hesitation, the other crewmen began taking their turns, one by one. The perilous ordeal instilled in even the hardiest veteran an unabashed feeling of fear. Said one man of this experience, after he had survived it, it was "a sickening feeling as we were swung up on the cliff," each heaving an audible sigh of relief.[10] "Sodden to the skin and obviously famished from the cold and prolonged exposure," the reporter noted, the crew were met by Red Cross workers, who promptly provided blankets, warm clothing, food and drink.

True to the oldest tradition of the sea, Captain Hickman was to be the last man brought ashore, Chief Officer Caird preceding him. The other crewmen, safe above, awaited their captain's appearance. Time passed, but he did not join them. Something had gone wrong. More time passed. Communication wasn't possible: the only way to find out was for one of the men to return in the breeches-buoy to the ship. Without hesitation the chief steward, Farley, stepped forward. Strapped in once again, he would tempt fate by risking a second and a third crossing to assist his captain.

When he reached the deck he found Captain Hickman with a fractured leg from a fall, helpless to assist himself. Within minutes Caird joined them; together they lowered the breeches-buoy down to deck level and lashed the captain into the apparatus, to be lifted and swung over the "yawning death between the ship and the shore."[11] Once safely atop the cliff, Captain Hickman was heartily greeted by his men, then placed in the hands of the Red Cross and taken off to hospital.

After several hours of witnessing the dramatic life-and-death rescue, the reporter spotted a surprising break in the storm clouds, remarking that "to us onlookers it seemed ironical that the moon appeared."

————

As Dubliners slept, the "gale steadily rose." Temperatures fell, and heavy snow began. By midnight the wind exceeded 50 miles per hour. By 1 a.m., 60. The storm was now gaining strength rapidly. Fitful sleepers were stirred by the wind's howling and snow pelting horizontally against their windows. The mighty air masses were in full combat.

In Dublin, with the dense snow now limiting visibility to only feet, "at 1.30 on Sunday morning the blizzard began."

Booth and O'Brien were on the road, having watched the weather turn nastier by the hour. They knew the roads well, had confidence in their van, even had "anti-freeze equipment on their windscreen." They had handled snowstorms before. But this was clearly going to be a longer delivery night than usual, as visibility diminished, roads became slippery, and snowdrifting began. Before long they had to creep in third gear, as it was becoming difficult to keep their vehicle on the road. The wind was now shoving their heavily laden van around, as trees along the roads swayed wildly, some limbs breaking off. A "heavy snowstorm," they were thinking. The notion of a "blizzard" was not yet in their consciousness. They'd be patient, they'd be late, but they would get their Sunday morning newspapers delivered. About that they had no doubt.

By 2:30 a.m. Dublin was being battered by the mounting blizzard. Snowfall intensified, "fell in sheets as the blizzard continued throughout the night." Accumulating at a rate of more than an inch or more an hour, it was covering the city, sticking to every surface:

> Whipped by the wind, the blizzard that raged during the night plastered snow against walls, trees, and anything with which it came into contact, as firmly as if it were put on with a trowel.[12]

It crawled up doorways and walls, coated windows. Railings and lampposts were ornamented with white icing. Tree limbs sagged lower and lower. Residents living around Merrion Square and throughout the suburbs were awakened by the sharp sounds of snapping branches and trees crashing. Hedges and ornamental shrubs were being crushed to the ground. The city's rickety, rotten tenement houses shuddered. Windows rattled, doors banged, loose bricks and slates were dislodged, crashing to the ground. Winds swirled through hallways, under doors, through every crevice. All over the city, drifts were piling up, foot by foot.

By this time Booth and O'Brien realised that they were not going to outrun or outlast any normal snowstorm. They were caught out in a *bona fide* blizzard. Then their van became trapped in a seven-foot snowdrift near Culohill, Co. Kilkenny. With no digging equipment, they were unable to extricate themselves. After some deliberation Booth decided to hike more than a mile through deep snow to procure a shovel at a farmhouse. Several hours later their van was freed. Ten minutes later it was stuck again.

It was the same story for other newspaper drivers around the country. All had been caught unsuspecting, with no warnings from weather forecasters. In Co. Sligo, Fred Crowley found the "roadways a death trap" as he skidded out of control and slammed into snowdrifts. Fred Brannigan, a veteran newspaper van driver, called the treacherous conditions along his delivery route to Galway the worst he had "ever experienced in his thirty-four years of driving ... frightful!"

Unknown to Booth and O'Brien, close to the same time they left Dublin another vehicle, carrying four men, left the city. It too was heading for Co. Cork. Four officials of Irish Shipping Ltd had been notified late on Saturday night that the *Irish Plane* had hit rocks and was being "mercilessly battered by heavy seas . . . feared a total loss." If so, it would be a terrible blow to the company, which was its own underwriter of the £150,000 insurance. Two of its other ships, the *Irish Pine* and *Irish Oak,* had been war casualties. They could ill afford to lose another ship so soon after the war years. The officials were determined to reach the shipwreck site as soon as possible to assess for themselves just how bad the situation was.

Having left Dublin in dark of night, like the newspaper van drivers, they had no inkling of a major snowstorm, much less a blizzard, that would catch them on the open road. Fighting at first the slippery roads and poor visibility, they proceeded at an ever-slower pace. Then they began encountering snowdrifts.

Several hours later the two vehicles encountered one another in the "middle of nowhere" in Co. Kilkenny. After greeting one another and earnestly commiserating for a few minutes, the six men decided to try to proceed in convoy, as a practical measure and for company. One shovel between them.

After about fifteen hours of constantly "stopping and digging more along their route" with the borrowed shovel, the six beleaguered men finally straggled into Cork at 7:15 that evening, along with the morning papers. Then Booth and O'Brien, for some fuzzy-minded reason, now sleepless for nearly twenty-four hours, having finished their meal decided to try a return trip to Dublin. They left Cork at 9:30 p.m. and on their way back were once again halted by snowdrifts, in the same Culohill–Johnstown stretch. Having no-one but themselves to blame for their predicament this time.

——

On Sunday morning Dubliners awoke flabbergasted. "Dublin went to bed on Saturday night with the wind howling around the houses," wrote the *Irish Independent,* "and awoke to find the city bogged in snow." The *Dublin Evening Mail* was more descriptive:

> When Dubliners woke yesterday morning they saw an utterly unexpected sight. A fierce gale had descended upon the city blowing down trees and poles . . . The snow fell for hours in bucketfuls . . . as people found themselves snowbound altogether, unable to leave their houses . . . For everybody it was certainly a day to be remembered.[13]

With their windows plastered with a thick coating of snow and doors frozen shut, people strained to gain a view of what lay outside. They looked out on drifts as high as a man's head, driven by a wind of 62 miles per hour. In memorable understatement, the newspapers wrote that the "blizzard took Dublin by surprise."

With the blizzard still fulminating, many people found themselves snowbound, unable to get out of their houses. Most early mass-goers prudently remained indoors. If they were able to emerge from their door and reach the pathway or street it was often covered with drifted snow up to their knees or higher. The elderly, to whom mass attendance was most important, had little chance. When a few newspaper or milk vans managed to roll sluggishly through a street they left tyre tracks that some people used as a path in which to follow on foot. Looking like a procession of pilgrims. But few dared to face the blizzard's rage. John Gallagher and a few of his neighbours along the Coombe quickly found that fighting the blizzard was painful, "like needles or pellets going into your face, it would cut you! You had to keep your head bent over walking." Throughout most of Sunday morning Dublin was as silent and still as a white ghost town.

The city's suburbs were the same, strewn with toppled telephone and telegraph poles, dangling electricity cables, fallen trees and broken branches that shattered roofs and blocked roads. Some residents foolishly tried to drive, but usually didn't get far. Harry Moscow of Orwell Road awoke on Sunday morning to find four large trees blown down on his garden during the night. Somehow he found several men who would work for three hours to clear them from his driveway. He then got into his car and crept down the road. A few minutes later he returned home—on foot, his car embedded in a drift. Throughout the day most Dubliners in the city centre and suburbs were content to remain indoors, as the blizzard continued to roar around them.

———

Country people were no less astonished in the morning when going to their windows. In fact, owing to colossal drifting over vast open landscapes, many were more stunned at what they encountered. As the blizzard swept across the country, several counties in the west, east and midlands got a particularly bad hammering. In Co. Carlow, Jim Nolan and his neighbours were caught off guard by the blizzard's suddenness and its severity:

> For two weeks we had a black frost day and night, with a strong east wind ... Then the snow started to fall. I can still remember the peculiar sound of that wind that evening and all through the night, as if it was coming from some big blower in the heavens. The snow blew right in through the keyhole in the kitchen door. When I got up the next morning and looked out I could not believe my eyes—all I could see were the tops of the trees.[14]

Parts of Cos. Galway, Mayo, Sligo and Donegal were buried beneath drifts. Nineteen-year-old Jim Maloney was on his family's farm in Co. Galway helping with the livestock. He saw how nature's deep-freeze prepared the ground for holding the snow atop it. When the blizzard struck it immediately changed the landscape and normal patterns of local life:

> The ground was blocked with the heavy frost, and that's what held the snow. The wind came from the east, the snow drifted, the roads were blocked, and no transport could travel. Deliveries were held up—no bread. Funerals were held up. It all came to a standstill.

The massive drifting sculpted the landscape into different forms, scouring some hills and mountainsides while filling in lowland valleys and depressions, covering stone walls and hedgerows, obscuring landmarks and familiar features:

> For miles on end not a blade of grass can be seen and only the tops of dividing hedges are visible in the fields. Boreen and side roads are indistinguishable in the general blot-out.[15]

From Killarney came news that the Arctic temperatures and blizzard caused the Lower Lake to become frozen for almost a hundred yards from shore. This had happened only once before in the previous fifty years. Throughout the country, people who could do so relied on horseback to get around. In 21-year-old Brian Kelly's part of Co. Donegal "at the onslaught of this bad winter there were no snowshoes, so people used to put socks over their shoes or little bits of hay ropes around their feet to walk in the snow."

———

Throughout Ireland, every town and village had its own predicament, its own story. In Straide, Co. Mayo, about ten miles north of Castlebar, the four hundred or so local residents had heard the rising wind whistling during the night as it hissed through crevices in their houses. Nearby lived the Ruane family. Self-sufficient farmers, they kept cattle and sheep and annually stocked up on food and dry turf for the coming winter. They had to be well supplied, for there were nine children, five boys and four girls, between the ages of five and twenty-one.

In family photographs Tony, the youngest of the lot, was clearly adored by the rest. Hard to imagine at the time that at the age of twenty-one he would bid an emotional goodbye to his parents and siblings and head for Dublin to become a garda. Or that he would become a champion boxer for the Garda Síochána, and later a fine writer gifted at chronicling his early life. In Tony's mind, the winter of 1946/47 stood out. "I have vivid memories of 1947, the year of the 'Big Snow' . . . houses in snowdrifts, and Mayo at a standstill."

It all began on that night of 1/2 February. For at least nine hours overnight throughout east Mayo there was a steady, heavy snow, whipped wildly by the wind into deep drifts. As the Ruanes slept, he recalls, "the high winds blew all the snow against any house or other obstruction in its path." By morning their house on the windward side was plastered several feet deep in snow, quite unknown to the family when they first stirred. On his going to the window his eyes widened. "Snowfalls of this magnitude were a rare occurrence, and the excitement generated made it a very special occasion indeed."

One by one his brothers and sisters took their turn in peering outside into what the local postman, Martin Sweeney, called "a world of snow." Then his father told the children to step away from the door as he attempted to open it. Young Tony watched:

> I can remember well being in our kitchen and my Dad pulling open the door with great difficulty. Then there was an avalanche of snow across the floor. Then my Dad started to dig with an ash shovel, the only tool available to him.
>
> Soon he had burrowed a path through the drift of snow. I did not have time to put my trousers on and I bolted through the door to see the spectacle. I was in my nightshirt and I recall my mother chiding me and telling me that I would catch my death of cold. Still in my nightshirt, I grabbed the ash shovel and commenced making a snowman.

Children throughout the countryside exulted in the thrill of such an extraordinary snow, as their parents and grandparents told them they would never see its likes again. Enjoy it for the few days it would probably last.

Among those also digging out in Straide that morning was a troupe of itinerant entertainers who had just arrived with their travelling road-show. Their intention had been to set up their stalls, stay for a week or two, then depart for their next rural destination. "But the heavy snowfall," quips Ruane, "put a halt to their gallop." The road-show—called a "hurdy-gurdy" show by most local people—was owned and operated by Phillip Mount, a travelling man of much savvy. And of good reputation. He saw to it that his performers behaved well and ruffled no feathers of the village elders or parish priest. So, when their colourful caravans were spotted setting up an encampment just outside the village, there was always excitement, and anticipation. In good weather they operated such rides as a Ferris wheel and small swing-boats. When poor conditions prevailed they still offered an array of tricks, acts, music. For country people, children and adults alike, it was always lively, exotic, and fascinating. Phillip Mount always had his seasonal agenda well planned, down to the last detail. Except for nature's role.

On the morning of 2 February he knew there would have to be a change of plan. During the night the blizzard shook their caravans and trailers so violently that some might have toppled over had they not been anchored by heavy pot-bellied stoves and equipment. Inside, pots, pans, tools, musical instruments, glass and china jiggled about, some falling to the floor. By morning everything was left topsy-turvy. Shortly after dawn, as the women were trying to restore order inside their vehicle-homes, the men were outside digging out. Mount ploughed through the deep drifts, consulting his men, assessing their situation. They couldn't erect their tents as usual, with several feet of snow on the ground, a half-gale still blowing, and sub-freezing temperatures numbing one's face and hands.

Nor could they pull out of Straide and hit the road in search of villages that might not have been smashed too hard by the blizzard. Local roads were heavily drifted over and all travel cut off. Clearly, they were stuck in Straide, and would be there until the roads were cleared or a major thaw occurred. There was no sign of either.

Always resourceful, Mount conjured up an alternative plan. If he could convince the parish priest to allow his troupe to set up their activities in the renovated former church building, now used as a community centre, two things might be accomplished: local people would be provided with some much-needed winter diversion, and his travelling group could at least earn enough money for food and fuel to survive the blizzard's blast.

He'd give it a try.

———

Meanwhile back in Dublin on Sunday, despite the blizzarding conditions, thousands of people trudged clumsily through the snow and cold, with a singular purpose. They were not to be denied their visit to the coffin of James Larkin, to pay their last respects. Since "transport was almost paralysed," most had to walk, some coming considerable distances. Those fortunate enough to find a bus or tram in service had to put up with long queues, frequent halts and breakdowns. It was often faster to walk, even in knee-deep snow. Where people had trampled a crude path, walkers frequently slipped and fell, many of them elderly, some who had marched with Big Jim under even more dangerous conditions.

The city's buses and trams were hours late getting started, as their drivers had difficulty reaching the terminals. Some of the most experienced men were bedridden with the spreading flu. Buses did not appear on the streets until nearly 11 o'clock, many quickly becoming embedded in drifts. CIE officials in company cars made the rounds with shovels and sand to assist with disabled buses. Within the first few hours a number of buses developed brake-drum problems in the snow and slush. When one bus became stalled, others were halted behind. At about noon, at Dolphin's Barn seven buses were lined up helplessly, unable to move forward or back. In disgust, some passengers disembarked and stumbled along on their own.

Trams had trouble from the start. Sections of track were badly drifted or ice-coated, as the heavy snow broke bumpers and motors burned out. Those that were running were a devil to control on a slippery track, which could render brakes useless. Tram-drivers cursed pedestrians, cars, and horse-drawn vehicles, which continually cut in front of them, risking injury. Paddy Lynch was well experienced, but that Sunday was the worst day he had ever faced:

Honest to God, you'd be frightened going out. The tracks were frozen and you wouldn't have *stopping* power, and you'd slide—there were accidents.

By early afternoon no trams were able to run on the Dartry and Terenure routes, while on the Dalkey and Dún Laoghaire lines some of the inward trams could only get as far as Merrion Square.

To those who did venture out of doors on Sunday, evidence of the blizzard's force and destruction were all around them. The cityscape had been given a good thrashing by nature, and telephone and telegraph communications were reduced to a jumble of torn wires and fallen poles. The wires of trunk lines were found in "tangled heaps along roads," looking as if they were writhing in agony. In many outlying districts, such as Clondalkin, there were so many wires and cables snapped and dangling that one resident described them as "lying like barbed wire" in coiled entanglements. Citizens were warned to stay away from any fallen poles or wires, as they could be highly dangerous, even fatal.

Dublin found itself "completely cut off from telephonic communication" with the rest of the country. Only the undersea cross-channel telephone lines survived the blizzard; the only telephone link with Belfast was through Liverpool. It was the most serious dislocation of the telephone service since its inception. Officials knew it was sure to generate public clamour for a big "underground movement" for telephone services.

The most serious problem was that of emergency services being cut off from contact—hospitals, doctors, fire brigades, Garda stations, ambulances, midwives. And without communications, people around the country were unable to contact family and friends to see how they had fared through the blizzard. This put quite an emotional strain on many, especially the elderly.

So long as the blizzard continued to blow into Sunday afternoon, little repair work could be safely attempted. Furthermore, the "electricity system along the east coast was badly disrupted," as it was throughout much of the country. The ESB's trunk network was seriously dislocated between the Ardnacrusha power station on the Shannon in Co. Clare and the eastern part of the country. When electric lights failed, people had to rely on oil lamps and candles. Where a complete black-out occurred, as in Bray, trams and clocks ceased working.

Over in the Phoenix Park, zoo employees faced their own emergencies. The blizzard, with its howling wind and snow, had blown over trees, frightened the animals, created drifts, making it difficult for the staff to carry out their duties. The snow, driven horizontally by winds of 60 to 65 miles per hour, had not only caked against buildings and cages but had frozen many locks shut. The staff had to use matches and cigarette lighters to thaw them out in order to insert a key—a tedious process. They were doing their best to keep wood-burning furnaces fired up to maintain an even temperature for the tropical animals, especially delicate birds and reptiles. Already one reptile had sloughed its skin and several parrots had fallen ill, while three new arrivals, touracos from West Africa, "sat huddled on their perch with their chins sunk in their chests like heavy-weight champions."[16]

Monkeys were always worrisome, vulnerable to cold. Several were succumbing to pneumonia. The bitter cold not only imperilled their health but upset their temperament. On Sunday morning the keepers found that "complete silence reigned in the monkey-house which was usually boisterous." They sat sulking, visibly displeased, and "maintained a disapproving silence about the prevailing weather."[17]

No-one in Dublin had more reason for dismay when they awoke on Sunday than the city's poorest tenement-dwellers. Those in Queen Street, Benburb Street, North King Street, the quays, Dominick Street, Gardiner Street and the Liberties lived in dingy rooms in buildings housing families of eight, nine, ten and more. Barely getting by with their meagre ration of bread, running out of fuel, or facing a fireless grate. Confined indoors by the weather.

Subsisting in primitive conditions, they used their slop buckets out of dire necessity, generally placed in a corner and covered with a hanging sheet. By morning the stench throughout the building could be sickening. Normally the buckets were emptied first thing, and windows thrown open for fresh air. Not in a blizzard. In tenement houses like Maggie Murray's in Queen Street, "during the winter you wouldn't *dream* of going down to the toilet in the yard, so the slop bucket was kept in the corner of the room," often near to over-flowing, inviting all manner of sickness and disease. With rear yards covered with snow and ice and the tap frozen, it was nearly impossible to empty and clean the bucket for the next night's use. In pitifully uncivilised conditions, tenants had to dispose of their waste in any way they were able.

All Dublin's Sunday sports and entertainment fixtures were affected by the blizzard. The cancellation of horse racing, football, rugby and other sports events was a great disappointment to sportsmen, who assembled instead in their local pubs to commiserate. Even contests within the pubs were called off. In the 1940s many inner-city pubs, especially around the quays, had their own ring teams. Inter-pub competitions were taken seriously, with teams from one house visiting others on a set schedule, packing the establishments and profiting the publicans. Such pubs as the Liverpool Bar, the Wharf Tavern, Campion's, Kelly's and the Lighthouse Bar were famous for their ring teams. Especially in dreary winter months, it provided important entertainment for the men. "The ring teams would travel around just like football teams," John Greenhalgh explains, "and their followers, the supporters, would go with them." Big entertainment, big betting. Great anticipation for major matches. But John Preston, who "used to do MC for the rings up in the Sligo Bar—all the top dogs there!" saw bad weather foul up everything when teams and followers couldn't travel across the city for matches. On Sunday virtually every inter-pub competition in the city was blotted out by the blizzard.

Even a big indoor contest, the National Bridge Tournament between Kerry and Dublin, had to be postponed, as travel was impossible.

Entertainment features were disrupted as well. The Gaiety Theatre found it necessary, "owing to inclement weather," to postpone Sunday night's performance of *To Kill a Cat*, giving assurance that it would be put on the following Sunday. Weather permitting. The Olympia suffered serious roof damage when a portion completely collapsed from the weight of the snow, and it had to inform patrons that it regretted being closed until further notice. The Theatre Royal, however, decided not to cancel its highly touted programme, featuring the Five Orlanders, a remarkable team of "acrobatic youngsters with their whirlwind antics," as well as song and dance numbers. It was one of their best presentations of the winter, playing to packed houses. On Sunday, however, only a scattering of brave but appreciative patrons showed up. Most of the city's cinemas remained open but did only a modest business, as people were reluctant to leave the security of their homes.

However, on instructions from her promoter "Miss Ima Weight" waded through the snow to go "on display" on Sunday afternoon before the handful of gawkers who showed up.

———

At about 3 o'clock in the afternoon the blizzard finally ceased. After nearly fourteen unrelenting hours. In late afternoon the temperature crept upwards, and a slight thaw set in. At first it was welcomed.

Along the south coast, when the weather improved later in the day, local people trekked towards the cliffs to gaze on the stranded *Irish Plane*, looking like a beached whale. A tug was on its way from Plymouth to see if the vessel could be removed from the rocks, but crew members were saying that the ship seemed badly holed, and it was doubtful whether it could be moved. A more immediate concern was the removal, or at least protection, of the valuable cargo. As shipping company officials conferred about practical matters, sightseers gathering atop the cliffs listened enthralled to accounts of the rescue. Especially awed by the vivid descriptions of the breeches-buoy transfers over the "gaping jaws of death" in the pitch-black of night. Sounding as if it were from an exciting Errol Flynn film. Everyone marvelled that not a single man had been lost.

The late-day "quick thaw," as it was called, was initially taken as a blessing. But by Sunday evening it was accompanied by rain, sleet, and wet snow, which "converted the streets into a quagmire," as one newspaper described it. Within a few hours the city was bogged in slush, and large pools made roads impassable. Cars and buses became disabled in deep water, and passengers were forced to abandon them and wade through calf-deep water. The sudden thaw also brought sheets of ice and snow sliding off rooftops, tearing away drains, endangering anyone below. Tenement roofs by the thousand leaked freely. In some cases water flowed down from one floor to the next. All over the city, water pipes that had frozen and burst now began flowing again, and much damage was done to private, public and commercial buildings. Plumbers' telephones were ringing incessantly, with frantic callers.

The quick thaw ended when nightfall brought temperatures below 32 degrees (0°C), and water, slush and wet snow once again began freezing into solid snow-pack and ice.

As people throughout the country went to bed on Sunday night they hoped that the blizzard had been winter's "last hurrah."

————

On the morning of Monday 3 February everyone in Ireland was anxious to read about the big "surprise blizzard," how it had affected areas beyond their own. Had it been a localised storm, or had the entire country been struck? They weren't disappointed, for newspaper coverage was expansive. Headlines were nearly identical: the *Irish Press* declared: "Blizzard lashes Ireland," while the *Irish Independent* reported: "Blizzard sweeps Ireland." The biggest weather story in ages.

As it turned out, such proclamations were not quite accurate. The blizzard had not ravaged all parts of the country. As communications were restored, one locale reported a remarkable anomaly. While the rest of the country awoke to face the blizzard's fury, it seems that the residents of Cork and the city's immediate environs rose on Sunday morning to find what was called a "bright, spring-like day—there was no sign of snow." Local people went so far as to gush that "summer conditions prevailed in Cork."

Weather experts were flummoxed. When the *Irish Press* reported that "the storm behaved with freakish inconsistency," it could offer no explanation, other than that it must be an oddity of nature. At first Cork residents were not even aware that any snow was falling elsewhere in the country. An *Irish Press* representative who had to travel by car on Sunday morning from Cork to Dublin had no inkling that a snowstorm lay in his path. Until suddenly, near Mitchelstown, he encountered the blizzard head on and within a few miles became caught in a deep snowdrift, finding it impossible to even open his car doors. He was forced to climb out the window. Eventually extricating his vehicle with the assistance of others, he cautiously crept along, a journey that ultimately took more than eight hours.

About the same time a passenger train from Dundalk to Carrickmacross went off the track when it smashed into a heavy snowdrift.

On Monday, in the immediate aftermath of the blizzard, the authorities began the monumental task of restoring communications and electricity networks. As this was slowly being accomplished, more reports filtered in from distant places describing harrowing experiences. Newspapers seized the stories and reported on dramatic events. For days the papers would sell out quickly, as readers devoured all the storm news. "Thanks be to God!" many were saying, that the blizzard had claimed no lives.

Perhaps blizzards weren't so terrible after all.

———

The *Evening Herald* saw it differently. It could only have been by pure good fortune that human life had been spared during such a ferocious blizzard. Crew members from the *Irish Plane* had barely escaped death, as had several people who probably would have died of exposure had they not been found in time. There had been, in truth, quite a number of close calls with death. People could call it "good luck," "fate," "destiny," or whatever they liked. But such thinking could create a false sense of security, a dangerous naïveté about nature unleashed in the form of blizzards.

In an editorial headed "Snow menace" the *Evening Herald* presented a hard, realistic view. Though conceding that a blizzard's "visitation, however crippling, is comparatively rare" in Ireland, it argued persuasively that protective measures should be adopted for the possibility of such storms striking. "In these latitudes we are not equipped for this Arctic weather," in clothing or footwear, snow-clearing techniques, or even psychological attitudes. When a blizzard struck, there was no defence against it.

The best the authorities could do was to send some crews of city council workers around with shovels and sand or straw to sprinkle about the streets— a largely futile exercise. By contrast, in cities such as London, Paris, Berlin and

Stockholm large snow-ploughs were ready to battle against snowstorms and blizzards. Active schemes existed for immediately clearing major roads, keeping transport moving and the city functioning. In Dublin, the Government did virtually nothing, passively leaving the public feeling helpless, at the mercy of nature, looking out their windows in dismay. Feeling exasperated, defeated by nature. Left only to hope and pray that the awful weather would leave them.

Newspapers generally contended that the Government was blatantly derelict in its duty of serving the citizenry during such times of crisis. Such negligence could put lives at risk. The *Evening Herald* charged it with pure malfeasance:

> Our cities and towns have been treated to a demonstration of their helplessness in the event of a heavy snowfall . . . making roads and footpaths virtually impassable and seriously dislocating traffic. A snowstorm of serious dimensions is regarded as a very unlikely event, and no preparations are made to deal with it when it materialises. Our methods of clearing away the menace are almost pre-historic—manual labour.
>
> The Government should procure some modern snow-removal equipment for winter emergencies. Otherwise, the city could be brought to a standstill and people put at risk.[18]

Though the Government shirked its responsibility, citizens were bound by ancient law to carry out theirs. According to a by-law first adopted in 1599, all occupants of business premises and private houses were responsible for the "clearing away of snow on the footpaths" outside their properties. After the cessation of a fall of snow "it must be cleared from the footway . . . without obstruction to traffic." But where were people to shovel it if not into the street?

Most residents had to use ash and garden shovels or coal shovels to clear their way from doorway to footpath, usually cutting only a narrow walkway, which quickly became packed down by feet into an icy composite. Many houses had no device with which to shovel snow. Ordinarily, when snow fell it was light enough for housewives to sweep away. In the inner city, where Una Shaw lived, women would often try to get rid of snow by "pouring hot water to dissolve it—but the minute that froze over you had a skating rink!" Then they would try to remedy that hazard by throwing ashes from the fireplace over the icy surface for some grit.

Irish people were neither snow-savvy nor prepared to cope with a real snowfall, much less a blizzard. In the absence of major assistance by the Government they were left pathetically helpless.

Owing to the vicissitudes of weather—rain, sleet, snow, wind, freezing, "quick thaws," refreezing—the influenza epidemic, now being called the "quick-fire" flu, was worsening daily. Its symptoms were unmistakable: "a sudden, blood-chilling fever, an 'explosive' sneeze and a sudden feeling of weakness," as one newspaper described it. All over Dublin, in streets and in shops, on buses and trams, was heard the raucous cacophony of wheezing, sneezing, coughing. Newspapers were publishing doctors' warnings: "Don't take chances with the flu, it is the forerunner of more serious diseases." According to a report by the World Health Organisation, it was feared that "another influenza scourge, similar to that of 1918, may be imminent."[19] As the greatest number of deaths was caused by the resulting pneumonia, it was recommended that "penicillin and sulphur drugs should be organised in advance." The potential threat was so serious that the WHO believed that the "fight against influenza deserves as much attention as the fight against tuberculosis and venereal disease [sexually transmitted disease]."

To make matters worse, rheumatic fever, called "juvenile enemy number 1" by the *Sunday Independent,* was on the rampage in Dublin, the chief cause of death and disability in children, especially those between the ages of five and eight.[20] According to the paper's medical correspondent, "this dread disease often hides behind what appears to be no more than a severe cold . . . and often develops following a sore throat." It was most prevalent in areas of poor housing, dampness, and "improper living conditions"—the tenement breeding-ground. Almost every tenement mother in the city had at least one child suffering from a cold, cough, or flu. If not the whole lot.

The wicked winter conditions were worrying mothers sick, and stealing their children away from them as death rates among the young rose.

Those in the city who could afford it sought treatment for the quick-fire flu from their doctor or chemist. The poor flooded into dispensary clinics. Tenement-dwellers also relied heavily upon old home cures, which they swore by. Most victims were bedridden, having to suffer through it day by day until they regained their strength. By Monday 3 February in Dublin, where the flu was particularly contagious, it was seriously "depleting factories, offices and workshops of many of their staff," causing some firms to close down.[21] In the city's large factories, such as Jacob's biscuit factory, it was estimated that the flu was knocking out one in every four. In some firms the figure was considerably higher. Some workers, fearful of losing wages, were not reporting their condition and so infected those around them.

In Clery's department store there were 116 victims on the flu list. At Grangegorman mental hospital it was said to be rampant among patients and staff. Within CIE's staff, hundreds had been placed on the sick list. It had truly reached epidemic proportions. The situation was exacerbated by the loss of hospital staff and medical personnel to the flu virus. By the first week of February, reported the *Irish Times*, an acute shortage of nurses was seriously "hampering medical men in their battle against the influenza epidemic."

Winter conditions were dangerous. People were falling seriously ill. Dying. The highest mortality was among the elderly, poor, frail, and young children. But people in Ballsbridge and Blackrock were victims as well. By early February the medical authorities expressed disquiet at the increasing death rate in the capital and other parts of the country, both urban and rural. Reports from hospitals, nursing homes, old people's centres, undertakers, mortuaries and cemeteries all verified that deaths were climbing at an alarming rate. Mortality figures would be watched closely throughout the winter.

————

The last place that elderly and ill Dubliners should have been on Monday morning was out in the snowy, slushy streets, where the temperature was hovering around freezing and a vicious east wind was blowing. A miserable day for a funeral—but one they were not going to miss.

Crowds began gathering more than an hour before Big Jim Larkin's 10 o'clock requiem mass, to be presided over by Archbishop McQuaid. They assembled in the church, stood outside, and lined the entire route to Glasnevin Cemetery. Devout Larkinites, they were willing to endure the physical discomforts, and health risks, of the day. Yet not all were able to make it. In their tenement house in Pimlico in the Liberties, Máirín Johnston's mother was terribly disappointed, for she had been a loyal follower of Larkin all her life, standing beside him during the most turbulent times. "My mother wanted to go, but the weather was cold and she just didn't have the warm clothes or proper footwear to go out in the snow, so she didn't go to the funeral." Weather kept many from attending—a real disappointment.

Every newspaper had a full contingent of reporters and photographers strategically placed to cover the entire event, from church to graveside. For those unable to attend the historic funeral, at least they would be able to read about it in great detail, with pages of photographs.

On the conclusion of the mass the crowd was hushed as the coffin, draped in the Starry Plough flag, was conveyed from the church to the hearse by members of the Executive Committee of the Workers' Union of Ireland. The cortege, led by old Citizen Army men, moved along Westmorland Street, O'Connell Street and Eden Quay to Beresford Place, where a halt was made outside Liberty Hall. Here the cortege passed through a guard of honour comprising 1,200 dockers under their union leader, M. Lennon. Many of the men were carrying their shovels, which "they handled like military weapons." The deep-sea men as well seemed "grimly proud to stand as guard-of-honour." But the *Irish Press* reported that the hordes of ordinary Dubliners showed just as great an outpouring of devotion:

> They all came out, men in dungarees with overcoats buttoned up to their throats, marching erectly as he told them to march, and women grown old since they struck at the 400 bosses at Larkin's will . . . they had to be there. The very air of the city seemed to be muffled . . . People were magnetised into the funeral "as if by common instinct."
>
> The south-easterly gale blows up the turbulent river crashing on O'Connell Bridge arches like Larkin's fist at the council table. Boots, heavy and grimy, polished and shiny, tramp, tramp, tramp, tramp through the slush on the streets. Joining the long, long queue, step and slither through the snowy slush.[22]

Among them was Maisy Flood, now ninety-six. "It was the worst of weather, and people were falling all over the place at the funeral." She heard no complaints.

All along the route the dense throngs of mourners stood in reverent silence as the coffin passed. As the procession moved by, people peered from windows or pulled blinds down, while customers came out of shops, swelling the crowd. Groups lining the pathways "waited, said nothing, then moved out, walking after the old grey men of the Citizen Army." Among them a young lad, Tony Behan, stood beside his father—"the *chill* in my bones!"—looking up at the emotion in the faces of those around them. On tenement steps mothers held up children to see, especially when spotting the "huge lorry of flowers, red and yellow and blue and lily-white." They all knew they were seeing Big Jim cross his city for the last time. Some mourners, commented one reporter, almost expected to see "a big black slouch hat on the coffin and a black pipe beside it . . . because you visualised Larkin swinging his huge shoulders as he headed to a meeting in the north city."[23]

Women, hankies in hand, dabbed their eyes as the hearse rolled before them. People removed their hats, bowed heads, even saluted. Some men cried. In public. Not a common sight in Dublin. A reporter for the *Irish Press* spotted a large policeman standing at the edge of the crowd, his face sombre and reddened, "and that's not rain on his cheeks. Praise be! At Larkin's funeral I have seen a policeman on duty—crying!"

Through the gates of Glasnevin Cemetery the hearse passed. Crowds outside thrust forward to see the coffin removed and placed on a trolley:

The "Last Post" sounds and the rifles crash a volley. The people tramp
back through the slush and snow, a bit dazed.[24]

Streams of mourners traipsed back home or to their local pubs to sympathise
and reminisce. Retell the great stories of Big Jim that would become part of
Dublin's history and folklore.

As they sat with their pints, "memoryising" about Larkin, publicans
reminded them of the new rules that went into effect that day. Guinness's
brewery had informed all publicans that their deliveries of porter and stout
would be cut, starting on 3 February. With the blizzard and Larkin's funeral
over the past forty-eight hours, many men had forgotten. Customers wanted
to know exactly what it would mean. Patiently, publicans explained over and
over throughout the day that their supply would be reduced by a whopping
30 per cent. It could possibly mean having to close the pubs for two or three
days a week. Leaving some regulars speechless for the first time in living
memory. Guinness claimed that the sharp reduction was absolutely necessary
because of shortages of grain but mainly because of their depleted coal
supplies from Britain.

The infernal winter weather was invading even pubs.

————

On Tuesday, harsh weather erupted again as the east coast was slammed by a
sharp north-easterly gale that continued throughout the morning. After a
rough crossing the mail boat, with four hundred passengers, had difficulty
berthing at Dún Laoghaire. Great waves dashed against the piers and
encroached upon railway lines along the south-east coast, catching the wheels
and splashing the windows of the boat-train after it left Dún Laoghaire for
Westland Row. All trains along the line from Bray were sea-sprayed as they
passed exposed points at Blackrock and Booterstown. The violent sea made
some passengers nervous, wishing they had not boarded the train in the first
place. Further south, at Ballygannon, Co. Wicklow, rough seas caused the
cancellation of the 9 a.m. Dublin–Wexford train. Passengers and luggage were
conveyed by bus.

Assessments of blizzard damage were now being released. The Post Office
(then responsible for the telephone service) placed the cost of the storm at
"more than a million pounds," a staggering sum at the time.
Telecommunications were in such ruin that it would take weeks, possibly
months, to restore normal service—weather permitting. The priority for
telephone repairs was given to hospitals, doctors, Garda stations, fire brigades,
ambulances and other emergency services. The ESB was doing its best, with
every repairman on extra duty. Most crucial was repairing the damage to the

Ardnacrusha power station and eastern trunk lines. Incessant winds made all repair work more difficult and dangerous.

In Dublin every plumber was working twelve or more hours a day to fix all the burst water pipes. There were not nearly enough to handle the demand. To worsen the problem, supplies of lead piping and solder were insufficient to meet immediate needs. This meant that the plumbers had to do many temporary "patch-up" jobs on pipes, just to prevent more flooding. But if more deep freezes, quick thaws and refreezes came, there was no guarantee that their work would hold up.

By midday on Tuesday disturbing information was arriving in Dublin from snowbound Co. Wicklow, the area hardest hit by the blizzard. People and entire villages were completely cut off. Downed telephone lines left no contact with the outside world. John Brophy, a postman in the Blessington area, reported that drifting snow was so deep that it had erased landmarks, disorienting even local people. It was difficult, he found, to tell fields from roads, as they were now "all on the same level." Though he knew every square yard of land along his daily route, he now had to make his way on foot purely by "instinct." Along the way he saw coffins being carried miles over the completely snow-blanketed landscape. How could they now be buried, he wondered.

Desperate descriptions of Co. Wicklow's countryside raised concerns about the welfare of the German and Polish orphans and the Sisters of Charity now marooned at Glencree. At the beginning of February the Red Cross in Dublin confirmed that it had food and supplies for about a month. Of normal winter weather.

R. M. Smyllie, enterprising editor of the *Irish Times*, saw the Wicklow predicament as a natural opportunity for a good news story. He decided to send a reporter and photographer on a journey to try to break through to Glencree and find out at first hand how the children and their carers were doing. The Red Cross agreed to provide a lorry and driver. If successful, it would be a scoop. Carrying shovels and hessian sacks to place under the tyres for grip, the two men set out with high hopes:

> In a Red Cross truck I tried to reach the home to see how the children are faring, after their rescue from the horrors of living in air-raid shelters. There was full confidence within me that it would be possible to reach Glencree. After Rathfarnham the snow had piled higher at the hedges and the lorry driver was forced to swerve to avoid drifts feet deep. Skids at corners showed that the surface was greasy, but for some miles there were no serious obstacles.[25]

Close to this same time, back in Dublin a crowd of people, mostly men, were admiringly looking upon quite a different sort of vehicle. Outside the Adelphi Cinema in Middle Abbey Street they leaned closer to get a good look at the new Jeep on public display. It was the first of its type to be assembled in Ireland and was being shown off to members of the Government, industrialists, farmers, and curious citizens. As the representative explained in detail the power of the four-wheel-drive vehicle and its capacity to handle the roughest roads and wildest weather, all were impressed. Inevitably, given the circumstances, viewers were heard commenting that the Jeep would be the ideal vehicle for tackling the country's snowbound roads.

Some miles to the south a Jeep would certainly have come in handy, as the adventurous reporter and his photographer were now getting a good dose of treacherous road conditions:

> We came to the hill skirting Hellfire Club mountains, the back wheels threw up snow and spun around without finding a grip. Sacks were flung beneath the wheels, but were of no use. The lorry was stuck in the middle of a steep hill.
>
> Glencree was still seven miles away. The back wheels were in a drift nearly four feet deep. Shovels were necessary then—and bending backs were straightened at the sound of a gruff voice. The speaker was an elderly man of the hills. "Go home," he advised, "it's *eight feet* up there!" He pointed up the hill where drifts were "up as high as the trees," he said.[26]

As the newspaper men were deliberating about whether to try to proceed onwards and upwards, down in Co. Cork salvage technicians who had just arrived from Liverpool were assessing the status of the stranded *Irish Plane,* firmly hung up on the rocks near Ballycotton. It was now possible to walk around the beached vessel when the tide permitted, allowing Commander Smith and his salvage team to make a detailed examination. The hull did not appear to be as seriously damaged as was first feared. The most immediate concern to shipping company officials was that some "pirates" from the sea, or local land marauders, might try to prey upon the stricken ship, loaded with valuable cargo. In addition to car parts, typewriters and wool were crates of fine whiskey bound for America. These could be easily stolen under the cover of darkness. Six crew members who had remained in Co. Cork volunteered to board the vessel and keep watch. They were the chief mate, second mate, third and fourth engineers, chief steward, and a deckhand. The six-man skeleton crew vowed to keep a close eye on the whiskey.

As all this was happening on Tuesday afternoon, the Government still had not issued any statement about the blizzard's crippling impact on the country. Instead, in Co. Clare, Éamon de Valera was being honoured for his thirty years as a member of Dáil Éireann at a celebration arranged by Ennis Comhairle

Ceantair of Fianna Fáil. Seán O'Grady praised the Taoiseach for his years of "loyal and unbroken" service to Co. Clare and to the Irish people:

> In the dark hours and in bright hours he had held the hearts of the people in a manner unequalled by any other Irish leader, not even exempting O'Connell and Parnell.[27]

Where, people wondered, was his leadership in these dark days of electricity black-outs, smashed telephone networks, snowbound roads and villages, and food and fuel crises?

The afternoon was dragging on, getting late. The *Irish Times* twosome, rather than taking the wise old man's advice, had proceeded to take the road higher up. When a large snowdrift finally halted their lorry they advanced on foot, doubtful about the man's claim of drifts higher than their heads:

> An eight foot snowdrift is something I wanted to see. So we walked up the hill. The snow lay in drifts, adding to the beauty and a touch of magic to nearby little cottages behind the snow which shut them in. The old man had not exaggerated—the drifts were eight feet and up to the tree-tops. This was as far as it was possible to even walk. The road leading to Glencree was barely distinguishable from the hedges and fields. It was impossible to even think of walking to the Red Cross home.[28]

Perhaps another day, they resolved on their way down. If the weather would give them a break. It would take a prolonged thaw, both agreed, to melt eight-foot snowdrifts.

———

Wednesday's newspapers had alarming news from Britain. In large type the *Evening Herald's* headline read: "Economic Dunkirk facing Britain."

The news grabbed headlines around the world. One Paris newspaper declared: "Dramatic week in England," requiring a six-column article to explain the crisis. The *New York Times* had an uncommonly lengthy headline: "English coal lack forces shut-down of mills—Commons thunderstruck—Crisis gravest in 20 years."

Nowhere outside Britain did the grim news carry greater import, or generate more angst, than in Ireland.

Britain had been struck by the same Arctic cold spell and blizzards that had swept Ireland. Wreaking havoc on coal production and the transport system. Ports were frozen shut, with railways, roads and mines snowbound. After two weeks of sub-freezing temperatures the country's limited coal reserves were being rationed at record rates. With the coal industry brought to a standstill, British industries were forced to reduce production and staff or close down. Simultaneously, large cuts were being made in the country's public transport and power services. The Government announced that further "drastic measures" would have to be taken. The severe weather was threatening to bring Britain to its knees, just as surely as Hitler had tried to do. This was a battle to be waged no less vigorously. And the call for sacrifice was essential.

As people throughout Ireland read with dismay of Britain's crisis, they understood that their coal imports kept Ireland afloat. When they put the paper down they were left wondering how severe a blow it might mean for them.

The answer came swiftly. The very next day, 5 February, the British Minister of Fuel and Power announced a ban on coal exports from Liverpool and other north-west ports. Up to that day colliers had been arriving in Ireland from Liverpool, Birkenhead, Preston, Barrow, Mayport. Now, suddenly, "it meant that the loading of coal at these ports for Eire will cease immediately."[29] At best, some last colliers already loaded or in passage might slip through.

The Irish Government and public were thunderstruck. People shuddered at the thought of what it meant. Following the war, imports of British coal had remained far below what they had been in 1939, making it a struggle for Irish people to adapt. But the country had somehow managed. Now it was a matter of survival.

Politicians, industrialists, businessmen felt stunned by the calamitous news. It caused "consternation in the Irish industrial, transport and catering services." CIE promptly declared that the country's railway system faced a "complete paralysis within a very short time" if the ban remained for a number of weeks. No less distressed, a spokesman for Dublin Gas Company soberly called it "disastrous," as its meagre supplies were already down to a "negligible quantity."

Upon hearing the news of the ban, P. L. McEvoy, president of the Federation of Irish Manufacturers, exploded: "This is the last straw." A prolonged stoppage of coal imports, he predicted, would result in the closure of many factories, and scores of people would be put out of work. Word came from Stormont that they too had no coal for the Six Counties. Summing it up bluntly, the *Irish Times* wrote that the coal ban would "cause a stranglehold on industry in this country."

Immediately, every coal-burning industry, institution and business sought to assess exactly how much it had remaining in stock. In almost every case, critically short. The general coal stock in Dublin was estimated to be sufficient for about three weeks. But the coal was of poor quality. Those most crucially affected were CIE, the ESB, Dublin Gas Company, foundries, hospitals, the

Irish Sugar Company, and bakeries. Managers of hotels and restaurants were frantic. For some it would be a day-to-day operation from now on. Hospitals faced a particularly grievous problem. Jervis Street Hospital reported that it had received only two deliveries of coal over the last three months, having to use it exceedingly sparingly. Now, it found, it was down to a paltry twenty-seven tons. It would have to try to use a mixture of coal, turf, and wood, an inferior and difficult heating system.

Repercussions were felt within twenty-four hours. The first major victim was the Hammond Lane Foundry in Pearse Street, the country's largest. One day after the ban went into effect the company announced that it would be forced to close down, and put some two hundred employees out of work. The cause was the lack of coke for the furnaces. The news sent shock waves through the country's industrial landscape. It was the first complete closing of any major industry since the fuel shortage began in the early stages of the Second World War.

Rumours had circulated about the "possibility" of a "partial" closing of the foundry. But, owing to its importance in the national economy, workers saw it as remote. Then the British coal ban drove the nails into the coffin. On Wednesday evening, all hope dissipated:

> When the hooter sounded in the evening at 5.30, it was for the last time. A long line of employees filed through the time office, punched their cards in the time-clock, pulled their coats more tightly about them, and stood at the bus stops, the snow mantling their shoulders as they watched the fully-loaded buses sweep by them.[30]

As disheartened men shuffled out of the factory, many with heads bowed, they were met by Jack Graham, the foundry manager, who said, with pained sincerity: "Sorry, lads, it can't be helped—we went on as long as we could." To which one man was heard to mutter, "I suppose there's nothing now but the dole."[31] Many of the men, instead of heading straight home, walked over to one of the pubs in Pearse Street to commiserate. Hoping the publican would uphold the long tradition of putting drink on the slate during tough times.

That same day in Wexford, Pierce and Company, manufacturers of agricultural machinery, also had to cease their operation because of lack of foundry coke, laying off 150 men. The closing of both firms so suddenly sent ripples of anxiety through the country's factory population, breeding "fears that other Irish industries may be forced to close down." Jacob's, Dublin's huge biscuit and cake manufacturers, stated that their firm had cut fuel usage to a bare minimum in hopes that they could "carry on for the present"—a vague statement that gave little feeling of security to their 1,300 or so employees. May Hanaphy, who had begun work in the 1920s at the age of fourteen, noticed the nervousness of her fellow-workers. No-one could be certain any more about what the next day might bring. Would they have a job, a wage packet to take home?

CIE was more direct, as it promptly gave notice that six hundred railwaymen were to be hit by the coal shortage, including drivers, firemen, and engine cleaners. Dublin Gas Company followed by stating that the consumer's daily ration would have to be cut by a full hour, thereby compounding the "worries of the already harassed housewife" trying to cope with Arctic cold, wet turf, flu in the family, and shortages of tea, bread, sugar. And a general insecurity about the days ahead.

Even the mighty Guinness's brewery was threatened. Though this was apparently not a fact that the brewery hierarchy wanted publicised. But William Tinnion, Liam Cradden and Dick Curtis, who worked at Guinness's, knew that the fuel situation was dire. It had been difficult enough for brewery managers to have to announce sharp reductions in deliveries of porter and stout to publicans; the public did not need to know that the brewing operation itself might be in jeopardy.

William Tinnion, now ninety-seven, sweated away in the boiler room and knew better than anyone just how precarious the fuel situation had become by early February. Ordinarily, as he puts it, Guinness's had *"mountains* of coal," never a thought of running short. But over the war years he had seen those alpine heaps eroded to hills. Now they were reduced to mounds. To him, the final indignity was having to resort to using coal dust to keep the brewery going:

> I was stoking the firing in the brewery, but we had a hell of a job, because the coal, it got *low*! And then the coal suppliers in Dublin, they had heaps of coal *dust*—they called it "duff"—and they sold *that* to the brewery. And we, the stokers, had to *try* and use that. Oh, we were desperate!

Tinnion and his mates shovelled the coal dust—inhaling half of it— wondering how long the "duff" would hold out. What would they do then?

———

When the coal ban was announced, attention became riveted on Ireland's domestic fuel: turf. The country's boglands and turf stocks had been devastated by the heavy rains of 1946. Early 1947 followed with freezing cold, heavy snow, and a blizzard. Leaving turf soaked, frozen, and disintegrating. By the first week of February it was declared that "almost all movement from the bog areas has been suspended by bad weather," and cut turf that could not be removed during the autumn, because of inclement weather, was "now under water."[32] Or beneath ice and snow. In something of an understatement, the

Irish Times wrote: "The shortage of native fuel is causing anxiety."

Food problems were no less worrisome. For many even more urgent, as the poor were now reported to be going hungry, especially in Dublin's tenements. Wheat and bread were of the greatest concern. Ireland had produced only a quarter of a million tons of wheat, of very poor quality, during the previous year, while the country needed half a million tons. Imports, however, had declined, because of worldwide shortages. The resulting bread rationing was causing real dietary deprivation for the poorer classes, who subsisted on it, and for many manual labourers, who were finding themselves weakened from lack of bread. So, in early February, the Government felt it necessary to allow a supplementary amount for certain categories of labouring men, such as dockers, miners, quarry men, cement and tannery workers, road labourers, and those in some building trades. Bread was regarded as human fuel for keeping the country's labour force going. The additional allowance was half the current domestic ration, or an increase of three pounds of bread per week.

In Dublin the morning of 5 February "began with intermittent gusts of rain and sleet, with a few sudden showers of hailstones . . . and a slight fall of snow." About this time Frank Hallinan, chairman of Grain Importers (Éire) Ltd, was arriving in New York on the liner *America* in the hope of arranging special shipments of American grain to Ireland. He would then travel on to Ottawa for the same purpose. In both places he endeavoured to explain that "grains were an absolute essential" to the diet of Irish people, that it was "not a meat-eating country." He knew he faced a challenge, as the United States was already having to limit its wheat shipments to war-torn European countries. If only he could impress upon the American grain authorities how desperate the wheat shortage was in Ireland!

As Hallinan was abroad making his case for wheat, back home there was bad news about potatoes as well. Historically an Irish staple, potatoes were now declining significantly in the markets, as farmers dared not open their pits because of the freezing temperature. And those who had protected stocks could not get them to the towns because of impassable roads. Vegetables were short as well. Dublin's milk supplies were also low, as deliveries from outside the city, such as from Blessington and Wicklow, were impeded by bad roads.

With food shortages tightening, Dublin's notorious black market was thriving, just as during the war years. It was the old story of the city's haves and have-nots. The affluent class, with money and contacts, could always manage to acquire food and fuel, even treasured tea, while the poor suffered from want of basic bread and potatoes. Once again the subject of Dublin's privileged versus impoverished classes was brought to light in the press as hard times grew worse by the week. On 6 February the *Evening Herald* published an expository editorial simply headed "Hunger," describing the immorality of the city's class system:

> In the present spell of bitterly cold weather, the poor are bound to suffer more than their better-off neighbours because of the lowered vitality caused by insufficient food. Despite efforts of charitable organisations, they remain inadequately clad, existing in a cold, dank atmosphere of stark poverty, but their principal need is food.
>
> We have banquets in this country—but a well-known Dublin preacher recently told of a widowed mother in the city who could provide her family of three a dinner of only crusts of stale bread softened in a pot of boiling water, in which her one solitary cube of meat extract had been dissolved.[33]

It was now being verified that the poor commonly had to either sacrifice food for fuel or fuel for food. In either case, it weakened their constitution, increased the risk of illness, and made their lives more miserable.

Three days after the blizzard several representatives of the Irish Red Cross Society attempted to drive to Glencree to check on the nuns and the orphans. They were unable to get more than two miles past Rathfarnham. That night more snow fell throughout Co. Wicklow's high country, making the roads more impassable, the villages more isolated. In the Enniskerry area places with 12-foot drifts were completely blocking the road to the Sally Gap. Some areas could be travelled only on horseback. A local farmer by the name of Walker was hailed as a "guardian angel" when he arrived with his horse-drawn sled to rescue the driver of a bread van trapped in a snowdrift, then taking him and his loaves on his regular rounds.[34]

The next day, undaunted by their two previous failures—and apparently not realising how much worse the conditions had become—the *Irish Times* reporter and photographer set out on another attempt to reach the marooned residents at Glencree. Stories were coming out of Co. Wicklow that snowbound inhabitants were now facing fireless grates and real hunger. Smyllie of the *Irish Times,* highly competitive, probably surmised that there would now be a race among the newspapers to be first to reach Glencree and capture a first-hand story. He may even have caught a whiff from the *Irish Press* editorial office, where plans were indeed under way to despatch a senior reporter and photographer in the quest to reach the "summit" first.

This time they were halted many miles from Glencree by drifts considerably higher than before. Accepting defeat early, they found a farmer who agreed to take them higher up in his horse-drawn cart. That might be a story in itself, they thought. Along the way they encountered local men shovelling the road, who told them about Mrs Kearns's farmhouse, which had snow piled up higher than her half-door. Perhaps they might want to check on her. With shovellers helping to clear the way, they reached her door and found that she and her three children had been without fire since 31 January. Her husband was off working in England, and they had barely enough food left. Every day they hoped for a thaw. Every day more snow fell.

"This," the reporter would write the next day, "was one of the stories of the 'Big Snow'"—a marooned family, hungry and fireless, only a few miles from the heart of Dublin.

Farther up the road they met two Augustinian brothers with a donkey and creel loaded with food supplies who were "calling at every house with a little food." Higher up they encountered three more of the brothers, who claimed to have reached Glencree on foot and were now returning. One had a four-foot blackthorn stick, which he said sank completely in the snow layer at Glencree. And drifts were three times that deep. They informed the reporter that the nuns and children were surviving for the time being, with ample food and fuel. But they would need to be resupplied within the next two weeks or so. "God willing." And weather permitting.

The extended weather forecast was not promising:

Pressure is high in a belt from North Russia to Greenland. Weather will be very cold in all districts . . . with periods of snow.[35]

Chapter 4 ∾

THE ARCTIC GRIP
TIGHTENS

Still in the grip of Arctic winter, lashed by a wind of extraordinary violence, the fuel shortage has become acute. In the city people have begun to strip their houses of woodwork to make a fire.

(*Irish Independent*, 10 FEBRUARY 1947)

Hemmed in by snow knee-deep to the doors, waist-deep to the boundary fence, and death to walk on further out, farmers dare not travel to check on sheep and cattle sunk in the snowy morass.

(*Irish Press*, 11 FEBRUARY 1947)

I got into the lifeboat . . . and we saw the ship sink about 100 yards from us . . . It was cold and the snow was falling . . . When I awoke the next morning [days later] I was the only man alive in the boat.

(JAN BORUCKI, *Irish Times*, 15 FEBRUARY 1947)

WEEKEND OF 8/9 FEBRUARY

Following the "surprise" blizzard the weekend before, Dubliners on Friday the 7th were hoping for a better one ahead. A wide array of sports and entertainment events was planned for Saturday and Sunday, and foul weather could once again ruin people's plans.

Late on Friday night an occluded front, associated with a depression to the north-west of Spain, was approaching from the south. By early Saturday morning a depression, now to the south-west of Ireland, was "almost stationary, and associated fronts moved only very slowly north-eastwards."[1] Warmer, moist air off the Atlantic was moving inexorably towards the high pressure and cold air to the north. Another collision of opposing weather systems seemed inevitable. Possibly a replica of the weekend before.

Neither Dubliners nor seamen were aware of the looming confrontation.

As the Meteorological Service did not then provide forecasts, weather prognostications were left to the newspapers' "experts." After their blunder a week before, completely missing the blizzard, Dublin's newspapers this Friday were cautious in their predictions. The *Evening Herald* told readers of "more snow and sleet, maybe." While another paper mentioned the "possibility" of some light snow over the weekend.

Messy weather, *perhaps*. No snowstorms forecast. And certainly not a blizzard.

———

Early on Saturday morning the sky was quiet and seas calm. Some distance from Dublin, out in the Irish Sea, a nineteen-year-old Polish seaman, Jan Borucki, was aboard the 642-ton collier *Ary*, which had left Port Talbot in Glamorgan with a cargo of coal (loaded before the ban) destined for Waterford. One of fifteen crewmen, he was among the youngest, strongest and most fit. His English was good enough for him to enjoy the company of his mates. Captain Edward Kolk, a 55-year-old Estonian, was a decent man and paid fair wages. Borucki was well fed and had a comfortable enough bunk at the end of his day's duties. Over the previous two weeks there had been some stormy, sometimes violent seas around Ireland and Britain, but this short journey along the east coast was expected to be uneventful. The *Ary* regularly carried coal from Wales to Irish ports, and the captain knew the waters well. A trip down to Waterford was regarded as an easy run.

Saturday morning in Dublin was pleasant enough, with people going about their shopping and social activities. O'Connell Street, Grafton Street, Henry Street and Moore Street were jam-packed, and the city's street dealers were doing brisk business. It was chilly outside, slightly above the freezing mark, with a steady east wind but no precipitation. No-one was heard complaining.

Many Dubliners were looking forward to events that afternoon and evening. Of particular interest was the rugby match between Ireland and England, to be held at Lansdowne Road. A crowd of British fans was expected to make the trip to see the event. Days in advance, straw had been strewn across the field to protect it from the elements. By 10 o'clock in the morning men were already in the process of removing the straw for the contest.

Thousands of people, having been confined indoors the previous weekend by the bad weather and cancellation of performances, were anxious to make the most of this Saturday and Sunday. Among a number of good films showing was a terrific one, *Ziegfeld Follies*, playing at the Capitol. The *Irish Press* film critic raved about the lovely singing of Judy Garland, Fred Astaire's "twinkling feet," and the "slapstick-cum-wisecrack humorists" Red Skelton and Keenan Wynn. Furthermore, "this is Technicolor in extremis," he promised. In Ireland's grey and bleak winters, colourful, fun films were always therapeutic as well as entertaining. Queues were sure to be lengthy, but so long as the weather was decent, people didn't mind waiting.

Shortly after 11 a.m. pedestrians felt a sudden change, as the force of the wind picked up and temperatures slipped. Their pace quickened as they pulled up collars and held hats. About midday the wind reached nearly 40 miles per hour. People gazed upwards and grew wary.

By early afternoon, along the east coast a mounting "fierce gale and mountainous seas" threatened ships caught unexpectedly in open water. At Dún Laoghaire the *Maev*, the first of the new naval vessels, which was to have put out to sea that day, was kept safely in the harbour. As violent seas broke over the piers, owners of boats feared for their safety, and some were damaged. At Greystones "angry seas threatened to sweep away the railway line," while in Wexford "huge waves were swept into the streets" adjoining the quays. Many houses were flooded, and a paling of railway sleepers was destroyed. All shipping in Wexford was suspended.

Throughout the afternoon the weather all over the country deteriorated, with temperatures falling below freezing and winds nearing gale force. In many places snow began falling. In the highlands of Co. Wicklow the snowfall was quite heavy. Off the coast of Co. Cork, near Ballycotton, seventeen men who had reboarded the stranded *Irish Plane*—six crew members and eleven from the Liverpool Salvage Association—felt the ship creaking and shifting. Realising they might be in peril, they once again abandoned the vessel.

Earlier that morning 65-year-old John Kelly, who lived near Glendalough, had gone to Moneystown to do some shopping. The district was rugged and could be treacherous in bad weather. When he departed the wind was gusty, but with no sign of a snowstorm. The two men with whom he lived expected him home by early evening. Towards mid-afternoon, when a steady snow began falling and the wind rose, they grew worried. But they were confident that if threatening weather developed he would seek shelter along his route. He was a sensible man.

At Lansdowne Road promoters and rugby fans were less sensible. Despite awful conditions by 2 o'clock, with snow falling and a wind whipping across the city, stinging people's faces, they were determined to proceed with the big match. Too late to cancel at the last minute, they argued. Diehard spectators streamed in, hoping that the "passing squall," as they saw it, would subside shortly. So, as one sports reporter described it, "with an icy wind blowing across the field and a ground which was hard despite the straw covering to protect it," the contest got under way before a crowd of stalwart but visibly shivering supporters.

Under such poor conditions the quality of play was conspicuously inferior, and some spectators trickled out. Those who saw it through were rewarded with a surprising Irish victory: 22 points to England's nil. At the conclusion "Irish enthusiasts filed out numbed by the Arctic wind," as the the *Irish Independent* summed up, pleased with what was called an "astonishing" triumph over a fine English team. Piling happily into the first warm pubs they encountered.

About the same time down in Co. Cork "sportsmen" of a different stamp were experiencing their own weather disruptions. Members of Cork Coursing Club were holding their bi-annual meeting. Much to their dismay, with the cold winds whistling across the fields they couldn't get the hares to run. After a disappointing first attempt the meeting was postponed until the following Saturday. Irish hares could be thankful for the harsh weather.

———

When Borucki and his crewmates on the *Ary* encountered rough seas at about 3 p.m. they also took it to be a brief squall, as no storm had been forecast. The captain apparently gave no consideration to changing their course. By evening, however, after some five hours of being tossed about on seas now grown violent, the captain and his seasoned crew knew they were in for a big blow.

By 8 p.m. John Kelly of Glendalough had not returned from his shopping trip. His companions were now sure they had cause for worry, as the Wicklow weather had turned dangerous, with freezing temperatures, powerful wind, and a heavy snowstorm reducing visibility to a few yards. By 9 o'clock he was still missing. At 10 o'clock they could only hope he had found shelter at a neighbour's along the way. But, with telephone lines down from the previous blizzard, they had no way to confirm this. Surely, they thought, he would show up in the morning.

By this time "the seas were roiling" and "the gale was blowing wildly, driving seas high above ships caught out in the open." It had become difficult to control the *Ary* on a safe course, as the blizzard showed no signs of abating. If anything, it was becoming more turbulent. Some time about 10:45 p.m. the vessel began to list to port. Immediately the captain ordered water to be pumped into the starboard side in an effort to right the ship. When this failed, all aboard realised the seriousness of their predicament. Distress messages were sent out, and flares whizzed aloft into the inky blackness above. Near midnight Borucki knew the "ship was on the point of sinking" as the captain gave the order for his crew to take to the two lifeboats. With eight others Borucki scrambled into one of the small boats:

I got into the port lifeboat, and we were not long in the boat when we saw
the ship sink about 100 yards from us. The ship sank near the Tuskar
Light. There were no oars, sail or engine in our boat. We heard the people
in the other lifeboat calling, but we could do nothing to steer our boat. I
do not know what happened to the other lifeboat, or if she got away from
the ship.[2]

Six men, including the captain, were in the other boat. From about midnight
the two small boats drifted helplessly apart in the pitch black, tossed about
madly in a tumultuous sea with screaming wind. Borucki and his mates could
barely hear one another speak. Not that there was much to say. They were
neither warmly clad nor shod. Within minutes their clothing became soaked.
With the temperature probably 5 to 8 degrees below freezing, the wind at gale
force, and the snow falling, the cold was penetrating. As they tried to huddle
together for warmth, young Borucki, the most physically fit among them,
curled up and said nothing.

By the time the *Ary* had settled on the ocean bed, the frightened men were
suffering from exposure. Within the first few hours the ship's steward, who
had been sick for days previously, fell seriously ill. The blizzard was
unrelenting as several drifted into fitful sleep.

John Kelly of Glendalough and Jan Borucki and his shipmates were caught
in the same blizzard, Kelly on land, somewhere in the rugged uplands of Co.
Wicklow, the *Ary's* crew somewhere off the south-east coast in an angry sea.
If their lifeboat were to capsize, drowning would surely be their fate. But so
long as their little craft stayed afloat they faced the same peril as Kelly: death
by exposure. All were at the mercy of nature. Completely blinded by dark and
snowfall. Physically and mentally struggling against odds growing worse by
the hour.

Death by exposure during a blizzard is a gradual, cruel, insidious process.
Quick death by drowning would be comparatively merciful. Kelly, of course,
had no such option.

Blizzard deaths can occur over a span of hours or days from hypothermia,
dehydration, and fatigue, as one eventually succumbs to the fatal
combination, hastened by the process of convection, which robs a victim of
heated air enveloping their skin—a transfer of heat by the movement of the
air itself. During a blizzard the incessant wind is the "breath that strips away
the warmth" from one's body.[3] Convection abets death through a
combination of cold and kinetics, exacerbated by the wind-chill factor.

Cold can bring about death on its own, but it takes longer. When cold and
wind conspire against the human body, loss of life is greatly accelerated.
Dehydration furthers the process. In the absence of gloves or a hat to help

retain some of the body's warmth, death is all the more swift. Victims become vulnerable to frostbite when the body's living tissue becomes irreparably frozen. Hands, feet and ears are the most susceptible, because they are the most remote from the body's central source of heat. Fingers, toes and other extremities are usually the first to go.

Struggling against a blizzard can actually hasten death, as exerting energy only accelerates the loss of strength and body heat. "Fear . . . even mild mental stress" also causes heat loss at a more rapid rate, and "terror and exhaustion are as efficient as wind in scouring heat out of the body."[4]

Owing to the wind-chill factor, Kelly and Borucki were suffering an excruciating cold that felt far below the actual temperature. Closer to zero, if not lower. In the winter of 1946/47, as victims of blizzards fought for their survival, an American scientists, Paul Siple, was working as a biologist on the Antarctic Expedition of Admiral Richard Byrd. It was he who would devise the formula for how convection brings death through the combination of cold and kinetics, and the wind-chill index. He conducted his research and calibrated wind-chill through a laborious series of experiments with water in plastic cylinders. His discovery of the loss of body heat through wind was startling. "At winds of 20 miles an hour, twenty-five times more body heat is lost than at 4 miles an hour."[5] Over the years his findings would be refined. According to the current revised, recalibrated wind-chill index (2010), when the wind is blowing at 30 miles per hour at a temperature of 25 degrees (−4°C), it *feels* like 8 degrees (−13°C).

On Saturday night, off the south-east coast and in the Wicklow highlands, temperatures were probably in the range 18 to 2 degrees (−8 to −16°C), with a Siberian east wind of 55 to 65 miles per hour. Feeling the unutterable pain of slowly freezing to death, Kelly and the *Ary's* seamen were surely shivering and shaking uncontrollably, which is "the body's last defence against the abyss of deep, potentially fatal hypothermia." For victims, spasms of wild shivering are frightening. Eventually, once shivering stops, "the chilled body falls quiet and then shuts down rapidly."[6]

On 8 February people in Ireland knew nothing of convection, kinetics, or the wind-chill factor. And no index had been devised to measure human fear.

———

On Sunday morning Dubliners awoke to face "another all-day blizzard." A near-replica of the weekend before, with heavy snow driven by "an east wind which cruelly whips in and wails around the houses like a banshee working overtime."[7] Once again telecommunications were knocked out and transport brought to a virtual standstill. Dutiful newspaper, milk and bread van drivers tried their best to make deliveries. Dublin Airport was closed to all traffic. The

Automobile Association warned drivers to stay off roads unless absolutely necessary. The Dublin–Belfast road was completely blocked by snow. Between Dundalk and Drogheda heavy snowdrifts trapped vehicles. At Blackrock, Co. Dublin, waves swept onto the railway platform, and people had difficulty getting in and out of the trains. Many mass-goers dared not venture out into treacherous streets, and people again had to accept home confinement.

Meanwhile, somewhere off the south-east coast—Borucki and his mates had no idea where—dawn's first light allowed the men to assess one another's condition, physical and mental. The slumped steward was still and silent, while others mumbled. Then Borucki realised that "I slept during the first night, and when I awoke the next morning the Steward had died." The men agreed to give him an immediate burial at sea, awkwardly shoving his rigid corpse overboard. After a few prayers, they said nothing. Without food, water, or oars, they continued to be carried blindly by wind-whipped seas, drifting in and out of consciousness.

By Sunday morning John Kelly had not returned. His two companions, sick with worry, were helpless, as the blizzard was still blowing and telephone lines were down. If he didn't appear by evening they would begin to plan a search for Monday. Around the country others were missing as well, especially in the midlands and in Co. Wicklow, where drifts now reached a height of eight feet and more. Continuing heavy snow and powerful winds were further resculpting the landscape. Blowing, drifting, piling up. Lowlands, valleys, ravines were filled in, covered, levelled. In places the wind blew snow into massive mounds and ridges. Rivers, streams and lakes had layers of ice—but no-one could be sure how thick. Local landscapes, normally as familiar as the back of a farmer's hand, became visually transformed beyond recognition. "It is a pity," wrote the *Irish Press*, "that people in this blizzard are practically lost in their own mountains." With features now hidden and mysterious, a farmer's own fields and bogs could be dangerous.

In Co. Leitrim on Sunday morning sixteen-year-old Charles James Healy headed into a snow-camouflaged bog to fetch some much-needed turf. As he had done countless times before, he left home with his ass and creel and trekked a familiar route. With poor visibility and reshaped terrain, his footing was not as sure as usual. Some deep bog-holes filled with water and with a layer of ice were now disguised beneath the snow blanket.

After several hours he had not returned. Though the bog was only a short distance away, it was not visible from the house. Concerned that he might have fallen, twisted an ankle or broken a leg in the icy, choppy terrain, several searchers set out to see what had delayed him. When they came upon his ass and creel, the lad was nowhere in sight. They forged ahead. Then one of the men spotted a pencil floating in a break in the ice of a boghole. Without hesitation another searcher, Francis Boyle, "dived into the bog hole, which contained 12 to 16 feet of water," and quickly found the body. Frantically, they tried artificial respiration, but without success. They lifted the pulpy body onto the ass and plodded homewards. No doubt wondering how they would tell his parents. Later, at the inquest, Francis Boyle would be praised for his bravery.

Blizzards would take lives in many unexpected ways.

Farmers were now facing a dilemma. They knew the risks of tramping across snow-concealed land in the midst of a blizzard yet could not passively remain indoors and let their stranded or buried cattle and sheep perish. As Brian Kelly had often seen in Co. Donegal, sheep were particularly vulnerable yet possessed remarkable survivability:

> The sheep is a silly old animal, and in the storm they went to the low, sheltery spot, and some of them stayed there until they were *completely* covered with snow. And perished. But the extraordinary thing, the snow was porous and the sheep could breathe their way out through the snow . . . with their hot breath.

Knowing that sheep caught or buried in snow could still be alive, farmers had to make a decision whether to trudge through the storm and try to find and save them. Facing snowdrifts waist and chest-deep and "death to walk on further out," some "dare not travel to check on sheep and cattle sunk in the snowy morass."[8] Those who did took their chances. Many farms extended over sprawling, undulating terrain, with uplands, depressions, blind cavities. Drifts ten feet high and bog-holes ten feet deep. Braving the worst, they would set out with a long pole on a mercy mission.

Sinking in the sea of snow, long shepherd's sticks gently prodding before them into the mounds that might be coverlets for dead sheep. Or maybe hoping that the breath of the sheep might have melted out a cave for itself to live in . . . as sometimes happened.[9]

Farmers finding stranded sheep and cattle still alive often realised quickly the sad folly of their search. For they were not able to dig them out, lead them to safety, or bring water and fodder to them. They were doomed. Many doubtless wished they had not found them at all, or at least had discovered them already dead.

————

After two weeks of Arctic temperatures and blizzards, word came from Dublin Zoo that "the animals are suffering much from the cold, owing to the shortage of fuel." The problem was not simply insufficient heat. The fluctuation in temperature was causing sickness and death to some tropical species. Having to use damp turf and logs, the zoo staff could not possibly maintain a safe heating level. Working around the clock, they relied on hot food, blankets, and other personal care. Nonetheless, some monkeys had fallen ill, and several died. An eighty-year-old mongoose expired when it could not be kept properly warm. Some snakes were by now "so badly frozen that they had to be thawed out." A tedious process of gently bathing them in warm water, which had to be gradually increased in temperature. It took about an hour to bring each snake back to normal.

The superintendent of the zoo, J. C. Flood, a man of complete dedication to his beloved animals, took a personal interest in every one of them. During the German bombing of the North Strand in 1941, in which one errant bomb fell in the Phoenix Park close to the zoo grounds, many of the animals were terrified, some thrashing against their cages to break free and flee. One huge bison smashed its way out. Sara the elephant, darling of zoo staff and visitors, managed to pull off a Houdini-style escape by unbolting her door with her trunk, then running free into the park. It was Flood who went in search of her, found her trembling in the high reeds beside the lake, and gently talked her into returning with him to her quarters. He had that sort of relationship with his wards.

During the first week of February he had just returned from England, where he had acquired a further collection of animals, including many tropical birds and snakes from West Africa, which needed special care during cold spells. He also brought from London Zoo two prized baby western boars. When they quickly became affected by the cold, "Mr. Flood carried them around his waist inside his pullover," the *Irish Times* revealed, "and this kept them warm enough to protect them against serious illness."[10]

Some snakes in Dublin—huge ones—were faring quite well. About a mile from the zoo, at number 8 North Earl Street, where Miss Ima Weight, "the world's fattest woman," had just concluded her engagement, she was replaced by Ty-Ana, "the world famous eastern snake charmer and her mighty pythons," on show from 2 till 10 p.m. daily. How her mighty pythons were kept warm and properly fed was not known. They certainly looked healthy to visitors.

On Sunday afternoon, with the blizzard still ripping across the cityscape, sports events were cancelled for the second consecutive weekend. It had become a serious financial and social problem. "The weather has had a lot to answer for regarding the poverty of play and paucity of patronage," affirmed the *Evening Herald*. "The bad reaction on crowds and 'gates' is worrying club officials." Club owners and promoters were losing big money. Athletes and fans were disgruntled. Shamrock Rovers, who had matches with Waterford and Cork United, were wiped out by the blizzards on the two Sundays.

In defiance of the weather, some rugby and football contests were held anyway, on appalling pitches—with the result, wrote one sports reporter, that "playing conditions were so bad at times that it became farcical." Paying patrons were not amused. Players were slipping, sliding, falling awkwardly like comedians doing falls for laughs on the stage of the Theatre Royal, leaving spectators to watch a comedy of errors rather than a seriously contested match. Many left grumbling that they wanted their money back.

Repeated sports cancellations had a social as well as a financial impact. Multitudes of Irish men addicted to sport and to betting on it were growing increasingly frustrated. It was disrupting their normal winter rhythm of life, causing some to drink more, become surly. In Dublin's pubs, distressed pubmen cursed the weather in colourful terms.

One athletic figure was not going to allow a mere gale-force blizzard to interfere with his Sunday afternoon plans. Not at all. James Green of 34 Merlyn Park, Ballsbridge, had taken a swim at Sandycove every year for the previous forty-seven years on 9 February, his birthday. Ugly weather had never deterred him from enjoying his sacred ritual. Nor was it going to do so now, on his eightieth birthday. To the astonishment—and admiration, no doubt—of family and friends, on Sunday afternoon in the wildest weather he set out for his birthday swim. "With a snow-laden north-east wind driving waves which broke with fifteen-foot spray along the east coast," he unflinchingly took "a plunge in at the Forty-Foot at Sandycove."[11] After which he refreshingly, smilingly "explained to his shivering friends, 'It was quite nice today.'"

Tradition was tradition.

At the same time that James Green was enjoying his birthday dip, Jan Borucki and his mates were drifting aimlessly in their lifeboat, as the storm was subsiding and waves diminishing. The whereabouts of the other lifeboat remained unknown to them. They spoke little but were probably thinking the same things. Wondering if any ships or lifeboat stations had picked up their hurried distress messages or seen the flares fired during the last minutes before they abandoned ship. As it turned out, Wicklow lifeboat station had spotted a flare, probably from the *Ary*. Late on Sunday afternoon, when the seas became safe enough, they "searched for some hours, without result." How close they may have come to the men's boat will never be known.

By nightfall they were losing strength, and hope. The men were famished, thirsty, numb, suffering from serious exposure. Several were only semi-conscious, delirium setting in. The clearing skies would cause the temperature to fall lower that night. Convection was robbing them of body heat, as the wind remained strong, keeping the wind-chill painfully low. Several had already lost sensation in their hands and feet as frostbite gnawed at their extremities. Borucki was holding on to life.

———

Dublin's Monday morning papers reported news of the widespread blizzard from distant counties, and even from abroad. Britain and much of northern Europe had been slammed hard as well. The Rhine was said to be frozen for miles, while around the Swedish coast ships were frozen in. The Baltic was rapidly freezing, and the sound between Sweden and Denmark was now described as "a solid block of ice." Throughout Britain and the Continent meteorologists and commentators were talking seriously of the possibility of a "new Ice Age."

In Ireland, distressing stories were now emerging from islands off the western and southern coasts. Islanders always endured hardships during a bad winter, being cut off from regular mainland services and provisions. Many of the islands were no more than barren slabs of rock—more like a lunar surface—with no boglands for turf, forest for logs, or decent fields for crops. Hardy folk, they somehow survived it all, year after year. But if they were cut off from vital provisions of fuel and food for a prolonged period, the deprivation could become desperate.

Island winters were typically chilly, bleak, and boring. But survivable. Owing to the normal influence of the warm Gulf Stream, spells of deep cold or snow were unusual and fleeting. In late January, however, islanders found themselves also victims of the freak Arctic regime, with bitter temperatures and slicing east wind. They always had food and fuel stocks put by for winter. In ordinary times, if they needed more food, coal or turf they could get it from the mainland. Now this was not possible, as mainlanders were themselves suffering shortages.

By 10 February some island families had already exhausted their modest turf supply in trying to keep warm. Each day thinking that surely the cold spell would end. Then they began burning hay and straw intended for their animals. By the second week of February the papers confirmed that on some islands the conditions had become so serious that inhabitants were now resorting to stripping wood from their houses for fuel. Even burning furniture. When Dubliners read of this in the newspapers they were appalled.

By mid-morning on Monday, John Kelly was nowhere in sight. His two companions notified the authorities in Glendalough, contacted friends, and organised a search party, to get under way that afternoon. Simultaneously Lloyd's of London reported the *Ary* as "overdue," having failed to reach Waterford on schedule. They would await further information before revising their report to "missing." Or worse.

Repair crews from CIE, the ESB and the Post Office were out again in full force. All still far behind in their work to restore services damaged during the first blizzard. This time a party of twenty-five men from the Signals Corps was despatched to assist the Post Office linesmen. Hospitals, doctors and emergency services anxiously awaited reconnection. Dublin Corporation (as the city council was commonly called) again relied on its primitive snow-clearance operation, sending out squads with shovels, sand, and straw.

In the early afternoon information came in from remote parts of Connemara and the Wicklow Mountains, where drifts were said to commonly be eight to twelve feet deep, enough to cover two cars, or a bus. Familiar features of the human landscape, such as stone walls, roads, railway tracks, fences, signs, outbuildings, telephone and telegraph poles, even small cottages, were blanketed or "wiped out" by a sea of snow.

From all accounts, the Co. Wicklow villages of Roundwood, Glendalough and Glencree were cut off from the outside world. Now, like islanders, short on food and fuel, they were forced to resort to desperate measures:

> In Glendalough and Roundwood it has been snowing for 24 hours . . . and now all the roads around the villages are again completely blocked . . . people are in a bad way for food . . . Cattle are badly off for hay . . . Many people have burnt articles of furniture for heating and cooking during the blizzards of the past week.[12]

The Red Cross Society grew more worried about the nuns and children in Glencree when word arrived that the roads had been made "even worse by the snowfall . . . The prospects now of getting motor vehicles through the deep drifts are remote." Realising the critical need for resupply of food and fuel, they announced on Monday afternoon that "a sledge is being built to maintain connection with Glencree." When it might be ready was not specified.

The *Irish Independent* decided to take up the challenge of trying to reach Glencree. It would send out a reporter and photographer, using a "secret weapon" of sorts: a new Jeep. Rugged, with four-wheel drive, special snow tyres, and the skilled driving services of P. McCarthy, service manager of Motor Distributors Ltd. Jeeps were war machines, reputedly capable of ploughing through, or over, almost any obstacles in their path. Nothing in Ireland was likely to stop them.

The paper confidently predicted that their "expedition" would successfully make contact with the "refugee children isolated from the outside for almost three weeks." It would try to reach their destination via Rathfarnham, Ballyboden, and the Hell Fire Tea Rooms, reporting on progress along the way:

The journey was made in the most appalling conditions . . . a nightmare drive up the Wicklow Mountains in a Jeep which at times ploughed through snow three and four feet deep. County Council workers were endeavouring to clear snow which was waist deep. As the Jeep progressed upwards the mountain drifts became deeper and deeper. About a quarter of a mile from Glencree we had to stop as the drifts were too deep, and we completed the journey on foot.[13]

As they approached the hostel, every window was filled with faces. On their arrival at the door Sister Patrick, who was in charge, greeted them with elation, blurting that "we were the first people they had seen from Dublin for weeks." Without telephones, electricity, or newspapers, the nuns were hungry for news. Had other parts of the country been similarly struck by blizzards? What was the Government doing to help? What was the weather forecast? The nuns and children huddled excitedly around the three men, firing one question after another, hanging on their every word about the "outside world."

Sister Patrick explained that "we were foresighted enough to get in a month's supply" of food and fuel before the "spell of weather set in," as she benignly phrased it. Now, however, they were in need of provisions. She heaped praise on Mr McCann, their local bread delivery man, for his "heroic work performance." Several times before the snow became too deep he had made his way by van and then walking, close enough to leave some loaves at a point where several of the younger, hardier nuns were able to retrieve it by hiking some distance. A godsend, she called it. Now short on both food and fuel, all they could do was pray every day for an end to the Arctic weather.

After saying their goodbyes, the three men began their trek back to the Jeep, following their original tracks, talking among themselves along the way about their experiences. "We found the thing most bothering the inmates being a sense of loneliness because of lack of communication with the outside world." A social and psychological condition now affecting thousands of others in snowbound, isolated areas. Their mission accomplished, at least in part, they began a thrilling return trip down the mountains and back to Dublin:

The Jeep slid all over the road and the driver had a trying time keeping his vehicle out of the ditch. The steering wheel at times whirled around in his hands as the car skidded on the snow-bound mountain road. The journey back was reminiscent of the dodgems in a circus or fancy fair.[14]

The reporter's forthcoming article about their adventure would make for interesting reading, something of a coup for the *Irish Independent*. But the

Irish mountains had defeated the American Jeep.

By dusk John Kelly had not been found. The search party had spent the day combing the local terrain for any sign of him. While they were hunting for him, another search team was trying to track down a missing man elsewhere in the rugged Wicklow Mountains. He too had disappeared during the height of the blizzard. "Men stayed out all night looking for the man who got lost way up in the ungettatable hills," wrote the *Irish Press,* and finally, late on Monday, "found him dead." Not yet identified, little was known about him. Other than that he died of exposure. The report of his death raised worries about others still missing.

———

Clear across the country, in Co. Mayo, where the second major blizzard in six days had further blocked roads and rail movement, the residents of Straide were feeling more isolated than ever. Like many small towns and villages, there was a sense of being cut off from outside communication. As Tony Ruane estimates, there were "only about three radios in the village," making it hard for most people to know what was occurring elsewhere in the country. The blizzards had knocked out telephone lines, and post and newspaper deliveries had been interrupted. What post had made it through by train could not now be delivered in the normal way, because Martin Sweeney's route was so heavily drifted. A better system had to be devised. Tony Ruane recalls:

> After about two weeks of isolation, an effort was made to deliver the post by donkey and creels. It was a common sight, the postman leading the donkeys through the snowdrifts, a mailbag on either creel, delivering letters and parcels. The mail *had* to get through at any cost . . . registered letters containing urgently needed cash sent by migrant workers in England.

Local people kept an eye out for him and if he got bogged down in snow would rush out to assist him.

Blizzards brought out ingenuity and resourcefulness.

Snowbound home confinement was a most unnatural human condition, for adults and children. Without normal romping and roaming, children grew fidgety and bored, filled with pent-up energy. Not being able to set foot outside the door for days could be torture. Naturally, this created stress for parents. In the Ruane household the mother wisely assigned her nine children specific household tasks, had the older daughters read books to the others, and stories were told around the turf fire. When a break in the weather permitted, the boys were set free in the nearby fields for purposeful activities, "gathering firewood, and we would set snares in the snow to catch rabbits," he recounts, "which would be brought home, cleaned out, skinned and put in the pot over the fire." Stay close to home, stay together, and don't remain out too long. Bad weather could strike without warning. The reward was rabbit stew, relished for "a flavour like nothing else."

Country men did not cope well with forced confinement. By nature and habit they were active, hard-working, busy almost every hour of the day. Some could feel "tied up," irritable, being home hostages. Under such abnormal circumstances the local pub assumed an even more important social role than usual. It provided a social outlet and psychological safety-valve for local menfolk. Even men who were moderate drinkers, or teetotallers, sought the pub's warmth and socialisation. Putting it on the slate if necessary to get them through the hard times.

In Straide, Heynes's pub was the sanctuary. Like most village pubs of the period, it also functioned as a grocery, carrying basic provisions that also drew women into the food section. Women too valued any opportunity to escape home confinement. Heynes's pub functioned as the vital centre for the exchange of news, gossip, and rumours galore. Every time some morsel of new information made it into the village, word spread by way of the Heynes's conduit. If a lorry driver made it through the snow, or a man from a neighbouring village arrived on horseback, he became the immediate centre of attention. "What's going on out there?" was the standard query.

As Tony Ruane tells it, everyone ended up in Heynes's for one reason or another, the most indispensable gathering-spot in the village:

> It was a kind of general store. You could get a pint of porter, a pound of sausages, rashers, or black puddin' . . . a stone of flour or a pair of Wellington boots, a shovel, a pickaxe or a hammer—whatever took your fancy.

But in the second week of February it was news that most people were most hungry for. What had the radio-owners heard from Dublin? Had anyone received informative letters? In the absence of verifiable news, rumours naturally flew wild. With the stock of supplies in the pub-grocery running low, speculation began that beer, spirits and tobacco were sure to run out soon if no lorries or trains made it through. An awful prospect for men to contemplate. Ruane senior, a moderate drinker, tried to keep up on the latest news and bring it home to his wife and nine children, as recounted in a poem written by his son many decades later:

> The paraffin lamp glowed,
> yellow on the wall.

Put that jute-sack
to the bottom of the door,
my father commanded.
Outside a tempest raged,
A very wild snowstorm.
The turf fire blazed
And the eleven of us were warm.
My Dad had just returned
from Heynes's Bar.
He liked a couple of pints
of plain black porter.
As he shook the snow
From coat and hat,
He told my mother all the news,
Like a "Western People" reporter.

Family members gathered around to listen. Coming from Heynes's, it was sometimes hard to discern fact from fiction. But it was always interesting.

Meanwhile Phillip Mount and his "hurdy-gurdy" road-show faced the reality that the second blizzard had probably snowbound them in Straide for an extended period. They settled in at the converted church, stacked at one end with a local farmer's straw bales. The reciprocal deal was apparently to the liking of both parties. As Tony Ruane puts it, "the priest was paid a rental fee and everybody was happy with this." At least so long as the attractions were "proper." Mount had the reputation of putting on a good show, giving people their money's worth, and then heading down the road. All the hammering, shouting and activity going on in the community centre created in itself an atmosphere of excitement among villagers.

It seemed that Phillip Mount's original bad-weather, road-blocked misfortune would be bringing good fortune to residents and neighbours of Straide. How long would the troupe of entertainers be staying? A good query for speculation down at Heynes's.

———

Far from Straide, on the evening of Monday 10 February, British citizens gathered around their radio sets to listen to the nine-minute address of the Prime Minister, Clement Attlee, on the BBC regarding the country's worsening fuel crisis. Irish people listened intently as well, knowing that their fuel fate was inextricably linked to that of Britain.

Following the second blizzard, British coal mines, ports and railways were so badly frozen up and snowed under that more industries had to be shut down and workers let go. Domestic fuel usage had to be further rationed, and London's tram and energy services were drastically cut. Citizens needed to understand, stated Attlee, that the coal crisis had become "dangerously critical" and that a "wartime dim-out" was needed. He explained that Britain had to be placed on "what virtually amounts to a war footing . . . with the same urgency as a military operation."[15] To accentuate his words he ended his grim speech by revealing that "no let-up in the freezing conditions" was forecast. Listeners in both countries could do little but sit silently and shake their heads.

Within twenty-four hours President Harry Truman in the United States responded by vowing that his country was ready to do everything in its power to help relieve the plight of the British people. This might be accomplished by diverting to Britain a number of American ships carrying coal to other war-torn European countries—but it would probably take a minimum of fifteen days for any coal to arrive.

If most British and Irish citizens were left mute by Attlee's worrisome words, George Bernard Shaw had something to say. After criticising British politicians for their myopia and poor judgement, he shared with the *Times* of London his "solution of the British fuel crisis." Very simply, they should for years have been harnessing the power of the tides in the Kyle of Tongue at the northern tip of Scotland. He informed the *Times* that he had suggested this very idea to both Government and engineers some eighteen years earlier. Ignored, he was not pleased:

> But they went on grubbing for power in coal mines, and now that the atomic bomb has wakened them, they are dreaming of nuclear energies, which are frightfully dangerous and enormously expensive. They do not seem to know that our tides, almost unique in the world, exist.[16]

On Tuesday morning the Irish authorities responded promptly. CIE announced that railway services would be further reduced, while the ESB warned of the need to cut usage to a bare minimum. Dublin Gas Company sliced the hours of usage from 8½ down to 5:

Morning, 6:30 to 8:30

Midday, 11:30 to 1:30

Evening, 6 to 7

"Horrible," housewives called it. The shorter midday hours intensified the lunch-hour rush in Dublin, with cooking time cut by a full hour. Hotels, cafés and restaurants had to adopt new schedules to meet the change. The city's legendary leisurely lunches were becoming a thing of the past.

Responsible citizens and institutions tried to do their part in easing the fuel crisis by limiting their use of gas, electricity, and oil. Homes, shops, factories, offices, schools, banks and pubs saw their meagre fuel stocks dwindle by the day. By now people had commonly taken to living and working—and for many sleeping—with coats, jumpers and scarves on. During the day they tried to keep the circulation going in their chilled hands and feet. Those with active work duties had an advantage in this regard over those tied to a desk or stationary job.

On Tuesday 11 February the internal heating of the GPO was discontinued, and the staff bundled up in cold chambers. By stark contrast, the occupants of Leinster House seemed quite unconcerned by the drastic heating cuts endured by others, snug in their warmly heated offices. Their furnaces consumed crude oil, of which "there was no scarcity," at a rate of 50 gallons per day. Owing to their comfort, many Government employees arrived early and left late. Seemingly oblivious of the misery of the multitudes of shivering Dubliners coping with wet turf or completely fireless grates.

Not only did shortages of coal and coke threaten foundries and other industries but the country's blacksmiths and farriers were now feeling the pinch in their forges. As Dublin still relied significantly on horse-power for haulage, the city's forty to fifty farriers were worried about how they were going to keep the horses safely shod with frost-nails. Already Galway's eight forges had announced that they were down to their last supplies of coal and coke, facing the "prospect of unemployment." By contrast, blacksmiths and farriers in Co. Donegal, owing to recent releases of coal from Fort Leenan and Fort Dunree, boasted supplies sufficient for another six months. Their shortage now was of iron.

Amid the tightening coal crunch, a story came to light in the newspapers about one enterprising Dubliner who let it be known that he was soon to personally receive a gift from a friend in America—*five tons* of coal! It was to arrive any day on an American ship. He did not divulge how this had been arranged, but his story elicited much interest and, no doubt, envy. As well as raising a good question: if an ordinary citizen had been able to negotiate terms in the United States for receiving tons of coal for his personal use, why had the Government not been able to do likewise on behalf of the citizens? Was one more energetic and enterprising than the other?

————

For three days the *Ary's* oarless lifeboat had drifted, as Jan Borucki saw his companions "die one by one from hunger and exposure,"[17] then being hoisted overboard into the sea without ceremony. By now the last few survivors were weak from hunger and thirst, semi-comatose, in a state of intermittent delirium. Young Borucki, the strongest, was surviving better than his mates, but his hands and feet were now largely devoid of sensation, as frostbite had set in. He doubted that any of them would live to see Wednesday's dawn.

At the first crack of light next morning, Borucki stirred. His first thought was surprise that he was still alive. Then, hazily, he realised that he was now the only one alive in the lifeboat. Immediately, he felt a fear of being beside the corpses.

About two hours later, near Minehead on the Waterford coast, some ten miles from Dungarvan, his small bobbing boat was gently washed ashore. No-one was around to witness it. Aboard was one man—who thought he was on the coast of France.

He lay still for several minutes, "suffering from acute exposure and in a state of collapse."[18] Gradually his senses were revived as he recognised that he had not washed ashore on a level beach but at the base of a high rock cliff. After three-and-a-half days cramped in a lifeboat in freezing temperatures, and weak from hunger and thirst, he had little sensation left in his hands and feet. It was difficult to stand erect and maintain balance. His mind was confused. He was, however, conscious enough to know that, isolated at the bottom of a cliff, he could die before being discovered. He had only one route to survival. He feared the cliff; but he feared death more. Without trying to assess which part of the rock face might be the safest to scale, he simply began climbing.

How long it took him he would never remember. With numbed hands and feet, "he crawled up the cliffs where the boat was stranded and made his way to a house." This was the home of a local farmer, Con Hourigan. "After climbing the rocks," the *Irish Times* reported, "he staggered half naked and in a state of collapse" to Hourigan's door.[19] Incoherent and in a "semi-delirious state," he was unable to inform the farmer of his ordeal. "Shipwrecked" was about all he could get out. Hourigan hurriedly took him to Dungarvan Hospital. Upon arrival, barely conscious, he was not able to give his name or that of the ship from which he had come. He was so severely frostbitten that doctors immediately gave him strong injections of morphia. He must have been remarkably strong to have survived, they said.

By late Wednesday afternoon the dramatic story of Jan Borucki's survival was being carried across the country by the press and radio. Everyone wanted the compelling details of how he had clung to life when all the others had perished. Reporters from all the Dublin papers converged on the small hospital, hovering outside his room, hoping to get the personal account. They were to have no luck that day.

———

Later on Wednesday, on the heel of Attlee's grave address, Seán Lemass addressed Dáil Éireann on his version of Ireland's fuel situation. It was, he stated, far worse than the public realised, because most people had been counting on native turf supplies to compensate for the absence of coal imports. But because of the long span of bad weather going back to the summer of 1946, this was now a false hope. The *Irish Press* summed up his discouraging comments:

> If bad weather continued, the country—not Dublin alone—was facing a first-class crisis in domestic fuel. Turf is sodden with water and virtually useless as a fuel. Lorries cannot reach the flooded bogs. Turf piled in dumps in the Phoenix Park is soaked. Under the worst conditions there would be *no fuel*—there was nothing to do about it.[20]

Ironically, the total quantity of turf produced in the whole of Ireland by Bord na Móna, county councils, private producers and individuals was as large as in any previous year. But, "entirely due to the severe and persistent weather conditions," Lemass affirmed, it was now sodden or unreachable.[21] There were more than 100,000 tons of *cut* turf that could not be retrieved from the bogs and transported to depots. Meanwhile, frigid temperatures had increased the demand for turf, fast exhausting the last decent supplies.

Lemass did not mince his words: it was a desperate situation that could become calamitous if warmer weather and drying winds did not arrive soon. His words of consolation to citizens were few:

> We can certainly pray for good weather in the coming weeks. If we get it, we will get through this period of crisis; if we do not, we are in for a very bad time indeed.[22]

Countless thousands of poor Dubliners were already having a "very bad time" of it, especially those in the most miserable tenement hovels. However, as the *Irish Independent* pointed out, there were those among the better-off classes who had apparently not fully comprehended the seriousness of the situation:

> Although most people in the country had known that a very difficult fuel period was ahead, the announcement by Mr. Lemass in the Dáil that the country was on the brink of a fuel crisis unless dry weather should come, created a shock.[23]

The paper, while lauding Lemass for his candour, added a note of criticism:

> The most disturbing feature of his speech was that he appeared to see no way of dealing with the situation if the weather did not improve. Dubliners are asking why large quantities of firewood were not being sought . . . It was contended that there was plenty of timber within 20 miles of the city.[24]

If turf ran out, could firewood save Dublin?

For the moment, only wet turf was in sight. From the onset of Arctic temperatures in late January there was exasperation among those who were trying to get the earthen sods to burn and throw off heat. Nearly every day it was the subject of newspaper articles, both whimsical and serious. *Dublin Opinion* featured jokes and cartoons about wet turf, most quite clever and amusing. At first. In the *Evening Herald*, "Uncle Argus" was forever poking fun at turf, often at his own expense. After one night when the temperature plummeted to 12 degrees (−11°c) he sought sympathy from his readers by telling them how he was "breaking icicles off his whiskers in the intervals of fumbling with numbed fingers at his frost-bitten typewriter." All this, he explained, because of his inability to get turf to burn. By the second week of February his patience with soggy turf was nearly exhausted, and he devoted an entire column to the maddening problem:

> My latest consignment of turf does not burn. The most you can do is coax it to smoulder. All that is left is a sulky red eye in a group of repulsive-looking sods. It continues to smoulder . . . it just glowers at you. I never met turf like it before.[25]

Though written in jest, it captured his readers' sense of frustration. And verified Lemass's contention that wet turf was "virtually useless" as a fuel.

Not according to Margaret Lee, however, who wrote an article on the society page of the *Irish Press* clearly intended for affluent readers. Its cheerful, encouraging heading was "Do not let wet turf get you down—It can be burned!" She first advised readers who had a "poky little grate" from which they could not draw a decent fire to simply "get a new fireplace installed." Then, she explained, "do not be afraid to pile the turf high . . . it will not fall onto the rug or carpet . . . neither will it set the chimney ablaze."[26]

This statement could only have astounded the city's tenement-dwellers, chimneysweeps and firemen, who were coping with the worst winter of chimney fires in their history, most of them caused by burning turf. Indeed the *Irish Times* had just reported that Dublin Fire Brigade was beset by a record number of fires in the city:

> The incidence of fires, particularly outbreaks originating in chimneys and spreading to other parts of premises, was far greater than in any previous year. The main cause of this remarkable increase is the widespread use of native turf, causing unclear flues and persistent smouldering ashes.[27]

James Rooney, the north side's legendary chimneysweep, who started out in the 1920s, was bedevilled by the widespread burning of damp turf in 1947:

Oh, turf is worse than coal, by *far*. The turf goes into *tar*, the build-up from it. And then the chimneys go on fire, and it cracks them. It destroyed chimneys.

Wet turf was both exasperating and dangerous. But it was all that people had to use.

———

Lemass's warning that "under the worst conditions there would be no fuel" made people panicky to find whatever turf they could get their hands on, regardless of its quality. Many people believed they could somehow dry it out if they could just get it home. Only those with a magic wand actually possessed such powers.

Along Protestant Row, off Wexford Street, twelve-year-old Margaret Coyne was sent by her Ma to get any turf sods she could. "Oh, God, we'd get the turf and the water'd be dripping out of it—but you *had* to take it, and we were glad of it at the time." People desperate to buy even the worst, often useless, turf profited the city's fuel merchants and black-marketers, eager to squeeze every shilling out of people's misery. By the second week of February citizens were storming the doors of their local fuel merchants. "Turf depots were literally invaded by customers seeking turf," the *Irish Times* reported. They pushed and shoved their way forward as the merchants' assistants yelled, "Get back now!"[28] Women tearfully cried out, *"Please,* mister, just a few sods!" *Irish Independent* reporters found that "small hucksters' shops in side streets" stopped even bothering to bring their turf deliveries indoors, as they were simply dumped "beside the kerb and the whole consignment is gone within half an hour."[29]

The miserable, strenuous task of collecting wet, heavy turf fell largely to women and children. Some newspaper photographs of long turf queues show no men. Pushing and pulling a rickety old pram or home-made handcart laden with soggy turf through cold, snowy, slushy cobblestoned streets was a great physical strain. Young Agnes Daly of North Clarence Street dreaded it but followed her Ma's orders: *"Everyone* had a boxcart, with two wheels off an old pram, out of a wooden box from a shop, and two handles—and I *hated* coming up the hill pushing it!"

The sight of frail grannies, pregnant mothers, young children heaving mightily through snow-clogged streets didn't bother most men. In the city's lower-income and working-class families of the 1940s it was seen as a "household" chore and therefore fell to women and daughters. Hefty men on their way to their local pub would walk past women straining with turf carts without so much as a thought of offering a helping hand. The publican John

O'Dwyer, who was working at the time at Lalor's pub in York Street, a real rough-and-tumble area, explains it was the culture of the time for men to leave such work to women.

By mid-February, some men did begin collecting turf. Heaps of it. Wealthy Dubliners with cars, large houses, garages and garden sheds had the means of buying turf in bulk from black-marketers and stockpiling it until it dried out. Black-marketers operated in many clandestine and shrewd ways, behind closed doors, under cover of darkness in the middle of the night. Sometimes a well-to-do man would be tipped off about the arrival of a turf lorry. He would then drive his car, often pulling a trailer, to the city's outskirts and flag down the driver, paying him two or three times the normal rate.

The city's multitude of poor, however, were left at the mercy of unscrupulous profiteers. "Oh, the black market was going!" recalls Maisy Flood, now nearing a hundred years of age, "and the poor ones really had a terrible time of it." The *Irish Times* exposed how the "tenement dwellers are suffering extreme hardship . . . There is profiteering in turf and the poorer classes are being exploited."[30] Profiteers inflated turf prices for those who could least afford it, forcing many to seek loans from moneylenders, who would hound them till their dying day for their mounting interest. Along Charlemont Street, one newspaper revealed, women had to "pay exorbitant prices for turf . . . selling at black market prices."

The *Evening Herald* brought the scandal to full light:

> It is shocking to find that some of their better-off fellow citizens take advantage of the plight of these poor people for their own financial gain . . . turf distributors taking lorry loads into the poorer districts after dark and selling it in small quantities at exorbitant prices. There is plenty of evidence that this occurs . . . this meanest form of profiteering.[31]

Why, then, wasn't the Government cracking down hard on the illegal profiteers? Everyone in the heart of the city knew at first hand how the black-market system operated on an unbridled, widespread scale. Those in the suburbs had every opportunity to learn about it from reading the daily newspapers, in which the abuse was explicitly documented. Most members of the Government, however, talked of it in terms of "hearsay" and "allegations," citing the need for "hard evidence" before legal action could be taken. Perhaps they could "look into" such charges of unlawful exploitation. From the windows of their warm, oil-heated Leinster House they couldn't seem to see any solid evidence of black-market operations.

———

There were other scoundrels at play in Dublin. Carrying out a different sort of illicit activity at the public's expense. Thousands of gas consumers were not abiding by the Gas Company's regulations about the off hours. These "cheaters," as they were being called in the press, were illicitly consuming precious gas by using the low-pressure trace left in the pipes during the off hours for a "glimmer." Taken in total, this "stolen gas" was estimated at nearly a fifth of the city's entire output, a serious drain on the gas supply belonging to all citizens.

N. J. Robertson, the no-nonsense general manager of Dublin Gas Company, decided to publish an open letter in the papers to "inform the public of the true facts of the situation." In straightforward terms, he stated that "we know of no further coal or coke which will be made available to us," while their paltry stock was of the "very poorest reject grade." It had a low yield of gas and would soon be exhausted. Those dishonest citizens who were secretly using the glimmer during prohibited hours were in effect robbing their own neighbours. For them, he had a stern warning:

> Should any of them be caught and have their gas supply cut off, they can hardly expect any sympathy when they go crying for it. And in the future more offenders are going to be caught.[32]

Caught by the legendary "glimmer men," the Gas Company's diligent inspectors who roamed the city streets, usually on bicycles. During the war years many housewives made something of a cat-and-mouse game of it, with all sorts of shrewd schemes to avoid getting nabbed. Most commonly they posted children at the ends of their street to keep a vigilant eye open for "yer man," with instructions to yell out if he was spotted. "It's the glimmer man! It's the *glimmer man!*"

In February 1947, amidst dangerously cold Arctic temperatures and vanishing fuel, it was a more serious matter. When newspapers revealed that cheaters were taking fully a fifth of the *people's* gas, it created resentment among the honest majority. There could even be ill feelings among neighbours and family members. Suddenly, gas usage was a personal, contentious issue in Dublin.

Nor was the ESB's plea for conserving energy being heeded. In fact during the second week of February consumption was running nearly a fifth higher than usual. This electricity could be supplied only by burning additional coal at the Pigeon House generating station, further reducing stocks. It had been alleged—and indeed found—that some affluent Dubliners with the luxury of electric heating and cooking had been serious violators. Not to be outdone by the Gas Company, ESB officials announced that they too were despatching inspectors to roam districts in search of electricity violators. The inspectors would be "patrolling the city and have the authority to demand each consumer's ration card," to make certain that consumption was proper. After which they carefully checked meters to make certain there were no "tricks" being played. The penalty for violation was disconnection.

Dubliners who were inclined towards cheating were now running a double risk of having both their gas and their electricity cut off. With no sympathy from authorities or public.

———

On 13 February, from Dungarvan Hospital came word that papers found on Jan Borucki's clothing confirmed that he was a member of the *Ary's* crew. By now he was also lucid enough to verify that his ship had gone down. But he could say little more. Reporters would have to wait longer for the full story. Later that day the body of another seaman from the *Ary* was washed ashore at Ardmore, about six miles from where Borucki landed. Towards afternoon, in London, Lloyd's bell would solemnly toll to officially announce the loss of the *Ary* on its voyage from Port Talbot to Waterford.

About the time the bell was rung, the searchers for John Kelly near Glendalough were scouring a heavily drifted area. That morning they had decided to expand their search area. It paid off when his hat was found some distance from the path he should have followed. This indicated that—typical of blizzard victims—he had probably become geographically disoriented by the white-out, eventually lost, then left to face the freezing wind-chilled temperature. As the processes of convection, hypothermia, fear and exhaustion slowly stripped life-giving heat and ultimately doomed him. Over how long a period of suffering, no-one would know.

In mid-afternoon searchers came upon his body, quite far off the path he should have taken. He may well have circled about until the last of his strength was sapped. Embedded in the snow, his body was carefully retrieved by gardaí and friends and began the journey home.

To Irish people reading about it, a man lost and freezing to death in a blinding blizzard sounded more like a story from Kansas or North Dakota on the vast American Great Plains.

———

In mid-February, after three weeks of Arctic cold, blizzards, influenza epidemic, fuel crisis, food shortages, and now deaths on land and at sea, the Government remained essentially passive, oblivious of the suffering of the people.

What, then, *were* they concerned about and discussing? Cosmic physics.

It was the most engaging, passionately debated topic of the Dáil's winter session. In the blizzard's aftermath, with the country's transport and

EVENING HERA

(INCORPORATING THE "EVENING TELEGRAPH")

VOL. 56, No. 26, DUBLIN, THURSDAY, JANUARY 30, 1947.   PRICE THREE

Dublin Still Shivering as Big Freeze Continues

COLDEST NIGHT FOR SEVERAL YEARS

But Youngsters Have The Time Of Their Lives

Two Degrees Short Of The Record

(" Herald ", Staff Reporter)

WITH 23 DEGREES OF FROST LAST NIGHT—THE LOWEST TEMPERATURE RECORDED FOR MANY YEARS, AND ONLY TWO DEGREES SHORT OF THE DUBLIN RECORD—DUBLINERS AWOKE TO-DAY WITH ACUTE DISINCLINATION TO GET OUT FROM UNDER THE BLANKETS.

The temperature had risen a few degrees when the big trek to business began, but the cold was still intense.

Ice floes were to be seen in the Liffey and the canals. Vehicular traffic again had to proceed warily and, in general, city life was slowed down considerably.

Snowball battle in St. Stephen's Green

She Doesn't Feel The Cold !

Antarctic Warmer than European Areas

1. On 30–31 January 1947 the temperature in Dublin fell to 7 degrees Fahrenheit (−14°C), colder than at the Antarctic that day!

2. In September 1946 Agnes Daly (*front*) and her friends hopped on army lorries to be taken out to farmers' fields to help take in the harvest.

3. During the first major blizzard of the winter the *Irish Plane* was driven aground off the Cork coast.

4. When early snows fell, newspapers showed photographs of children happily at play with snowballs and snowmen. This "fun" aspect of the snow soon changed.

5. Dublin Corporation workers using primitive shovelling methods to clear snow and dump it into the River Liffey.

Ice Floes In Dublin Docks

6. The Liffey became jammed with large ice-floes several inches thick and even froze over in places.

7. In early winter, Dublin children had fun breaking off pieces of ice in the fountain in St Stephen's Green.

Repairing The Damage

8. A man in Dublin shovelling heavy snow from the street and gutter.

9. Barefoot tenement children, such as these at Henrietta Place, risked frostbite during the Arctic spell.

10. Wet snow and slush would freeze solid, making conditions dangerous for motorists and pedestrians.

11. Outside Sligo, men helping to shovel free an *Irish Independent* van that became stuck in a drift.

12. A lorry with county council workers aboard barely squeezing through a narrow cut in the snow in Co. Wicklow, where drifts reached 12 to 20 feet and higher.

" Listen, Kavanagh, if this morning's official calculations said there'd be no more snow, then there IS no more snow."

13. *Dublin Opinion,* Ireland's humorous magazine, regularly used comic relief during the harsh winter. "Expert" weather forecasters were favourite targets of jokes—and sarcasm.

14. A crowd of desperate Dubliners waiting patiently in a snowstorm at a local turf depot with sacks, prams and carts.

" The old bus is pulling well . . . considering we've got a full load on."

15. *Dublin Opinion* found amusement in the serious problem of turf shortages.

16. At the age of seventeen Una Shaw worked at Resnick's clothing factory in Dominick Street. Going to work during blizzards, she would be "holding on to the railings, because the blizzard and wind would knock you off your feet!"

17. By mid-February most tenement rooms in Dublin, such as this one in the Coombe, had fireless grates and little food.

18. A Moore Street dealer, May Mooney, recalls that "we used to be *freezing*, but we had to put up with it. *Every day.* Snow and all weather . . . We'd survive."

19. Seán Whelan remembers, "These blizzards . . . the strong winds *slapped* into your face, because it was very icy and it *hurt* you … dreadful, *terrible*."

20. The *Evening Herald* caption read: "Mrs. McGovern trying to remove water from her room at 22 Lwr. Gardiner Street. The tenement house was completely flooded after the blizzard."

21. Desperate tenement-dwellers in rooms such as this in New Market Street tore out banisters, beams, floorboards and door frames for firewood.

All Eyes Were On The Fuel Front

22. A crowd awaiting their meagre ration of wet turf in Seán MacDermott Street.

23. Women heading home, happy to get their ration of wet turf. This rigorous chore was mostly a woman's burden.

24. With Dublin's death rate doubled and then trebled, hearse-drivers such as these at Fanagan's undertakers were pushed to their limits. Coffined bodies had to be stockpiled or put in "snow-pits".

25. Coopers like Robert Dunne of Smithfield had to work in cooperage yards open to the worst elements of cold, wind and snow.

" I always keep a bottle handy in case of an emergency. . . . You never know when you might get a glimmer man."

26. *Dublin Opinion* published jokes about the legendary "glimmer man" of Second World War fame when Dublin Gas Company again had to send him out on the prowl for violators in 1947.

27. Blizzards paralysed the country's transport and communication systems, creating havoc, isolation and fear.

communications systems crippled, they were comfortably ensconced in their warm chamber, waxing eloquently on matters of "cosmic" importance. In short, de Valera and his Government were enthusiastically proposing that £24,000 of taxpayers' money be spent to create something called the School of Cosmic Physics—whatever that was!—within the Dublin Institute for Advanced Studies. In truth, very few knew. Its many opponents did know, however, that it was an immense amount of money to appropriate for some "futuristic" field of vague higher intellectual enquiry. After weeks of contentious discussion, on the 13th it reached boiling point, in what the *Irish Independent* called a "fantastic atmosphere of debate." Impassioned speeches and protestations rang through the chamber, until almost everyone felt flummoxed and fatigued:

> A somewhat dazed Dáil wrestled with abstruse abstractions. Nine-tenths of them could not have formulated a reasonably comprehensive definition of what the phrase "Cosmic Physics" means.[33]

With the possible exception of a few "Einsteins" in Trinity College or UCD, no-one could honestly comprehend its deeper meaning, or value. To most newspaper readers who followed the verbal combat it was pure "cosmic nonsense." Under the extraordinary circumstances of the severe winter and its dire consequences, the public could but wonder how their Government could be so obsessed with cosmic matters rather than earthly ones just outside their doors.

ST VALENTINE'S DAY, 14 FEBRUARY

There was little to feel cheerful about on St Valentine's Day. Food and fuel were more on people's minds than Cupid. A few ounces of tea preferable to a box of chocolates. Life's basic necessities, as well as pleasures, were now in short supply: coal, turf, gas, electricity, flour, bread, sugar, tea, paraffin oil, candles, Guinness, cigarettes. And CIE was cutting back on its passenger and goods train services. The very quality of daily life was depressingly diminished. Mary Frances Keating, writing for the *Sunday Independent*, summed up the prevailing glumness:

> The general hardships . . . short supplies and shorter resources. How are mothers to feed their families and keep them in health in these cold winter days? How are we to be cheerful and happy under the intolerable circumstances of life in Ireland to-day . . . days of gloom and muddledom *in excelsis*.[34]

St Valentine's Day brought more bad news. A report on world tea production revealed that it was far below demand, thus ending all hopes of an "early cessation of tea rationing in Ireland." It was not only a lack of quantity but of quality as well. For weeks housewives had been complaining that the taste of their tea did not seem quite the same. The *Irish Independent,* in an article headed "why tea does not taste so good," confirmed women's suspicions that "the brew has acquired a taste that is not at all acceptable to the Irish palate." The reason was that tea importers had to purchase "an unduly large proportion" of Ceylon tea, which is much lighter than, and has an entirely different flavour from, Indian tea. This was a matter of no little importance to Ireland's multitude of ritualistic tea-drinkers.

With more British factories closing, it was announced that "tobacconists expect an acute shortage of cigarettes as long as the severe weather" continued. Tea for women and cigarettes for men were two of the most calming substances in their increasingly stressful lives. In the winter of 1946/47 they were needed more than ever.

Down at the Cork car factory of Henry Ford and Sons the management chose St Valentine's Day to announce that they had to lay off 150 men and put all the rest on a four-day week. This was because they had not received the consignment of car parts still on board the stranded *Irish Plane.*

―――

By late morning on St Valentine's Day, Jan Borucki had recuperated sufficiently to talk to reporters, who had patiently hung around for days to get his story. Eager for the facts, they clustered around his bed, notepads in hand. He had suffered severe frostbite, and doctors found that the gangrene in his two feet was so extensive that it might require "surgical treatment," as they put it. Though he was still weak, his memory had generally reconstructed his nightmare experience.

As the only one of the fifteen crew members to survive to tell the tale, his every word was of interest to reporters. He began by saying: "I got into the lifeboat . . . It was very cold and the snow was falling . . ." He proceeded to explain the hardships of having no oars or sail, no food or water. How the ship sank so quickly before their eyes. He clearly recalled the death of the steward the first night, how he had been given a proper burial at sea, with prayers. Beyond that point he became hazy about days and deaths. One by one he had watched them die—that's about all he knew. With frostbite numbing his bands, and his strength failing, it became increasingly difficult to roll their bodies overboard into the water. He didn't mind admitting that he was frightened of being beside corpses:

> When I awoke [on Wednesday morning] and was the only man alive in
> the boat I put the [last] bodies overboard because I was afraid to remain

in the boat with them. I then drifted until I came to the rocks where the boat grounded. There were high cliffs . . . and I climbed them. I kept going until I reached a house. I asked for a cup of tea, or anything they had. And then asked where I was. When they told me I was in Ireland I could not believe it—I thought I was in France.[35]

How he accomplished the incredible climbing feat he couldn't explain. Survival instinct, he guessed. He answered the reporters' queries as best he could, usually with few words. Yes, he had been terrified by the blizzard. Yes, he thought he might die. Yes, he was grateful to Con Hourigan for rushing him to hospital. Yes, the doctors and nurses had been exceedingly kind. Yes, he knew now that he was the only survivor.

Did he want to go to sea again? Hesitation. He didn't know yet.

He preferred that it be left to reporters and newspaper readers to interpret the meaning of his remarkable story of survival. He was not about to call it a "miracle," as some were.

———

Mr Robertson was right. Only forty-eight hours after his warning, and his prediction that more gas "thieves" would be caught, the glimmer men had discovered more than a hundred violators, and cut off their gas. Newspapers called them a "serious menace" to the welfare of law-abiding citizens. They deserved no mercy.

Some were going beyond merely using the glimmer and had devised other ways to cheat the system. One afternoon at about 3:30, Gertrude Gahan of Cooley Road, Crumlin, the mother of nine children, was caught "stealing a quantity of gas, value not less than 2/5 and not more than £1-8-9." Her husband was unemployed, and the family were suffering from cold and hunger. When the glimmer man called to her house he found that the gas supply had been disconnected from the meter and bypassed with a connection made with a bicycle tube. The tube went behind the meter and was hidden by it. An ingenious, but dangerous, contrivance. The purpose, she explained, was so that she could light the cooker and have her family sit around it to heat themselves. The glimmer man pointed out to her the high risk of her action.

Judge Hannan in Dublin District Court was not sympathetic. He sentenced Mrs Gahan to one month's imprisonment, adding that if she thought him too hard he fixed two bails of £7 10s each, and she could appeal. The story of her sentencing made all the papers, no doubt sending a chill through many housewives. Which was just fine with the Gas Company. Had this been Judge Hannan's intention?

There was far more distressing news in the papers. From both city centre and suburbs came reports that people desperate for fuel were now resorting, like the islanders, to stripping their homes of wood to burn in the grate. Ripping out anything that would burn: floorboards, doors and frames, window sills, banisters.

Seventeen-year-old Richard Gerster of Kevin Street and his neighbours had been "collecting timber at houses getting demolished," scavenging for anything that would burn. When that resource was depleted they began stripping within their own homes. One morning, to his surprise, his mother took the pictures from the walls and carefully removed the contents. With curiosity, he watched. Then he understood. "My mother burned the picture frames off our walls, to keep us warm." Not even those of the Blessed Virgin or the Pope were spared. Around the city, walls were being stripped bare.

Next came furniture. By mid-February the *Irish Independent* confirmed that in many parts of the city "people are burning furniture." First using the least valuable items, usually plain chairs. Then small tables. Breaking them into pieces for the grate, trying to make them last as long as possible. Not only in the tenement districts but in suburbs as well. Along Clonard Road in Crumlin, "people who had been without any turf for the past five days are forced to burn furniture," it was verified, to get through the freezing nights.

When the smaller furniture items were burned, larger pieces were eyed.

———

St Valentine's Day fell on a Friday, and many Dubliners set out on the town for a night of entertainment. There were some highly acclaimed new films. At the Corinthian was the rousing *Strike Up the Band,* starring the unbeatable combination of Judy Garland and Mickey Rooney. A real heart-warmer was showing at the Capitol, *Our Vines Have Tender Grapes,* featuring Margaret O'Brien. The Irish were among the biggest film fans in the world, and they followed titbits from Hollywood with great interest. On St Valentine's Day they were buzzing over the news that Barbara Stanwyck and her dashing husband, Robert Taylor, were to arrive in Dublin within the next day or two for a visit. Less happy was the news that the Irish-born actress Greer Garson, star of *Mrs Miniver,* had just announced that she would be separating from her husband, Richard New. Who, by the way, had played her son in the same film.

Night owls on St Valentine's Day thought the ESB heartless to have begun its new outside lighting ban on the traditionally romantic evening. The prohibition was on all signs and outside display lights. After-hours shop-window lighting was already prohibited to save electricity. The "customary brilliance of the city streets was noticeably toned down last night," said the

Irish Independent, "when most of the bigger signs on business houses, and cinemas were switched off." A pall fell over the normally radiant College Green and O'Connell Street areas. It "brought back the gloomy atmosphere of the Emergency to cities and towns," as if someone had pulled the plug and cast people back into the dark of the war years. Though it did create darkened nooks and crannies for Dublin's courting couples.

Though the winter's cold and darkness may not have been conducive to romance, it is verified by oral history that many men were prompted towards sexual activity by the confined conditions. This news did not make the headlines of the newspapers.

In the working-class culture of the 1940s, when "wet days" caused men on outdoor jobs to be temporarily laid off, this often meant having to spend more time at home in their tenements or other dwellings. Which, in turn, commonly led to increased sexual activity. It was simply "customary," a result of man's will and dominance in marital arrangements of the times.

By St Valentine's Day, three weeks of bitter temperatures, snow and blizzards had kept men uncommonly housebound. Because of limited money, they couldn't spend all their spare time in the pub. Confined at home for long, boring periods, their attention could turn to sex. Regardless of their wives' wishes or protestations. As Máirín Johnston put it, men simply "claimed their 'conjugal rights'!" For a few minutes of privacy (which is all many men needed) they scooted the children out into the hallway. Seán Whelan explains it:

> In this winter, the men were at the pub, and then they came home and looked for their food and their marital rights. And that was also a way to keep *warm!* I don't mean to be crude, but that's true, that's reality. It generates heat. And their marital rights meant there'd be more children.

Having more children was the last thing many tenement mothers wanted; they already had more than they could properly feed, clothe, and care for.

Noel Hughes lived in Coleraine Avenue, off North King Street, one of the city's most densely populated tenement districts. He witnessed how winter's forced confinement ballooned the local population nine months later. Church dictates and male culture gave women no choice in the matter, a moral injustice that angers him to the present day:

> It was vicious cold weather. And there was *more* children conceived in 1947—due to the bad weather! 'Cause of the sexual activity that went on. She couldn't say "no" if she wanted to, that was forbidden by the clergy. She would be *condemned* if she refused her husband! And she'd have to

tell the priest she refused her husband—and *he'd* tell her off!

Una Shaw lived in Lower Rutland Street, just a few paces from Summerhill's sprawling tenements. It was the same story there, she testifies, as harsh weather brought misery to a mother in many ways. The added stress of having to submit to a husband's sexual demands at such a difficult time was a terrible torment, she feels:

> The men hung around the house in the bad weather—and the women *suffered*! And that's what happened! In nine months' time there'd be a new birth in that house—that's the way the birth rates went up then. That's the way it was.

"Blizzard babies" some would be called in after years.

———

For the multitudes of inner-city children, life was commonly hard and unfair. Tenement ragamuffins suffered in this worst of winters. Ill-fed, ill-clad, many barefoot. Racked by epidemics of flu and chilblains and rheumatic fever. Many were victims of TB. Stuffed in dingy rooms with eight or ten or more other family members, before a fireless grate, never enough food to go round.

By St Valentine's Day, ladies of fashion were complaining that at Clery's and Brown Thomas "there were no warm winter boots to be bought," as the stylish spring footwear was already out. Meanwhile the poorest of children went completely without footwear. Every day Mary Dunne saw "children barefoot in the snow, like the paper sellers, kids at Humphreys' pub, at the Five Lamps, *barefoot!*" A commonplace sight to Una Shaw as well around Summerhill:

> The boys, they'd be barefoot—in *that* winter! And a pair of short pants and a jumper—that's all they'd have . . . with *ice* on the ground. And their little faces were pinched because they weren't well fed—and they had this winter to contend with!

In February an "epidemic of chilblains" was declared by the medical authorities. It was impossible for children to stay warm and dry, as they were bedevilled by the constant irritation. As Noel Hughes found, "*everyone* got them. I got them myself. Oh, chilblains was a devil. They were little red buggers—oh, they hurt you!" Typically they began with an annoying itch, advanced to redness, swelling, and pain, then often breaking open and turning into septic sores. Victims found them maddening.

There were different treatments and claimed cures. Every granny had her sworn home cure, every chemist his own concoction. The legendary chemist

Harry Mushatt of number 3 Francis Street did a great business during the winter months selling his own substances for a few pence, a treatment for every ailment:

> A *lot of* chilblains from the cold and frost! Their fingers or feet would swell and get red. Like frostbite. So we'd make up a rub from sweet oil and ammonia, make it thick and put a little wintergreen oil into it, to give it a bit of heat.

Specifically for chilblains, those who could afford it bought iodine, Iodex or penicillin tabloids. But Josie Sheehan and her neighbours around the Liberties relied on their time-proven remedy: "Now for chilblains, we used to use our own urine—oh, everybody believed in it!"

———

Hungry children from miserably cold tenement rooms could at least look forward to a bit of relief and comfort at school. A heated classroom and the promise of milk and bread, maybe with a swipe of jam, was something to look forward to. It sustained them from day to day. At Rutland Street School one teacher, Peggy Piggot, knew what it meant to them:

> A lot would come to school without anything in their tummies. They'd look pale and small . . . delicate. And a lot of illness—flu, colds, sore throats. And consumption.

Schools were comforting. Most teachers caring. The building warm.

Until 1947. Then the fuel ran low. School buildings could be only partially heated—or no longer heated at all. Some furnaces could be run for only a few hours. Children kept their coats on. In classrooms with a high number of children the body heat helped. Fourteen-year-old John Gallagher from the Coombe was attending Francis Street School:

> In school you'd be *really* cold. There wouldn't be enough fuel to keep the furnace on. You'd have fifty in a class, at least, so there'd be some body heat . . . but *unpleasant*, you know, with the wet clothes, that wouldn't be clean . . . and always a smell. People couldn't wash or bathe as often in this winter, and couldn't open the window.

As a consequence, infection spread easily, and children fell ill more readily with flu and other sicknesses. In some classrooms the children sat shivering and trembling all day. With minds dulled by cold and hunger, learning was greatly impaired.

When the fuel ran so low, or was completely depleted, and the cold became nearly unbearable, some principals dismissed the pupils and closed down. Others did not, and pupils were made to sit and suffer. "We didn't have to go to school some days," Josie Sheehan recounts, "or we'd be *sent* home, because they couldn't light the fires—and we were *so cold*."

During the coldest spells, some mornings when children entered the school building it was found that the inkwells had frozen overnight. When Alderman Alfie Byrne learnt that city-centre schools were freezing cold or being shut down when suburban schools were not, he was furious. Then he found out that many schools were no longer even giving children their glass of milk or bread. Of the Government he demanded to know why there was "neither fuel nor milk available" in those schools. Why were soldiers and army lorries not supplying decent turf to schools, where the little ones were left to shiver all day? The military barracks were heated! It was an outrage that the Government would place children's physical health and mental well-being at risk while, in their warm Leinster House quarters, they proposed spending £24,000 on cosmic physics.

Within days, children's mistreatment in the city's schools came to full public light in the newspapers. Parents and sympathisers wrote letters to the papers condemning the Government for shameful malfeasance. On 15 February the *Dublin Evening Mail* published several letters exposing the barbaric conditions:

> Sir,—There is a great deal of talk about starvation and fireless houses in the poorer districts of the city, but what about the shivering, poorly-clad children in schools without *any* heat whatsoever?
>
> Could it be believed that in this age of civilisation little helpless children are herded into damp barracks of schools. Thus are the seeds of T.B. and other diseases laid. Surely some form of heating could be supplied for these unfortunates.[36]

Many personalised their letters by citing the experiences of their own children's suffering in fireless schools, pointing their finger directly at the Government:

> Sir,—All last week my children came home shivering, having sat all day in an unheated classroom. It's *inhumane*! My kids will stay at home until some heating is introduced. Why risk lives with colds and flu in such conditions? I would like to know what the Government means by having the schools unheated in the present weather.[37]

Did members of the Government not know that there was a medically documented influenza *epidemic* already sweeping the city? And, many inner-city residents wondered, were *their* children attending unheated schools?

One parent, A. T. Jordan, submitted a letter to the *Dublin Evening Mail* describing how his children had to "sit in cold classrooms without any heating whatsoever . . . with teeth chattering." Ending with a pithy, provocative thought:

I'm sure the Dáil would soon adjourn in similar circumstances.[38]

————

Mid-February marked three consecutive weeks of Siberian cold. Two fierce blizzards had swept the country, causing deaths on land and at sea. Lakes, rivers and canals were freezing over. The *Evening Herald* conjectured: "Blitzed by blizzards, we've gone back to the Ice Age." The total number of hours of sunshine in Dublin during the first two weeks of the month could be counted on the fingers of two hands. A gloom hung over the land. And fear of what the second half of February might bring.

D. E. Foster, one of Dublin's most respected weather analysts, gazed long and deep into his crystal ball. He examined the anticyclonic regime entrenched from Russia across northern Europe to Greenland, took into account the Atlantic currents, charted high-pressure and low-pressure systems and the prevailing wind patterns. Then he shared his conclusion with the *Irish Independent:*

The cold air over Siberia and Northern Europe is beginning another onslaught in this direction.[39]

Chapter 5 ❧

"KING WINTER RETURNS TO BATTLE"

Snow-swept Dublin was again struck by a blizzard yesterday for the second day in succession . . . Roads in places were sheets of ice . . . On the road from Glencree to the Sally Gap there are drifts of snow from 10 to 16 feet deep.

(*Irish Independent*, 22 FEBRUARY 1947)

King Winter returned to battle with renewed vigour in Dublin last night, frost and snow combining in an onslaught which caused general paralysis.

(*Sunday Independent*, 23 FEBRUARY 1947)

Huge *mounds like marble, solid* ice—*four and five feet high! They glistened!*

(JOE KIRWAN, 80)

SUNDAY 16 FEBRUARY

Sunshine made headlines.

When it broke through the leaden skies in one of its rare, fleeting appearances shortly after noon on Sunday, the next day's *Irish Independent* heralded its return in large type: "The sun shines again."

By the third week of February, people were in the doldrums, victims not only of Arctic cold and blizzards but of sun deprivation, a medical malady though not clinically well documented at the time. The prolonged, seemingly interminable bleakness of the harsh weather was taking a toll. Sunlessness was afflicting many with not only a cheerless mood but depression. So, "sunshine was rarely more welcome than when it made its brief appearance" at midday on Sunday, wrote the *Irish Independent*, as the "glimpse of the sun took people out doors." They flocked outside to look up, absorb the warm solar rays, a natural therapy. But, alas, as if timid, its presence was brief.

The psychological and emotional effect of combined cold, snow, ice, sunless skies, confinement and fuel and food shortages was now a common topic among citizens and in the press. At first journalists had treated it lightly, using amusing stories and humorous articles to depict people's growing frustration with winter's gloom. John D. Sheridan used wit in his *Irish Independent* column. "The meteorological people regard a depression as a cause of bad weather," he wrote, "but my milkman takes a more sensible view—he regards it as an effect."[1] *Dublin Opinion,* the humorous monthly, regularly published jokes and comic sketches about people shivering in the cold, trying to burn wet turf, standing in bus queues during blizzards. Early on, humour did indeed provide some comic relief for everyone. But as the human condition worsened in late February even *Dublin Opinion* was prompted to sardonically quip:

> The weather was enough to make cheerful hearts find neuroses underneath the snow.[2]

In serious vein, the *Irish Times* speculated about the "effect of the weather on the human body (and, by extension, the human mind), a subject about which there has been surprisingly little research."[3] How was a person's "temper, equanimity . . . disturbed by the weather?" the paper asked. In the *Evening Herald* the usually humorous Uncle Argus decided to give his grim slant on the subject. He devoted his column to telling readers how the conspirators of cold and sunlessness were now working on his brain, inflicting on him what he called "mental frostbite":

> Those blanketing grey clouds, the sub-Arctic temperatures that have beset us for weeks seem to have got into the old noodle—and brought the machinery to a full stop. I am sorry for myself in a dim, pathetic way. I wonder what can have happened to the old grey matter . . . We are suffering from a new form of frostbite, and may not recover until the warm weather arrives.[4]

Ending in a lighter vein, he described how he fantasised about the day "when forecasters will talk about *heat waves!*" In the meantime he shared with readers his own treatment for winter's discomfort and depression: collecting "gaudy travel brochures, trying to warm myself with pictures of tropical scenes."

By 16 February the *Sunday Independent* regarded the prevalence of winter-induced pessimism and depression, even despair, among the population as serious enough to devote an entire editorial to it, headed "The importance of optimism":

> The citizens fighting the losing battle against the turf fire . . . insolvable

problems of commodities . . . weather forecast victims facing the "wintry outlook" day after day . . . have alarmingly increased the numerous army of pessimists. Too much of the cold and hungry world has little warmth in its heart.

In this boreal and abominable season the citizen has never had better reason for his despair. Still, the philosophy of optimism in the midst of distress must be preached.[5]

The plea for optimism over pessimism, hope over despair, was also preached from pulpits throughout the country. The need to have "faith," belief in the power of prayer to bring about better times. Doctors also warned against depression as a dangerous condition, undermining one's general health. For the elderly especially it could weaken the determination to fight off illness, even erode the human spirit and will to live.

For most people, like Una Shaw, there seemed no relief from it, no end in sight. "It just *kept on* . . . We thought it would never go!" The seeming interminability of February's dark, freezing days inspired G. M. Hawksley to write a poem simply entitled "February 1947":

Grim are the February noons, and dear!
The month drags on through bitter sunless days;
No snowdrop tips its frozen ice-green spear.
No blossom stars the prunus tree's dark sprays.
No matins and no evensong is sung
By choristers once practising for spring;
And gulls, far inland, steal the morsels flung
To little garden friends who used to sing.
The alien Arctic currents surge and flow
Across our land beneath a leaden sky.
And starveling birds drop weakly on the snow
By drift-beleaguered villages, to die.
Yet every day the hidden sun mounts higher
And waits to show us his life-giving fire.[6]

Meanwhile, "eternal optimists" who went around blithely dispensing such platitudes as "Winter can't last for ever!" and "Spring is just around the corner!" could be annoying.

With the onset of the fourth consecutive week of the Siberian cold spell, people were obsessed with warmth. "To tell the truth," wrote the *Irish Independent*, "the chiefest trouble with citizens is to keep warm." It preoccupied their thoughts night and day. People began sending in tips for keeping warm. One man wrote to the *Dublin Evening Mail* suggesting to readers that they "simply sew or pin sheets of brown paper or newspapers between the blankets—and it is surprising how comfortable one can be." Another reported that he headed daily for the National Library—the "hottest spot in this city," he found. One can only imagine how the staff of the library greeted this suggestion for public consumption.

Those who worked in heated offices, shops or factories were much envied. For the majority of people, the cinemas, theatres, pubs, restaurants, libraries and bigger shops provided the most reliable warmth. Patrons browsed and dallied in the finest heated shops as long as they could discreetly get away with it. Pubs were more packed than ever, heated further by the body mass. Explained one pub regular: "How can men manage to keep out of public houses when they are cold and tired? . . . I cannot really afford it but it is very tempting . . . the warm and lively atmosphere." Even teetotallers who never set foot in public houses were now commonly seen ensconced in a corner sipping a mineral or hot coffee.

Actually, the warmest places in the city were probably the forty to fifty forges, where the ring of the anvil was now heard up to sixteen to eighteen hours a day. Customers awaiting frost-nails for their horses, and cronies of the farrier or blacksmith, enjoyed a setting around the fire that provided heat unmatched anywhere else. If they didn't mind the smoke and the sparks.

At the opposite extreme, guests at the Shelbourne and Gresham Hotels were given heaps of blankets and hot drinks and were welcome to sit before a warm fire from morning till bedtime if they wished. And some did. Paddy Fogarty, a pageboy at the Gresham, had orders to tend to the guests' every need for warmth and see that the fire was fed continually. "It was a big open fire with turf in the residents' lounge that guests liked to huddle around," including Dwight Eisenhower, John McCormack, and the actor Victor McLaglen.

For ordinary citizens, cinemas offered the double benefit of warmth and escape, especially if the film showed scenes of tropical beaches or the clear blue skies and sunshine of the American West. It worked wonders for patrons, many of whom were willing to see any film showing outdoor scenes in glorious Technicolor, regardless of cast or plot. For a few hours it transported them from the frigid, slate-grey bleakness of Ireland to a bright world of solar heat, tropical sands, tanned figures, and leisurely life-styles. An enchanting escape, for those who could afford it.

Fortunately for Ken O'Flaherty, a young medical student at UCD in 1947, he could afford the cinema purely for its warming qualities, especially those that were now being heated by oil because of the fuel shortage. It was an interesting time to be attending the university, with the likes of Charles Haughey, Ulick O'Connor and other luminaries-to-be as fellow-students. He was also in luck, as his pre-med class was in the Science Department, then in the old Royal College of Science building in Upper Merrion Street, and had central heating during the day. Other times, however, he found himself out in the cold. Then he discovered the perfect solution to the numbing problem:

> The only warm places of refuge were picture houses and pubs. Most of us non-drinkers went to the pictures almost every week night and twice on Sundays. When we had seen all the films in the city, we moved out to the suburbs. We were seeing the same films for the second time.
>
> I kept a diary in which I recorded seeing 42 films over a six week period. I did not return to a cinema for two years.[7]

Some cinema ushers could not enjoy the warmth available to their patrons. At the city's grand cinemas the younger ushers were assigned the toughest duty: tending to the long outdoor queues for up to eight hours a day. At the Savoy in O'Connell Street, Herbie Donnelly was a neophyte on the job. "I was *constantly* outside . . . The weather was so bad that I had two pairs of gloves on me." Up and down, back and forth along the queue he'd stroll. Through sleet, snow, blizzards. Trying to generate enough circulation to combat the cold and numbness. All the while, envying the patrons as they crowded through the doors. His typical day lasted from two o'clock in the afternoon till the "last of the queue went in around nine." And he dare not make a complaint to the management. At the end of some nights he felt frostbitten.

––––––

Far to the west of the Savoy Cinema, the residents of Straide and surrounding district of Co. Mayo could not enjoy a choice of cinemas, theatre productions, or swanky restaurants. But they were quite happy to have what may have been the best entertainment in their part of the rural west, provided right at their doorstep, thanks to two blizzards. Phillip Mount and the cast of his "hurdy-gurdy" road-show were settling in for a long forced visit. As they began setting up their array of indoor attractions, the confined, bored local people found it a dazzling display of colour, sound, and movement. Everyone was delighted that the travelling troupe were stuck in their village till the weather improved.

Walking through the doors of the old church, converted now into a village social centre, with its lights, music, and gaming displays, was like entering a kaleidoscopic emporium. And, because of the crowds, it was quite warm. Hundreds of people showed up, milled about, smiled, dared to take a chance with one of the games. Tony Ruane, his siblings and their pals watched the whole pageant. There were attractions for the entire village, from kiddies to grannies. Puppet shows, roulette wheels, fortune-telling. It was a scene he remembers well:

They did a *great* business. There was always an audience . . . crowds to play pongo [like bingo] and other games. *Any* games that could be set up were used indoors. A shooting gallery with air rifles and roulette and a raffle wheel that was spun for prizes. There were actors who put on plays in their fabricated theatre—and records they played, and Phillip Mount had a piano accordion.

A Theatre Royal crowd back in the capital could not have been more pleased. Little skits and humorous or dramatic plays drew an appreciative response from the audience drawn close to the stage. Women and children mostly up front, men standing at the back.

Even when wind and blizzards felled electricity lines, the show went on, for Mount had concocted his own power system, generated by a two-stroke petrol engine that, Tony Ruane recalls, went "bang . . . bang . . . bang . . . putt . . . putt." Sometimes it would slow down and the lights would dim threateningly. Then, as the motor regained momentum, "the lights would brighten and there would be loud applause and cheering from the audience." The engine's sputtering and pausing provided as much drama as the acting on stage. Everyone inside the building seemed delighted with the goings-on, nearly enough to make them forget for a few hours the Arctic atmosphere outside. When they were departing to return home, a Siberian blast caught them as they stepped through the doorway—an instant reminder.

Mount was savvy. He knew that he had to do more than draw a good crowd for a night or two, have their curiosity satisfied, play a few games. He needed a steady income. His road-show was trapped, in need of food and fuel from day to day. He had to bring local people back again and again for as long as his troupe were marooned in Straide. This meant relying on some regular advertising. So, he devised a simple but effective public address system, which, when turned up loud, could reach almost everyone in and around the village:

> On their PA system they played records through a huge bugle-type loudspeaker mounted on a village telephone pole, to attract crowds. And the record they played most was "Let It Snow, Let It Snow, Let It Snow"— I can remember hearing that song echoing across the snowy countryside.

Before long, everyone was repeatedly singing or humming the cheery refrain. Most important to Mount, those who were not attending his show knew what they were missing.

———

Sunday's newspapers published a bit of good news. Archbishop McQuaid announced in his Lenten regulations that, owing to the extraordinary hardships of cold, hunger, and illness, he would be granting a dispensation from the rule of fasting. There would be no abstinence on Wednesdays, with the exception of Ash Wednesday. To hungry tenement-dwellers who barely got one meagre meal a day it was of little consequence. Though he showed lenience on fasting, McQuaid reaffirmed his warnings about "mixed marriages," non-Catholic schools, forbidden societies, "evil books," and certain places and circumstances of dancing. And the city's packed dancehalls were among the warmest places in Dublin, generating nearly as much heat as a forge.

———

Throughout Sunday, as people perused their newspapers and sipped their weak tea, more bodies from the ill-fated *Ary* were washed ashore along the south coast, some as far as Youghal. All were wearing life-jackets. Medical examination would show that they had died from exposure rather than drowning, consistent with Jan Borucki's testimony that he had watched his shipmates die before his eyes, one by one, before they were put into the sea. By now a total of twelve bodies had been recovered. Two days later they were buried in a mass grave, somehow hacked out of the frozen earth in the shadow of Ardmore's thousand-year-old round tower. As the coffins were lowered, the snow was again falling.

Of the fifteen crew members, only Borucki had survived. Though not in his original form: to save his life, doctors had to amputate both his legs and several fingers.

On Monday the 17th it was revealed that Dublin's fuel thieves were on the rampage, stealing gas, electricity and turf at an unprecedented rate. Dublin Gas Company reported that over the previous few days more than three hundred households had been disconnected for illicitly using the glimmer gas. Many more had received warnings. These "gas pirates," as they were now dubbed by the papers, were plundering the city's last meagre supplies. Realising the widespread nature of the problem, the Gas Company decided to treble the number of glimmer men.

Similarly, the ESB was experiencing a significant increase in the number of customers exceeding their allowed consumption. Many, apparently, were from affluent areas, with central heating and electrical appliances. Each day more scoundrels were being caught and cut off, but the problem persisted. In the third week of February the ESB made a public announcement that forthwith *all* "electricity consumers are 'on trial'," liable for severance for any "cheating." Adding that if electricity usage was not voluntarily reduced the board would be forced to impose further mandatory cuts on everyone.

Dublin's majority of law-abiding fuel-consumers were fuming. Growing increasingly intolerant of their selfish neighbours, who put the limited public supply at risk. Honest people should not be penalised for the acts of law-breakers. In a tough editorial, the *Irish Press* branded them "public enemies":

> A grave fuel crisis has hit our homes and our industries . . . Gas and electricity are cut severely and many grates are fireless. People who strive to outwit the regulations and get more than their share are the enemies of the public good.[8]

Such strong condemnation by the press prompted citizens to begin reporting violations by greedy neighbours, even relatives. It was perceived as an immoral act—exposed for the public good.

Fuel-robbers were also now pilfering the piles of coal and turf in the Phoenix Park and outside hospitals and other institutions, and wherever else it was accessible. The Gardaí were ordered to keep a watchful eye out. Garda Senan Finucane was put on special duty to be on the look-out at night for fuel thieves. He knew for certain that buckets of coal were being stolen from supplies outside hospitals, and turf sods taken from depots. Around his part of the Liberties, tenement-dwellers were poor and desperate, many with six, eight, ten or more children. With little food and sometimes no heat. When he nabbed a fella, or a mother, stealing a few lumps of coal or turf he was inclined to give them a gentle reprimand for their first violation. But he told them he had his duty to perform and could not overlook a second offence.

The situation had grown so serious by mid-February that the *Evening Herald,* affirming that thousands of families had "not seen a fire for weeks," declared that Dublin now faced a "fuel famine."[9] By coincidence, the same day the *Irish Independent* used the same fateful word in historical context:

> Let us not this year forget 1847. Let us commemorate in our rosaries the multitude who died during the Famine.[10]

To Irish people, mention of "famine" evoked powerful historical remembrances. In coming weeks, it would assume contemporary meaning.

———

CIE was already confronting its own fuel famine. On Monday, as the ESB and Dublin Gas Company launched their new crackdown on violators, officials announced that very soon the "railway passenger service on c.i.e. main lines will be brought to a standstill." And no extra provincial buses were to be put into service to compensate. Furthermore, parcel post would now be carried only three days a week, instead of the present five. This meant that about three thousand men in the passenger service saw their "employment threatened almost immediately." The suspension of passenger train services was described as a "severe blow" to the public.

Then came a worse one. "Unless coal supplies become available very soon," declared CIE officials, "the *entire* system will have to close down." A complete shut-down of the railway system would mean temporary unemployment for nearly twelve thousand men. The prospect of no railway service was unimaginable. CIE's top brass confirmed that the situation was "unparalleled in the history of Irish railways."[11]

With a drastic reduction in the goods train service, attention promptly shifted towards increasing cargo haulage on the barges along the Royal Canal and Grand Canal. However, the owners of these barges let it be known that they were already "working to capacity," carrying "almost every kind of goods," from grains to Guinness barrels. Furthermore, with the prolonged cold temperatures the canals were now freezing over at night, slowing barge traffic to a crawl as bargemen broke their way through the ice barrier. Hindered by the ice, lashed by the constant east wind, and strained by unusually heavy loads, bargemen were beleaguered.

Besides the bargemen, other outdoor workers—postmen, newspaper sellers, market dealers, dockers, draymen, drovers, tuggers, lamplighters—received much public sympathy. But behind the scenes were other workers, often inconspicuous, who typically suffered more from the brutal weather. Various craftsmen were hidden behind fences or walls, in yards, down alleys, tucked in niches of the cityscape. Forced by the nature of their craft to toil outdoors under abominable conditions without protective clothing, gloves, fires, or proper tea breaks. Confined all day to a bench or standing stoically at their small work space carrying out what many saw as "slaving" in "inhumane" conditions. These stonecutters and carvers, coopers, shipwrights, signwriters, coffin-makers and others were the "unseen sufferers" of the Arctic siege. Sufferers also of rheumatism, arthritis, chest and lung ailments, bad back and legs, flu. Captives of their outdoor crafts, they dared not miss a day's work for fear of losing their job. Never had they experienced a winter like that of 1947.

No craftsmen laboured in more primitive or painful conditions than the legendary "stonies," who cut and carved granite. Some worked at large firms, such as Harrison's of Pearse Street, others in small yards around the city. Slashed by wind and nearly frozen numb, they took up hammer and chisel to sculpt granite the colour of their faces. As one carver, Brendan Crowe, described it, "no fires allowed—you just went to the bench, picked up your ice-cold tools, and you'd be standing on ground clay . . . *dreadful* conditions!" And no gloves.

John O'Donoghue, born in 1908, was working as a headstone-carver at Mount Jerome Cemetery in Harold's Cross. Before he could begin his day's work he had to chip off the ice:

> Just the movement of your hands was the only activity you had. The tools
> were steel, the stone was cold, and with the east wind blowing you would
> *freeze inside*. You couldn't wear gloves, because in freehand work there's a
> sensitivity in your hands. How we survived it I don't know.

Many coopers had it no better, working in open yards or beneath lean-to
sheds affording no real protection from the cold, wind, or snow. Like the
stonies, they could not wear gloves, because of the precision of their craft.
Their fingers would stick to frozen metal tools and hoops. At Guinness's,
where Liam Cradden was fortunate to have an indoor office job, he watched
with sympathy through the window at coopers working outdoors in open
yards, doing the repair work on casks. For this type of labour he saw that some
devised "home-made rubber gloves" from the inner tubes of lorry tyres.
Garages would give coopers old inner tubes, and they would "just slice them
the right length and cut a little hole in it and put their thumb through." This
provided some protection for hands, though only for certain jobs.

Every morning, regardless of storms, Eddie Dunne showed up for work in
his family's cooperage in Smithfield, knowing the discomfort he faced. "The
north-easterly wind was the worst I ever experienced, the coldest I can ever
recall." Bare-handed, holding a hammer and driving hoops savaged his hands.
"My hands would be hurting, raw and open. I used mutton fat on my hands
and covered them with gloves when I'd go to bed." At day's end, coopers had
their own ritual of "repairing" their hands for the next day. David O'Donnell,
a 27-year-old cooper at Guinness's, devised his own treatment:

> Ah, in that winter your hands would crack like a horse's hoof, and quite
> deep. I often stitched it up with a piece of thread when it would be really
> open. It was like leather, you wouldn't feel a thing. Then I'd put tallow or
> goose grease on my hands, in front of the fire.

Shipwrights and coffin-makers faced similar conditions. When Joe Murphy, a
shipwright, and his mates showed up for work at their yard in Ringsend each
morning they had to begin by "sweeping the snow off to find the screw holes
you bored the day before . . . You'd no protective clothing, no fires, and your
hands would go hard." Even signwriters, when they could find no indoor jobs,
often had to work on shop fronts and fascia boards. Intricate lettering
required great sensitivity in one's fingertips, meaning no gloves. Kevin
Freeney wore mittens with the fingers cut out, but on some days "the *cold*—
you just *couldn't* work. There was as much snow in the pot as there was paint!"
And the east wind, which often reached half-gale force and higher, was a real
hazard. "On a wild, windy day the ladder could shift! Times were hard . . . but

you had to just keep working."

By comparison with craftsmen forced to work outdoors, fully exposed to winter's severe weather, Dubliners complaining about their cold, unheated shops, offices and factories had cushy jobs.

———

On the morning of Wednesday 19 February the *Irish Times* published news that readers found shocking. With everything else seemingly on the decrease, one element of life was on a startling increase: the death rate:

> The death rate in Dublin has more than doubled since the beginning of the cold weather. There has been a big increase in the number of admissions to the city's hospitals, and undertakers say they were never so busy. Some of them are not able to deal with the numbers of funerals they are asked to carry out.[12]

The sudden sharp increase was attributable to multiple factors: cold, hunger, influenza, pneumonia, other illnesses, depression. All conspiring most cruelly against the city's elderly, poor, and infirm. Dublin's worst tenements were already known as "fever nests," "human styes," "death traps," long before the Arctic winter of 1946/47 struck. Now racked by freezing temperatures, fireless grates, virulent influenza epidemic, and gnawing hunger, many were doomed.

Sixteen-year-old Seán Whelan saw the deadly consequences around his north-side district:

> Very few people escaped that flu. It was a terrible epidemic altogether. And there was no recovery from it, because you hadn't got heat, and people couldn't afford to buy fuel. Lots of people died from that flu.

As Dublin's death rate more than doubled and was in danger of trebling, many country people were faring no better. From many counties came reports that rural deaths were rising at a similar rate:

> For the elderly, those bone-chilling weeks presented a deadly nightmare. The plummeting temperatures triggered respiratory problems, heart attacks and strokes. With no access to GPS or hospitals, hundreds of elderly souls in rural Ireland succumbed.[13]

Throughout the country, undertakers, mortuary staff, coffin-makers and gravediggers were being pushed to their limits trying to cope with all the bodies now accumulating, awaiting burial. Hearse-drivers and their horses were getting little sleep. Joseph Fanagan, now eighty-three, of Fanagan's Undertakers, one of Dublin's oldest firms, dating from the 1850s, recalls that "we'd be doing up to fifteen funerals a *day*. You could keep the body in preservation in the wintertime." All undertakers were working to their capacity. Fanagan's hearse-drivers had to have their horses securely frost-nailed, meaning "they might be getting up at four in the morning—and getting home at ten at night." Meanwhile, in the undertaker's rear yard, Tommy Hoban, a coffin-maker, and several mates were now forced to make two entire coffins each per day, sometimes taking twelve hours. Cold hands and feet made the work all the more difficult. But they put the wood shavings from the elm and oak to good use. "In those winter months we used the timber cuttings for a wood fire, and we stood around the fire" to thaw out limbs periodically. At tea break he might grab a few minutes of nap by going indoors and crawling into one of the coffins.

Conducting funerals no longer necessarily meant carrying out burials. As the ground became frozen more solidly during February, the coffined bodies could no longer be promptly buried. Gravediggers at Glasnevin, Dean's Grange and Mount Jerome did their best at first to try with pickaxe and shovel to hack open graves, but it was a gruelling job, and they felt more like quarrymen. Passers-by peering through the gates at Glasnevin, seeing the gravediggers picking away at nearly impenetrable frozen ground in temperatures of 25 to 15 degrees (−4 to −9°c), with an east wind of 30 to 40 miles per hour strafing their hunched-over forms, had only pity for them.

Surely there was no worse job in the winter of 1946/47 than that of gravedigger.

By the third week of February people were dying and being coffined faster than gravediggers could keep up with them. They began piling up, being "backlogged" at undertakers and cemeteries. Relatives were simply told that their loved ones had to wait for a proper burial. A lot of elderly poor around the Liberties were dying, including John Gallagher's granny from the Coombe. "With my grandmother there was a long delay. The ground at Glasnevin was too hard. You'd just have to wait your turn—just kept in the coffin." The only positive aspect of the situation was that it justified extending wakes, where the living found warmth huddled together.

Newspapers published reports from all provinces of mounting death rates and burial backlogs. From every county the stories were much the same: "in both town and country [the] elderly succumbed to cold and exposure," to hunger and flu, at a rate two to three times higher than normal. There was no mistaking the core cause behind it all, confirmed the *Irish Times*: "harsh weather is blamed for the high mortality rate."

Mortality reports from every county verified that most deaths "occurred among aged poor people." It was the prolonged cold and hunger that took such a toll. By 18 February it was found that the practice of sacrificing food for fuel, or fuel for food, was very widespread. In newspapers, articles about hunger, now a common topic, led to documented cases of actual starvation among both Dublin tenement-dwellers and some isolated country people. Letters from compassionate readers began filling the newspaper pages. The *Irish Independent* published an entire section entitled "A plea for the old," in which the following letter from a distressed citizen was included:

> Sir,—Our Government . . . are allowing the poor of this country to starve. I know of people who have no means apart from the old age pension. Out of this they are expected to provide rent, food and fire. The amount they are getting would not even provide a fire. What is their diet? A couple of loaves a week and tea.
>
> Many of them must be dying of slow starvation. I know of one old lady and I have often gone to her house and found no fire, even in the coldest weather, and no food in the house. She is starving to death, and there are many others like her.
>
> She told me death would be a merciful release.
> —"Charity at Home."[14]

The *Evening Herald* cited a "grey depression," often a sense of despair and despondency, that was dooming many elderly people just as surely as were cold and hunger.

———

Late on Wednesday morning Dublin got a scare. "Borne on an east wind which had been blowing hard" throughout the night, snow began to fall, "growing in intensity until midday." Then it abruptly ceased. It turned out to be a rather strange, highly localised snowstorm, limited to Dublin and its suburbs. Bray saw no snow. Dún Laoghaire had only a very light fall. By afternoon, Dubliners were relieved.

That evening in London, at the Royal Meteorological Society, Wing-Commander Poulter gave a presentation on the highly abnormal cold temperatures and blizzards that had swept Britain and Ireland over the previous month. An expert on the subject, he regretted having to tell his audience that the extraordinarily harsh weather was "continuing without remission up to the time of the meeting—and showing no sign of abating."[15] He stated that it was already rivalling, if not surpassing, the famously severe winter of 1894/95. If the brutal weather persisted for much longer, he conjectured, the winter of 1946/47 might set some weather records.

His words seemed prophetic. As he was speaking, frontal systems were again gradually aligning for another collision over Ireland and Britain. Slowly, a deep depression moved east-north-east into the Bay of Biscay, ever closer to the realm of high pressure to the north and the path of the indomitable east winds from Russia.

In complete contradiction of what the elements of nature were brewing in the upper atmosphere, on Thursday the 20th the *Irish Times* told its readers what all Irish people had been hoping and praying for. Their weather experts were in agreement that winter's siege appeared to be finally nearing its end. According to their data, "conditions of freezing temperatures and heavy snowfalls over the past weeks have been highly 'unusual' . . . [but] now the glass was rising quickly." This sign, they concluded, meant that "only some unexpected change in weather conditions can bring snow again."[16]

Smyllie and his staff were eager to share the wonderful news—in large type and simple terms. "Experts say snow has gone," said the headline:

> Weather experts believe there will be no more snow. There may be frost, but heavy snowfalls are not expected.[17]

Readers were elated.

————

With the assurance of "no more snow," Dubliners went to bed on Thursday night looking forward to a storm-free weekend, with a full slate of sports events and entertainment. There was to be an important rugby match between Ireland and Scotland, and big races at Baldoyle. No worries about cancellations this weekend.

Throughout the night the low-pressure system from the south intensified as the moisture-laden oceanic clouds gathered. On Friday, "by early morning there was a 'complex system' over the British Isles which was moving slowly east-north-east."[18] Perfectly poised over Ireland to encounter "strong north-east winds reaching gale force," creating heavy snowfall and "frost to continue day and night." There was no escaping its intention.

Shortly before 7 a.m. Dubliners awoke to the now-familiar howling wind and dense, horizontal snowstorm. As this third blizzard roared across the country, the city was positioned to take its full force. As it gathered strength, by mid-morning the "blizzard snow piled up to four inches an hour." It was essentially a repeat performance of the blizzards of 2 and 8 February. As the *Evening Herald* described it in its headline, "Dublin takes another snow 'blitz' to-day."

This blizzard, however, unlike the previous ones, struck on a work day. People had to leave their homes. Indeed Friday was always the busiest weekday, when streets were most packed and shops crowded with customers. Consequently, thousands of Dubliners ventured forth into the storm in an effort to carry out their job and personal duties. Streets and footpaths quickly became snow-clogged and slippery. As usual, Corporation crews armed with shovels, sand and straw went about their futile attempt to manually dig the city out of snowdrifts several feet deep. Telephone, telegraph and electricity lines and poles were again down everywhere, and traffic paralysed. By midday the Dublin–Belfast road as far as the border was completely drifted over, and motorists were warned about trying to drive outside the capital. Within the city they were told to "exercise greater care than ever in the vicinity of schools," as many children were being sent home again soon after they arrived. Simultaneously, "robust persons were invited to assist" the young, old and infirm across streets. Many of whom should not have been out in such conditions. Postmen with their heavy 38-pound bags fought to keep their footing.

Friday's vehicular and pedestrian traffic grew more chaotic and dangerous as the "blizzard continued throughout the day with little respite." Cyclists put themselves and others at risk as they zigzagged through the streets in front of vehicles and people, skidding and slipping on icy tram tracks and cobblestones. Sometimes falling in the path of a bus or tram. Throughout the day many would be injured. Percy Hughes of Richmond Avenue was cycling to work when his bicycle suddenly slipped sideways, tossing him off, and he struck his head on a hard surface. Passers-by rushed to his assistance. A Fire Brigade ambulance was called to the scene at once, but by the time he was brought to Jervis Street Hospital he was pronounced dead.

Seventeen-year-old Joe Kirwan had a perilously close shave, which could well have been fatal. A messenger-boy, he had confronted all horrendous weather conditions since the Arctic spell set in during the last week of January with the "Big Freeze." Ill-clothed and shod, he swerved through snowy streets with an imbalanced heavy bicycle. He was typical of other youths doing much the same to help out their tenement families. He never missed a day's work. He always hurt with cold and hunger:

> My clothing . . . it was cruel. I had a bare head, never had a cap . . . money was so scarce. I had short pants, canvas runners, sometimes old socks on my hands. And a pullover. With the frost and ice you would be numb with the cold . . . and I was always hungry.

He had survived the first two blizzards without mishap. But the blizzard that struck on 21 February caught masses of people on a work day with streets jammed with vehicles acting crazily. Icy tram tracks were the worst hazard for all cyclists: "Oh, if your wheel got caught in one of those you were gone!" This day the streets were chaotic, and, blinded by the snow, he could not be as cautious as usual. With an awful suddenness the heavy bike with laden basket flipped out from beneath him:

> I fell under a tram at Kelly's Corner. Got caught in the tracks and just went under the tram, and the driver was very alert . . . He mangled the bike but I was just inches away from probably losing my legs. 'Cause the bike was mangled—and that was steel.

The next morning, Saturday, he was out on the streets again on a different bike.

———

Bus-drivers again bore an awful burden during the blizzard.

Busy Fridays were difficult under the best conditions. These were the worst conditions.

Packed as heavily as possible with passengers—actually overloaded—buses were extremely difficult to control on slippery streets. Passengers found they had their own problems. With people sitting or standing in every square foot of space, they were deprived of the normal view out windows. To exacerbate matters, the windows became coated with frost, snow, and ice, often making visibility nearly nil. "Bus windows were so frosted over or covered with snow," reported the Irish Times, "that passengers sat in buses not knowing where they were."[19] Many missed their stop; some even passed right by their own house without knowing it.

On streets with an incline, sharp corner, or curve, drivers found it difficult to properly accelerate, navigate turns, or stop safely. Commonly, when a bus got stuck in a patch of snow or on a sheet of ice a few hefty male passengers would disembark, walk to the rear, and "get behind the bus and lean their weight against it," trying to shove it forward, or backwards. Often falling themselves in the effort. By Friday afternoon, wrote one newspaper, "all around the city passengers were assisting bus-drivers in snow and icy conditions."

No-one could assist the driver. When a pedestrian, motorist, cyclist or horse cut in front of a bus—which was often—the driver automatically hit his brakes, usually causing the vehicle to slide out of control in any direction, even up onto a pavement. Maisy Flood was on buses that flew suddenly out of control. "The buses, you know, would jack-knife!" Sending pedestrians scattering and frightening passengers. Some closed their eyes and fingered their rosary beads. As the Evening Herald described it, "bus drivers everywhere performed prodigies of skill in steering their skidding vehicles over the icy stretches."[20] Inevitably, a number of accidents occurred, most not serious. The driver of a number 83 "had a narrow escape" when a turf lorry crashed into the front of it at Kenilworth Square in Harold's Cross. Luckily, the lorry driver was able to jump clear, but the windscreen and front portion of the bus, which had a full load of passengers, were smashed.

By late afternoon, with the blizzard still blowing, some bus-drivers had been on duty for eight or nine hours. CIE was short of drivers because of the flu epidemic and had to work its men to the limit. In something of an understatement, the *Irish Times* wrote: "Bus drivers had an anxious day, for in many places, particularly on corners, brakes were useless." To the drivers, "terrifying" would have been more fitting than "anxious."

At the end of their duty on Friday some drivers, physically and mentally fatigued, "reported that they were not prepared to take the risk of keeping their buses on roads which, in places, were sheets of ice."[21] CIE officials agreed, deciding that on the most treacherous routes "the buses had to be taken off" altogether. The risk to passengers, drivers, pedestrians and other motorists was simply too great. Leaving the regular bus passengers to wonder how they would now get to and from work and home.

As drivers crept back to their garages late in the day, some were visibly nervous wrecks. A few spoke to reporters. Declared one frazzled driver: "I have been driving a bus for ten years and I do not remember snow, frost, rain or any kind of weather like today's for the strain it put on me."[22] After three weeks of snow and ice, quite a few drivers sounded as if they were seriously contemplating swearing off bus-driving for good.

Pedestrians were falling and sprawling all over the city. Around the Liberties, John Gallagher saw, "many people fell and got bruises and cuts and worse. Breaks. And they'd have to be carried." Sixteen-year-old Chrissie Lyng of York Street made it to work that morning at the Ever-Ready battery factory at Portobello Bridge but fell several times along the way. By closing time the streets were worse. "The pavement was so bad 'cause ice was all over, and I had a couple of falls, and my father was coming to my work to walk me home." All along O'Connell Street, Grafton Street and Dame Street people were seen on the ground. By early Friday evening Dublin's hospitals, which were already coping with the flu epidemic and increasing illnesses, were severely strained, as reported by the *Irish Times*:

> Hospital staffs in Dublin had one of their busiest days in years on Friday, when many people received injuries from falling on the slippery streets and pavements. There was a continuous stream of patients to accident wards.[23]

At the Mater Hospital alone five people were suffering from fractured femurs and there were twenty cases of fractured ribs, while two people who fell at Westland Row had serious head injuries.

On Saturday morning Dubliners climbed out of bed expecting the worst. But the blizzard had ceased. Leaving the city, however, coated with frozen snow and ice. R. M. Smyllie, editor of the *Irish Times,* having confidently predicted "no more snow" the day before, sat unhappily eating humble pie. The morning's *Irish Independent* rubbed it in with its headline "King Frost still reigns."

Shortly before noon the "sun shone bravely and for moments even brilliantly for a blue sky this morning." Its intense glare on the snow and ice caused people to squint, to cover their eyes. It was as if the dull cityscape had been lit up by bright stage lights. There was suddenly a high definition of features, with light and shadow. Buildings, shops, streetscapes were again three-dimensional. The sun was just warm enough to nudge the temperature a degree or two above freezing. Barely enough to bring about a slight thaw on the surface of the snow and ice.

Once again, to the great dismay of spectators, weekend sports events were cancelled. In addition to GAA hurling and football matches, the Baldoyle Races were called off, as the racecourse was declared "frost-bound with a covering of snow." With sporting contests so often wiped out, some punters quipped that perhaps they should begin betting on the weather itself. To which the *Irish Press* retorted: "It would be unwise to gamble on the climate." It seemed that only billiards, chess, bridge and cards were impervious to King Winter's shenanigans.

With one exception. The cessation of snowfall on Saturday morning, with the brief appearance of the sun, convinced the organisers of the big rugby match between Ireland and Scotland to proceed with their plans. Shortly after 10 a.m. they announced that the match was on. A huge crowd was expected to see an excellent Irish team strive for the Triple Crown of international rugby. The field had been heavily covered with straw for protection. But no-one knew for certain what lay beneath. By late morning the straw was being raked off by a large crew of men.

It was a decision that would later be regretted. For beneath the straw they found the "ground slippery and treacherous ... as deep snow lay behind each goal line." Spectators got to see the contest, all right, but it was hardly top-notch rugby. Three times during the match there were heavy falls of snow, and both teams "could be excused for resorting to safety-first tactics." Players could not be as competitive and aggressive as usual. Admitted one sports reporter, "It was, in fact, a dull game to watch, for a greasy ball became increasingly hard to handle." Nonetheless, supporters could leave with the satisfaction that Ireland had defeated Scotland by one try (three points) to nil.

Most Dubliners muddled through the day, confused by the sun's appearance early, then snowfall, slight thaw, temperature fluctuations, and unrelenting east wind. Wondering if the storm was really exhausted.

At about 6 p.m. snow began falling steadily. The temperature was again below freezing, and slipping. Nonetheless, throngs of Dubliners, hoping that the worst was over, headed out on Saturday evening to cinemas, theatres, restaurants, dancehalls, and parties. Determined to retrieve something enjoyable of the weekend. Not realising that the slight thaw during the daytime had perfectly prepared the surface for ice glazing. By about 7:30 the cityscape was getting a "glassy" appearance as the night freeze began. The temperature dropped from 26 degrees ($-3°$c) to 24, to 21, downwards towards 18 ($-8°$c). As the *Irish Independent* described it, the process of continual snowfall, freezing, thawing and refreezing was coating the face of Dublin with a layer of ice inches thick:

> Changing within twenty-four hours from a great freeze-up to warm, and back again, Ireland alternately froze and thawed. The sunshine thawed the hard surface of snow, hours of snow then followed, and then came the worst conditions of the month . . . roads and streets highly-glazed and extremely slippery surfaces on which buses, cars and cycles become difficult to control.[24]

By nine o'clock "conditions were worsened by further heavy snowfall," wrote the *Evening Herald,* "as the new layer was quickly frozen into crystal hardness over the icy coating already covering the streets."[25] The crystallisation of snow, slush and fresh snow was creating layers of compacted ice, interbedded as perfectly as layers of a Jacob's fancy cake. Between 9:30 and 11:30, when Dublin was packed with night-goers, "the ground surface was turned into a veritable skating rink."[26] Driven by winds of 40 to 50 miles per hour, snow crystals blowing horizontally stung people's faces. The *Irish Press* called it an "ice blizzard."

There ensued what one newspaper described as the "night of mishaps." Ambulance bells rang incessantly around the city as hospital wards, lobbies and corridors began filling with accident victims. The "skating rink" had formed so quickly that night-goers found themselves caught out on streets and paths so highly glazed that they had great difficulty walking, or even standing erect. When patrons emerged from cinemas, theatres, dancehalls, they were surprised to encounter a treacherous glaciated world. The Gresham Hotel had its usual Saturday night dancing from eight till midnight, with its resident orchestra and its singer Frankie Blowers. When the dance crowd disgorged into O'Connell Street at the stroke of midnight they were stunned. All night long, people were grasping for anything—or anybody—to stabilise themselves and keep from falling. A feeling of helplessness.

While newspapers likened the city's surface to a skating rink, it was actually far worse: at least a rink's ice is smooth. Dublin's face was carved into frozen ruts, ridges, craters and human and tyre prints nearly impossible to stand on. Young Tony Behan had to walk all the way home from the city centre to Ringsend. "Walking home was a nightmare! The ice had frozen on the ground and formed egg shapes, which made it so difficult to walk that I got pains in my legs."

Trying to walk and remain upright in a million frozen footprints in the dark of night, perhaps after a few drinks, was nearly impossible for many. People simply wanted to make their way home safely. Creeping, edging a few feet, or inches, at a time. The usual Saturday night late rush for buses was brought to a crawl. Many knew they would never make it. All around central Dublin men and women headed home by trying to hold on to walls and clinging to the city's ubiquitous iron railings along their way. "You were holding onto the railings, trying to get along," explains Una Shaw. But they too were coated with ice. Along some streets a string of teetering figures stretched the entire distance, catching onto railings, looking like a line of skiers holding onto a rope lift pulling them up a slope.

Had it not been so serious it would have been hilarious. O'Connell Street was quite a sight. People slipped, fell, sprawled, simply plonked down on their posterior. Toppled forwards and backwards. Women's shoes were a curse. Chivalrous men sought to assist women, sometimes at the expense of their own dignity. At times it looked like a Charlie Chaplin or Buster Keaton film, as people clung and swung on lampposts, or held on for dear life to a wall or building. Even crawled a few feet seeking better footing. When falling, people's expressions encompassed startled, embarrassed, fearful, pained. Some were harmlessly ludicrous, causing pals to laugh uproariously. Eighteen-year-old Eddie McGrane found the entire scene sheer "mayhem."

The staff of Dublin's hospitals found no humour in the night of mishaps, many of them serious. Already straining to cope with mounting cases of flu, pneumonia, other weather-related illnesses, they were short on space and stamina. Then unexpectedly came the flow of accidents on Friday. By Friday night they had stated that they had reached their capacity, could not possibly take in any more injured patients.

On Saturday night they *had* to.

From early evening the steady stream of accidents began. Many too serious to possibly turn away. They were placed on trolleys or beds and put in lobbies or hallways. Most were cases of a broken wrist, hand, arm, elbow, leg, ankle, shoulder, ribs. Broken backs and skulls. Concussions. "Nearly a hundred patients were treated for fractured limbs" in city centre hospitals by mid-evening. No count was kept of the hundreds more with sprains and bruises.

It was chaotic, reported the *Irish Independent*:

> The biggest crop of accidents due to snow and frost that the city has
> experienced in many years. In some cases the hospitals presented typical
> "behind the line" scenes as dozens of victims awaited attention.[27]

The Mater and Jervis Street were forced to initiate a type of military triage
system, treating the most critically injured patients first. Veteran members of
the hospital staff could compare it only to the havoc of 31 May 1941, when the
North Strand area was bombed by the German air force. At that time some
forty-five people had been killed and at least a hundred seriously injured.
While this was not a "panic" situation of that magnitude, the hospitals
reported their staff working under exceedingly high pressure over a period of
forty-eight hours.

Unfortunately, the Adelaide Hospital in Peter Street had been forced to
close a forty-bed block only days before because of inability to keep it heated.
In many hospitals, such as St Kevin's in James's Street, nurses who had already
been working longer shifts than usual were fatigued and sleep-deprived
before the third blizzard hit. Now they were being called back for emergency
duty. Even when they got a break to go home for sleep they found they "must
freeze before a fireplace grate because the sods of damp turf reduce
themselves to ashes."

Throughout Saturday night havoc reigned in the city's streets. Drivers of
cars, buses and trams found they had no grip, no traction for starting and
stopping. As the *Evening Herald* portrayed the wild scene, "motorists found
their cars executing all sorts of weird tricks," sliding sideways, spinning
completely around, jumping kerbs, smashing into shop windows, scattering
pedestrians. It could well have been an old Keystone Kops film. One reporter
wrote that "a Dublin motorist of 30 years' experience described the conditions
in O'Connell Street about 9.30 p.m. as the worst he had *ever* seen."[28]

Bus-drivers concurred. By all accounts, the most treacherous road
conditions of their entire career. In truth, no buses should have been out on
the roads. But, like people, they also got caught out when the city began to
crystallise throughout the evening. Then it was too late. With brakes and
steering gear largely useless, they couldn't control their behemoths on glazed
inclines, corners, and curves. Their vehicles simply glided smoothly out of
control. Whatever was in their path, they struck. When a bus was stalled or
had an accident on the roadway, it backed up all the traffic behind. A blockage
that closed down the thoroughfare and stranded drivers and passengers
behind them. As the city's arteries became plugged up, the flow of transport
slowed or ceased, and frustration grew.

At 10:15 p.m. there occurred the "extraordinary sight of about 60 buses, outward and inward," held up between Nelson's Pillar and the traffic lights at Dorset Street corner.[29]

By the end of their duty on Saturday night a number of drivers admitted to supervisors, and to reporters, their fear of the dangerous, stressful conditions. They were clearly suffering from jangled nerves, mental-emotional strain. Resulting in insomnia, a nervous condition, and general jitteriness. They dreaded facing the icy streets. One driver candidly shared his feelings:

> I've never experienced anything like it. The *strain* of constant concentration while driving crowded buses over the past weeks is beginning to tell on me. Brakes are useless on a slippery surface. All you can do when a bus begins to swing about is to shove it into low gear—and pray.[30]

An expression representing the feelings of his many fellow-busmen.

———

Following the most treacherous ice blizzard in anyone's memory, Sunday morning dawned relatively calm and quiet. Revealing the astonishing beauty of Dublin's cityscape, looking like an ice palace. Lamplighters first saw it on their early morning rounds to put out their lamps. Tom Flanagan had worked as a lamplighter in the Phoenix Park since 1924, making his rounds with pole and carbide torch, but never had its scenery been so breathtaking. Like sparkling diamond earrings, the "icicles were hanging off the lamps, and I'd have to knock them off," one by one. St Stephen's Green was bejewelled in icy splendour, awing those who saw it in early morning. Joe Kirwan never saw Dublin so exquisitely adorned, before or since. Everything was iced and shining: streets, trees, railings, balconies, lampposts, Georgian fanlights. Great heaps of snow had been transformed into glittering solid silver-white ice capsules:

> There were *huge* mounds of what had been snow but what now was like marble. *Solid ice.* Four and five feet high. Now in this country that was unheard of! Like ebony, they shined. They *glistened.* This ice shined . . . *so cold* that there was a shine.

Dublin *gleamed.* A sight never seen since, those who witnessed it testify.

Such splendour was also dangerous. Early Sunday morning mass-goers faced the decision whether or not to risk life and limb by setting foot outside their door. Many wisely remained at home. Those who managed to get their hands on a newspaper read that the blizzard had also hammered parts of Britain and the Continent. Ice was further locking up British coal ports, mines, and railways. Dense ice-floes in the North Sea were proving a serious menace to shipping. As the floes drifted they carried away buoys marking shipwrecks and safe channels between war-mined areas.

Apart from the big news of the ice blizzard, other items were typically mixed. On top of all the existing shortages, rations and bans came the announcement that the ration of butter was now to be reduced to only two ounces per person weekly, which "came as a bombshell to people." City-dwellers grumbled, asking why there should be such a shortage in Ireland. Farm folk, like Ora Kilroe, knew well enough and had no sympathy with their complaining:

> They would not be so surprised at the cut in the butter ration if they could see our cows going gaunt and dry-coated on their meagre rations, tied up in stalls day after day. And women shoppers in the towns, who know nothing about the production of butter, might grumble a little less if they understood the farmer's difficulties.[31]

Any light or amusing news was welcome these days. Some Sunday readers enjoyed the photograph of a polar bear in Dublin Zoo with the caption "Quite at home in his icy pool." On another page they were puzzled by a news announcement from the United States about something else with a "polar" name. A "Polaroid." As they read further they found it to be a new "wonder camera," capable of producing photographs in sixty seconds. Right in one's hands! As if there were a tiny photo lab within the hand-held camera. Photography enthusiasts were eager to see its appearance in Dublin soon.

The *Irish Times* devoted its Sunday editorial to a "Tribute to the bus drivers," the beleaguered men behind the wheel:

> At the best of times the bus driver's job is trying and nerve-racking. His mind and eye must always be alert and quick. Every day the safety of hundreds of citizens is entrusted to his keeping. But we doubt if the bus drivers of this country, and particularly of Dublin, have ever had a more difficult time than they have experienced of late.
>
> They have done their job magnificently and it is proper to place on record the admiration of the public for their patience, skill and endurance.[32]

And the *Ballina Herald* added: "The busmen are not one whit less heroic than those who go down in ships to bring us our food." A chorus of "Amen!" could be heard from bus passengers throughout the country.

So also were the country's roundsmen being widely lauded by the public and press for their gallant efforts: the breadmen, milkmen, postmen, newspaper deliverers, messenger-boys. In cities and countryside they were exhibiting an unfailing sense of duty to those whom they served, under the most difficult, often dangerous, conditions. Milkmen who had abandoned their stuck vans and carried heavy cans on their backs for miles. Breadmen doing the same with loaves to reach families and villages they knew to be desperately hungry. Postmen and newspaper deliverers who kept isolated people in touch with the outside world. Apart from thanking them in person, citizens were now writing to newspapers to express publicly their appreciation. One newspaper published a special "Tribute to the roundsmen," in which Leila Cadiz of Ranelagh sent her letter of thanks:

> Sir,—I would like to express my gratitude to the milk servers, bread servers, etc., for the fine way they kept up supplies, working through the ice and snow and bitter cold. All these men deserve the highest praise ... and I don't forget the dumb beasts who gallantly helped. God bless them all.[33]

Out in the countryside the landscape was coated in crystallised snow and ice. Everything glistened. Everything was frozen still. "The heavy snows have frozen hard and picks are now necessary for roadways," confirmed the *Irish Times*. "Even if a real thaw were to set in, it would take weeks to melt the hardened snow-ice."[34] The road from Enniskerry to Glencree was now declared "snowbound with frozen snow, making it well nigh impassable." There weren't enough pickaxes in all Ireland to hack the petrified landscape free of its frozen face. Nonetheless, an effort had to be made.

On Sunday morning after mass the sound of shovels and pickaxes on ice could be heard from Cos. Donegal, Mayo, Sligo and Galway, across the midlands, through Cos. Dublin and Wicklow and down to Wexford and Waterford. County council crews along with gangs of local volunteers chipped away at interbedded layers of frozen snow and ice that looked like sedimentary rock formations—but felt more like solid granite. Like quarry men, or "stonies," they hacked away and sliced at the ice, wearing no gloves or goggles to protect their eyes from flying shards of sharp ice that could injure a man's face and eyes. Those trying to break through the ice with shovels heard the "twang" and felt the reverberations ripple through their arms and shoulders. After a few hours with pick or shovel a man's brain could feel rattled. It was no work for weak men.

Where the frozen snow and ice was granite-solid and several feet thick, sticks of dynamite would have been a better solution. An idea not that far-fetched, as near one Czech town on the Austrian border, planes were now being used to break up dense ice barriers on the Danube by dropping bombs on them. Unfortunately, in the battle against King Winter the Irish were armed only with hand weapons.

With the heavy snowfall and gale-force winds of the third blizzard the Irish landscape was further transformed, sculpted into new, unfamiliar forms. Rivers, streams, lakes and watery boglands were solidly frozen and snow-covered. Even sections of the sea looked strange. "The temperatures remained below freezing day and night," testifies Keith Collie. "Rivers and canals were frozen and even the sea turned to slush along the east coast."[35] From the hilly districts around Blessington came reports of snowdrifts "measured at fourteen feet," more than twice the height of the tallest garda. On the road from Glencree to the Sally Gap drifts of from ten to sixteen feet deep were common. There were other reliable accounts of drifts reaching twenty feet.

No-one could be sure what was buried beneath them.

In the aftermath of the storm, Wicklow County Council was in crisis mode, describing areas around Roundwood and Glencree as "worse than ever . . . many people in the mountains cut off" completely from the outside world. Unreachable. Around the country, county councils expressed frustration on finding that the most recent blizzard had nullified much of their previous shovelling work. In the worst-hit counties it was being said that many roads "would not be open for traffic for some months."[36]

The *Irish Press* published lengthy articles about the "ice blizzards, frozen rivers, impassable roads," animals dying, and people running short of food and fuel in the Dublin Mountains. Some city-dwellers may have wondered if it could be so dire. The newspaper despatched a reporter to travel as far as he could get into the foothills to see just how desperate the conditions were:

> Of the hundreds of houses we passed, only one chimney showed a wisp of smoke . . . and we saw children peering through the windows of fireless cottages. We knocked at a cottage to ask the way and looking inside saw a fireless grate. The housewife said their small stock of fuel was completely exhausted and her husband had gone out to look for logs or turf. An almost deserted appearance over the countryside . . . cattle struggling through chest-deep drifts to get at small tufts of grass in the hedges.[37]

He was told by people that they had not had any bus service for over a fortnight. Nor supplies from Dublin. How much longer they could hold out they couldn't say.

———

Animals were an urgent concern. They were trapped, buried, dying by the countless thousands. It was winter's "slaughter," some were saying. "Losses of live-stock in the country, especially in the mountain districts, are heavy," confirmed the *Irish Times*. "These animals become buried in the snow and were dead when found by their owners."[38] In the Wicklow Mountains and in Connemara they were perishing in appalling numbers. In Co. Wicklow it was heard that "some residents believe there will be no sheep left alive."

When the severe winter weather first set in, some farmers made every effort to take in and protect their animals. Provided they had ample barn space and fodder, as had the fortunate Ruane family of Straide, Co. Mayo. Most farmers, however, were not so prepared. Furthermore, back in late January, when winter's blast was first felt, farmers did not expect it to last— and could not have imagined the blizzards to follow. So, many left their animals to the fields, hills, and mountainsides. But as the snowdrifts deepened and ice crystallisation formed, it became more risky to go in search of stranded or buried sheep and cattle. With each day the odds of saving them diminished. It was a difficult decision facing farmers:

> Sheep farmers on the highlands have been out of touch with their flocks since the beginning of the month. It may be weeks before a count can be made. Sheep have been known to live under snowdrifts for a fortnight or longer . . . but if not near a place where they can be fed if rescued, there might be little point in searching for them.[39]

This was their awful dilemma. For the farmer and all his family there was anguish in having to abandon their animals while still alive. Yet even when found alive they often could not be saved for lack of food and water. One farmer in Co. Wicklow told of risking his own welfare during the blizzard of 21/22 February to find and assist his flock of sheep, "only to lose them through lack of fodder" soon after.

Animals would sometimes be found standing *in situ*, frozen statue-like, as if preserved by a taxidermist.

Live animals, especially sheep, when stranded, starving, growing weaker, could be eyed by hungry predators. Famished foxes waited impatiently at a distance, creeping ever closer, watching and fidgeting until the moment was right to tear at them. Others didn't wait. There were accounts of events when "flocks of starving birds swooped down on snow-marooned sheep . . . and devoured them."[40] While still alive. The *Irish Times* verified cases where "grey crows have picked out the eyes of helpless animals caught in the snow."[41] Sheep were found with empty eye sockets. Hideous scenes of nature, animals driven mad by hunger.

Cattle were suffering and dying as well, in great numbers. By the third week of February even stabled, protected cattle were in danger of starvation as a farmer's fodder ran out. Snowbound roads prevented bringing more in. Even goats, which were "regarded as domestic animals only during the seasons when they give milk," were now found "at or near the starvation point."

Whenever possible, farmers tried to get their sheep and cattle to market for sale while there was still some flesh on them. Those closest to Dublin had the best chance. Dublin drovers, such as Christy "Diller" Delaney, then in his twenties, worked for farmers outside the city, driving their herds into the market during the most wretched weather. Drovers were a tough bunch, but this winter the weather "hurt." Outfitted in "very little clothing to cover ourself . . . me leggins, hob-nailed boots, a cap and hankie around me neck," he and his father and a few other fellas had to be out in the farmers' fields at 1 a.m. to begin the drive citywards through sleet, snow, and a ripping east wind. With ash stick and trained dogs, "we'd have maybe hundreds of cattle and sheep . . . in bitter cold." Upon completion of their work, soaking wet, frozen numb, they collected their paltry wages and headed directly to the pubs at the Dublin Markets, which at that time opened at 6 a.m. After a few hot coffees laced with whiskey and treacle the drovers said they almost "felt human again." They talked of little but when the atrocious weather would end.

The longer the winter lasted, the poorer the condition of the animals. By the latter part of February, Dubliners got a grim first-hand look at their emaciated bodies in the market pens in Prussia Street. When the railway cut back on the service of conveying animals, farmers had to try to get them to market by lorry or by driving them long distances. Snowbound roads often prevented this. And many animals were no longer strong enough to be driven any distance. Penned-up cattle and sheep were viewed by prospective buyers, who shook their heads when seeing their condition.

In the third week of February there were more than a thousand fewer cattle on offer at the market than the week before. Of the 3,840 sheep on offer, "with the exception of one or two pens, they were only 'skin and bone'."42 Scrawny, ribs showing, dull eyes, barely able to stand, some of them. It was obvious that farmers had not been able to feed them and were trying to get rid of them in any way possible. An altogether pitiful sight for animal men.

———

Wild creatures suffered as well from cold and starvation. Sometimes driven by hunger to unnatural behaviour. Famished foxes and badgers daringly raided the coops and hen-houses of farmers, who had already lost great numbers of hens from the cold. Around Kilroes' farm, "at night I heard foxes crying around the house, and a wild, eerie sound it was."43

Some deer were actually tamed by King Winter. It was reported that deer in Powerscourt Demesne "lost their timidness through hunger and now allow themselves to be hand-fed." Throughout the Wicklow Mountains many hundreds of deer descended to the lowlands in search of food, daring to enter the realm of Man for survival. As "hunger made them lose their natural timidity . . . they wandered in the neighbourhood of cottages" in search of food.[44] Conversely, the hunting of weakened deer provided food for some farm families who still had the means of cooking the meat. At Kilmacanogue it was reported that "a fine male specimen of 195 lb. was shot."

Other deer were freed by nature. In 1860 Lord Powerscourt had imported from Japan some sika deer, which he prized. They were safely protected in an enclosure with a fifteen-foot fence. Here they thrived, and multiplied. With the third blizzard of 1947 the snowdrifts piled up and reached fifteen feet and higher, allowing the deer to blithely walk out to freedom. Over the years they interbred naturally with the local red deer, creating a multitude of hybrid deer. Leaving a very visible legacy of the "winter of 1947" throughout the Wicklow countryside.

The plight of wild birds was particularly sad, as they struggled and died by the score. Many species were not equipped by nature to survive Arctic conditions. As land and trees were coated with snow and ice they couldn't find food. When rivers and lakes froze they couldn't find water. Throughout the countryside it became a common sight: birds weak and flapping on the ground, falling from trees, lying still with eyes open. In desperation, blackbirds, thrushes, chaffinches and others were driven from country fields into city gardens in search of food. Few people could spare crusts of bread to help them.

Country folk had great affinity for the bird life around them, and it was painful to have to watch them suffer and die. In Jim Maloney's part of Co. Galway the loss of birds was conspicuous everywhere. "A lot of birds died of hunger. All the wild ducks and mallards and swans would be going around flying from one place to another to find food . . . and get running water." It was distressing to see them perishing in such an awful way:

> In my little area the little rivers froze over and the mallard and the lapwing all congregated, looking for a bit of sustenance. Oh, the birds were *really suffering!* And shooting them was easy then, but there wasn't much flesh on them. And the pheasants didn't survive.

Bird-lovers could do little but witness their sorry sight. Some threw grain out, but it was too valuable to waste. One housewife told how tragic it was to see birds dying in such a way:

> Flocks of starlings were so frantic with hunger that they'd come into the kitchen. And the wild, lonely curlews were dying on the boglands. I tried

to catch one, but he fluttered off into the bushes, using his long bill as a prop. No-one will ever be able to count the loss of bird life this winter.[45]

Many weak and disabled birds were quickly put out of their misery by foxes and other animals only trying to survive themselves.

As word increasingly reached Dublin of the plight of suffering animals, alarmed citizens expressed interest in helping them. But how? In some circles there was the suggestion of "organising hikers and other vigorous young people from the city" to assist farmers in trying to save their imperilled stock. To the urban mind it seemed logical; to farmers it was well-meaning poppycock. A bunch of Dublin "do-gooder hikers" acting as animal rescuers, tramping across unknown terrain with chest-deep snowdrifts and hidden frozen rivers and ponds, armed with their knapsacks and high ideals, was a worrisome image to farmers. They politely rejected the offer, "on account of the danger that some of the searchers themselves might become lost." Or worse.

————

At midday on Sunday 23 February the sun in Dublin peeked through parting clouds. From its overnight minimum of 13 degrees (−11°c) the temperature rose into the upper 20s. The solar rays made it feel warmer. On some of Dublin's lakes, ponds and canals, children and even adults were seen skating or playing on the ice—though newspapers had continually warned about the risk of the ice breaking. In years past there had been some tragic drownings because of carelessness.

By early afternoon some better-off citizens with cars were taking advantage of the sunshine and snowy slopes. At about two o'clock "a stream of motorists drove along the Enniskerry road carrying toboggans on the roofs and luggage grids . . . Skis stuck out from sunshine roofs and windows."[46] All in festive mood under the rare Sunday sun. Many were from Ballsbridge, Blackrock, Howth and other privileged districts. They brought wine and food, "as camp fires were even lit and sausages cooked." Before long it took on the appearance of what the *Evening Herald* called a "Swiss holiday resort."

During Sunday afternoon there existed a paradoxical human situation. Several miles behind the "Swiss resort" crowd, back in Dublin, were thousands of impoverished tenement families now in their fifth week of cold and hunger. A truly Dickensian world. At the same time, miles ahead of the tobogganists and skiers, in the countryside and mountains of Cos. Dublin and Wicklow, were farm families and villagers snowbound and isolated from the outside world, also facing hunger and fireless grates. Starving animals. Fear of what the next day might bring. High up in Glencree some forty-six German and Polish orphans and Sisters of Charity now marooned and short of food and fuel. All facing an uncertain future.

Between the suffering tenement-dwellers and distressed country people were the merry "Swiss resort" partiers.

In the last week of February, if there was anything that Irish people throughout the country shared it was the question foremost on everyone's mind. Mary Dunne heard her mother and all her neighbours along North William Street asking it every day:

> It was the *freezing, freezing* cold—and the *snow*! There was no *let-up*! The mothers all grumbled . . . Ah, yes, 'Is it *ever* going to stop?'"

Chapter 6 ∾

| NO WARMTH IN WORDS

The country's position has never been so grave.
(SEÁN LEMASS, 24 FEBRUARY 1947)

The prongs of hunger and cold have penetrated the homes ... The pinched, drawn look on their faces spoke of hunger and hardship.
(*Dublin Evening Mail*, 25 FEBRUARY 1947)

The Government cannot be blamed for the abnormal weather, or for the collapse of the British coal industry. What the Government must be held responsible for is the utter inactivity shown during the past month.
(*Irish Independent*, 25 FEBRUARY 1947)

The meteorologists ought to be thankful that they are living in a very tolerant country. In some places they would be put to death as enemies of the people.
(*Dublin Evening Mail*, 21 FEBRUARY 1947)

MONDAY 24 FEBRUARY

It was the twenty-ninth consecutive day of the Arctic nightmare. People's patience was nearly exhausted, nerves on edge. *"Fed up!"* was the going phrase: fed up with the wicked weather, inert Government, bungling forecasters, the food and fuel shortages, wet turf, profiteers—the whole lot.

Volcanic talk was a release, a safety valve. Talk and criticism and blaming and cursing. Talk in pubs, homes, shops, offices, factories, outside churches. Possibly in the confession box. On buses and trams. At weddings, christenings, wakes.

Citizens faulted politicians. Politicians criticised one another. Everyone lambasted the weather "experts." Bus and tram drivers cursed zigzagging cyclists, drivers of horse-drawn carts and pedestrians who cut in front of them. Gravediggers cursed the frozen earth. Postmen, milkmen, breadmen, papermen railed against icy streets and snowdrifts. The elderly muttered about confinement and missing mass. Children whined about being kept indoors. Pubmen talked profanely of sports cancellations, the shortage of cigarettes and Guinness.

Ladies in Bewley's lamented the rationing of tea, bread, sugar, and butter. And limitations on their social life.

––––––

Monday brought more bad news. It was announced that seventeen more foundries—in Dublin, Cork, Waterford, Wexford, and Athy—employing more than a thousand workers, would be forced to close within a fortnight because of a lack of coal. Smithfield Engineering Works in West Arran Street, which had twenty-one employees, "will be closing to-day for the last time," the bosses said. The closure of these factories was a serious blow to the entire country, as they produced a wide range of essential products, including ploughs, harrows, other agricultural equipment, galvanised tanks, gutters, gas pipes, kitchen ranges, man-hole covers, cinema seats, and metal bases for school desks, among other things.

Word was leaking out of Jacob's biscuit factory that their fuel was now precariously low and being monitored from day to day. May Hanaphy and her pals working in the special cakes department were seriously worried about losing their jobs. So were all the other 1,300 or so employees, many of whom lived in the city's tenements and depended on their weekly wage for rent, food, fuel. Survival. Every morning now they would punch the time-clock, walk to their work station, then hope and pray the managers would not announce bad news that day.

News from CIE grew worse by the day. On Monday it was revealed that it was now literally scraping the bottom of the barrel. Down to its last stocks of coal at the depots, which was "of the lowest grade." Much of it had become "mixed with dirt and earth from the bottom of the dumps." Ordinarily it would have been unthinkable that CIE would have used such inferior fuel. Statistics defined its problem. Coal consumption per locomotive-mile had now risen to a figure well beyond even the maximum of the most severe period of the war years, at 103 pounds, compared with 42 in 1939. Every evening railwaymen like Paddy Whelan, an engine-driver, gathered at the Royal Oak pub near Kingsbridge Station (now Heuston Station) to commiserate about their jobs being lost and the uncertain future. He thought he saw the writing on the wall, the same as during the war years, when, "oh, we had no coal, we ran on turf and logs . . . shovelling it in, 'cause you had to put a hell of a lot of it in to fire it!" After the war he thought he'd never see such days again. Now it looked like they might be just ahead.

From around the country came more disturbing reports of dramatically rising mortality rates. Limerick verified that between 1 and 21 February seventy-one bodies had been interred in Mount St Lawrence. Half these deaths had occurred during the previous week alone, when thirty-five funerals took place. During the entire twenty-eight days of February 1946 there had been only sixty-three. Word arrived from Clare County Home and Clare Mental Hospital, where "the aged and infirm are undergoing a trying ordeal as a result of the intense cold," and the number of deaths totalled nineteen during the previous fortnight, compared with five for the corresponding period the previous year. Nearly a fourfold increase. In Cork, Galway, Sligo, Wexford and elsewhere the story was much the same.

One more death was added on the 24th when it was reported that the body of Joseph Ennis, aged fifty-nine, a British army pensioner, was found embedded in deep snow near his house outside Rathdrum, Co. Wicklow. The coroner's inquest would determine that he had died "from heart failure due to exposure" when caught out in the blizzard.

Daily news had become so grim that it was hard to find anything good or light to read—other than the reliable cartoon characters Mutt and Jeff.

———

It had now reached the point where it was declared nearly "impossible to get dry turf." Ireland was snowbound, waterlogged, ice-encased. Turf could neither be cut nor transported. What had been stocked was nearly gone. At the Phoenix Park the remaining small dumps were in "appallingly bad condition," and the *Evening Herald* predicted that the end of the turf was close at hand:

> Thousands of homes have been without fires for weeks . . . with the fuel situation steadily worsening and the bleak prospect of what little turf is still left in the capital being used up in a short time.[1]

As the last of the turf dwindled, people grew more desperate to get their hands on even a few soggy sods. Alfie Byrne testified that in Seán MacDermott Street he had personally witnessed a woman standing in a turf queue at 2 a.m. Even guesthouses were now giving notices to boarders that they would have to close down, no longer able to provide heat or cooking.

In frustration, Oscar Love of Blackrock decided to write in to the *Irish Times* to document the incredibly wet condition of turf. "I weighed a nice water-laden sod of turf and it tipped the balance at 3 lbs. 6 oz.," he wrote. Two weeks later, after somehow managing to dry it out, "I weighed the same sod of turf—it weighs 1 lb. 10 oz." Summing up his scientific experiment, he posed the question: "I wish to learn who obtains the money paid for the 1 lb. 8 oz. of water."[2]

With turf fast vanishing, Dublin became a city of scavengers. Swarms of people, children and adults alike, scrounged around in search of anything that would light and throw off a warming flame for a few minutes: bits of newspaper, cardboard, books, old shoes, disused canes and artificial limbs, twigs, bark, children's toys. A branch was a real find, either on the ground or torn off. In one suburban house a reporter learnt that the "Sunday joint was cooked at the expense of a 25-foot wireless aerial pole," which provided fire throughout the day. People combed demolition sites and dug through dumps. Under the circumstances, some people had to put their dignity aside. "You had to have a fire," explains Joe Kirwan, "and so people burned everything!"

In North Clarence Street, Agnes Daly's Ma sent her young sons out to the railway yards "to collect cinders in a bag and bring it home for fuel." What didn't fit into the bag could be stuffed into trouser pockets. There was plenty of competition as inner-city children swarmed like cockroaches across dump sites, picking up the smallest items that might ignite.

Wooden setts embedded in the city's streets, originally implanted to dull the sound of the iron-clad wheels of carriages and carts, became real treasures. People were now mad to get their hands on them, because, as Una Shaw recalls, "with all the creosote on them they'd burn for days on end." Along Chamber Street, Mary O'Neill and her neighbours were lucky when the Corporation began tearing out some setts from an old section of road and giving them to needy residents. "They'd blaze up the chimney!" Entire families crouched around the heat.

In the poorer tenement districts, stealing setts from the streets under cover of darkness became widespread. Young Garda Paddy Casey had just come on duty at the Bridewell Station in 1947 and saw people plucking them out like bad teeth:

> *Savage* hardship around Queen Street, the quays, Dominick Street, North King Street. Terrible, terrible difficult that winter. And the poor would come out with picks and *hack up* the street and take the wooden setts in sacks for fire.

It would have taken a heartless garda not to turn a blind eye.

By the last week of February even William Tinnion and his fellow-stokers at Guinness's were having thoughts about scavenging. For weeks they had watched the heaps of coal dwindle, then vanish. Forced to begin using the coal dust, or "duff." Now even that was running out. Without their furnaces fired, the titanic brewery would be shut down. Feeling stymied, he and his mates began slowly surveying their surroundings; and then "the old brain" began working overtime.

———

Elsewhere around Dublin the talk turned to logs. "Ah, sure that'll keep us going," many people were saying. It sounded feasible enough.

Already men were seen around the city breaking limbs off trees and trying to saw or chop up poles blown down by the blizzard—looking like buzzards picking at some large carcase. At every fuel merchant's in Dublin "the telephone rang almost incessantly," with people wanting to know if any logs had come in yet. Their expectations had been mistakenly raised by articles in some newspapers claiming that timber was the solution to the fuel crisis. According to the *Irish Press,* there were "thousands of trees suitable" for cutting and use as firewood "within easy reach of the city." However, the *Irish Independent* rebutted this facile notion, contending that "after the continuous cutting in recent years, little timber remains in the vicinity of Dublin to supply merchants." Leaving the public confused.

When a lorryload of logs did rumble into the city, delivered to a fuel merchant, his "premises were besieged by crowds" trying to secure even a single log to haul home. As with turf, black-market profiteers were eager to get their clutches on logs, using the same unscrupulous tactics and reaping big profits. The poor could afford to buy only a single log or two at a time, perhaps three, while affluent customers with cars and cash could buy in bulk to fill their garages and garden sheds. Noting that "firewood has now been added to the huckster racket," the *Evening Herald* described how a small dealer managed to procure a load of timber and "immediately proceeded to sell it by the stone at a profit of anything up to five hundred per cent, or even more."[3] The poorest of the tenement-dwellers were particularly exploited, and many "cases of overcharging by bellmen and itinerant wood-sellers have come to light . . . asking as much as two shillings for one log of wood." One log, often wet, that neither fitted their grate nor burned.

As with turf, the task of collecting logs fell largely to women and children, who hadn't realised how heavy wet logs were until they began struggling to lug them home. Fourteen-year-old John Gallagher was sent by his Ma to collect some. "You had to queue for *hours* at a fuel yard up in James's Street to get wet logs to carry in a sack." Then straining to haul them back to the Coombe. The *Evening Herald* told of a five-year-old girl at a fuel depot who stood for "almost five hours waiting her turn to get two stone of timber. When she got the logs her hands were too cold to lift the sack."

Lugging logs home was not only an arduous but often a futile chore, as they commonly failed to fit in the grate or to burn properly. Most inner-city dwellers knew little, if anything, about types of wood or log-burning. To them, "wood was wood." Country folk knew better. As a public service, the

Irish Independent published a series of articles on the "art of the wood fire." Beginning with wood types, it stated that "naturally, old (dry) wood is best," with oak, holly, dogwood and hazel being excellent for burning. Ash was probably the best of the lot. Conversely, such woods as birch and fir were to be avoided, as they burned too quickly. Most city people hadn't a clue what type of wood they were buying.

As for the proper technique, the old maxim was to be followed: "One log can't burn, two logs won't burn, three logs may burn, four logs will burn, five logs make a good fire." Provided, of course, there is the "ideal hearth," with flat brick floor measuring three feet by one foot nine inches. A writer for one newspaper wrote an article in the "Women's Parade" section—clearly intended for better-off readers—explaining that "it is not a matter of great cost or difficulty to have an ordinary fireplace enlarged and bricked." As for those less fortunate residents, a poky little grate is indeed "ill-suited for wood fires."

Nonetheless, many a poor Ma sat hopefully before her little grate with a single log sticking partially out, holding a match beneath it, waiting for a fire to warm her family.

As some timber-cutting and log delivery began, it created new problems. Men venturing into the countryside to fell trees often had no experience of using saws or axes and were not knowledgeable about safety techniques for this high-risk job. Accidents, and some deaths, resulted.

In Co. Wicklow, John Campbell, his son and several other men were out felling trees. About midday they were having tea on a lower road when they heard a rumbling above them. Next thing "he saw his son lying down, bleeding from the head, mouth and ears." Two other men on an upper road, out for timber as well, had rolled a section of a tree down the slope, having no idea of the men below them. Later that day young Campbell died in the County Hospital.

Logs were presenting problems in the city centre as well as they were being delivered in bulk to factories, institutions, and businesses. Dubliners were now "grousing against huge lorries from which loads of wood blocks are being removed in narrow thoroughfares at busy periods," reported the *Irish Times*. The lorries were disrupting traffic in the city, blocking some thoroughfares, alleys and narrow passages for hours at a time, and tempers flared. As the paper explained, "before the Ice Age, when we had coal, it took next to no time to unload a ton of coal" through the cellar holes in the city's pavements. Now, to feed a ton of wood blocks through one of these holes "is an afternoon's job."[4]

The only welcome aspect of wood deliveries was when logs fell from rumbling lorries onto the road and were snatched up in seconds before the driver had a chance to retrieve them.

Now into their fifth week of Siberian weather, Dublin's poor were suffering multiple miseries. They faced a life of fireless grates, flu, TB, malnourishment, overflowing slop buckets, frozen pipes, broken windows, leaking roofs. Hungry and numbed by cold, in dark, damp, fetid rooms. Little wonder their death rate was doubling and trebling.

As the general public was learning more about the plight of the poor, it became apparent that many privileged Dubliners living in elite suburban enclaves knew little of the suffering of the impoverished at the bottom of Dublin society. An article in the *Irish Independent* during the last week of February was starkly illustrative of the city's old, entrenched class system. The article "Good grooming" told readers:

> Everybody—yes, *everybody*—needs a bath every day . . . [Even] with the present shortage of fuel, how many can honestly say that they cannot provide themselves with a jug of water, a basin, soap and wash flannel? Having washed, to then stimulate your circulation . . . rub a scented toilet water or skin perfume all over your body.[5]

The writer recommended the enchanting fragrances of "Tweed" and "Green Velvet." But, if necessary, a bottle of lavender water or eau de cologne would suffice. For tenement-dwellers, perhaps such lovely fragrances might also cloak the stagnant, suffocating odours of congested bodies, slop buckets, wet, smouldering turf, and sickness.

The poor were, as always, essentially mute and powerless. A voiceless class within greater Irish society. However, after nearly five weeks of suffering, their pitiable life was being increasingly exposed by sympathetic citizens and a conscientious press. Editors, dismayed over the Government's failure to assist the needy during the winter crisis, printed their often-emotive submissions, knowing they would elicit compassion and generate controversy. And, of course, boost readership.

Several papers began devoting their entire "Letters to the editor" section to the subject of the poverty-stricken in society, under such headings as "Appalling scenes of want in Dublin" and "An appeal for the poor in Dublin." Far more letters landed on editors' desks than could be printed. In contrast to earlier weeks, when citizens' letters were generally detached observations on the poor, they now became poignant eye-witness accounts, such as that sent to the *Dublin Evening Mail* by Nancie L. Hatte of 50 Adelaide Road:

> As I sat on the bus home I felt a little nauseous. For I had just come from a tenement with a fireless grate, housing seven children, a father and mother. The fingers of the little ones were blue with cold, and they were

crying. The mother tried vainly to warm them by wrapping them in a tattered quilt. The father, silent with the silence of despair, sat in a corner. He makes a little money by selling newspapers.

Sometimes Paddy, the second boy, brings in 3/- [3 shillings] daily on papers, six days a week. It is hard work, and cold work, knocking about O'Connell Street in this icy weather and a heavy cold in your nose—but it keeps starvation from the door. His earnings on the city streets in this Arctic weather are keeping the family in existence.[6]

It was the combination of cold and hunger that was so debilitating, that made victims stuporous. As sixteen-year-old Seán Whelan experienced, it weakened one's physical constitution, mental functioning, one's very spirit:

I have recollections of shivering, *real trembling*. It was dreadful. It was not getting enough to eat, as *well* as being cold. You didn't have food to warm you *inside*. So it was the deprivation of good, nourishing food *and* the deprivation of sufficient heat. Children'd be crying with the cold and the hunger.

Newspapers published uncommonly lengthy letters vividly portraying one insufferable case after another:

Sir,—Can nothing be done as regards the appalling conditions which the poor of Dublin are expected to live under? The prongs of cold and hunger have penetrated working-class homes . . . and duly left their mark. Recently, I had occasion to visit Keogh Square. Here I saw poverty on a large scale. Barefooted children, half-naked and under-fed, were running around searching for turf. Elderly people were to be seen huddled in groups speaking in hushed voices, and the pinched, drawn look on their faces spoke of hunger and hardship.

At the fuel depot a large queue of poverty-stricken folk waited patiently for their supply of turf. While I was standing there one old lady fainted and I went to assist her. She was nothing but a bundle of rags and bone. When I brought her to shelter and warmth she said she had nothing to eat since the previous evening. I took this poor, unfortunate woman to her home—and what a miserable hovel that was. A filthy flight of stairs led up to this poor being's home. The stairs were never lighted and I had to grope my way along the wall. This poor woman made the best of her miserable lot.

When I came out I was shocked at the sights that met my eye. Window frames without glass or any protection against the hard wind, sewerage pipes burst and waste matter flowing all over the place. Men standing around had that listless, unseeing gaze in their eyes that clearly showed they had no interest whatsoever in life.

They saw their children wither and fade like flowers before them through lack of food. Those children had dropped to the level of animals, with only one idea and that was to get food—anywhere.

—Uncle Remus.[7]

The newspapers were lauded not only for printing lengthy, explicit testimonial letters—many truly reading like dark Dickensian tales—that enlightened the public but also for printing photographs showing the actual face of poverty in the city. Many better-off citizens, by their own admission, had never ventured into tenement districts. Never seen "withering" children reduced to the "level of animals," or the mute elderly sitting silently in a stupor as a result of prolonged cold and hunger.

Such letters and photographs opened many eyes, and hearts. One appreciative citizen wrote in to say that "the *Independent* newspapers have done a national service by publishing photographs of these Siberian wind-swept fuel queues of the poor." He proceeded to express regret that "some of the lady reporters from the Press who so accurately describe (in sketches) expensive dress creations" at the city's lavish functions and banquets did not bother to take their pens and drawing pads down to the tenement districts. He had a suggestion for them:

> Draw pen pictures of the poor old women literally shivering in remnants of shawls, cotton frocks and slush-filled canvas shoes ... many obviously racked with t.b., with brains suffering from destitution.[8]

The reference to TB was timely, as the results of a three-year study on tuberculosis in Dublin had just been published, conducted by Dr William Kidney under the auspices of the Irish Red Cross Society. It confirmed that between 40,000 and 80,000 people in the city were actively infected, of whom 2,700 were sufficiently ill clinically to need treatment. Dr Kidney stressed that "tuberculosis was definitely related to poverty, overcrowding and ignorance." It was no wonder that Valentine Morgan, a butcher in North King Street whose shop window looked directly across at some of the most wretched tenements in Dublin, called them "coffin boxes," because so many inhabitants were dying of TB, other sicknesses, cold, and hunger.

One reporter, Anna Kelly of the *Irish Press*, was motivated to go into a tenement district and stand in a fuel queue to get a first-hand story. She chose a turf depot in Bridge Street run by a kindly but gruff Mr Buckley, of local renown. Amidst wailing women, she clandestinely slipped into the queue:

> The cold oozed up from the ground where the slush was ankle deep. The darkening air was trembling with snow as it drifted down and settled

heavily on them. Women gave out a wail, "Oh, Mr. Buckley, *open the door and let us in!*" It is grim, it is terrible in its urgency and misery. The women talk about nothing else. The search for fuel has eaten so deeply into their time and energies that there is no room for any other feelings, any other topics of conversation.

They have babies stored away at home in rags and wrappings, sick husbands roaring and bawling out for this and that. Mr. Buckley opens the door, holds it against a surging mob. There is a frail woman with a bent back. She tries to lift her sack but it swings low on the floor between her weak wrists. "Ah, give the woman a hoist!" They swing the bag on her back and she staggers off, bending over lower than ever.[9]

Some citizens wrote to the papers to lament that the general public had not got a better understanding of how appalling living conditions actually were in the inner city. One woman submitted her idea to the *Dublin Evening Mail* for enlightening the better-off classes in the suburbs:

I wonder if all those comfortably dressed people one sees in fashionable thoroughfares were to see into some of the places where human beings live in Dublin, would they not immediately turn sick, and go and do something about it.

I think they would, because I believe that most people, at heart, are kind; but they are ignorant. What we need is someone who will take a cinematograph of some of the living conditions prevailing and flash them on every screen in Dublin. It might cause a commotion, all right, but it would be a good one![10]

Volumes of words spoken, words written. But there was no warmth in words.

————

And where were the voices from Leinster House? Why were food and fuel not being provided by the Government for the multitudes suffering?

In the days immediately following the third blizzard, ordinary citizens and various organisations clamoured for the Government and the army to act, to provide food and fuel and promptly establish meal centres and food kitchens throughout the poorer districts. Real hunger now pervaded tenement rooms, as cases of malnutrition were being documented. It was verified that some were now actually suffering slow starvation. The Catholic Social Service Conference, established by Archbishop McQuaid, provided dinner centres around the city but not nearly enough for the expanding hungry population. The *Irish Press* vigorously championed the cause, arguing that "good and valid reasons have now arisen for the setting up of municipal kitchens and communal feeding centres."

The city manager, P. J. Hernon, jumped on the bandwagon, asking the Minister for Defence to establish, without delay, emergency municipal kitchens around Dublin to ease hunger and hardship. The Committee of the Irish Housewives' Association gave its "wholehearted support to the plea" for the immediate opening of such kitchens. Mrs A. D. Skeffington, secretary of the association, asked sternly: "What happened to the Mansion House kitchens? Why haven't they been opened to provide hot meals for those who have no fuel?" A Labour Party councillor argued strongly for the provision of army field kitchens, especially for the old people who could not venture out on icy, dangerous streets. "If field kitchens were placed on Army lorries food could be brought to their homes." The paper supported the idea that the army should promptly "lend a hand with its field kitchens in Dublin."

Most tenement mothers who in the past had declined to accept food from local meal centres, not wanting to be seen as a "charity case," were now well beyond the point of allowing such pride to stand in the way of feeding their hungry family.

But despite the outpouring of pleas, neither Government nor military brass acted on behalf of the cold and hungry.

————

On Monday 24 February there finally occurred a dam-burst of criticism directed at Government members, who sat cosily in their oil-heated chambers in Leinster House week after week, apparently oblivious of—or uncaring about—what was taking place beyond their doors. Dismissive of all appeals for assistance, for action.

Impassioned criticism came from the public, press, and political opponents. Critics presented a litany of what the Government could, and should, have been doing over the five weeks of the Arctic siege and blizzards, by making use of their combined resources of money, manpower, and army equipment. Most blatant were the failure to provide fuel and food, to despatch hardy soldiers with army lorries to clear snowbound roads, to rescue and assist marooned passengers in stranded vehicles and isolated villagers, to begin cutting and transporting timber from distant counties, to send rescue squads to search for missing people, to aggressively crack down on black-market activities and profiteers, to set up shelters for tenement-dwellers whose buildings were windowless, leaking, and utterly unfit for human habitation, to establish food kitchens. Furthermore, de Valera should have been sending special envoys and delegations overseas at the highest levels to explain in person how desperate Ireland's food and fuel crisis had become.

Instead, Government members, who had the authority and the means to act in such ways for the public good, had inexplicably remained passive, insouciant and, some argued, outright arrogant in their inaction.

Until the third blizzard struck, the newspapers had essentially exercised restraint by not directly faulting the Government for negligence. Immediately afterwards they became blunt in their criticism, as the *Irish Independent* expressed it:

> The Government cannot be blamed for the abnormal weather, or for the collapse of the British coal industry. What the Government must be held responsible for is the utter inactivity shown during the past month.[11]

A move was made by the Labour group on Dublin Corporation and referred to the Minister for Defence, strongly urging "that the Army come to the aid of thousands of Dublin families shivering in fireless homes" by using their lorries to obtain and distribute decent turf and logs to city depots—without further delay. The motion explicitly warned that if the Government and army failed to come to the assistance of needy citizens "a major emergency may result in more deaths in the city." To which the *Dublin Evening Mail* sharply added:

> The Army should have been utilised in this serious crisis. The Government is too high and mighty to listen to suggestions from anybody—or has been so far.[12]

Fine Gael, measuring mounting public discontent with the failures of leadership, seized the opportunity to act. No more time could be squandered, it argued, putting forward a motion in the Dáil:

> The Dáil condemns the failure of the Government to make better provision for the supply of fuel for public utility service, and for general industrial and domestic purposes, which has resulted in dislocation of public services and of employment, and caused extreme hardship to all sections of the community.[13]

The Government was asked to afford time in the Dáil on Tuesday 25 February to discuss the motion, which had been placed on the order paper in the names of Richard Mulcahy, John A. Costello, T. F. O'Higgins, and Daniel Morrissey. All of them regarded the Government as being bankrupt of imagination and initiative, while ignoring ideas presented by members of the opposing party, the press, and the public. Indeed Dr O'Higgins had asked the Minister for Industry and Commerce if he would "take steps with a view to leasing one of the small Welsh coal mines to be worked by Irish labour" for the use of the Irish people. He received no satisfactory reply or action.

———

On Monday evening the Minister for Industry and Commerce, Seán Lemass, hoping to counter the strong indictments of the Government, made an address to the nation on Radio Éireann. Citizens listened attentively in anticipation of hearing solutions to the winter's problems. He began by declaring that "the country's position has never been so grave. Not even in the worst period of the war" had Ireland to face a complete stoppage of coal imports, accompanied by the ruination and depletion of turf reserves in the eastern areas of the country. All this, he emphasised, was due to the highly abnormal winter weather—over which Man had no control.

In short, it was a crisis "more severe than anything the country had ever experienced previously," stated Lemass. The small remaining supply of coal had to be used for transport, gas, electricity, and a few vital industries.

In its editorial headed "The lesson," the *Irish Press* summarised the hard realities presented by Lemass:

> The hope of many industrialists and merchants that coal would soon be plentiful has proved a pipe dream, an opium dream . . . There are no coal boats arriving and there are likely to be none for a long period of time. Turf must be our main domestic fuel for years to come.[14]

What, then, were his *plans* for coping with the crisis? Why had the army not been used? Were food kitchens now to be established? As Dubliners were now asking "why large quantities of firewood were not being sought," would the Government, with its resources, initiate a timber-felling campaign?

Lemass did at least touch on the last query. He explained that, contrary to popular perception, there wasn't much timber left to be cut, especially near Dublin, as "many trees that our country needs so sorely" had been felled for firewood during the war years. Furthermore, "logs are an unsatisfactory fuel for the great majority of city furnaces, ranges and grates." Nonetheless he would consider making some tree-felling permits available. Apparently for the benefit of those with large fireplaces.

At the conclusion of his address Lemass queried his listeners—"You may ask what you can do to help the position"—and proceeded to tell them they could "avoid the selfish practice" of using off-hour glimmer gas, and reduce their electricity usage. In other words, *citizens* needed to *sacrifice* more. In lieu of offering Government solutions, his words of "comfort" were to tell people that they must have patience and perseverance—and pray.

The response was fast and furious. Disappointment, frustration, outrage. The consensus was that the Government were shrugging their shoulders, blaming it all on nature. In his broadcast, the *Irish Press* wrote, "Mr. Lemass made it clear that, apart from the most rigid economy on the part of all consumers, there was no solution." As a consequence, the public's hopes were dashed, as acknowledged by the *Dublin Evening Mail*:

> A broadcast by Mr. Lemass has come to mean . . . something unutterably grim . . . to cause an immediate depression of spirit. We were told that the fuel position could hardly be more serious. What was depressing was the apparent lack of any coherent plan on the part of Government for dealing with the position.[15]

In its editorial aptly headed "Cold comfort from Government," the *Irish Independent* tersely commented:

> It scarcely needed a Ministerial broadcast to make the public aware that the fuel position "could hardly be worse." Mr. Lemass's broadcast will give little warmth to the fireless homes in Dublin.[16]

———

If the Government was devoid of imagination and resourcefulness, at least some citizens exhibited ingenuity in offering solutions for the country's fuel and electricity shortages. A number of these were submitted to newspapers for the public to ponder. One woman wrote to say that she had just attended one of the city's largest cinemas, where she went into the women's cloakroom. "I noticed there were seven electric lights in use, all shining brightly. Three would have been ample." Here, she felt, was a lesson to be learnt in conserving electricity.

Another letter-writer indignantly criticised the ESB's "somewhat hysterical appeal for ordinary citizens" to economise in their use of electricity when city officials had done no more than impose a ban on outdoor lighting and display lighting. In his opinion they could do a far better, more egalitarian job:

> Sir,—I suggest the E.S.B. put the following restrictions into force immediately: (1) Impose drastic cuts in all places of amusement, cinemas, clubs, theatres, etc. (2) Cut off all supplies to breweries and factories making non-essential goods which use electric power. (3) Make all public houses reduce their consumption by at least 50 per cent.[17]

One particular letter to the *Dublin Evening Mail*, from J. F. Hoey, stirred quite a bit of interest, both for its historical perspective and its future potential. Dubliners displeased with the city's lighting ban, which made their nights on the town gloomy, doubtless read it with interest:

> Sir,—We hear a lot these days about the scarcity of gas owing to the want of coal. Yet in the year 1823 the Directors of the Dublin Gas Light Company obtained from the patentee, Mr. John Barlow of Belfast, the privilege of lighting the city of Dublin with turf gas. And from

experiments made at their works they had no doubt of being able to adopt its general use.

Surely the Gas Company in 1947 could do likewise to light the city of Dublin with gas made from turf.[18]

No less intriguing was a paper read by Cyril Fry at the meeting of the Engineering and Scientific Association of Ireland in Dawson Street. The title was "Some Lesser Known Facts in Connection with Irish Rail Transport." Not, seemingly, a paper to stir much interest among the general public. However, one of Fry's lesser-known facts not only aroused considerable interest among his audience but made the *Irish Times* the next day. "According to geologists," he asserted, and based on an 1896 map of the country, "Ireland has the largest coal fields in the British Empire."[19] Huge coal fields were alleged to exist in Cos. Clare, Kerry, Limerick, Cork, Roscommon, Sligo, Leitrim, and Cavan. One of these fields was estimated to be "16 miles long and 16 miles broad." It got some people wondering, all right.

———

By the last week of February some of the choicest criticism was reserved for Dublin's weather "prophets." There had been no warmth or comfort in their words. Rather, deception and grief. Astonishingly, they had missed all three blizzards. Great destruction, suffering and death had occurred.

Earlier in the winter the public had been forgiving of their "miscalculations." They were the butt of jokes and witty commentary. Failing to forecast the second blizzard, they were viewed with less humour and amusement. As John D. Sheridan wrote in the *Irish Independent*, more in sarcasm than jest:

> I take my weather from my milkman. As a prophet he has been right on target for the past six weeks. And there is no "outlook unsettled" nonsense—when he says "brutal," he means "brutal." And when he says "diabolical," you can see his horse shiver under his sacks. And his parting salute is, "We're going to get more of it—mark my words."[20]

When the third unpredicted blizzard raged across Ireland, bringing death to animals and humans, destruction to transport and communications networks, marooning road passengers and isolating villages, their blunders were seen as sheer incompetence. Now viewed more as pariahs than prophets, they became targets of scorn and derision. One newspaper contended that, despite all their supposed analysis of charts, graphs, and the "glass," their forecasts were no more than guesswork. Another newspaper jabbed: "Amongst the old people, many regard 'the rheumatics,' or condition of their corns, as the only reliable barometer." The *Evening Herald* concluded that there was now a prevalent lack of faith in forecasters among the public:

> It is clear that we are still a long way from the time when we can trust weather forecasts implicitly. The abiding distrust that induces large numbers of people to disbelieve every attempt to forecast the weather is strong.[21]

The *Dublin Evening Mail* threw the hardest punch:

> When they do tell us, more often than not, they do not tell us accurately. As things are, the guesswork of any layman is almost as reliable as the most laboured calculations of the true scientific weather report.
>
> The meteorologists ought to be thankful that they are living in a very tolerant country. In some places they would be put to death as enemies of the people.[22]

Under the barrage of such criticism, by Monday 24 February it was understandable that Dublin's weather experts were inclined to "play it safe" in their projections, being deliberately abstruse in their wording. Openly disagreeing with one another, they further confused the public. Some exhibited all the indecision of a nervous, reluctant bride. Reported one newspaper: "Some weather experts foresee a change with to-day's new moon—but whether the change will be for the better or worse they do not say."

Scarcely thirty-six hours after the cessation of the third blizzard, Dublin's newspaper weathermen issued almost absurdly contradictory projections:

> One meteorological expert promised a radical change, basing his prognostication on the fact that the very strong high pressure which has caused the present cold spell by hovering persistently over Western Europe during the past weeks appears now to be slackening.[23]

That very day, others saw it differently:

> A more dismal outlook is that of the weather prophets who foretell of Arctic or near Arctic conditions until the vernal equinox towards the end of next month.[24]

The *Evening Herald* presented its own slant, stating that the arrival of the new moon has "aroused in the breasts of freezing Dubliners hopes of an immediate improvement." Most weather experts, however, were "by no means sanguine," some predicting that people would have to endure the "present Arctic conditions for some time longer—but they cannot say how long."

By this time, many people had ceased even reading the weather forecasts in the papers.

"Did'ja hear the good news from Russia?" By late Monday afternoon and into the evening everyone was talking about the *Evening Herald's* dramatic late news bulletin. It claimed that there might really be a disintegration of the anticyclonic regime and high-pressure realm from Siberia across northern Europe to Greenland. The good word was spreading across the Continent, through Germany, Scandinavia, France, the Low Countries, to Britain and Ireland; then from Dublin onwards to Sligo, Galway, Donegal, and Kerry:

> A cable from Russia to-day has the weather experts buzzing, talking thirteen to the dozen. From Moscow came news that there is scattered rain over most of western Russia. Temperatures at 8 a.m. were 33 degrees Fahrenheit—a considerable rise.
>
> The reason for the meteorological hubbub is the fact that the piercing weather we in Ireland have been subjected to for a month has come from Russia. One weather expert hopefully said, "The warmer weather in Russia may at last indicate that Europe's icy spell is ending."[25]

Citizens were jubilant.

They had been fooled before. But this weather news appeared genuine. It was not based on the amateurish calculations of local weather prophets but had originated in Russia and been verified along the way by Continental meteorologists. In Berlin it was now "clear and warmer." It was reported in Paris that "the snow has stopped and the sun has broken through." London had nine hours of sunshine and warmer temperatures.

This news seemed to have a real stamp of credibility. Even the BBC and Radio Éireann were broadcasting the positive forecasts. Dublin's newspapers hopped on the bandwagon. The *Irish Press* blared: "Warmer Moscow may mean a thaw." Proclaimed the *Irish Independent*: "Hopes for a break in cold spell."

People believed it to finally be the beginning of the end. "Halleluya!" was heard on the streets of Dublin, Cork, Limerick. In small towns and on farms. In the small Mayo village of Straide.

Confident of the seemingly authenticated weather news coming from Europe, the *Evening Herald* told readers that the next day—Tuesday 25 February—should be one of the best in some time:

> A ridge of high pressure over the country will maintain fair or fine weather . . . There will be moderate south-east winds . . . with good bright periods.[26]

A dandy day ahead.

Chapter 7 ❧

| "THE DADDY OF THEM ALL"

Dubliners awoke to find the streets already covered to a depth of two feet of snow, and the blizzard raging with greater severity than ever. Flakes fell so thickly that visibility was reduced almost to nil.

(*Irish Independent,* 26 FEBRUARY 1947)

Snow seven feet deep in inland areas . . . at least one 50-foot drift near Glencree. The hamlet of Moneystown at Roundwood has been "lost" in the snow.

(*Irish Times,* 26 FEBRUARY 1947)

Three men died in the Sligo countryside on the night of the worst blizzard. One of them had gone only a hundred yards from his home. This story might have come from some Polar Expedition. It is almost unbelievable that such conditions could exist in Ireland.

(*Irish Times,* 13 MARCH 1947)

TUESDAY 25 FEBRUARY

In the middle of the night of 24/25 February, somewhere out in the North Sea, the captain of a Swedish ice-breaker radioed Stockholm: "It is nothing but an inferno out here in the sea . . . During my 20 years as master of ice-breakers I have never encountered anything similar."[1]

Dubliners had gone to bed comforted by the good news from Moscow that heralded the demise of King Winter's cruel reign. Anticipating a fine day ahead, with warmer temperatures and "bright periods."

Irish weather forecasters were so buoyed by the promising news from Russia, far to the east, that they apparently failed to glance over their shoulders at what was slowly, ominously, approaching from the west. Here a "vigorous low just west of Ireland had been poised to take a more northerly track than the previous ones . . . with the threat of heavy snowfall."[2] Throughout the night the deepening depression "moved north-eastwards across Ireland with gale force winds." Under the cover of darkness it gathered strength, churning across Ireland like a mighty steam engine, drawing the deep low-pressure and high-pressure systems into another inevitable collision. This one the most violent and devastating.

It would have a name. Christened the "white enemy" by the *Evening Herald,* old-timers would long remember it as "the Big Snow," or "the Daddy of Them All."

———

It struck at different times around the country. About midnight Dubliners heard it howling like a banshee through the city's streets. It ripped along the Liffey, down O'Connell Street, through tenemented rows, into alleys, across the Phoenix Park. Everything was set in motion. Windows, slates, loose chimney bricks, shop awnings, traders' stalls were shaken and dislodged. Smaller objects, such as boxes, boards, and bottles, went flying and rolling around the streets like tumbleweeds across Wyoming's high plains.

Despite the awful clamour, most sleepers at first probably took it to be a gusty squall racing through, as no storm had been predicted. By about 1:30 a.m. it blew so furiously that snow blasted its way through door and window crevices, into keyholes. Accumulating inches by the hour, the wind drifted it up against buildings and barricaded doorways.

Meanwhile it was smothering the countryside. In Brian Kelly's part of Co. Donegal, farm families like those of his parents went to bed on Monday night to a few snow flurries, utterly unsuspecting:

> It started slowly. A light snow and a wind came up and blew it—and then it became a blizzard! This snow blew and blizzarded . . . blew and blizzarded all the snow on the lower roads and low fields. And on the hollows where the animals were sheltering.
>
> And then every door passage, and church door, was blocked, and it was up to the height of a car . . . and you didn't know what you were walking on. And the temperature dropped down. Everything froze over. Froze. *Froze!*

According to Canon Martin Halloran of Sligo, "the 'big snow' continued without a break . . . People woke up to a landscape resembling a white desert."[3] In Boyle, Co. Roscommon, Christy Wynne slept contentedly through the night, only to awake and peer out the window in astonishment:

> As I went to bed on that Monday night the first flakes were beginning to fall. The next morning I woke up and looked out on the street below and I could barely recognise it. Shop fronts, shop windows, hall doors had

literally disappeared under a huge blanket of snow.

An eerie silence hung everywhere, and there wasn't a human being in sight . . . There were drifts fifteen feet high. The town began to look like a lost village in Siberia.[4]

In Longford, Miriam Sweetman's 89-year-old granny, Annie Gillespie, was ill and nearing the end of her life. She departed just as the blizzard arrived:

As the snow started to fall, Gran quietly slipped into eternity. The snow continued to fall all night, and the next morning the whole country ground to a standstill.[5]

Others would die as well during the blizzard, but not so peacefully.

———

Dubliners awoke flabbergasted. More than two feet of snow already covered the ground, drifted to five feet in places. Snowfall so dense that it created a white-out. Those who *had* to be up and out to work before dawn—lamplighters, milkmen, bakery men, newspaper deliverers—made the first footprints in the pristine scene. William Tinnion waded through hip-deep drifts to arrive at Guinness's on time at 5 a.m. to stoke the big furnaces. Miles away, out in Whitehall, Dick Curtis, a barrel-checker at the brewery, was up and dressed, wondering how he was going to make it into town. He never missed a day of work. His best bet was to release some air pressure from his bicycle tyres for a better grip and hope to follow in the tracks of some delivery vehicles already out on the roads. It would be treacherous, and probably take three times as long as usual. Similarly, David O'Donnell, a Guinness's cooper in his twenties, was fit and would make it to work, blizzard or not.

Guinness's directors would be coming in late that morning, in their large black cars, waiting hopefully for the roads to clear for their journey from the suburbs. Weather might bring the rest of Dublin to a standstill, but it would not halt the brewery. At least, it had never done so before.

Early morning milk, bread and newspaper van drivers had learnt hard lessons from the previous three blizzards. They were better prepared. The *Irish Press*, like other papers, now provided their drivers with assistants and with "shovels and strong ropes to dig and pull their vehicles from snow drifts." Many brought along picks, chains, hessian sacks and sand as well. Their shared mantra was they "must get through." People *depended* on them.

This was the outlook of Donald Kelly and Harry Morgan, drivers for Boland's bakery. They knew that in these hard times especially, the loaf on the table was the central component of meals for most families. In the poorest houses it was the only solid food they could count on. Both experienced drivers, they left Dublin early on Tuesday morning at a crawl, with a full load, knowing it was to be a far longer day than usual but hopefully not one marred by mishaps. Harry Morgan drove cautiously along snowy roads towards the Blessington district, Donald Kelly angled his van in the direction of Glencullen and Stepaside. Both looking forward to full morning light and a clear sky soon.

Their brethren the milkmen were doing the same, trying to get milk into homes for nourishment and health. Well before dawn, the main milk distributing firms in north Co. Dublin, Meath, Louth, Kildare and Wicklow were despatching their lorries to make their morning collections of milk cans from farmers. All their drivers were equipped with "extra crews, chains, ropes and shovels." As they crept along the rural roads outside Dublin they grew more apprehensive with every mile.

Back in the heart of the capital, many managers and supervisors were up hours earlier than usual, facing decisions about the day's operations. CIE's supervisors bore the heaviest burden. Would the country's public transport run? Buses, trains, lorries. Most had early-morning departure schedules. Could their drivers even reach the depots? Would passengers be safe aboard them? Supervisors had to make the judgement. With much of the country's telephone and telegraph network knocked out by the blizzards, most had no way of communicating with other districts to check on road and rail conditions. Decisions would be a gamble. And the stakes could be high.

By about 7:45 a.m. at CIE head office in Dublin, M. Mohan and his colleagues were sipping strong tea, consulting about the problems they faced. Most important were provincial buses. Some had a journey of five to seven hours—under *normal* conditions—across some remote and wild territory. If trapped by snowdrifts, passengers could be marooned far from any help, meaning food, water, shelter, medical attention. Just as surely as if they were on an Arctic expedition. During the previous blizzards there had been some harrowing experiences for buses and passengers along isolated stretches of road.

As supervisors around the country were deliberating, most were surely hoping that the blizzard would cease at any moment—as no storm of any type had been forecast.

Not only were CIE's buses needed to transport passengers, but trains carried food items, mail, and assorted vital goods, while lorries hauled farmers' animals to market and brought fodder for starving beasts. To some farmers it was a matter of life and death for their stock. A day's delay could be crucial. Some cattle and sheep collected by CIE lorries destined for Dublin's market were already scrawny, barely fit for selling.

Between 8 and 9 o'clock many important transport decisions had to be made. The blizzard clearly was not abating. Nonetheless, many bus supervisors decided to go ahead. L. Aughney, in charge of CIE's road freight, considered conditions "a nightmare experience" yet felt he had to try to keep the fleet running. Close to 9 a.m., several dozen CIE lorries were sent from Dublin to Cos. Kilkenny, Tipperary, Meath, Offaly and Wicklow to collect cattle on farms and bring them to the market. As they pulled out of the garages, their supervisors yelled, "Good luck!"

Gradually throughout the early morning many buses, lorries and trains were ordered out on their normal schedules. Others were temporarily suspended or cancelled.

———

In Galway a bus was scheduled to depart at 8 o'clock sharp for Dublin. A cross-country trip through the wide-open midlands, parts of which were flat terrain, a treeless landscape with boglands and small, separated farmsteads. Remote, isolated stretches of road with long distances between towns and villages. Vulnerable to sweeping winds, snowstorms, and heavy drifting. Where earth meets sky on distant horizons.

By 7:15 a few passengers were arriving for the bus, to get settled in their seats early. The driver and conductor assisted with luggage, tried to answer their queries. No, they didn't know how long the blizzard might last, how bad the road could be ahead, how late they might arrive in Dublin. As the driver stood by the door of his bus smoking a last cigarette, his supervisor was inside making his determination about the final go-ahead. Surely, he thought, the blizzard would have ceased by the time the bus reached Loughrea. He wished he could phone ahead along the route to check on conditions.

A few minutes before 8 o'clock the driver flicked his cigarette butt into the snow, checked his watch, and looked up at his supervisor. His orders were to proceed. Cautiously.

Though some passengers appeared a bit nervous, most were calmed by the comfortable bus and the companionship of others. They were in good hands, all agreed. There was even laughter. Along the way they planned to read, sew, knit. Nap. Chatting always shortened a trip. Children were excited drawing on the frosty windows. Promptly at 8 o'clock the driver gave his supervisor a farewell wave, adjusted his seat, gripped the wheel, and rolled out. Dublin-bound.

Throughout the morning similar scenarios were enacted by other supervisors and bus-drivers in every county. Dutifully seeing to it that the national public transport operated in all weather. Knowing that there were always some passengers who had to reach their destination for the most serious of reasons: medical treatment, a death in the family, a wedding, christening, important family matters. CIE could be counted on.

_____

Tuesday being a work day, individual citizens had their own decisions to make. To try and get out to work on time or wait until the storm subsided? Shop-owners and factory managers were not about to keep their doors shut. Business hours were to be kept. Dubliners were not about to risk losing their jobs.

City buses and trams ran sporadically and slowly, if at all. Bicycles had to be pushed more than pedalled. Throngs set out to try to walk to work along snow-clogged pathways. Gardaí were duty-bound. Around the artisans' dwellings of Stonybatter, Davy Sheridan, a postman, slung his 45-pound canvas bag over his shoulder, dropped his head against the cutting wind, and shuffled forward. "You weren't supplied with gloves . . . The frost would slit your fingers. Ah, it would be terrible sore." On the worst-weather days he was always sympathetically invited into a few houses for a quick cup of tea and moments of warmth. "The rules said 'no' . . . but sometimes you'd go in." This would be one of those days.

By about 7:15 Mary Dunne and Una Shaw could wait no longer to decide. Both valued their jobs: they'd go. Fifteen-year-old Mary had just left St Vincent's School in North William Street to take a job with a high-class tailor, a woman named Moore. Her job was described as "runner": going for messages, making tea, sweeping up, getting buttons and thread from the haberdashers. Mrs Moore ran an elite shop. "Oh, all the ambassadors' wives came to her to make up their garments, like dresses and ball gowns. Oh, she was the fashion designer of her day." And she insisted on punctuality. Even during blizzards. For Mary it was a plum of a job. Of her 7 shillings a week she gave 5 to her Ma. She couldn't dare to lose her job. Normally it was a 35-minute walk. Today it could take three times that long.

The crowds of citizens trying to get to their work had to fight against the blizzard, which was reaching its full ferocity between 7 and 10 o'clock. About 7:30, eighteen-year-old Una Shaw was dressed, had finished her breakfast, and was peering out the window of her home in Rutland Street, dreading having to open the door and face her walk to work. She was employed at Resnick's clothing factory in Dominick Street, usually a twenty-minute walk. Today she wasn't sure she could make it at all. She bundled up with all the warm clothing she had, gave her Ma a goodbye and faint smile. The second she opened the door and stepped out, the gale-force wind caught her as she balanced herself for the trek:

The blizzard was that bad that I could barely see, and I remember having a scarf over my mouth, 'cause you couldn't breathe it was so cold! I can remember *vividly* how cold it was . . . It'd penetrate *right through you!*

With the struggle getting to work I literally had to hold onto the railings of the houses, 'cause with the blizzard it would *knock you off your feet!*

And I particularly remember the struggle getting up Dominick Street, because the factory was right at the top, and you were holding onto the railings going along. And I'd have to stop and wait until I got up enough steam.

When you were inside the factory you were quite warm, with the machines going. But then you had to go out and face the same thing coming home.

In every street in the city people were seen inching their way along, clinging to railings, halting to get their breath, wrap their scarf tighter, forging onwards tentatively. The elderly were conspicuously having the hardest time of it.

About the time Mary Dunne reached Mrs Moore's establishment without mishap, sixteen-year-old Seán Whelan was making his way from his house in Ballybough to Bolton Street Technical School—quite a trek. Along the way he saw people and horses falling. Both received immediate attention. "People were so willing to help back then, extremely helpful." Fallen horses were a sad sight, the beast's eyes showing great fright. "They had to unyoke it from the shaft and lift the shafts up and get the horse back on his feet again." He didn't have time to stop and watch. For most of his journey to school he had to keep his head bowed down against the blizzard's whipping:

You were walking *into* the wind, and the snow came down and drove into you. It just came down in *sheets*—it just *slapped* into your face. Driven by this strong wind, it *hurt* you when it hit your face, you know, because it was icy. You were nearly ice-bound on the front. It was terrible . . . *terrible.* The worst blizzard I ever experienced in my life.

Joe Kirwan showed up for work as a messenger-boy at the chemist's shop. Having just escaped a close shave during the previous ice blizzard a few days before, when his bicycle toppled on the tram tracks at Kelly's Corner, he was very wary this morning. Clad as usual in short trousers, jumper, and canvas runners, he pushed off with his first delivery of the day, determined not to fall again.

About the same time, eleven-year-old Anthony Naylor of Hagan's Court, off Lower Baggot Street, was crossing the road at Baggot Street Bridge when he was struck hard by a lorry and flung to the ground. Bystanders were at his side within seconds. He was alive but in a serious condition when an ambulance arrived to take him to the nearby Royal City of Dublin Hospital. Those gathered around the accident site were saying that it was no-one's fault—unavoidable under the blizzardy conditions of bad visibility and poor braking power. There would be many more such accidents before the day was out.

———

Most Guinness workers had managed to arrive on time, or shortly thereafter. Coopers, brewers, stokers, draymen, bargemen, office staff and others had fought their way through the blizzard. The directors and senior managers were in no hurry. Because of bad conditions around their fashionable town-houses or suburban homes, they decided to remain inside for a while longer. Some suburbanites found themselves stranded, as even taxi-drivers "refused to take people outside the city limits." Many would not dare venture beyond the city centre.

Around mid-morning twenty-year-old Liam Cradden, who had a job in the Guinness office building, looked out the window to see the "bosses," as he called them, arriving one by one in their big cars. With some amusement, he watched:

> On that particular day there were places in the brewery with four feet of snow! But they brought in a man with a tractor and a scoop, and he started at the front gate and he drove up the yard to *clear it,* so the directors could get in—and drive their cars *right up* to the directors' offices. And also for certain other managers and "quality" people to park their cars. So they didn't have a problem.
>
> But we did have a laugh when we saw them clearing the yard *all the way up* to the directors' parking area.

Having then only to walk a few paces on ground that had been shovelled and sanded. Barely a sifting of snow on their shoes. Neither Éamon de Valera nor Archbishop McQuaid were treated more reverentially than Guinness's royalty.

Meanwhile, flocks of children were plodding through heavy snow, sometimes up to their waist and higher, trying to make it to school. But by later in the morning, when the blizzard had showed no sign of abating, teachers and principals began to worry that the children might not be able to make it back home later in the day. So, only an hour or two after the children arrived, many schools began closing. The children were elated, not realising what they faced. Among them was Keith Collie of Ballycorus, near Shankill in south Co. Dublin, who was attending school in Ranelagh. "It was ten in the morning and snowing when the science master came into the class and said that anyone living outside the suburbs should go home, *now."* So he and a number of other pupils reached for their coats and scrambled out the door to try to catch a bus home:

> I was on a single-decker bus by 10:30, the roads were white and the driver was finding it difficult to see through the windscreen. When he could see out, it was all white anyway. By Dundrum we were in virgin snow, but making progress. Then things got worse and worse.[6]

It was about this time, many miles away, that James Gallagher, a 55-year-old farmer from Garvagh, Dromahair, Co. Leitrim, and his family ran out of turf. With the blizzard blowing hard, their house became cold very fast. Not wanting to face a fireless night, he pulled on his boots, bundled up, opened the door against the wind, and trudged out towards a neighbour's house to get a sack of turf. He'd be back soon, he assured his wife. By the time he was no more than twenty yards from home his figure faded away in blurring snowfall.

During the morning members of the Dáil and Seanad who lived outside the capital, many in distant counties, were deciding if they should try and make it to Dublin for the day's important proceedings. Some normally travelled by train, others by car, a trip that took most of them from an hour to three or four hours. A nice journey, during which they conversed, read, studied documents, reflected. Important matters were on the order paper for that day, among them a vote on Fine Gael's censure motion against the Government for failing to protect and assist the public during the fuel crisis. Road conditions varied from county to county. Some legislators were deciding for, others against, the trip.

———

Far to the west, the Galway–Dublin bus was just pulling in to its stop at Loughrea, well behind schedule. The driver, navigating his vehicle through what was being called a vast "sea of snow," already showed signs of nervous tension. And uncertainty. A seasoned driver, he was not easily rattled, but conditions had become exceedingly treacherous. Visibility was reduced to no more than ten to twenty yards, the windscreen was becoming clogged with snow and ice, and the wind bullied the bus all over the road. Some patches of roadway were swept clear by the wind, while a few yards farther ahead would be drifts several feet deep. It was completely unpredictable—and unnerving. Passengers could not appreciate the conditions he was facing.

Upon arriving in Loughrea he could not phone to his supervisor in Galway for instructions about proceeding, as the phone lines were down. If anything, the weather was becoming worse. The journey ahead across the midlands was long and forbidding. He, and many other provincial bus-drivers, found themselves in a position similar to that of a ship's captain in distress. The bus was his vessel; he was the navigator. Unfortunately, a bus-driver had no first mate, second mate, trained crew, radio equipment, emergency supplies, or flares. He was completely reliant on his own skill and judgement to provide for the welfare of his passengers. There might be a few safe harbours along his way, but they were far apart and possibly unreachable. He feared being stranded but said nothing of the sort to his wards.

As the driver was mulling over such thoughts, passengers were stretching their legs, wondering themselves what lay ahead. It is not known whether at this point any expressed their worries, or fears, to him, or asked him not to continue on the road. What is known is that he was a firm believer in the democratic process. He decided to put the critical question to his passengers; it would be their decision. "The driver, on reaching Loughrea," reported the *Irish Press,* "left it to the passengers to vote—for or against proceeding."[7]

It is not recorded how long their deliberation lasted, nor exactly what the tally turned out to be, but the majority "decided to continue the journey." The driver, however reluctant he may personally have been, abided by their decision. He flicked another cigarette butt into the snow, closed the doors, gripped the wheel tightly, and turned his bus once again onto the road.

Had the passengers known what was taking place to the east and west of them by this time it might well have swung their vote the other way. "Road conditions in the Midlands and north-west were worse than ever before remembered," creating perilous conditions in which "cars and lorries which became snowed-up had to be abandoned and were lying half-buried."[8] Before long, many would become completely buried, mere lumps on the white landscape. Some would not be found for weeks. To the west, in Connemara, near Recess, several buses had encountered a 2½-mile snowdrift some six to eight feet high in places. The buses became trapped, forcing passengers to set out on foot in search of shelter.

Railways weren't faring much better. Icy tracks and mounds of snow bedevilled drivers of the most powerful locomotives. Like roads, railway tracks could be highly deceptive, blown clear in one spot but with snow whipped into an eight-foot pile a few yards ahead. With poor visibility and curves, the driver never knew what to expect from one moment to the next. It was impossible to react quickly by putting on the brakes in a rolling train on slippery track. To make matters worse, it was reported that the electric signal apparatus was damaged on many lines, and "points are frozen, causing delays." Trains were not only being blocked but derailed.

Soon after departure, two Great Northern Railways trains were snowed up. The 7:50 a.m. train from Drogheda to Oldcastle became stuck in a snowdrift between Virginia Road and Oldcastle. Elsewhere, goods trains were held up by snowdrifts, and derailment was reported to be a growing danger. There occurred a serious "derailment of two wagons at Moyvalley and a further two at Castlerea." Some of the large locomotives had been fitted with snow-ploughs, but these were often of no use against five to ten-foot crystallised snow and ice barriers. Large ploughs were making some progress on the track between Sligo and Carrick-on-Shannon and between Athlone and Westport. Then a Sligo train encountered a drift estimated at "more than six feet high and 150 yards long." When stymied by such gargantuan drifts, special crews carried along for the purpose had to hop off with shovels and picks and begin hacking away. On stalled or derailed trains, passengers sometimes became understandably fearful. In one instance Mick Higgins, a railway porter from Claremorris, "walked the line from Claremorris to Kiltimagh, a distance of 9½ miles, in drifts up to his hips to assure people that the snow-plough train was coming soon."[9]

In Dublin, by mid-morning snowbound roads were bringing transport to a standstill, as it was declared that "grocers' and milkmen's rounds were impossible." Milkmen and breadmen who had gone out at dawn in the hope that the storm would pass now found themselves helplessly bogged down in snow on roads around and outside Dublin. In Cos. Dublin, Meath, Kildare and Wicklow they came upon "snow drifts up to ten feet," particularly on the by-roads leading to farms where milk awaited collection. To further exacerbate problems, the failure of electric power was interrupting pasteurisation and bottling in some of the distributing firms.

By now the Boland's bakery drivers Harry Morgan and Donald Kelly were far beyond the point of being able to turn back. They had managed to make their early deliveries, but as the snow mounted on the rural roads they knew they were in trouble. At about 10:30 a.m. Morgan encountered a drift near Blessington that halted him in his tracks. Shortly thereafter Kelly became stuck in a white mass in the Glencullen area. Surveying his predicament through his van window, he buttoned up his coat, yanked his cap down in resignation, and embarked on what would be an eight-mile hike to shelter.

Some distance away, on his way home from school, Keith Collie sat worriedly on the bus now crawling along. Neither driver nor passengers could see anything but a white whirlwind out their windows. All sensed that they were not going to make it much further:

> On a bend beside Kilternan Church we were engulfed in a snowdrift— and there the bus remained for the next two and a half weeks. We set off on foot along the road in a white semi-darkness. The driver said he'd had enough when we reached the pub at the Golden Ball (where I believe he stayed for several days).

I continued on, by this time up to my knees in snow, waist-deep in drifts and breathing in as much snow as air. I was dead-beat by the time I made it the mile and a half home.[10]

————

Co. Sligo was being battered by what was being called its "worst blizzard for a century," leaving the town of Sligo now completely isolated. By the next morning residents would be struggling to "dig their way out of their houses as snow drifts ten feet high piled up all over town."[11] Before it was all over it would be regarded as the worst blizzard of *any* century.

Next door in Co. Mayo conditions were no better, as the Ruanes of Straide got word that Westport "was badly snowed-in and isolated with drifts as high as fifteen feet." Through the window young Tony saw drifts whipped into towering forms. To a child's eye it may as well have been the Alps. Indeed the next day, when he could finally trudge through shovelled passages where snow was heaped high on both sides, creating a maze-like landscape, he recalls that "walking through channels in the snowdrifts was like going through a mountain range for a youngster." Neither neighbours' houses nor horizon were in sight. A strange, distorted world of snow he would never know again.

In the most absurd contrast—and one of the most freakish phenomena of the entire winter of 1946/47—Cork and environs had been left untouched by the violent blizzard. The city was calm, bright, sunny—and warm. Like the tranquil eye of a raging, swirling Caribbean hurricane, as described by the *Irish Times:*

> Cork City enjoyed spring-like weather, fine and dry, with occasional sunshine. The temperature was 47 degrees—the blizzard did not touch the city.[12]

So, on Tuesday morning three members of Dáil Éireann nonchalantly departed for Dublin as usual, unaware that the worst blizzard in human memory was raging throughout the rest of the country. With telephone lines now working but no newspapers delivered yet, they probably surmised that some other parts of Ireland were experiencing a local storm of some sort. Éamonn O'Neill, the "popular Leas-Cheann Comhairle" from west Cork, and T. J. Murphy of the Labour Party left for Dublin by car, with full confidence that they would arrive, as always, in plenty of time for business. Another member from Cork, Patrick McGrath of Fianna Fáil, boarded his early morning train, as was his routine. With not so much as a thought of concern about the journey.

The authorities were certainly worried. Up since dawn, the top brass of CIE, the ESB, the Post Office, Dublin Gas Company and the Red Cross Society were in full emergency mode. By about 11 o'clock the first fragmented assessments of blizzard disruptions and damage were filtering in. An ESB spokesman announced:

> The disruption of the Board's network is extremely bad—very much worse than that following the blizzard of three weeks ago. Conditions beggar description.[13]

He confirmed that "damage caused to the trunk lines is greater" than in the previous three blizzards. The main transmission lines between Ardnacrusha and Dublin were broken near Nenagh. In the area between Dublin and Port Laoise "low tension wires were short-circuited or broken by the weight of the snow and by telephone and telegraph wires which fell across them." One after another, like dominoes, all across the country, electricity, telephone and telegraph poles snapped and toppled, bringing down others adjacent to them. Leaving acres of fallen poles and broken, curling, tangled wires, some blocking roads.

Radio Éireann was knocked out of service when the Athlone transmitter was brought down. In time of crisis the national radio system was more important than ever, linking worried and frightened people together, giving comfort through information and verbal communication. When large ESB poles were felled at Mullingar, much of the midlands was blacked out, leaving people to rely on paraffin lamps and candles, which were also in short supply nationally.

At the same time the Post Office reported: "The entire telephone trunk line is again badly disrupted . . . Communications are in chaos."[14] It was impossible to telephone Athlone, Clonmel, Claremorris, Ballina, Limerick, Kilkenny, Longford, Roscommon, Tipperary, Thurles, Shannon Airport, Port Laoise, Ennis, Cavan, Blessington . . . and so on. Almost the whole of Ireland was disconnected and disrupted.

Within Dublin "thousands of telephone subscribers whose instruments have been out of order since 2nd February have now been joined in isolation." Once again, hospitals, doctors, fire brigades, the Garda Síochána and ambulance services could not be contacted in emergencies.

Finally, the Government and Department of Defence agreed to lend a small helping hand. It was announced that "all Post Office engineering staffs, assisted by detachments from the Army Corps of Signals," were setting up skeleton services on the main telephone and telegraph lines in the hope of reconnecting emergency services. With the blizzard still at high pitch, ESB and telephone repair crews found themselves working under slow and dangerous conditions.

CIE supervisors grew fitful as the morning wore on. They had given the go-ahead for early bus and lorry departures on the assumption that the "storm" would pass by mid-morning. Instead it had worsened, becoming a blizzard beyond description. Now its drivers, vehicles and passengers were "out there" somewhere, unaccounted for, on their own. In the absence of communication with different counties and terminals, they could only speculate about what might be occurring.

When a few of the closer provincial buses did roll into Dublin, drivers and conductors gave grim accounts to their supervisors of conditions on the road. In mid-morning at Aston Quay, Joseph Nicholson, a conductor who had just arrived from Tullow, Co. Carlow, gave a dramatic account of the bus having to battle the blizzard every mile of the way, repeatedly becoming stuck in drifts and "having to dig in the snow for three hours" by asking every strong man aboard the bus to do his part.

Such accounts made supervisors wonder what conditions must be like in the barren midlands, the wilds of Connemara, and the Wicklow uplands. Over the next hours and days they would keep a list of buses marked "late," "missing," or "lost."

By late morning many schools had dismissed their pupils and closed. Teachers too were worried about getting back home. A number of shopkeepers had sent their staff home early. Factory managers were contemplating letting workers off around mid-afternoon. Approaching midday, office workers in Dublin were glued to their windows, wondering whether to head for lunch or for home. Their chances were better in trying to catch an early bus or tram, with services now so disrupted that schedules were meaningless. And every hour fewer were running.

Keith Collie's father made his decision, clearing his desk, grabbing his coat and hat, and heading straight for the railway station:

> He decided to come home from his business in Dublin at lunchtime, as the city had come to a halt under a thick white blanket and nothing was travelling on the roads. He walked to Harcourt Street station, got the train to Carrickmines and somehow crossed the golf links and Russell's Hill to our home. That was over two miles and by then the snow was probably eight feet deep in drifts.[15]

This would have been about the time that Deputies O'Neill and Murphy, who had left the sunny "riviera" city of Cork earlier that morning, had a rude confrontation with King Winter. A short while after leaving Cork they met some high winds and blowing snow, but nothing to worry them. Then, near Cahir, Co. Tipperary, "they encountered the full force of a terrific blizzard," reported the *Evening Herald*, "and at that point almost despaired of reaching the capital."[16] Throwing their car into low gear, they moved ahead with great caution. Meanwhile their colleague Deputy McGrath, who had left tranquil Cork at about the same time, was peering out the train window at a sweeping white hurricane. The train was rolling slowly, halting at many points, forging forward again. By now the journey was less than half covered but had taken twice the time.

James Gallagher had not returned with his sack of turf from a neighbour's house. Nor had the Galway bus arrived in Dublin. Nothing had been heard from CIE's dozen cattle lorries sent out early in the morning. Milkmen and breadmen failed to show up at their delivery destinations. By early afternoon some morning milkmen, their vehicles stuck in the snow, were seen "carrying churns of milk on their backs" in an effort to reach customers. Ambulance-drivers too were doing their best under the worst conditions. With telephone lines down, family and friends of the sick had to try to reach the ambulance service on foot to plead for assistance. Sometimes they made it only part of the way. In one case an "ambulance taking a patient to the County Home in Rathdrum could not complete its journey, and the patient had to be carried in a chair" through the blizzard the rest of the way.[17]

————

Amidst the havoc the *Irish Press* got a bright idea. That afternoon it would try to send out a reporter and photographer not only to get a riveting story of the monster blizzard but also to deliver survival food to the orphans and nuns at Glencree. The paper called it a "relief party." The key to success, it was confident, was two tough vehicles, a Jeep and a tractor, both to be handled by expert drivers. In the comfort of the editorial office the scheme seemed feasible.

The newspaper selected two of its best, a reporter identified only as J.B. and his photographer, Sam Hughes. They would depart daringly—some surely would have said foolishly—in the early afternoon, at the storm's peak. Nonetheless their driver, Tom Donnelly, assured them that his four-wheel-drive Jeep could scale Mount Everest if necessary. After a full lunch they loaded the vehicles with provisions, and the four-man expedition ploughed its way out of Dublin, headed towards the highlands of Co. Wicklow:

> We left Dublin shortly after mid-day, when the blizzard was at its height. Already, motor transport was in difficulties and the roads deep in snow. Gardaí told us that Glasnamuller was completely cut off, and people there were in distress. Our party was to try and get through with supplies of canned meat, macaroni, tomato soup, sausages and flake-meal.[18]

Seventeen-year-old Eddie McGrane was already in the Wicklow Mountains and wishing he weren't. He and a few pals, all enthusiastic members of An

Óige, had got themselves into a bad predicament on foot. All due to their youthful exuberance and naïveté. They had been on an outing for several days, hiking around, feeling challenged by rugged mountain terrain, staying at any shelter they came across. But hardly equipped to survive a blizzard:

> We were walking, about eight miles—and we walked *through* the blizzard. Snowing and snowing! We'd always have some food with us, but we hadn't got the proper equipment. Wearing light boots, and we didn't have pull-ups ... Some had short pants! And scarves around our face. And we were going into snowdrifts—and the snow was up to your chest. Oh, it *was!* And we were walking on *top* of the snow. I can actually see it now. Oh, we were foolish, we were *stupid!* There was danger—absolutely.

Late in the afternoon he shouted to his mates that he had to find a place to sit down for a moment: his feet felt raw, and blood was seeping through his boots. He had just bought a new pair—for a great low price—only to find out now that "they weren't real leather—I'd been *robbed* at the boot shop." The nails had punctured through and cut into his feet, "and my feet were bloody ... They had to carry me."

Far to the west, about forty miles outside Ballina, Seán Lang, a strong young man in his twenties employed by CIE, was having his problems. The day before the blizzard he and a workmate had been sent into the country to repair a lorry with a broken axle. "I was sent out in the back of an open van with the driver and axle for a lorry that was broken down. It was going to be a tough job out on the open road." Especially without warm clothing and gloves. "We brought a tarpaulin with us to put over the front of the lorry so we could get at the front axle" in case of snow. On Tuesday morning, with the worst of the storm approaching their area, they struggled to hold the tarpaulin above them against the wind as they worked at replacing the axle. They had just completed the job when, "the next thing, the *big* snow came down, and because of the wind the snow was on the road and between the ditches." With the snow quickly covering the road, they tossed their tools into the van and headed for Ballina, hoping to make it before nightfall.

Back at CIE head office in Dublin, with some telephone lines temporarily hooked up again, troubling bulletins were steadily coming in from around the country: "Near Newry, nine buses abandoned on roads ... Goods trains held up in snowdrifts ... One bus at Dromintee buried in seven-foot drift ... Railway wagons derailed ... Cattle lorries' whereabouts unknown ... Lorries and buses abandoned and lying half-buried ... Buses bound for the midlands snowed up ... Mullingar and other districts in the worst storm belt now isolated, roads blocked ... Missing, missing, missing ... No information, no information."

J.B. and Sam Hughes were making steady progress. At a very slow pace, however. But they expressed no discouragement, at least to one another. Then, unexpected problems began occurring:

> The tractor fell out at Cabinteely when the blizzard whirling in the unprotected driver's face forced him to give in. The food was loaded into the Jeep in a wild snowstorm. With Sam and myself aboard, Tom pointed our snub nose up into the wilderness of driving snow. Visibility was only ten feet at the most. Windscreen wipers were not capable of dealing with the snow which plastered itself in thick cakes on the glass before our eyes.
>
> And the road itself had disappeared. Our only guides were the tops of the hedges on both sides—and they were fast disappearing under the gathering drifts. The hill was growing steeper.[19]

Back in Dublin, life was moving sluggishly as well. Many buses and trams had broken down, stalled, or were taken out of service. It was becoming clear to thousands of city-centre workers that they were not going to be able to get home that night, even if they waited in the queues for hours. They had better begin searching for overnight accommodation, as hotels and bed-and-breakfasts were filling up fast. By mid-afternoon more and more factory managers were letting workers off early. Many workers, realising the futility of trying to catch a bus or tram, began trudging homewards or in search of night shelter, often following in single file in one another's beaten-down tracks, slipping and falling along the way. Younger workers bravely tramped through the snow, delighted to be off early, sometimes arm in arm, singing away. At least at first.

Dozens of young women who worked in the Urney chocolate factory in Tallaght knew they were trapped by the blizzard and decided to sleep in the village. However, "a few of the more adventurous girls employed in the factory made their way into the city on foot," reported one newspaper. At some factories it is likely that a number of employees, and certainly managers and owners who lived out in the suburbs, ended up sleeping overnight in the factory, though there is no record of this fact.

By about 3 o'clock in the afternoon, with the blizzard still in full throttle, desperate passengers aboard provincial buses that had become stuck on the road in snowdrifts were seeking shelter before nightfall. Local villagers, townsfolk and farm families sympathetically took in those marooned, providing shelter from the storm and, if possible, some food. In Co. Sligo, clobbered especially hard by the blizzard, "buses, lorries and cars were abandoned in deep snow drifts, while their occupants took refuge in nearby houses." As they came straggling along desolate country roads, "approaches to farms and dwelling houses were cleared by local men with spades and shovels" to allow them passage to safety.

——

Co. Mayo was blizzard-blasted as badly as Sligo. The Ruane family and their neighbours found themselves barricaded in by alpine snowdrifts. Roads throughout eastern Co. Mayo were snowbound by heavy drifts, leaving the marooned passengers of cars, buses and lorries both helpless and frightened. During the daylight hours of Tuesday many abandoned their vehicles and began searching for shelter. Kindly residents, including Tony Ruane's family, took in as many as they could. He saw their small figures in the distance along the road, heading towards his house, looking like wartime refugees seen on the cinema screen. Ill-clothed, weary, hungry. Struggling every foot of the way through the sea of snow. A narrow path was cleared to their door:

> Buses travelling from Ballina to Galway became engulfed in snowdrifts and had to be abandoned. The passengers, drivers and conductors had to take refuge in rural houses—and some had to stay for over two weeks! I remember there was a bus driver named Harold Lewis and a conductor, John Timlin, both from Ballina.

Welcomed into the Ruane household, the bedraggled wanderers were taken at once before the turf fire, given food and drink and assurances that they were safe. Despite having a family of eleven, the Ruanes took in every weary soul possible. Fortunately, food and fuel were not yet in short supply in the house. "Food did not pose a problem: we had a good supply of potatoes and vegetables, plenty of salted bacon home-cured, milk from the cows in the byre."

The sudden hubbub in the house fascinated the youngster. Probably a bit shy at first in the presence of strangers, he was quiet and observant, taking in all the unusual activity. "As a child I remember the strangeness of all the unfamiliar visitors, and having to dig passages out of our house through the front door" to accommodate them. The house was enlivened with new voices, laughter, harrowing accounts of the blizzard. Extra sods were placed in the grate, and the chatter was ceaseless until bedtime. As days passed, the strangers would become friends.

One can only imagine how Phillip Mount and his road-show family were enduring the mighty blizzard. Perhaps the already compacted snow and ice surrounding their flimsy vehicles actually stabilised them, preventing toppling. Though it is not known how they fared as regards damage, they survived—and the show went on. In the wake of the blizzard the "putt, putt" of the engine would be heard again, as lights flickered on and the music again wafted across the surrounding Siberian plains. By this time some of the snowdrifts were nearly the height of the loudspeaker affixed to the telephone pole. "Let it snow, let it snow, let it snow . . ."

———

Towns with local Red Cross volunteers did their best to find any sort of shelter for road refugees: church hall, barn, shop, forge—anything to protect against the wind and the blinding, mounting snow. By the later part of the afternoon there were so many stranded vehicles in some counties that there was almost a steady stream of marooned passengers into nearby towns and villages:

> There were hundreds of vehicles stuck in drifts between Longford and Newtown Forbes, three miles distant. Buses to Sligo, Westport, Ballina and Athlone were grounded near Longford and passengers desperate for shelter and accommodation. The Red Cross worked tirelessly to have people taken in by residents in private houses when all the b&bs were filling up.[20]

By this time the *Irish Press* "relief team" might have wondered if they would soon be among the marooned, as their Jeep "pitted its strength" against now nearly impenetrable snow and ice barriers—straining, clawing and climbing its way upwards with its four-wheel drive grinding and snow tyres spinning as much as gripping:

> As we bucked and plunged our way up, some of the boxes of canned meat broke loose and tins began to rattle. The Jeep was doing all it could, slowed to a grinding five miles an hour. Turning a bend, we got the weather right on our windscreen . . . It felt like a gale and howled as it heaped our struggling Jeep with snow and ice. "There is no use in trying to take a picture in this!" said Sam. The blizzard was just like a handkerchief held in from of the lens of the camera.[21]

Deputies O'Neill, Murphy and McGrath were confronting a similar white-out on their journeys to Dublin. With visibility limited to about ten yards, they could not identify exactly where they were. But by now they knew they were not going to make it to Dublin in time for the day's proceedings in Leinster House. Nothing was lost, however, for King Winter had now shut down the government. Even many members living in Dublin's suburbs were not able to make it into the city. "As might have been expected," wrote the *Evening Herald*, "the grim weather and transport difficulties had a serious effect upon attendance."[22] As it turned out, only 38 of the 138 members of the Dáil showed up. The Seanad did better, with 29 out of its 60 members present. The blizzard had prevented 131 legislators from carrying out their governmental duties. The invader had, in effect, knocked out the Irish government at the moment it was most needed.

––––

By 3:30 in the afternoon Mary Dunne found herself glancing out the front window of Mrs Moore's tailoring shop every few minutes, fretting about how she was going to make it back home at 5:30 when dismissed. Then came a nice surprise. Firstly, her sister Lily showed up; and then Mrs Moore, a real stickler about punctuality, showed heart:

> Lily came to see me on the job, as a surprise. It was *bitter* cold, so Mrs Moore let me go home at about four o'clock. And I could *barely* hold the door open for her, with the wind. There was no *let-up* with it! So, instead of walking home we said, "Let's get the bus"—a bad move, 'cause the queue was that long in Earl Street. So we said we'll wait a while.
>
> So we went up a little street beside Downes's bakery. There was a side-show, a snake charmer, with live snakes. So we went in, one shilling entry. That was Lily's Confirmation money. It was very *warm* in there. We touched the snakes and were very surprised at them being so dry, not slippery at all.

They had happened upon "Ty-Ana" and her mighty pythons. The warmth alone was worth the price of admission. But time was passing, and their mother a worrier. They returned to the queue and waited it out, talking of their snake experience. It helped pass the time:

> Eventually we got the bus home. It slithered and slid all along the way to O'Connell Street, Abbey Street, Amiens Street and finally to North Strand Road. By this time it was about half six—my poor mother was in bits!

With the late afternoon light fading, J.B. and Sam Hughes knew they were fighting a losing battle against the elements, their enthusiasm drained:

> Our jeep ploughed its way up before burying its nose in an impassable snowdrift. We sat and talked gloomily. This one finished us. We gave up the fight. The shovels dug us out. The run back to town was a parade of snowbound, abandoned cars against a disappearing landscape.[23]

They may have stopped along the way to assist a few stranded motorists with their shovels, exchange a few minutes of chat; but they could hardly help everyone. They could do no more than wave sympathetically as they rolled past.

––––

Dusk, and the spectre of nightfall, brought fear. On roads throughout the country countless passengers in cars, buses and lorries found themselves marooned and clearly beyond help that day—and night. By 5 o'clock the blizzard had been raging unremittingly for eighteen to twenty hours in most parts of the country. Stranded victims in the white wilderness felt their apprehension growing as darkness descended over the landscape. They feared facing the night without shelter, warmth, food, water—and the possibility of being buried by the drifting snow. Legitimate fears.

By late in the day, some had been lucky. Seán Lang and his CIE mate made it into Ballina just before dark, where a kindly woman put them up for two nights, offering dinner, a turf fire, and a comfortable bed. Eddie McGrane and his fellow-hikers found shelter as well with a local family. Most of CIE's cattle lorry drivers who had become stuck in drifts had managed to walk to safety, leaving the beasts packed together to endure the blizzard.

A good many marooned road passengers were fortunate to reach a town, village or farmstead before dark, where they found safe accommodation. In most communities, when small local hotels and B&Bs filled, residents gladly took in the rest, as a simple humanitarian act. When a packed double-decker bus became snowbound near Stepaside, all the passengers were taken into nearby houses for the night, while the driver and conductor were accommodated in the local Garda station. This charitable spirit typified almost every country community.

There were, however, a number of instances, disclosed in the following days and weeks, in some towns and villages where greedy hotel-owners and B&B proprietors—even ordinary home-owners—exploited the desperation of blizzard victims:

> Some unscrupulous people tried to make money out of some unfortunate passengers and charged people 10 shillings per night to sit in an upright chair in a room without a fire. At that time the charge for a B&B was seven shillings and sixpence.[24]

Refugees from the road, of course, often had no choice but to pay such exorbitant fees simply to be put in a room out of harm from the blizzard's reach. Many were so weary and traumatised from their ordeal of trekking miles to safety through the storm that they were probably glad to pay such an inflated charge. As they saw it, it was for *survival*. However, in later years it would be remembered by local people as shameful.

By 6 p.m. most vehicles stuck on snowbound roads were destined to remain there for the night. Some for weeks.

Along many roads, when the first bus or lorry had become trapped in a drift, it then blocked others coming up behind, so forming a chain of stalled vehicles and creating a small community of marooned passengers, who at least found some comfort in their shared crisis. Most frightened were those caught out on the open road alone, with darkness looming. Within the first few hours of being halted, a vehicle could become half-buried by the gale-driven wind, piling drifting snow higher and higher. Buses could soon become covered to the bottom of their windows. From that point passengers trapped inside had to watch it ominously climb higher. No passengers dared set out on foot after darkness fell.

Bus drivers and conductors—though hardly trained for such blizzard duty—did their best to comfort their wards. The elderly and children fared worst. Before long a car or lorry became nearly as cold inside as the temperature outside. Inside buses the passengers collectively generated body warmth—the more the better. Where motorists were stranded alongside buses they could pile into the bus as well, increasing the passenger population and creating additional warmth, and feeling of security. At least they were out of the cutting wind. People shared the little they might have: sandwiches, biscuits, apples, raisins.

Everyone longed for a cup of hot tea, or a cigarette or puff of a pipe.

Enveloped by blackness, they huddled close to one another, the wind screaming, hissing through every door and crevice, as if trying to reach them. Rocking their vehicle with unnerving constancy, all the while everyone wondering how high it was drifting up around them as the night wore on. On some buses the passengers sang hymns. Mothers hummed lullabies to children. Women fingered their beads, some murmuring the rosary aloud. Many sat mute. Those who were able to drift into sleep were envied.

How many wondered, "Could a bus actually become *buried* beneath snow?" A question that would be answered by next morning.

———

In Dublin, scores of workers marooned in the city overnight, unable to get transport home, were making the best of it. By about 8 o'clock every hotel and B&B would be filled. Red Cross members were scouring the city for temporary shelters to accommodate those still stranded, and many charitable home-owners began taking in complete strangers. No-one went hungry, and restaurants and fish-and-chip shops were crammed to capacity.

Although the blizzard was still blowing hard, many workmates, stuck together in their predicament, decided to brave "going out on the town." Little mobs of men and women, walking quickly, with heads bowed against the wind and stinging flakes, were seen along O'Connell Street, some seemingly in festive spirit, laughing and joking. Pubs, from the rough locals along the quays to the elite watering-holes of the suburbs, were packed shoulder to shoulder. Warmed by the stuffed bodies.

Cinemas were the most desired destination of thousands. Hordes of city-stranded residents from Malahide, Finglas, Tallaght, Blessington, Enniskerry and everywhere else outside the city were mad to get into any cinema for its warmth and comfort. Under the circumstances, funny films were the biggest attraction. At city-centre cinemas every showing played to a packed audience. By good fortune, on that fateful day there were some wonderfully humorous, outright hilarious films. After their day's ordeal, patrons had never been more appreciative of a whimsical or plain crazy film. Two favourites that night were *Monsieur Beauclaire* at the Savoy, starring Bob Hope and Joan Caulfield, and the antics of Abbot and Costello in *Time of Their Lives* at the Theatre Royal. Others preferred the Queen's Theatre in Pearse Street, which was presenting a performance described as "a colourful, gay and carefree show in 16 sparkling scenes." Its title: *Keeping Warm*.

At 7:40 p.m. the Dublin transmitter operating on the Athlone wavelength was temporarily repaired and kicked back on, allowing Radio Éireann to return to the air. For those who could receive it it was immediately comforting, a connection with the outside world.

Many lights were still on at CIE head office, and would remain so throughout the night. Supervisors and senior staff were on around-the-clock crisis duty. They had an unknown number of what were now being called "phantom" buses, "missing," "stranded," "lost," around the country. Occupied by uncounted hundreds of marooned, surely frightened, passengers, many of them elderly and children. Some perhaps ill. And what about those who had disembarked to trek through the blizzard in search of shelter?

The garage superintendent at Broadstone, M. Mohan, and his colleagues found themselves in an unprecedented, previously unimaginable, emergency situation. Suddenly responsible not only for the welfare of CIE's passengers but for their *survival*. Scattered across the entire country. The information they had to work with was extremely sketchy, and unverified for the most part. Rumours were now flying about wildly. It was impossible to sort one from the other. As telephone and telegraph lines were repaired, more information trickled in, but most of it was superficial and fragmented. There were few detailed, substantiated accounts from their staff in the field.

A number of veteran CIE supervisors had experienced bad snowstorms in past years, going back to the difficult winter of 1917 and a few in the 1930s, but nothing remotely of the scale and severity of what confronted them on the night of 24/25 February 1947. There was nothing in CIE's training that prepared authorities, drivers or conductors for fighting against blizzards and for saving lives. They were a transport service, not a rescue organisation. But on this night, and over the coming days, they would have to assume that role:

> c.i.e. headquarters were [eventually] well informed . . . Officials of all departments were in the front lines on rail and road in the gallant response to the call of the wild blizzard. c.i.e. men had to drive and dig through the snow and ice hurled at them . . . through a blinding snowstorm. They risked being marooned in "no man's land," miles from town or village, and finding themselves in drifts of snow of up to ten feet deep.[25]

They would not hesitate to place their own welfare at risk.

By 8:30 p.m. Mohan and his fellow-superintendents were organising rescue squads to despatch towards known trouble spots with stranded vehicles. Men were selected according to experience, judgement, strength, and stamina. Those who were unflinching in their duty. Many were eagerly volunteering. Some had trudged from home through heavy snow from distant parts of Dublin to offer their services for duty during days long to be remembered as cie's finest hours.

The rescue squads, generally numbering twenty to thirty men, were equipped with shovels, pickaxes, pneumatic drills, chains, planks, sand, and torches, as well as rations of food and water for several days. Rudimentary medical supplies were included. At head office there was the feel of a military operation under way, a rush of adrenalin and undeniable excitement about the challenge. All rescuers were frankly advised of the risks they were facing. They would hit the road in cie lorries, buses, and staff cars. And might well end up on foot, like throngs of other marooned victims of the blizzard.

By great good fortune, cie had recently acquired two aec Matadors, big eight-ton diesel-engine lorries, which were equipped with a large scraper that could "charge the drifts, bull-like . . . at anything up to thirty m.p.h."[26] They would lead the assault on snow and ice-bound roads. If the behemoths became temporarily bogged down, a small brigade of men with shovels and picks would hop off accompanying vehicles to hack away furiously to free the Matadors. At least, that was the idea.

It was known that there were serious log-jams of cie and private vehicles throughout the midlands and west. But superintendents had to realistically identify regional rescue targets that could be *reached*, especially in Cos. Dublin and Wicklow, where their chances of success were highest. One particular jam was pinpointed and verified by reliable information. It was in the Port Laoise area, estimated to involve *at least* forty-five vehicles, a conglomeration of cars, buses, and lorries, all stuck along a highly drifted stretch of road. Eight of the vehicles were thought to be buses carrying a great many passengers. Mohan, capable and respected, was put in command of this rescue mission. He wanted to get his forces on the road without delay, within the next hours. He had no intention of waiting till daylight. It would be a midnight rescue operation.

As CIE rescue crews were preparing to leave Dublin, a few bus-drivers and conductors were still straggling in. Close to 9:15 p.m. the bus from Galway rolled into the depot after its thirteen-hour journey. Passengers were fatigued, visibly relieved. A few took a minute to tell a reporter of their cross-country ordeal, how they had democratically voted at Loughrea to proceed across the blizzarded midlands. How the driver had managed to hold the wheel to fight the wind. He apparently gave no public statement when he climbed down but surely met CIE officials to brief them on conditions "out there."

Shortly thereafter the Cork–Dublin train lumbered into the station, caked with ice and snow, looking like the Trans-Siberian Railway. Among the passengers wearily stepping down was Patrick McGrath, the Fianna Fáil deputy who had left Cork that morning in spring-like weather. He had "tried his luck by train," reported the *Evening Herald,* and "only finally reached Dublin more than twelve hours later," the longest train journey of his life, he said. At several points it was questionable whether he would make it at all. In any case he arrived safe, in good spirits, but tired. There is no record of when, or if, his colleagues, Deputies O'Neill and Murphy, who had set out by car, reached the capital that day.

James Gallagher had still not returned home with the sack of turf. The worst was now suspected.

———

By this time Mohan's squad, headed by their Matadors, were barging their way along the snow-packed roads south of Dublin, headed for the Port Laoise area. In the early going, as the Matadors' large scoops cleared the way for those behind, the men periodically halted to assist stuck motorists. During the first hour and a half, "in the course of clearing the road, they set 17 stranded private cars on their way again," it was reported. However, taking the time to free cars, and graciously accept the praise heaped upon them, was jeopardising their primary mission. Mohan made the difficult decision to thrust onwards towards Port Laoise without any further delays.

Shortly before 10 o'clock the worst of the blizzard ceased in most eastern parts of the country. It had raged for nearly twenty-six hours.

Though the heavy snowfall lightened in their area and winds diminished from gale force, they remained strong enough to cause continued troublesome drifting. The CIE men, heartened by the break in the blizzard, forged ahead with greater confidence than ever, as they could now see the road far better by the illumination of their vehicles' headlamps. Finally, "as they were approaching the Heath, near Maryboro [Port Laoise]," they saw in their headlamps the monumental cause of the log-jam, more imposing than they had imagined: "a stretch of snowbound road over three miles long."[27]

The Matadors began charging the drift repeatedly in a back-and-forth motion, as men alongside with shovels and picks and strong backs did their part. Working relentlessly, perspiring in the frigid night air, they made steady progress. Sometimes, when a Matador bulled its way forward it might clear a long patch of snow. Other times it could stall after ten or twenty yards. Because snowdrifts were often crystallised, frozen into solid ice in sections, it was impossible to know what one faced with each forward thrust. Nor was it possible to know whether the marooned passengers on the other side of the great barrier knew that their rescuers were working their way towards them, either by hearing their engines or seeing the lights of their vehicles.

It was well after midnight when the rescue squad broke through the last snowdrift, greeted with loud cheers. But their work was far from over. They quickly found that every vehicle, some more than half buried, now had to be shovelled free. After this was accomplished they took a count and recorded that they had "reached eight stranded buses, eight c.i.e. lorries and 31 private cars, all stuck in the vicinity of the Heath."[28] Then they checked on everyone's physical condition, identifying no serious injuries. But quite a few cases of shattered nerves.

No-one thought to count the total number of rescued passengers aboard those vehicles for the historical record. A reasonable estimate would be in the range of 200 to 240 people. Additionally, on the return trip "seventy passengers who had made their way to Maryboro [earlier] on foot were collected there" and taken back to Dublin. Bringing the total closer to 300 people retrieved. A good night's work for the cie men. Indeed:

> "Remember '47" will be the rallying cry for many years hence of c.i.e. men who had to drive and dig through snow and ice![29]

Some time after 2 a.m. Mohan gave his troops the order to "move out!" Thus began a triumphant return to Dublin:

> All the vehicles were released, then the ten lorries (including two Matadors), eight buses and thirty-one cars set off for Dublin in a convoy carefully controlled by the c.i.e. garage superintendent who was in charge of the rescue work.[30]

On the return trip they encountered patches of road drifted over again, but these were easily cleared by the Matadors and the weary men. For all, it was a satisfying trip home.

During the hours of rescue another most peculiar weather aberration occurred, another meteorological twist in the already bizarre winter weather. During the last few hours of the blizzard the temperature had remained a fairly constant 27 to 28 degrees Fahrenheit (2.5°c). When the major part of the storm subsided at about 10 p.m. on Tuesday the skies became clearer. But instead of the temperature dropping lower during the later night hours, the opposite happened. The *Irish Press* called it "the strangest phenomenon of the blizzard":

> As the blizzard ended shortly before 10 p.m., a warm front which had emanated from the Azores passed over Ireland, causing an immediate thaw. By midnight, the temperature had risen to 37 degrees and remained high until 5 o'clock the next morning, at one stage reaching 38 degrees.
>
> At 6 a.m., however, on Wednesday, the warm front passed over Scotland and in the district of the Baltic, with the resultant drop in temperatures.[31]

Slipping below freezing again.

Most Irish people had slept right through the "heat wave" that had visited their country overnight. Only the next day did they read about it in the papers, doubtless shaking their heads once again over nature's fickleness. In a classic understatement the *Irish Times* concluded: "The weather has ceased to be logical."

Dublin's weather experts were more flummoxed than ever. They had now missed the fourth, and worst, "surprise" blizzard, followed immediately by a ten-degree temperature surge, then dropping quickly again below freezing. An atmospheric roller-coaster that would leave any sane meteorologist or forecaster exasperated. The next day, one of Dublin's most prominent weather experts would issue a personal prediction:

> It was another "freak day." I do not remember anything like it. I think I will give up trying to forecast what the weather will be.[32]

WEDNESDAY 26 FEBRUARY

At 6:20 on Wednesday morning the curious CIE rescue convoy, comprising assorted vehicles and passengers, pulled into Dublin. A few reporters who had got wind of the story were on hand to get the details. Neither marooned passengers nor exhausted rescuers were in much mood to talk to the press after their long and arduous ordeal: hunger drove them straight to breakfast. After which, in a surprise footnote to the whole episode, "some of the rescue squad, having had breakfast, volunteered for further urgent duty in releasing snowbound buses elsewhere."[33]

By morning, everyone was eager to get their hands on a newspaper to see how bad the blizzard had been in other parts of the country. Had there been any deaths? Were victims still marooned and lost? For the past thirty-six hours editors and reporters had been scrambling to piece together the information they had been able to gather, to organise it into a coherent "big picture" of the whole country. With telecommunications down, their material was fragmentary and difficult to verify, and they drew upon whatever reliable sources were available to them. The *Irish Independent* reported:

> When hopes were beginning to be entertained that the end of the weeks of Arctic weather was at last in sight, Dublin and the rest of the country was experiencing a fierce blizzard which raged . . . the heaviest snowfall yet leaving widespread havoc.[34]

Considering it by far the "worst" yet, the *Irish Times* sought to give readers a condensed portrait of the storm's visit:

> Blacked-out towns and villages, main roads impassable, passenger bus service suspended, homes without food and fuel, turf bogs under six feet of snow—this is the general picture of desolation left by Tuesday's great blizzard.[35]

In the great blizzard's wake, a mood of despondency hung over the country. People felt defeated, hopeless against nature. In a bleak editorial headed "On nothing," the *Irish Press* wrote gravely and with an uncharacteristic sense of dejection:

> "Now is the winter of our discontent . . ." One is very sure about the discontent—nature is now only a graven image of herself. The days are steely; the things we love are petrified. The east is purple cold. There is a skin of snow on the ground; only once in three weeks have we seen the stars.[36]

―――

Digging out began at dawn. People's first task was to dig their way out of their own house, as many had snow piled high against their doors. The fortunate ones began to extricate themselves immediately, "with shovels they had wisely brought indoors when the snow started." Others, without vision or shovels, had to wait for outside help. Many would be trapped indoors for days, some for weeks.

In Dublin, hefty dockers wielded their coal shovels to free people and clear shopkeepers' doors for business. Dublin Corporation sent out its full force of men with shovels, sand and straw to begin the massive job of trying to clear the city's streets and pavements.

Even the army finally responded. Several detachments were ordered into action to shovel snow and break up mounds of ice, load it into lorries, and take it down to the Liffey to be dumped into the river. Early on Wednesday morning 22-year-old James O'Dwyer heard a bit of hubbub outside his house in Thomas Street in the Liberties. Peering out his window, he saw a party of soldiers marching to duty, armed not with rifles but with shovels, picks, and pneumatic drills. He and a few pals dashed out to follow them. "Oh, they brought the army fellas out! With jack-hammers and picks to break up the ice." Something unusual to watch.

When the soldiers tramped past John Gallagher's home in the Coombe his mother shouted, "The army is out! The army is cleaning up the streets!" He and other children clambered outside to watch the show. "It was a bit of excitement, you know . . . a bit of glamour about the army." It gave people something to watch, to talk about.

Some army officers saw it quite differently. Eddie McGrane's brother-in-law was a colonel in the army and disagreed vehemently with the decision to use soldiers for such mundane, demeaning duty:

> He objected *strongly* to the army being used to clear off the snow, even outside Government Buildings. They were *soldiers*—they weren't *cleaners*. Oh, he was emphatic about that.

Might the resistance of some of the army's top brass have been a factor in the Government's long reluctance to call out soldiers to assist citizens during the winter crisis?

Country people were left on their own to dig out. They awoke to a smothered landscape, more dramatically transformed than before. "Driven by persistent gales . . . the entire island became a vast ashen wasteland."[37] In Co. Carlow, Jim Nolan and his neighbours were stunned on looking out to see only the "tops of the trees" exposed.[38] Some towns and villages had been visually reduced to clusters of rooftops and chimneys. The *Irish Times* reported that not only had cars, buses and houses been lost beneath snowdrifts but even an entire village:

> The hamlet of Moneystown at Roundwood has been "lost" in the snow. It is now three weeks since there has been any news from its inhabitants. County Council workers who tried to "find" the village had to abandon their attempts to cut their way through, and it is not known how people are faring.[39]

Ireland had been submerged in an ocean of snow, leaving a world of white that was simply fantastical. To James Clarke, "it just changed the whole atmosphere."[40] Around Jim Maloney's parents' farm in Co. Galway, "oh, it was over your *head* . . . It was that heavy from the drifting, and you'd only see that much of a telephone pole." Because of the cycle of sub-freezing temperatures, brief surface thawing, then refreezing, many snow surfaces had frozen hard, allowing people to walk atop it, or burrow beneath in tunnels. Both were strange sensations.

After barely making it home from school on the day of the blizzard, Keith Collie awoke in his house in Ballycorus the next morning to find a frozen snow-world outside:

> The snow had a hard crust and we would walk on it. Yes, the snow was over the hedges and gates, and only the tops of trees stood out . . . Higher up in the hills the snow covered the telephone poles.[41]

One story seemed to top another. In Co. Sligo, particularly hard hit by the blizzard, people found themselves digging out for survival's sake, to clear air passages for their houses and excavate tunnels in which to move about. Snow tunnels were always dangerous, especially for children, because they could so easily collapse. With Sligo now completely isolated, there was no outside help. Thomas Crosby, a resident of the town, looked out over a landscape now unfamiliar. "Driven by a penetrating east wind, it drifted . . . and the landscape assumed the appearance of a vast white desert."[42] Trees and telephone and power lines simply "disappeared under the massive burden of snow." He and other residents found on Wednesday that in the immediate aftermath of the blizzard they were actually able to "walk without restriction over submerged trees, pylons and buildings." Hugh McCormick vouches that when he watched road gangs trying to clear the snow with shovels, some of the men, heating up, "could hang their coats on the telephone wires."[43] And from Co. Leitrim, where some drifts climbed high on poles, came the story of Jackie Doherty of Kiscarbon, who "found his way home by clambering up a drift and using the telegraph wire to guide him and maintain his balance."[44]

Many were the stories that would beggar belief in later years for those who had not lived through the winter of 1946/47. Yet verified at the time by the most reliable citizens.

———

At first, digging out could seem hopeless. "As bulldozers weren't part of the scene then," says Jim Maloney, "dwellings and farms were cleared by men with shovels and spades." Feet and yards at a time. Throughout his county of Galway, every physically fit man and lad was expected to step forward and grab a shovel:

Every able-bodied man who had a shovel was employed by the local authority, to go out and shovel snow. In other words, if you could stand up and use a shovel, it didn't matter if you were fourteen years of age or ninety, you were employed. Oh, everyone wanted to do their bit. You did your own house, but then you did the main roads.

In many towns, once the roads were cleared sufficiently for people to move about they descended on the local provision shops, and a flurry of panic-buying broke out. As most shops were already low on commodities, it didn't take long to empty their shelves. Hunger and fear could drive some people to behaviour that was not characteristic of their best nature. Conversely, crisis also brought out the best in many people, who looked after the community's needy by sharing food and fuel.

In Sligo and Westport and many other towns, deliveries of bread, milk, groceries, newspapers and other basic commodities were completely cut off when road and railway transport were paralysed. In Co. Donegal, Brian Kelly saw how men in the local pubs grew agitated over "no whiskey coming in!" Just when they craved it most. And pipe tobacco was running out as well. A genuine crisis.

All through Wednesday morning, missing persons were reported to the authorities in many counties. Altogether there were dozens. Most were men who had left their home to go to a nearby town, a neighbour's house, or out to get turf or logs. Others were out searching for imperilled animals. The early hope was that they had found shelter along the way. However, with telephone lines down it was not possible to contact neighbours to verify this. James Gallagher was still missing. In Aghafad, Carrickmacross, another farmer, 63-year-old Edward Walshe, had left for Ardee but had not returned home. Even under the best weather conditions the walk could be a strenuous one. In inclement weather he would logically stay at a neighbour's house. His son hoped he had done so this time. Martin Delaney of Tubbrit, near Moate, Co. Westmeath, lived alone, so there had been no-one to miss him at first. It seemed that little was known about him, as newspapers referred to him simply as "an aged man." In snow-packed Co. Sligo at least three men were reported missing.

In Co. Roscommon, Johnny Gormley, a well-liked postman, was caught out on his bicycle in the teeth of the blizzard in a rugged valley area. Suffering from hypothermia, fatigue, and growing fear, he eventually collapsed in the snow. By a stroke of good luck a local farmer out searching for his sheep came across his fallen form and brought him to his house, where he recovered.[45] It was a very close shave; but the story of his discovery and recovery would give hope to others with relatives still missing.

In Dublin, as Corporation men and soldiers were shovelling and picking away at the ice mounds, the awful racket of their chattering pneumatic drills sounding like machine-gun fire, there was a quiet announcement from the Royal City of Dublin Hospital in Baggot Street. Eleven-year-old James Naylor had died from the injuries he suffered during the blizzard when struck by a lorry at Baggot Street Bridge. He had held on, unconscious, for twenty-four hours.

Throughout the morning Dublin's transport, telecommunications and electricity authorities were hard at work assessing damage and organising repair plans. Many had spent the entire night on the job. By the time the CIE rescue convoy had pulled in from Co. Wicklow at 6:20 a.m. other rescue units had been formed and despatched. One of these, working in the Dunlavin area, quickly discovered "23 passengers who had been trapped in their snowbound bus overnight." Cold and distressed, but unharmed, they were immediately brought back to Dublin. For the next ten days CIE teams would be sent out from Dublin to "rescue buses which had 'disappeared' in the blizzard with passengers and crews."[46] The anxiety and worry increasing with the passing of each day.

No longer were buses listed as "late." Only "missing" or "lost."

Entire trains were now missing as well. Somewhere "out there," between departure and arrival points. On the track or off. Because of the lack of communication, no-one knew. As one CIE man put it, "'ghost train' might be a better description of it, for it was difficult to ascertain its whereabouts."[47] In one instance, after a train was snowed up in a ten-foot drift at Carrick-on-Shannon, a snow-plough was sent from Dublin to cleave a way for it. But six to twelve feet of crystallised snow proved too much for it, and "a small army of railwaymen with shovels and picks had to finally clear the track." Meanwhile another snow-plough that was clearing the railway from Dublin became stuck near Kilfree Junction, Co. Sligo, in a massive drift.

As CIE crews were on the hunt for missing buses and trains, it was reported that "five milk lorries belonging to one Dublin firm are missing in snow-bound country areas." There were no rescue forces to come to their aid. It was hoped that the drivers had found shelter. Three lorries from another milk firm carrying 1,500 gallons of milk had also disappeared. One milkman who made it back into the city told of "snow drifts of up to ten feet" not far from the centre of Dublin. All the while, the milk was freezing in cans and bottles.

A similar number of bread vans was now missing as well.

By mid-morning the ESB and Post Office had only a sketchy knowledge of damage to their systems. It was simply reported that communications were in a shambles, "full storm havoc not yet known."[48] Every available repairman was on duty, with all Post Office engineering workers, assisted by a detachment from the Signals Corps, kept busy setting up skeleton services. As before, hospitals, doctors, fire brigades, the Garda Síochána and other emergency services received priority.

———

About midday on Wednesday "the sun shone for the first time in forty-eight hours, breaking through dark snow-filled clouds, causing a slight thaw." Which meant the night would bring more freezing temperatures and another ice-over.

Throughout Ireland, in cities and countryside, the sight of the sun brought people outdoors. In a crystallised world the burst of bright sunshine created an intense glare from shiny surfaces, causing visual discomfort to many. "That sunshine, that was terrible hard on the eyes," recalls Jim Maloney, "because the sunshine was reflecting back up from the ice and snow." It was an age in which not many people in Ireland owned sunglasses. It posed a particular problem for farmers having to go in search of their animals, for road-clearing crews and rescue squads, for repairmen. But no-one was heard complaining.

The sun's visit, though brief, was enough to revive the *Irish Press* "relief mission" to reach hungry Wicklow families and refugee children. Undaunted by the previous day's travails, J.B. and his photographer, Sam Hughes, were eager to have another go at it. They couldn't have known how much worse the conditions had become after the quick thaw and immediate overnight freeze. Cheered by sunny skies and a temperature now a notch above freezing, they mounted their Jeep, with Tom Donnelly again at the wheel, and rumbled out of Dublin, fuelled by fresh optimism:

> At 2 p.m. we re-loaded the Jeep with canned meat, luncheon sausage, flake meal, macaroni and all the rest. Up on the mountains where we were going, people in the highest village in Ireland [Roundwood] were isolated and hungry. There was a blue sky overhead and no blizzards. We piled in the back of the Jeep on top of sacks and boxes, gripped our shovels hopefully, and shoved off.[49]

Before long they were passing cars, lorries and buses that had been stranded overnight, hopefully awaiting assistance from CIE rescue crews. After exchanging a few encouraging words, they went on their way. The sunshine brought out their laughter.

In Dublin the early afternoon sunshine and slightly warmer temperatures created both beauty and danger. The deep snow and glistening ice gave the city a primaeval appearance, a natural cosmetic covering that hid its blemishes. It looked unspoilt, untarnished. St Stephen's Green and the Phoenix Park had never looked more stunning. "Oh, it's as lovely as a

Christmas card," admirers gushed.

However, as the *Irish Times* warned, "loose snow and treacherous ice was setting traps for unwary pedestrians." Because of the thaw-freeze cycle, huge dangling icicles that glittered radiantly in the sun were a sight to behold—but dangerous to walk beneath, as some pedestrians found out. Seán Whelan was cautious. "I saw these icicles, some quite large, hanging from the gutters," and he kept his distance. Others, quite oblivious, walked right under them, when some cracked and pierced downwards like daggers, splitting apart or sticking neatly in a snow-pile as if it were a pin-cushion. Thick layers of snow and ice on rooftops were even more dangerous for pedestrians unaware of what lurked above. Often the only warning was a sudden "crack!" or "swoosh!" as an icy avalanche slid down on unsuspecting people jostling for walking space on the pavement below. Loud roof slides could also frighten passing horses and cause them to rear up or bolt. Children, of course, delighted in plucking icicles from railings to suck.

Throughout Wednesday every newspaper in Dublin felt the pressure of gathering accurate information and piecing together the story of the worst blizzard in living memory. There was a natural competition to produce interesting, verified articles, accompanied by photographs. All newspapers were under the same constraints: telephone lines down, roads impassable, no possibility even for some staff members to get from their snowbound suburbs into the newspaper office. Newsrooms had not been in such a frenetic state since the German bombing of the North Strand in 1941. Under such conditions it was a challenge to gather, cross-check and write up coherent stories to cover every aspect of the great blizzard. They knew there was a huge public hunger for the latest news—and guaranteed massive sales.

Blizzard stories were genuinely sensational: there was no need for embellishment. Death by exposure, people lost, passengers marooned on country roads, villages isolated, food and fuel running low, animals buried alive, buses and trains missing—the news could hardly have been more dramatic. A once-in-a-lifetime story for editors and ambitious reporters. They also wanted to chronicle it accurately for the record. Some authenticated facts sounded almost too unimaginable to print, such as the *Irish Times* reports of "at least one 50 foot snowdrift" in Co. Wicklow, and "lost" villages. All newspapers were printing accounts of snowdrifts deep enough to bury several double-deck buses. Day after day, readers followed the latest news as if it were a serial film at the cinema. "What's the latest?" . . . "Did they find so-and-so?"

Newspapers jockeyed for advantage. On-the-scene coverage by reporters such as J.B., describing their battle with the blizzard, their Jeep bucking up mountain roads, had an adventurous flavour that readers liked. And it sold papers.

On Wednesday afternoon reporters were covering an emergency meeting of Dublin Corporation and city officials. The City Manager, P. J. Hernon, and his staff were under enormous pressure to act on the fuel and food crisis, to use their authority to compel the Government to finally take an active role. The blizzards had brought the greatest hardship to the poorest, most helpless people. The Government's belated actions over the previous thirty-six hours in sending out some soldiers with shovels and picks, and a handful of Signals men, was a paltry, token effort. The public's patience with Government inaction and ineptitude was nearly exhausted. Massive action was needed.

Newspapers were now using the terms "starvation" and "freezing to death," as the *Evening Herald* wrote:

> Residents of tenements in the poorer districts are entering their fifth week of the severe weather in a pitiable plight from which there is no immediate promise of relief.[50]

The poor and elderly were succumbing to hunger, cold and illness at an increasingly high rate. Only the Corporation and Government could provide relief.

Members arrived at the meeting looking sombre, engaging in none of the chit-chat that normally preceded business. Order was quickly called and the fuel crisis immediately addressed. The continuing severe weather and worsening fuel shortage, explained Hernon, constituted an emergency requiring the "exercise of exceptional powers by the Government and the Corporation." Why, then, had the Government not acted *weeks* ago, one member asked, to protect turf reserves and provide timber? Prompting Councillor Elinor Butler to speak her mind, charging that it was not only negligence but outright cowardice, as "no-one had the courage to say that there was a state of national emergency—for fear of starting something they could not handle."[51] This lack of leadership was unconscionable for the misery it had wrought upon the most vulnerable citizens. Cormac Breatnach TD agreed, stating that he "deplored the fact that nothing had been done to cut down the thousands of tons of fuel" in the Phoenix Park and St Anne's Estate.[52] In support, councillor M. O'Higgins stated that he had "reliable information" that in the Park there were at least three thousand trees, averaging 1½ tons of fuel per tree, that could be cut down without damaging the Park environment. Furthermore, he estimated that at least as much timber could also be cut on St Anne's Estate. Another person chimed in to say that in Santry Court there were dozens of trees that would eventually have to be taken down to make space for the new sanatorium.

On the conclusion of the discussion a motion was proposed that the Government allow the maximum amount of timber to be cut in the Phoenix

Park for fuel, and that "Army transport and men should be released for the work."[53] It was further proposed that "the greatest amount possible of timber suitable for fuel" be made available from St Anne's Estate.

As the meeting was taking place, searchers came upon a body on the slope of Garvagh Mountain in Co. Leitrim. It was that of James Gallagher, the farmer who had gone to get turf from a neighbour's house. No-one could know what had gone through his mind in those last hours. It appeared to have been a classic blizzard death by exposure: a white-out, lost visibility, disorientation, meandering, fatigue, fear, eventually succumbing to a wind-chilled cold that robbed his body of life-giving heat.

But his body probably wouldn't be buried for some time. The earth was now more solidly frozen and snow-covered than before. Bodies had to stay put. In rural areas, coffins were transported on improvised sleighs, usually barn doors taken from their hinges and pulled with ropes, to where the remains could be "temporarily buried in snow until graves could be opened" in the frozen ground. In many instances "bodies were put in snow-pits for up to six weeks until their graves could be dug."[54] While it was distressing for relatives that their dearly departed had to be delayed on their final journey, it was accepted under the circumstances, as the snow-pits provided natural preservation of the body.

———

The Jeep threesome were ploughing forward and upwards. With sunny skies, Sam Hughes was finally taking some gorgeous photographs. But their confidence began to wane before long:

> A half mile up, the snowdrifts began, smooth curving humps of dazzling white. They reared up every ten yards or so. We got out and began to shovel a path for the Jeep. Again and again, brought to a halt, driver Tom Donnelly would reverse a few yards, bang it once more, reverse again, and so on until the way was clear.[55]

Banging and barging ahead ten or twenty yards at a lunge was tedious, and discouraging. Passing farmhouses along the way, they waved to people trying to dig themselves out of the snow that was climbing up the walls of their houses. At one place "three youngsters put us to shame with the amount of snow they were able to hurl over their shoulders." The lads were toughened by farm life, they reckoned.

In a distant county a reporter for the *Irish Times* was concentrating his attention on the widespread loss of animals following the blizzard. The greatest blizzard had eradicated whole herds from sight. "In Louth I saw farmers trudging up to their waists in snowdrift," he found, "carrying food for sheep weighed down with the snow on their fleeces."[56] The sheer weight of the clotted snow and ice could bring animals down. On Wednesday afternoon one farmer in Co. Wicklow managed to plod across his land in chest-deep snow, only to find that he had lost 170 of his 200 sheep.

In mid-afternoon two human bodies were found. Edward Walshe was discovered by his teenage son near Carrickmacross in a field, partially buried by snow. He knew at once that it was his father. Similarly, Martin Delaney, the "aged man," was found at Tubbrit, Co. Westmeath, "near his house where he lived alone." Both victims of the blizzard. In coming days, news of other deaths around the provinces would reach Dublin. Some, however, remained local, never appearing in the national newspapers.

At the meeting of Dublin Corporation several members wanted to acknowledge the generosity of private citizens in helping with the fuel shortage. Lord and Lady Talbot de Malahide were thanked for offering two hundred trees for fuel. Similarly, W. J. Kelly of Naas had given the Corporation, free of charge, some hundred trees. And on the grounds of one convent the nuns were allowing trees to be cut down to relieve the suffering of the poor. The City Engineer then revealed that he had received from an undisclosed source in Maynooth nearly four thousand trees. T. and C. Martin, the building supplies firm, had offered to have logs sawn into blocks at their North Wall works free of charge. It seemed that citizens were more enterprising than members of the Government.

Councillor Eugene Timmons, however, made a cogent point, noting that not all citizens were so generous. Some, in fact, seemed unappreciative. It was his opinion that farmers near Dublin who had ample timber available on their land "had not displayed the same sense of co-operation as the people of Dublin had shown the farmers" six months earlier, when they "flocked in hundreds to save last year's harvest."[57] An indisputable point, members agreed.

As it turned out, the Dublin Chamber of Commerce was holding its annual meeting on Wednesday. Understandably, most topics on the agenda were dropped and full attention was concentrated on the weather and the crisis. The chairman, Joseph Walker, praised the work carried out by the CIE rescue squads, county council men and others who had so generously rushed to help others in need. In the same breath he took a verbal swipe at those who had not done so. Following each of the four blizzards, he stated, calls went out from various agencies for citizens to volunteer in clearing roads outside the city and throughout paralysed Co. Wicklow. The response had been pathetic, he reported, as only a handful of individuals showed up.

What most irked Walker was to see instead throngs of Dubliners, many better off, in the wake of blizzards engaging in snow sports. From the Phoenix

Park to Enniskerry, with its "Swiss resort" atmosphere, privileged citizens played in the snow while so many others were battling snowbound and ice-packed roads with pick and shovel, their backs sore and hands blistered. He took this opportunity to make a pointed plea:

> Let the young people in the city leave their toboggans and skis at home and come out with picks and shovels.[58]

At least other countries were responding positively to Ireland's misfortune. By Wednesday afternoon, as more information about Ireland's latest blizzard reached London and Washington, the two governments pledged urgent assistance with fuel. The British Cabinet Coal Committee, despite its own dire fuel shortage, offered Ireland a special allocation of five thousand tons of coal and five hundred tons of coke to help keep transport, electricity and gas going for a few more days. Likewise, the US Government contacted the Irish Government to promise 34,000 tons of good-quality coal. On behalf of the Irish people, de Valera's Government "expressed gratitude for that action." However, the emergency consignment of American coal, which was presumably being diverted to Ireland from its original destination in war-torn European countries, would probably not arrive for ten days to two weeks. It was to be earmarked for CIE, the ESB, the Gas Company, and possibly a few vital industries.

Meanwhile a most critical item was raised by Hernon at the Corporation meeting: the urgent need for food kitchens. It was now verified that thousands of the poorest tenement-dwellers were barely subsisting, some "slowly starving," it was said. The provision of food kitchens seemed the best immediate form of assistance. Proponents had been arguing for this for weeks, their words falling on deaf ears. Councillor Butler reminded the council that the Government had resisted providing army field kitchens, which could be set up easily and quickly, claiming that "these could not be put to use because a state of emergency had not arisen."[59] From the windows of oil-heated Leinster House they apparently saw no condition that qualified as an "emergency." Were they not reading the daily newspaper accounts of human misery in the heart of Dublin, caused by hunger and cold?

Alfie Byrne, though incensed by the Government's neglect of the needy, spoke prudently. Conceding that members of the Government had "all broken down on their job and failed miserably in the task given them"—to care for the public good—he contended that it would not "help to indulge in carping criticism of the Government" in a time of such crisis.[60] Rather than rebuke he believed the corporation should forcefully *"demand"* from the Government and Department of Defence the immediate "release of hundreds of lorries that were lying idle . . . and the release of Army men to man the lorries." They should be put to the task of setting up food kitchens throughout the city and distributing fuel to those with fireless grates. Lastly, he called on the Government to control the black-market operations by unscrupulous profiteers exploiting the most vulnerable citizens.

———

As the sun faded and clouds gathered, J.B. could feel the temperature dropping. Their Jeep was now up around the Goat's Pass, where they "felt the high wind of the uplands in our faces." Growing weary, they now had to hop out every few minutes to shovel their way clear:

> We took turns with the shovels. Then we sat, as directed, on either the front or rear of the Jeep to give the necessary weight; then we pulled and hauled and perspired in the bitter wind for almost three hours.[61]

They came upon a hardy band of men in a "reconnaissance party" that had been sent up the road on foot, apparently by county council officials, to assess conditions. They informed the "newspaper fellas" from the big city that the road ahead got *far* worse, impassable even for the strongest Jeep.

Perhaps not wanting to admit defeat in their presence, the three colleagues half-heartedly pushed on a bit farther. Shortly thereafter "the Jeep finally was stopped by snowdrifts of a depth of twelve feet and over. We gave up then."

On their return trip they came across the farmhouse of Norman Fox, who agreed to take their supplies and distribute the food as best he could to the neediest families in the area, at least those he could reach. Feeling at least partially successful, they rolled back into Dublin in the dark.

By now the afternoon papers were out on the street in the hands of people eager for the latest news of the blizzard's wrath—tolls of damage and deaths. The hard facts. The *Dublin Evening Mail* was crammed with dramatic and sad stories of lives lost and people trapped in perilous circumstances, noting that the full tragedy would not be known for some days to come:

> Stories of harrowing distress in many country places were reaching the city . . . There may be many grim discoveries, as it is believed that many people have been caught in the storm and left unrescued. But rescue squads have been working night and day to free marooned passengers and private motorists who have existed under appalling conditions on lonely roads, until rescued.[62]

In the following days there were indeed "grim discoveries." Some counties would report multiple deaths. A triple-death tragedy in Co. Sligo was front-page news in all the papers, as described by the *Irish Times*:

Three men died in the Sligo countryside on the night of the worst blizzard. One of them had gone only a few hundred yards from his home to feed a sick beast in the fields. The young man had apparently been driven blindly before the blizzard, and there were evidences that he moved in a circle, not knowing which way to travel, and crossed and recrossed a tributary of the Owenmore River four times in all . . . The body was found near a bank of the little river, 300 yards from his home.

This story might have come from some Polar Expedition. It is almost unbelievable that such conditions could exist in Ireland.[63]

———

Over Wednesday night the temperature in Dublin clung to 25 degrees Fahrenheit (−4°c). As usual, everything iced up again. By 8:30 on Thursday morning the temperature had risen to 41 degrees (5°c). Morning newspapers were again filled with the latest blizzard news, noting the mounting deaths of both humans and animals. Stories confirmed that, regardless of age or fitness, anyone caught out in the blizzard was at mortal risk. With people still missing, more bad news was sure to come.

Other articles reported on the effect of the severe winter on business. Two Dublin laundries were forced to close down because of lack of fuel, and the country's property market was struck a blow when "the weather got the upper hand, as sales were adversely affected." Auctioneers complained about telephone breakdowns and travel problems. With business shrivelling, many simply took properties off the market and postponed transactions.

No organisation was more irritated with the latest storm than the GAA. For five consecutive weeks the weather had ruined its sports schedule. Frozen ground, wild wind, snow and ice-covered fields had conspired to make playing conditions impossible. Big money was being lost. Organisers, players and spectators were exasperated. As the *Irish Times* summed it up, "weather is still the G.A.A.'s nightmare."

After its postponement of proceedings on blizzard day, the Dáil was back in session on Thursday. On the agenda was the motion condemning the Government for "failure to anticipate and guard against the present fuel famine," moved by Richard Mulcahy and supported by John A. Costello and Daniel Morrissey, among others. It was summarily defeated by 46 votes to 23.

In sharp reply to Fine Gael's censure motion Seán Lemass went on the offensive, asserting that "there would not have been a complete stoppage of coal if the severe weather had not brought a crisis to Britain's transport."[64] It was an act of nature—a natural calamity—unpredictable and unavoidable. He scolded Fine Gael for its "cynical effort to turn the sufferings of the people to party advantage." It was regrettable, he continued, that they had not wanted to "discuss this national difficulty on a constructive basis, to pool ideas and suggestions." National "difficulty"! Opponents sat fuming.

Lemass took the opportunity to announce that, in response to Dublin Corporation's urgent request for the felling of trees, the Government was granting permission for "as many trees in the Phoenix Park [as] are suitable for firewood, to be cut down . . . with the greatest despatch," with a view to "relieving the deplorable shortage" of fuel among the "poorer sections of the community."[65] Curiously contradicting his earlier statement that logs were essentially useless for the small grates of the poorer classes.

Opponents of the Government contended that it had taken a fourth "killer" blizzard to finally spur politicians into belated action on a paltry scale. The day's session generated even more heat in the already warm Dáil chamber.

CIE officials and county councils around the country were not interested in polemics but in immediate action. Shovel gangs were working feverishly to clear impassable roads and liberate snowbound towns and villages. Roundwood and Glencree were now helplessly cut off by mammoth snowdrifts, twelve to twenty feet high. "Vehicular traffic is out of the question," reported the *Evening Herald*, and might be so for many more weeks, if not months

With the nuns and orphans at Glencree hopelessly beyond reach by road and in serious need of food, fuel, and possibly medical aid, Red Cross officials were now talking of an aeroplane drop of supplies. In Britain isolated villages were being supplied through emergency airlifts by the air force, identical to a military operation. The relief authorities pondered the possibility of at least some sort of aeroplane drop of food. Dublin grocers were vowing to do their part by contributing basic food items. The challenge would be working out how to drop food parcels accurately and safely where they were most needed.

By early Thursday afternoon the sun "shone brilliantly in a cloudless sky," the temperature in the upper 40s (about 9°C). Ideal flying conditions. At about 2 or 3 p.m. the whirring of a plane's engine was heard over Co. Wicklow. That of a small plane. Below, farmers and villagers, taking advantage of the good weather to shovel out, paused and looked up. As the plane was flying very low, some waved. As it soared ever lower over the white-carpeted landscape, people wondered what the pilot was up to. His mission was verified by the *Irish Times* the next day:

> The isolated village of Roundwood had some food dropped from an aeroplane yesterday, but it is still cut off from the rest of the country.[66]

No further details were revealed. Who had funded and carried out the airlift? It was not a military aircraft. If it had been a Red Cross operation the Society surely would have announced it; and logically food would also have been delivered to Glencree. A good Samaritan? When the airlift made the newspapers, and the food eventually reached the hands of the isolated people, it gave country towns and villages the idea of preparing petitions to be presented to the Government and the Red Cross Society, asking for an airlift to relieve their hardship.

CIE's relief missions were sluggishly land-based. With every restored telephone line or opened roadway, new reports reached head office verifying cases of still-stranded buses, lorries, and cars. Because of the urgency of the crisis, rescue squads were being sent out around the clock:

> A squad of over twenty men with pneumatic drills, picks, planks, gear of all sorts, and three days' rations left Dublin at night to look for passengers in six or seven buses which have not been heard from since Tuesday when they were swallowed up in the snowstorm between Longford and Ballina.[67]

It would be found that "swallowed up" was an apt term.

———

Friday 28 February was the final day of the shortest month. For those who lived through it, the longest month of their lives. It was the thirty-fifth consecutive day of the Arctic siege.

Undaunted by their blunders and discredited reputation, most of Dublin's weather prophets were at their game once more. Again dispensing conflicting predictions, some bleak, others hopeful. Certain forecasters, playing it safe, were deliberately obscure. Others, like a poker-player, were hoping for one good hand to offset their losses and redeem credibility.

With unsullied March approaching, every newspaper naturally wanted to present a positive outlook. The country needed "brighter" prospects. The *Irish Press* based its end-of-month forecast on information gleaned from several weather analysts, who the paper boasted had relied upon "science." What these experts were hoping for, it explained, was a deterioration of the anticyclonic regime and high-pressure system from Russia to Greenland, a weakening of the east wind, and resumption of the normal Gulf Stream influence over Ireland. Upon such "hope," they issued their forecast:

> Our weather experts have worked out this forecast scientifically . . . In two days' time General Winter may abandon the onslaught he began on Ireland 35 days ago . . . with hopes to an end of the weather "blitz" after that.[68]

By contrast, the *Evening Herald* offered its readers no "hopeful" or "wishful" scenarios:

> Dubliners had high hopes that at last the month-long Arctic spell was beginning to break, but now there are no solid reasons for believing that the country is at last emerging from its "Ice Age."[69]

Leaving people bewildered about what to expect of March.

As if in defiance of both hope and science, on the last night of the month King Winter dropped the mercury 21 degrees below freezing, to a painfully cold 11 degrees Fahrenheit (−12°c). A cruel return to January's "Big Freeze," the slashing east wind bringing the wind-chilled cold well below zero (−18°c).

In Siberian conditions, thousands upon thousands of Dubliners faced another night with fireless grates. Wondering what the month of March would hold for them when they awakened the next morning.

Chapter 8 ～

"SNOW ARMY" ASSAULT

With an army of 700 men, Wicklow County Council made a concerted attack on snow-covered roads. In approaching Glencree the men ran into snowdrifts 12 feet deep.

(*Sunday Independent*, 2 MARCH 1947)

Every day and everyone one meets brings fresh tales of desolation.

(*Irish Press*, 22 MARCH 1947)

As far as the eye could see there was nothing but a rolling plain of snow-covered wasteland . . . what the steppes of Siberia must be like. The whole north-western part of Connaught was completely isolated . . . [It is] feared that the final disappearance of the snow would reveal many tragedies.

(*Irish Independent*, 4 MARCH 1947)

WEEKEND OF 1/2 MARCH

Following sinister February, the mere arrival of unsullied March seemed redemptive.

It began favourably. At about 3 a.m. on Saturday the temperature began to climb from 11 degrees (−12°C), nudging above the freezing mark at about 9:30. By the time Dublin's streets were alive with Saturday activity the skies were mostly clear, with a bright sun beaming down. Conditions were ideal for the "snow armies," as the papers were now calling them—CIE, the ESB, Post Office and county council road gangs—to launch a full assault on snowbound Ireland. An urgency was felt to make the best of the good weather, wary of what the next day might bring.

Their task was gargantuan, as "the countryside was entombed in a still, white, eerie blanket."[1] In effect, de Valera's postwar Ireland had "ground to a complete standstill."[2] Leaving the frozen, petrified landscape strewn with stranded or missing buses, lorries, cars, "ghost trains"—many buried or half-buried; marooned passengers, isolated towns, "lost" villages, virtually vanished houses and farmsteads snowed in to their chimney-tops, vast herds of dead animals.

An unknown number of people were still missing, some probably perished by now.

Only an expansive "snow army" campaign throughout the country would open roads, restore communications, rescue people, liberate towns and villages, and combat the paralysis of snow and ice. An endeavour that would take weeks rather than days.

Citizens liked the military parlance as newspapers wrote about the snow armies "attacking" or "assaulting" snow barriers and "winning the battle" against King Winter. Against what one newspaper called the "snow enemy." Terms such as "front-line battalions" and "back-up forces" were reminiscent of the Second World War. Ireland was divided into the "Western Front" and "Eastern Front." Under the circumstances it had a legitimacy.

In the earlier blizzards the eastern and midland counties had suffered the worst battering, most notably Co. Wicklow. This time the western midlands, far west and north-west were struck as hard. Meaning that the snow armies had to spread their efforts over most of the country. They varied in size from "battalions" of seven hundred to eight hundred men down to squads. County council forces could number in the hundreds, while CIE superintendents preferred to organise squads of twenty to thirty men. Then there were the locally organised shovel-and-pick gangs that typically had a dozen or so men. Anyone who was willing and able to wield a digging or chopping tool was welcome to become part of this national "army." Ordinary citizens stepped forward to do their part, without need for sworn oath or uniform.

Keith Collie's father, who had barely made it home to Ballycorus from his office in Dublin on the day of the blizzard, would set out with two other men, forming their own little squad of snow soldiers:

> My father led an "expedition" comprising the local postman and a neighbour . . . to Glencullen in the Dublin Mountains. There they found the village totally under snow, and the locals moving around in tunnels.[3]

The Government did not despatch thousands of soldiers, lorries and equipment in a mission to break winter's paralysing grip on the country. Forces of the "snow armies" were a *citizens'* army. A "liberation army," to assist and free their fellow-citizens.

On Saturday morning the strategy of the snow armies was to "break through" to the isolated west, viewed now as a blockaded, frozen frontier land. As one member of a CIE squad put it, "the entire western world beyond Longford was just a snow-covered mystery—as to the rest of the west north of Galway and south of Sligo, all was silent." Leslie Luke, a public relations officer for CIE, accompanied a rescue convoy forging westwards. Upon seeing buried Connacht he exclaimed that he could compare it only to what he "imagined the snow-covered steppes of Siberia to be like."[4] As far as his eye could see there was nothing but a "rolling plain of snow-covered wasteland." Wondering how humans and animals could survive in such a barren Arctic environment, he openly expressed the fear that when the north-western parts of Connacht were cleared—or thawed out in the spring, or summer—the land would "reveal many tragedies."

Snow armies marching westwards were essentially heading into the great unknown. With telephone and telegraph lines down they were unable to obtain information about what lay ahead in Cos. Longford, Roscommon, Galway, Mayo, and Donegal. Only sporadic contact with Sligo was being made, obtained on the telephone by way of Belfast and Liverpool. Physically and telephonically severed from the outside world, these counties may as well have been Arctic outposts. And it was impossible to judge the reliability of the fragments of information that did come out. To the first rescuers, some stories sounded too astonishing to be believed:

> Fantastic rumours were coming through about the size of drifts. Towns and villages, where buses were marooned with their passengers, were said to be starving.[5]

By mid-morning, CIE, the ESB, the Post Office and county councils had despatched their best rescue and repair crews. But with telecommunications inoperable, they were going ahead blindly, unable to communicate with one another or co-ordinate their efforts. This caused much confusion and frustration, not to mention valuable lost time. Each agency was really dependent upon the other for performing at their fullest. For instance, the ESB squads "were plodding away somewhere in the snow to get the electricity going again," but they needed clearance squads to open the roads for them first. Conversely, CIE rescue teams were anxiously awaiting telephone repairs so they could call ahead and find out where they were most needed to assist stranded buses and marooned passengers. Without normal inter-agency communications and co-operation, snow armies were greatly impeded in their urgent work.

As in a military operation, their progress could be slow, sometimes measured "yard by yard hacking their way through the icy ring that has cut off large sections of the West."[6] With each new road cleared, village reached or telephone line restored they were met with more "stories of the devastating effect of last Tuesday's blizzard filtering through."[7]

———

The challenge of the snow armies was typified by the experience of one of CIE's rescue squads, which had been sent out from Dublin at about 9:30 on Friday night, comprising about twenty-five men with a Matador, a coach, and a staff car. Fully outfitted with shovels, picks, pneumatic drills, chains and ropes, as well as petrol and food for several days. "Even *stout*," confided one member, "of which some thoughtful person had provided a supply in the bus." After all, to the hard-working man in Ireland stout was known as "liquid food," replenishing strength and stamina.

The men were on a top-priority assignment and had been carefully selected. They already possessed blizzard-busting experience, as "all week we had been busy in counties Dublin, Wicklow, Kildare, Laois and Offaly, rescuing snowbound buses." With little rest, and no hesitation, they were now taking on the west. In retrospect, they would admit that they were charged by surging adrenalin as well as feelings of challenge and excitement. High adventure, high stakes:

> Now we had to make our way to the west. The whereabouts of almost a dozen buses were unknown at that time. In particular, we were worried about a bus with a load of passengers which had left Ballina on the Tuesday morning directly before the blizzard began, at 8.30 a.m. For all we knew, its passengers and crew might be under some enormous snowdrift.[8]

Shortly after 2 a.m. they reached Longford station, where the "signalman made us feel welcome . . . We had tea cooked on the fire at the stationmaster's office."[9] Just what they needed at that stage in their journey. About 7:15, after nearly ten hours on the road with only sporadic bits of sleep, they neared Strokestown. Many times along their way they had to halt and shovel their way out of drifts in the road; but it was just outside Strokestown that their real ordeal began:

> We hit the first heavy, long snowdrift. The hard work began here and the pattern of it was much the same all the way to Ballina: charge the drift, bull-like, with your Matador lorry, at anything up to thirty m.p.h. When she bogged, the diggers came up to clear her, and away she went again, the rest of the vehicles following for a run of 200 or 300, or perhaps only 20 to 30 yards.[10]

A pace of slow, steady progress and great exhaustion. As with all snow armies, local people along the way greeted them with appreciation and generosity, sharing what little they had. Sometimes "it was difficult to find water, food, fuel and lodging," one participant recounted, "but the hospitality was never lacking. We found it in presbyteries, Garda stations, garages, shops and, above all, in every farmhouse where we halted."[11] Even sleeping in a barn on straw, out of the wind, could feel luxurious.

————

No hospitality was better than that found in the Ruanes' house at Straide, Co. Mayo. Marooned visitors were provided not only with shelter and food but with the best of companionship. Over days and weeks real friendships would develop. At night, as everyone gathered around the blazing turf fire, chatting amiably, Tony, the "baby" of the family, was allowed to stay up a bit later to take it all in. He observed and listened carefully, cultivating what was to become a remarkable memory. When eventually he grew drowsy his mother had a warmed bed waiting:

> Lasting, long friendships were forged around turf fires in the paraffin lamplight. My knowledge came from listening to the chat around the fire, the flagstone floor freezing my arse as I looked up at all those adult faces.
> Before being dumped into a freezing bed a few round stones, about egg size, would be put into the fire and heated, dropped into a woollen sock and placed between the blankets. During the "Big Snow" that was pure magic.

Within the village of Straide, friendships of a different sort were being nurtured. Phillip Mount had added a new social attraction to his road-show. When local people naturally tired a bit of the games and regular performances, he added nightly dancing. Country people never seemed to tire of dancing, able to swing and sashay around the floor so long as the music played. Keep the music flowing, and regulars would return night after night— that was his plan. With a collection of records and his piano accordion, the "band leader" could put on the right music for all crowds: youngsters, teenagers, middle-aged and "oldies." Ruane remembers that dancing became almost infectious in the village during those bleak winter weeks:

> Phillip Mount had his piano accordion, and later in the night the seating would be pushed to the walls to make space for a dance. All the lads and lasses would take the floor, a couple of hundred. The dance at the end of the night, that was the highlight . . . resulting in many romantic adventures . . . and a few broken hearts in the bargain.

The younger crowd—and some older couples, no doubt—took full advantage of the opportunity to dance in the low-lit building, especially down at the far end, where the stacked straw bales offered dark shadows and private niches for stolen romancing. Behaviour not missed by the parish priest, who determined to keep his eye on any imprudent couples. Yet he apparently didn't want to cancel the dances and jeopardise his income from Mount. So "the young people danced there in the light of the paraffin lamps," confides Ruane, "and sometimes when a guy got off his mark he might invite his partner up to the dimly lit corner of the golden straw for some moments of love."

His subtle admonitions having gone unheeded, the priest finally felt compelled to put a stop to the licentious behaviour of some young dancers. He decided to do this in the most public and intimidating manner. "The priest called them out from the altar one Sunday," says Ruane, and "roared about debauchery and carrying on in the old hall."

It may have been about this time that some of the village elders decided that perhaps it would be best if the travelling entertainers packed up their road-show and moved on to a different village. But this was not possible. Like all travellers, they had to wait until the snow armies had safely cleared the roads, especially for their wobbly, vulnerable vehicles.

This delay was fine with young Tony, who was hardly interested in dancing anyway: he was fixated on jabbing, feinting, landing the right punch. Over the previous weeks he had befriended one of the showmen, who took a liking to the scrappy youngster and decided to teach him the rudiments of boxing. It might serve him well in life:

> One guy with the road-show, his name was Tommy, and he was the first to teach me how to box. He stood me up on a keg and got me to put my guard up and showed me how to feint with a left jab and follow through with a straight right.

Pugilistic tactics he would use masterfully sixteen years later when he boxed as a member of the Garda Síochána. The great blizzard of 1947 had bred a top boxer in the ring.

All the while, outside in the frigid night air, skimming across the crystallised surface, "Let it snow, let it snow, let it snow."

———

J.B. and Sam Hughes had had a bellyful of shovelling and picking away at mounds of snow and ice. Their editor at the *Irish Press* had come up with a better scheme this time. Apparently drawing good readership from their previous exploits in the Jeep, a grander "relief mission" was envisaged for reaching Roundwood and Glencree. One that would allow the intrepid reporter and photographer to laugh at tormenting winds and snowdrifts.

This time they would *fly over* the impenetrable landscape.

By late Saturday morning, with the weather clear and sunny, ideal for flying, they were packing the cargo section of a small plane with parcels of tinned food donated by Alexander Findlater and Company, to be dropped from the air to isolated, hungry people. Shortly after noon, with the sun gleaming on the wings, they took off in their three-seater Auster aircraft, provided by a Dublin car and aircraft dealer and flown by an expert pilot, Dan Fincher. Within minutes they were out of the city and over dazzling, pristine countryside. Sam Hughes poked his camera through a window slot, taking once-in-a-lifetime photographs of a completely unblemished white landscape. They swooped low over roads dotted with vehicles stuck in drifts, wondering how many still had passengers in them. Then they dropped low enough to clearly see people against the white canvas:

> Some of the "lost people of snow-bound Wicklow" waved at our relief plane as it hedge-hopped about fifty feet off the ground. Over the lost hamlets we watched villagers chiselling their way through the snow that has isolated them for weeks. They waved with their shovels to us as we hedge-hopped past.[12]

Below them, as they soared with ease and grace, were "upwards of 800 workers smashing their way to victory" in a battle with the snow and ice-coated roads of Co. Wicklow.[13] The aviators could well empathise with those infantrymen of the snow armies.

Throughout the sunny day in every county more volunteers poured out to join the snow soldiers. In age they ranged from fourteen-year-old lads to stooped veterans of the First World War, the 1916 Rising, and the Civil War. Some had fought with the British in the Anglo-Boer War. Now, in their own country, they fought the "white enemy," as imposing a foe as they had faced.

————

At CIE head office Michael Dowling spent Saturday engaged in what would be called the "herculean work" of organising efforts to break through to Galway, Sligo, and Ballina. And along the way to rescue "a score of buses that were snowbound and isolated."[14] With passengers or without? No-one knew.

His priority was to despatch a special rescue team to try to reach and open up Sligo, which was in particularly dire need. For days the town had been completely cut off, with no goods trains or delivery vans coming in. Some residents were growing panicky. The rescue squad numbered thirty men, in several lorries, a coach, and a staff car, carrying the standard digging equipment. They were also ordered to assist stranded motorists along their way. By the time they neared Longford they were picking up an odd collection of marooned vehicles and passengers. Among them were an *Irish Independent* van, a new hearse on delivery from Kinsale, two Ford lorries on which were perched two new motor cars on their way to Letterkenny, and an *Irish Independent* car carrying a reporter and photographer. All were thankful to find company and to work together in pushing forward.

As the convoy crawled its way along, regularly halting to dig through drifts, every man was expected to handle a shovel, including the reporter, whose hands would be blistered by the time he sat down to type his own story days later. Finally, approaching midday on Saturday, the curious convoy of mismatched vehicles broke through the last barrier and rolled into Sligo, to the wonderment of a crowd of onlookers:

> The Angelus bell tolled over Sligo, as people on the footpaths stood and welcomed a bizarre line of vehicles rolling into town to re-open road traffic from the rest of the country. The newsagents were besieged by townspeople eager to read their first news of the outside world in a week.[15]

Other dramas, small and large, were being played out on Ireland's "Western Front." A bus from Boyle to Sligo continually became halted by drifts, with the driver, conductor and twenty-five passengers taking turns for eight hours in digging out. Aboard was a reporter for the *Sunday Independent*, who had unwittingly become a participant in his marooned passengers' story. Like all the others, he had to handle the shovel and push the bus from behind, time after time.

Unknown to them at the time, from the opposite direction a county council work gang from Sligo were shovelling their way towards them at a slow pace. "The bus had been pushed and dug out through thirty miles of the deepest drifts," the reporter would write. "My hands are frozen and sore from many hours of painful shovelling."[16]

In frustration, a few of the more hardy passengers decided to set out walking the remaining fourteen miles to the town. There is no record of their experience. Those remaining aboard the bus eventually made it into a village, still some miles from Sligo, at the bottom of a hill too steep for the bus to climb. By good fortune, the reporter and several other determined passengers, having scoured the village, found a set of tyre chains that actually fitted the bus, proudly presenting them to the driver, only to have him inform them that CIE regulations gave him "no authority to buy them." Unhesitatingly, and doubtless with some annoyance, the reporter "then bought the chains and the hill was safely negotiated." It made a good story.

J.B. and Sam Hughes were having a considerably easier time of it this day. By 2 p.m. or thereabouts they had circled large sections of Co. Wicklow, and Hughes was capturing stunning photographs. The three men could not help but be awed by both the beauty and the destruction of the "daddy of them all" blizzard:

> We began to see the kind of snow that had buried buses in the past week, waves of it . . . It rose around the houses, and channels showed where inhabitants had dug their walls and windows clear. There was so much snow that landmarks were obliterated and hamlets and villages became anonymous. The roads in these parts were quite impassable.[17]

"Buried buses" were not a reporter's fanciful hyperbole, a fact to which Seán Lang could personally attest. After he and his mate had replaced the broken lorry axle, barely made it into Ballina, and been put up by the sympathetic woman, they were quite comfortable. Then, on Saturday, the two men received orders to join a detachment of CIE rescuers trying to find several buses that had "disappeared" along their route. "So we were sent out to look for these buses—because they were thought to be covered with snow."

When they first set out he doubted that anything as large as a bus could actually be hidden by snow. They began seeing hedges, high stone walls, sheds blanketed. Then shrouded cars. Eventually they saw houses covered to the roofs, with only chimneys poking out. When they encountered drifts over fifteen feet high they seriously began looking for hidden buses:

> It took us two days to get about ten miles. And the wind blew snow from the fields and it *covered* the buses. Covered. It was hard to *imagine*—that a bus could be *completely* covered with snow! We came across a bus that we didn't know was *there!*
>
> Local houses around the area put the people up that were in the buses. Oh, and when we came into towns people were standing in front of the shops *cheering* for us, for rescuing them.

Hailed locally as heroes, they were treated as such in the newspapers as well. However, as the *Ballina Herald* wrote, "there are no medals for the heroes of the blizzard."[18]

———

Western and midland towns along the railway line hoped for an early resumption of a proper train service, which had already been cut back because of fuel shortages. Many had not seen a train for days, some for a week or more. Shops were running low on basic supplies. Seeing bare shelves made people anxious. Pubmen had grown grouchy when beer and whiskey had to be rationed. Some towns were completely out of cigarettes and pipe tobacco. Smokers and drinkers—meaning most men—could become cantankerous at home. Their wives hoped a goods train would get through before long.

The railway authorities in Dublin faced myriad problems: acute fuel shortages, men laid off, trains blocked by snowdrifts and ice mounds, some derailed, others missing. To exacerbate matters, "points, water columns and tanks were frozen ... Snow was at the level with some station platforms." Even where trains were still running it was reported that "locomotive crews worked against enormous odds with poor fuel," having to use coal of such poor quality that it would have been rejected under normal circumstances. It made performance poorer and their job harder.

Railway supervisors studied their route maps, dotted with trouble spots. Places where trains had been halted or derailed—or might be. Several serious derailments had been verified. Having learnt lessons from the previous blizzards, they knew that snow-ploughs affixed to locomotives often failed to gouge their way through the densest barriers, and some broke down. Therefore, on several major lines they assigned special crews of men armed with picks and shovels to travel with them, hop down when necessary, and hack the track clear. With good weather on Saturday, all railway gangs were out working to clear lines, such as the Dublin–Wexford and Wexford–Waterford lines, where one of their largest snow-ploughs "ran into drifts 20 feet deep at Palace East." The railwaymen stood looking up at it.

Even the strongest railway ploughs were not ice-breakers. The recurrent cycle of heavy snowfall, slight thawing and deep refreezing had created granite-like blocks of ice that would have posed a challenge to quarrymen. On the Sligo–Mullingar line, where a powerful locomotive had been humbled by a huge ice formation, the crew despatched to dig it out reported to Dublin that they had encountered drifts "eight feet deep which are *frozen solid.*" Such glaciers had to be picked away one swing at a time. Even when bad patches of track were cleared, the difficulty was then keeping the line clear. It could be discouraging, as described by one railwayman assigned to work at it:

> Snow ploughs did an important job in clearing railway lines, but would have been useless without the accompanying gangs of diggers. In the West, lines were opened, closed, and reopened. The main difficulties were in cuttings where space for snow removal from the line was limited, resulting in the strong winds blowing the snow back on to the permanent way again.[19]

Meanwhile, like the *Irish Press* aviators over Co. Wicklow, the ESB was taking full advantage of the clear weather to do some aerial reconnaissance of its own. It needed to assess blizzard damage and identify priority repair points. To accomplish this, Shannon Aero Club provided it with a plane that could fly low to scout the ESB network. With perfect visibility, at midday several ESB officials flew over the Shannon scheme, from Ardnacrusha along the western seaboard and inland areas for a general survey. Soaring low, it was possible to identify toppled poles and snapped cables—at least where they were not buried. They also spotted some of their own linesmen in trouble. In Co. Mayo they saw electricity repairmen obstructed by "100 foot long snowdrifts." In a particularly bad part of Co. Galway they observed that "Army authorities in Galway had sent an armoured car" to help clear a passage to Swinford for the purpose of reconnecting the ESB lines.

Loss of electricity imposed serious problems for hospitals and homes for the elderly and feeble. The County Hospital in Roscommon had been without electricity for three days following the blizzard and had already used nearly a thousand candles but was now nearing the end of its supply. Throughout most of the country, people were running short on paraffin oil, candles, even matches.

Apart from checking on their own system, the ESB surveyors dropping low in their plane noted road conditions and telecommunications damage to pass along to CIE and the Post Office for their repair work. Along the way, farmers and villagers waved to them, many probably out of distress as much as friendliness.

———

The far west had its own desperation. Its remote, "frontier" character presented problems for inhabitants under even the best of conditions. Contact with the east was essential for access to basic provisions and services. Their links with the outside were largely by way of narrow, rough roads, some barely wide enough for a car, much less a bus. They could be washed out with a good thunderstorm. People didn't mind their isolation so long as they could rely on contact with towns such as Galway and Sligo, and could reach Dublin when necessary. But they didn't want to be "cut off."

Inhabitants of the mountainy country of Connemara and Co. Donegal were renowned for their toughness and independence, hardened by centuries of hardship. A people not easily defeated, even by famine. "Connemara folk are proud survivors of a cruel land, where rocks and death are part of life," it was written.[20] In parts, a wild and isolated land where a blizzard could submerge little roads beneath an ocean of snow and swallow up cars and even buses.

Indeed, CIE head office in Dublin soon got word that several of its buses were missing on roads west of Galway. Several rescue squads were sent from Dublin to take up the search. Clear across the country. Their primary goal was to reach Galway, replenish their supplies as necessary, then move westwards towards Clifden—as far as they could get. And to assist any marooned passengers along their way. One CIE rescue team halted and helped "more than 100 people, picked up at various places, then brought to Galway." Setting out again, they weren't sure what they might find when they got well west of Galway on the worst roads. Many Dubliners thought of Connemara as a "no man's land," hauntingly beautiful but mostly a barren, rocky patch of human frustration, where people retained old customs and begged the land for a subsistence living.

On open stretches of Connemara road one could become marooned at any season of the year. So, it was with some trepidation that, on the first days of March, CIE men from Dublin left Galway and headed towards Clifden. They quickly found the land smothered in snow and caked in ice, animals dead and frozen by the thousand, their carcases sticking out in pained forms. The wind howling and not a human voice to be heard. Here farmers no longer dared to venture out to check on their animals. They knew better. The only sounds to be heard along the way were those of local work gangs hacking and chiselling with blades and picks. Upon finding abandoned cars and lorries, they could only wonder what had happened to the passengers.

When they reached the area of the Maumturk Mountains and the Twelve Pins they encountered a new enemy: avalanches.

Not the high-altitude type, as in the Alps, but avalanches nonetheless. The cycle of quick thawing and freezing, followed by more heavy snow, combined to create ideal conditions for avalanches. Always accompanied by the strong winds, the slippery layers embedded in the upland drifts allowed the natural force of gravity to carry volumes of snow downwards, picking up force along their path. The same principle as large alpine avalanches, only on a smaller scale. Connemara avalanches could be triggered suddenly, plugging up a narrow valley or road within seconds, halting or trapping vehicles and passengers. CIE supervisors and leaders of county council squads warned their men to be vigilant, as conditions were ripe for repeated avalanches following the greatest blizzard of all, which had packed a great weight of new snow atop that already layered on slopes. By Saturday afternoon, with temperatures in the 30s (0 to 4°C), CIE crews found the avalanche danger at its peak:

> Conditions in the region of the Twelve Pins have worsened within the past few days . . . A strong east wind, reaching gale force at times, has been driving avalanches down the mountains on to the roads, blocking the stretch between Maam Cross and Leenane. County Council workers have been working on the Galway–Clifden route to keep the road open, but almost as fast as they clear away the avalanches, others take their place.[21]

CIE recruits had been taught nothing about fighting avalanches: it was strictly a learn-on-the-job experience, under stressful circumstances. A deep, swooshing sound ahead or behind told them of another slide, and they hoped it was not across a road. Digging out of avalanche depositions using manual shovelling would make a great tale to tell their grandchildren in years to come. In Ireland!

―――

Clear across the country, three men in a small plane were now meandering in the skies over Co. Wicklow in search of Roundwood and Glencree—which they couldn't *find*. They had not anticipated that the thick snow blanket would have completely eradicated familiar landmarks. Not only roads were covered but railway lines. Rivers and lakes were frozen and camouflaged with snow. Features of different villages were so obscured that from the air they all looked much alike. Even when Dan Fincher swooped low right over rooftops it was nearly impossible to distinguish one settlement from another. So, unfamiliar with what they were seeing, the three aviators were, in a sense, now lost themselves. With the afternoon waning and fuel running low, Fincher suggested that they do their best and begin dropping parcels wherever they could make out clusters of farmhouses:

> Near a lonely farm house on Calary Bog, we let one parcel of tinned food go . . . and there was a danger of parcels striking our own tail. Before dropping our load we circled the farm house and saw the farmer and his wife wave. Then we swooped low over a nearby field and pilot Dan Fincher slid the package out the window.[22]

As they veered away they could see the recipients struggling through the snow to reach the "miracle" relief parcels.

Below them, in the snowy morass, were hundreds of workers under the leadership of the county council. They had been divided into gangs of twenty to forty men and assigned duty at the most strategic points. By mid-afternoon some had been at the pick for nearly six hours. Their work, though gruelling, drew no complaints. So long as the good weather held, they were determined to reach and free isolated outposts where people were in need of food and fuel. Their principal target was Roundwood, where, by now, residents probably regretted that theirs was the famous "highest village in Ireland." The new strategy for reaching outlying villages was not to clear the full width of the road but just to carve out a passage, as it was being called, through which bread, other food and if necessary an ambulance might be brought in. By about 3:30 p.m. several work gangs were making considerable progress in the area from Rathdrum to Laragh and Ashford. The sky remained clear, and at least a partial moon was being predicted. If so, many of the men would volunteer to continue working by moonlight.

By this time the CIE rescue squad that had left Dublin at 9 o'clock the night before and fought their way through Longford to Ballina, finding buses and digging out marooned people along their route, were nearing their twentieth hour of duty. Their stock of stout remained untouched but no doubt was in their minds as they worked up a great thirst. Their new orders were now to concentrate on the areas around Elphin and Ballaghaderreen, Co. Roscommon, where several buses were known to be missing. With the sun faded and temperatures falling, one squad member recalls their welcome into Elphin:

> We arrived in Elphin at 5 p.m. People had assembled to watch us arrive, they had heard it was the Army coming, probably because they had seen the Army-grey colour of our vehicles. We were the first vehicles into Elphin since the blizzard and found the people had been in sore straits. The town's food supply was low, timber for fuel was coming in on sleds. A coffined corpse had just been dragged on a sled through the streets to the church.[23]

Other bodies were turning up that day. With the afternoon's sunny weather, search parties had been out in force in several counties looking for people missing since the blizzard. Martin Mullen, a 49-year-old farmer from Ballintober, Co. Roscommon, who had been missing since Tuesday, was found dead of exposure in the snow.

The big news was that of "a triple tragedy of the blizzard" at Corcullin, Bellacorick, near Bangor Erris on the far western seaboard of Co. Mayo. The victims were the McAndrews brothers, Alex and Patrick, aged 76 and 69, and 28-year-old Patrick Rowland. The brothers, who lived by themselves, were thought to have become lost during the blizzard when they went to get turf from their rick on the moor about three hundred yards away. The blizzard had suddenly worsened during their trek, and they apparently became caught in the deadly cycle of disorientation, fatigue, hypothermia, fear. Full exposure to the blizzard.

Young Rowland had ostensibly gone out to look after cattle during the earlier stages of the blizzard. However, at least one account claimed he had "left his home in the first instance to go to the assistance of the McAndrews." This will never be known. Whatever his motivation, he failed to return. Despite his youth and assumed fitness, he was not immune to the blizzard's entrapment. His body was recovered on the moor at about 3 p.m., some six hundred yards from his house.

Winter's death toll was mounting. People were dying in myriad ways: exposure, drowning at sea, falling through ice on rivers and lakes, being struck by vehicles on icy roads. But the greatest number by far were the elderly and poor, who were succumbing at an alarming rate to cold, hunger, illness, depression, loss of the will to live, and various combinations thereof. As snow armies broke through barriers to reach snowbound towns and villages they learnt from local people how winter's hardships were taking lives at an unprecedented rate.

In urban Dublin, hundreds more were succumbing in the tenements, and elsewhere, for the same reasons. Still no records were being kept on weather-related deaths for the archives.

People were dying in record numbers—but most were still not being buried. By early March the ground was more deeply frozen and snow-packed than before. Both in towns and in rural areas, bodies were coffined and placed in storage for eventual burial, with natural refrigeration preserving the bodies in snow-pits. Some would remain in this limbo for more than six weeks. In Dublin, coffined bodies were stacked up at some undertakers who had the space. As a Liberties youth, Liam Cradden, now eighty-three, and a few pals liked to peek at the backlogged coffins:

> See, in Glasnevin they had to use pickaxes for graves. But then the snow got five foot thick and more. And they couldn't get them buried. They didn't have places to put them, really—and they couldn't just bring the coffins up to the graveyards and leave them exposed. So the undertakers had their coffins full. I *remember* in the Coombe looking at the coffins stacked on top of one another . . . yes, 'cause they *couldn't* get them buried.

In country areas, where old customs run deep, relatives made every effort to at least get their deceased out to the cemeteries, even if they had to be placed in a snow-pit there for the time. But many families took advantage of the delay to have an extended wake. The challenge of transporting a heavy coffin over six to ten feet of crusted snow and ice was daunting. But over the weekend of 1/2 March many country people took advantage of sunny skies and warmer temperatures to get the remains of their loved ones out to the cemetery.

In the Cloondra area of Co. Longford several coffins were seen being carried "five miles through the snow to reach the cemetery." Commonly, makeshift sleighs were used, made of anything that was flat and would slide across the snow—barn doors, wooden planks, or corrugated metal panels. They could be pulled with a rope by horses or men. Often, however, coffins had to be shouldered by men, working in shifts. It was a common sight in Brian Kelly's part of Co. Donegal. "The coffins had to be manually shouldered. I know of funerals carried three miles to the graveyard. It was a feat of human endurance to do that!" Coffin-bearers and mourners struggled to keep their footing, as it was easy to break through crystallised snow layers.

A few of the dearly departed did get a proper burial. In Longford, Miriam Sweetman's granny, Annie Gillespie, who had "quietly slipped into eternity" just as the first snowflakes of the blizzard began to fall, was one of those so fortunate. As she had been critically ill for some time, her grave had been dug in advance. It would be easy enough to get her granny into the ground, if only they could get her to the cemetery. "Our problem with Gran's funeral was to go to Ardcane Church of Ireland near Boyle."[24] The undertaker managed to "get a hearse and coffin to our house in Main Street . . . as half a stone of salt was thrown on the footpath." It was then taken by railway wagon to Boyle, where the hardest work began:

> In Boyle a lorry with 30 men carrying shovels waited. They got the coffin aboard and set off for Ardcane, three miles away. Three times they got stuck in a drift and the men jumped off and dug it out . . . got to the graveyard and up the steep hill to the grave.[25]

Canon Martin Halloran can match that story with an equally challenging burial in his part of Co. Sligo:

> In Templeboy a local man, named Hughie Golden, died. Two men from his home in Kingsmountain had to walk miles to get the coffin, as others carried whiskey and porter supplied by Carvey's Pub to his home. Then the County Council workers, helped by volunteers, some of them using hay knives, began the task of cutting away huge blocks of snow, [wide] enough to carry the coffin two abreast to the graveyard.
>
> Finally, the gravediggers had to dig down 13 feet through the snow into the ground hardened by six weeks of frost.[26]

Why a simple temporary snow-pit was not acceptable for Hughie under the circumstances is not known.

––––

At the close of the afternoon, Dan Fincher told J.B. and Sam Hughes, who by now had a treasure of photographs, that it was time to head back to Dublin:

> We turned again in a last effort to locate Roundwood . . . but the pilot abandoned the search for familiar rivers, roads and railways. The mountains and valleys were looking less inviting every minute . . . We turned for home.[27]

Below them, CIE and county council squads pushed ahead to try to carve out at least a narrow passage—an oxygen tube to the smothered village. Encouraged by their progress during the improved weather, they vowed to continue when night fell. "Working all day and by moonlight," reported the

Dublin Evening Mail, they fought their way forward in hopes of "clearing a passage to Roundwood and Annamoe via Ashford and Laragh from Rathdrum."[28] Sheer adrenalin charge kept them going by the moon's light, some would later say, in the knowledge that their rescue efforts could mean lives saved.

At the same time the CIE rescue squad that had triumphantly marched into Ballina and Elphin that day, freeing numerous vehicles and passengers on the way, had now been sleepless for nearly twenty-four hours. Struggling to stay awake, they sought lodging in Elphin but with no luck, for some inexplicable reason. Under the clear, moonlit sky the temperature was falling fast and by midnight would reach 14 degrees (−10°C). Hardly particular at this point, the exhausted men were ready to sleep anywhere:

> There wasn't lodging for our men in Elphin . . . so we slept in the coach, or rather *tried* to sleep, on the top of a hill, a few miles beyond Elphin. That was the *coldest* night, the heaviest frost of all. We could not sleep and most of us walked about to keep warm. Even the stout in the bus was frozen in the bottles that night.[29]

———

Sunday 2 March dawned even clearer and lovelier than the day before. A radiant sun nudged temperatures steadily upwards. It looked like another perfect day for the snow armies on both the Eastern and Western Fronts. No-one seemed to remember when the last consecutive pleasant weekend days had occurred. It must have been some time back in 1946.

In Boyle, Father Mulligan was determined to make Sunday more successful than the previous day. On Saturday the CIE and county council forces had done a superb job at road clearance, but he was displeased with the poor turn-out of local men in his parish. He knew that between his town and Sligo stood the "biggest snowdrift yet encountered, extending for 500 yards." Many more workers were needed. It was urgent, because the mammoth drift had trapped a number of buses and cars, their marooned passengers now no doubt frightened and hungry. There could be no excuse for shirking one's responsibility in such a crisis.

At Sunday mass he stepped up to the pulpit with a personal message. He told those before him that he had been sadly disappointed at the poor volunteer turn-out, and that, as "no action had been taken, he must appeal to his parishioners to show their charity towards those who had been on the road for days," suffering from their ordeal.[30] Every man in the parish was personally known to Father Mulligan. Some probably lowered their heads and stared at their lap as he spoke.

They took his words to be more than an "appeal." Within minutes of mass ending, volunteers were stepping forward. By noon there were more than forty fresh recruits, ready for road work with shovels and picks.

Around the country, scores of people had not been able to attend mass on Sunday because of the treacherous weather. Even if it wasn't blizzarding, the pavements and streets were icy and dangerous. People had safely stayed inside, especially the elderly. This Sunday many finally made it to mass. At Wheathill church in Co. Fermanagh people had not been able to attend mass for three weeks, because conditions had kept the priest away. To end this deprivation a very determined Father John McGrail of Killesher mounted a three-ton tractor early on Sunday morning and drove it some twelve miles, "passing through snowdrifts of over six feet deep," to celebrate mass at the church. When word got out of his arrival, nearly everyone trudged through the heavy snow in the bright sunshine to attend.

Shortly after noon the weary men who had tried to sleep aboard their freezing CIE coach near Elphin progressed onwards to Ballaghaderreen, liberating more marooned passengers along their way:

> At Ballaghaderreen we found one of the missing buses and freed it from a snowdrift. On our way we picked up many people who were stranded, including priests, women, children and others.[31]

Their good work was carried on throughout the afternoon as temperatures rose to nearly 40 degrees (4°c) under the welcome sun. By about 3 p.m. the men regarded their good deeds as deserving of a modest reward. As one member recalls it, "on Sunday there was brilliant sunshine, striking off the unending carpet of snow, enough to give one sunstroke—so we had iced stout, thawed out at our turf fire."[32]

Residents of Sligo were rewarded as well. After an ill-starred five-day journey, a goods train that had left Dublin on Tuesday finally rolled into town. It had been one of the missing "ghost trains," as CIE officials had no idea of its whereabouts for days. It was eventually discovered that it had been snowed up in a ten-foot drift at Carrick-on-Shannon. A snow-plough was sent out "to cleave a way for it, but even this was held up until a small army of railway men with shovels and picks" showed up to clear the track once and for all.[33] There was great rejoicing in Sligo, as the train carried much-needed food items and other household supplies.

———

With the weekend's calm, clear skies and comfortable temperatures, farmers throughout the country were able to venture out to check on their animals. At least what was left of them after six weeks of Arctic cold and four blizzards.

Newspapers also sent out reporters to tour the countryside and assess how badly the cattle and sheep had been stricken by the prolonged Siberian spell.

Few were prepared for what they found. Mass discoveries of animal carcases by farmers and snow armies brought horror. Hillsides, mountain slopes and valleys, from Co. Wicklow to Connemara, were littered with dead sheep, cows, horses, donkeys, goats, deer. Foxes, badgers, rabbits. Birds. Some cattle, sheep and horses were frozen in place, in grotesque forms. Snow armies came upon hundreds of animal carcases around them, sticking partially out of the snow. As if nature had slaughtered all the beasts of the land.

From Cos. Galway, Sligo and Roscommon came reports that the "continuous blizzards are taking a disastrous toll on the sheep population, now in the middle of lambing and weaning season." Near Westport one farmer told of taking seventy-five dead sheep out of a single snowdrift. The Rev. Mark Curtis of Glencullen, in the Dublin Mountains, in a half-mile walk from his house came across four dead sheep and seven dead horses. Passing one farm, he saw "cattle unable to rise because of starvation."[34] In Glendhu twenty-one cattle and two horses belonging to a Mrs McMahon were slowly drying before her eyes for want of fodder. Each day she watched them grow weaker, their eyes more dim.

On Sunday afternoon a reporter from the *Irish Press* drove out as far as he could on some roads outside Dublin to see if the stories of animal starvation were as tragic as he had heard. It didn't take long to find evidence:

> Starving animals standing in snow-covered fields were whipped with a cruel wind and were hungry. It was clear that if some lay down they would not get up again. No live sheep were seen. At one of the houses I watched 6 to 8 month old calves being helped to their legs when they tried to walk down the hill to drink. They were literally skin and bone. The wife of one farmer told me it is costing her husband a pound a day to get fodder to his stock. "They are not worth the money, but we can't let them die," she said.[35]

For farmers, worse than discovering their animals dead in the fields was coming upon those still barely alive, in the final, awful throes of starvation. The bellowing, moaning, guttural cries. Pleading eyes. Knowing that nothing could be done to alleviate their hunger or terminate suffering. That was the most excruciating to witness. Leaving indelible images in their minds.

Many farmers found themselves helpless. Even if snow armies cleared the main road near their land, the secondary roads leading directly to their farms remained under deep drifts. So, they were unable to bring fodder in or get their animals out to market while they still had some flesh on them. And many of those who were able to clear their road for transport realised that they could not afford fodder, which, as it became more scarce, was soaring in price. In early March, at Killarney, hay was selling at £16 a ton, which in an average season would fetch about £4 to £5 a ton.

Those fortunate farmers who were able to somehow get their cattle and sheep to Dublin's weekly stock market in Prussia Street sat in the bar of the City Arms Hotel or nearby pubs commiserating with one another and with buyers about the most God-awful winter they had ever experienced. Sipping pints or hot whiskeys, they matched gory stories about their scrawny animals. And their proof was just outside in the market pens, where animals little more than skin and bone were barely strong enough to stand. The men talked of nothing else:

> Farmers from widely separate parts of the country consoled one another with accounts of their fodder position and state of their livestock. Cattle dealers who had been marooned in the west recounted their experience for farmers from the eastern and Midland counties . . . and told of hundreds of sheep and cattle suffering from snow-blindness and drowned in snowdrifts.[36]

Farmers concurred that "a continuation of the Arctic conditions for another week" could wipe out their remaining emaciated animals.

Some men told stories of desperation as they brought into their house a goat or lamb. "Owners of ewes are having a time of it," one farm wife related, "the ewes don't want to take on with the lambs and the lambs are too weak to suck—everyone has pet lambs in the kitchens."[37] Poultry farmers added their stories of great loss, as immense numbers of hens had perished from cold and hunger, with no way to keep their sheds and coops warm enough for survival.

Nothing, it seemed, had been spared.

———

Snow armies had a large part to play in animal survival. It was up to them to clear the roads so that lorries could carry fodder and could transport animals. Farmers in every county were banking on them to open passages in time to save their animals.

Getting fodder to the farms was only half the task. Then it had to be carried across snow-packed terrain, sometimes great distances, to where trapped cattle and sheep were starving.

Efforts were made to inform the public of the deteriorating condition of the country's stock. Newspapers were now regularly issuing regional reports and publishing lengthy articles that were alarming to read. The Dublin Committee of Agriculture sent out documents on the crisis of starving animals, stating that "stock caught in the snow are dying for lack of fodder," explaining that it was the worst year such snowstorms could have happened, because the people on "high farms got no chance to make hay last season." Roads must be opened to farms so that fodder could be brought in.

One member of the committee, J. G. Litton, reported that he had seen farmers "carrying bundles of straw on their back for two miles" through deep snow. And these were not young men. The chairman, J. McGrane, added that he knew of a farmer in Co. Wicklow who had lost all but a few of his more than two hundred sheep. Meanwhile P. J. Burke TD, divisional director of the Irish Red Cross Society, issued an "urgent appeal to clear the snow-bound roads" in the Dublin and Wicklow Mountains, where "conditions were appalling . . . sheep and cattle starving and dying" in shocking numbers because fodder could not reach them.

In the Dublin papers calls were made for volunteers to help with shovelling farmers' roads clear and carrying fodder across snowy fields to desperate animals. Hopes were high for a massive turn-out on the sunny Sunday. Volunteers were directed in the newspapers where to report for duty, at Garda stations and other specified points. Here they would be provided with equipment, work orders, and transport. Organisers were anticipating a volunteer spirit similar to that of the "Save the Harvest" campaign of the previous year. This would be a "Save the Animals" effort. Many Dubliners had rural roots and would surely respond sympathetically to the animal crisis.

By 11 o'clock on Sunday morning, under a glaring sun and with temperatures already in the 30s, confident organisers waited for volunteers to begin streaming in to help the farmers with their animals. After a good breakfast they'd be ready for a full day's work. It was a day that was sure to bring everyone outside, as the next day's *Irish Independent* would gush:

> Spring seemed not far away in Dublin—another day of bright sunshine from an almost cloudless sky, which brought thousands out into the fresh air again after weeks in blizzard-bound homes.[38]

At noon, organisers at the volunteer centres stood puzzled. Where were the helpers? Only a few were trickling in to grab a shovel. Because of a natural sensitivity towards animals, especially among Dubliners with farm backgrounds, it had been assumed that the turn-out would be large. By 1 o'clock it was clear that this was a faulty assumption. Conversely, by the thousands sun-starved Dubliners were flocking to the Phoenix Park, St Stephen's Green and Fairview Park with sleds and toboggans to enjoy a delightful day of recreation.

By the end of the day, at a volunteer centre at Stepaside Garda Barracks, where hundreds had been expected, "not more than 25 showed up." The story was much the same at the other meeting-points. Organisers were disappointed. And perplexed. One organiser groused: "Only a few people answered the appeal for help on Sunday—but 600 people were skiing" south of the city at the "Swiss resort" areas.[39]

An estimate that was probably quite low.

Chapter 9 ༁

| QUARRY POND TRAGEDY

Chance is always a silent partner in disaster. Bad luck, bad timing, the wrong choice at a crucial moment.

(DAVID LASKIN, *The Children's Blizzard*, 2004)

The pond, since the blizzard, has attracted children to skate on the frozen surface. Civic guards have been trying to keep children from skating on the pond . . . but as soon as they chased the children away they returned by another route.

(*Irish Times*, 4 MARCH 1947)

A particularly poignant feature of the tragedy was that one of the boys who eventually disappeared was seen to pull at least four children to safety.

(*Irish Independent*, 3 MARCH 1947)

SUNDAY 2 MARCH

Among the crowds of Dubliners luxuriating in Sunday's sunshine and warmer temperatures were many skaters who had been itching for a nice day to get out on the ice covering the city's canals, ponds, and lakes. Newspapers, however, had repeatedly warned citizens that it was not safe to do so. Despite the prolonged freezing there had also been a number of "quick thaws," which had weakened ice platforms. These warnings were backed by reminders of tragic drownings in past years. And several this winter as well.

Indeed just that week Joseph Naan, aged eleven, of Belturbet, was drowned in the River Erne when skating with other children. A gallant attempt to save his life was made by Eileen Dolan, also eleven. She caught hold of the boy when the ice broke but was also pulled into the water, nearly drowning herself. She was barely rescued by a man on the scene, James Sullivan, who risked his own life in passing a long stick to her, pulling her to safety.[1] That same day, not far away, a similar tragedy was averted only by good fortune. Bernard Fitzpatrick and Cornelius Gallagher from Enniskillen, both fourteen, experienced what the *Irish Independent* called a "remarkable escape from drowning" when the ice on Lough Erne broke under them. Only with the lucky assistance of a rope were they saved.

There was yet another near-accident when a foolhardy young lad, William Boyd, took a gamble on Lough Erne's ice, plunging into the water when it broke. William Gillen was nearby to hear his shouts for help and pull him to safety by using his coat. Otherwise, within minutes he would have succumbed to the numbing cold and perished.

Reports of near-drownings were common around the country. Several people had not survived. In Dublin there had been some very close shaves. Yet the temptation to test the ice was irresistible to many.

Most Dublin children had a healthy fear of walking on ice. But that did not always stop them from doing so. "The canals were frozen and people were walking on the canals," remembers Joe Kirwan, "and lives were lost—oh, yes." Although Carmel Byrne knew better, she and her young pals would often take the chance. "When the canals were frozen we would cut across instead of taking the long way around." And boys were always throwing heavy objects onto ice surfaces to see if they could break them.

Parents were constantly reminding their children to stay off the ice. Most children were obedient, others simply forgetful or dismissive. Seán Whelan took his mother's words seriously. "All the rivers and canals were frozen up. It was very dangerous. My mother would *never* let us on the ice." Lakes and rivers with deeper water were the most hazardous. Like most savvy city children, Richard Gerster knew the difference:

> We used to skate on the ponds in the Green [St Stephen's Green], 'cause if you fell through it wouldn't matter, because it's only about two feet deep. But the Liffey was frozen—and you could walk across *it*. You wouldn't *think* the Liffey would freeze, but it did! It was that *cold*. I wouldn't have been brave enough to walk on it . . . 'cause if you went through the ice . . . And it happened to a few of them, went down and they were drowned.

By far the most popular and safe place for skating was on the lake at Dublin Zoo. During cold winters it was opened to public skating, but only after the authorities carefully measured the thickness of the ice at various points and were positive of its safety. They had a method for helping nature along. Several nights before opening for skating the lake was "flooded to take advantage of the night's frost in thickening the ice."[2] Four to five inches was usually considered a safe layer. On the delightfully sunny weekend of 1/2 March, Dublin skaters were thrilled when zoo officials announced in the papers that the pond was open to the public. Great numbers showed up to play on the ice, young and old. With skates and without.

Some people, especially children, may have taken the zoo's

announcement of skating safety on its pond to apply to all the city's lakes and ponds.

———

By midday the temperature was in the high 30s (2 to 4°C) and surely headed towards the 40s by afternoon. Such glorious weather was not to be squandered. After mass, every child in the city flew home, yanked off his church clothes, grabbed a bite to eat, and tossed a "goodbye" to his Ma as he barged out the door to join his pals in play outside. Having been confined indoors for so many dreary, sunless weeks, Dublin children were about to burst with pent-up energy. The streets came alive once again, teeming with happy, yelling, squealing children "on the loose." Dashing around with the pure joy of unrestrained freedom. Seeking fun wherever they could find it. In their exuberance they felt unusually carefree, perhaps even a little careless. Adults out strolling on the fine Sunday afternoon found much pleasure in seeing the city's parks and streets enlivened with the laughter and antics of children.

Tens of thousands of Dubliners had other plans. That afternoon at 3:30 in Dalymount Park there was an important, much-anticipated soccer match between very good Irish and Spanish teams. An exciting international contest. Dublin sportsmen, after so many weekends of cancellation disappointments, were charged with enthusiasm, knowing that it was definitely on. A huge crowd of excited spectators was expected. Even many women planned to attend, anxious to get out of the house into fresh, sunny weather in an exhilarating social setting. Their confinement had been claustrophobic as well.

By early afternoon flocks of people were heading towards the Phoenix Park, the zoo, Fairview Park, and St Stephen's Green, where paths and walkways had been cleared to accommodate visitors. Most children from Kimmage and Crumlin were content to play locally, where they had plenty of streets and open spaces. In the 1940s parents had little worry about their children gallivanting around the district. Parental warnings were mostly to be polite, watch out for horses and vehicles, don't get too dirty, don't be too loud—"use your head, now—and behave!" Most children were mindful and obedient. Perhaps forgetful. Occasionally foolhardy. Normal childish failings.

Mothers and fathers in Kimmage and Crumlin felt their young ones to be quite safe when they set out for a day of play.

———

With one glaring exception. The Ramparts, as it was known locally. A deep pond in an abandoned quarry that gave many parents plenty of worry.

The quarry, off Sundrive Road (now the site of Éamonn Ceannt Park), had been owned by Mount Argus Brick Company. Disused for nearly fifty years, it covered almost three acres and varied in depth from 20 to 30 feet; however, some pockets were alleged to be 50 feet deep or more. Some called it a "death trap," and for good reason. Over the years it had taken a number of children's lives. No-one seemed to know for certain just how many, but in 1947 local people knew well that over the previous five to eight years it had taken three or four lives. Parents took its dangers seriously; children too often did not.

After each tragedy there had been the usual outcry for safety measures. A fence had been erected after the last drownings, but children had no trouble getting through, over or under the fence if they had a whim to swim on a hot summer's day, or skate in the winter. In a short time the fence had been torn apart.

The Ramparts had its moods. Its different faces. Some attractive, seductively inviting. Others sullen, dark, foreboding. The water and rock changed with the seasons, lighting, time of day, colour of the sky, winds. To local people it had a fascinating split personality that made it worthy of viewing as one passed by. Some people were quite taken with the old quarry pond, regularly pausing to gaze upon it. Its grey, craggy contours were a unique feature of the local landscape. At certain times—dusk, nightfall, during storms or cold grips—it could look particularly murky and dark. To some, menacingly mediaeval.

It *always* looked mysterious.

Children were both attracted to and repelled by the old quarry pond. Every child had heard of the danger, the drownings. But on a hot, stuffy August day its shimmering silvery water looked cool and inviting for a quick swim. Or at least to skip some stones or to dangle one's feet in the water. In the winter, when ice-capped, it called out for a good game of ice hockey or skating. Or a bit of daring sliding. While the majority of children were fearful enough not to dare risking their life, others exhibited a youthful, reckless abandon. Especially those who liked to boldly show off before their pals, or be part of the "action."

Then there were those who simply had memory lapses . . . or moments of poor judgement.

On the afternoon of Saturday 1 March the local gardaí had chased a bunch of careless youths off the ice. On duty that weekend were Sergeant Roche, Garda Steele, Garda Donnelan and Garda Lannin from Sundrive station, only a short distance from the pond. They knew the Ramparts and its dark history. And they knew the local children. Making their daily rounds in summer and winter months, they often had to shout at children to get away from the water, or the ice. But this weekend, after such prolonged confinement, the children seemed unusually rumbustious, prone to risky behaviour. The guards understood this, as they too were in high spirits with the invigorating weather.

Ordinarily, the guards would first fling a few friendly shouts towards the children to clear them off the ice. This Saturday they called a number of them over and explained to them the serious risks they were taking, in a gentle, paternal manner. All good kids, they knew most by name and behaviour. But there were the usual few reckless ones or rebels in the gang. Usually the children got off the ice and wandered away. This weekend, however, there were more children on the ice than ever before, and this worried the guards.

A number of youngsters were engaged in a spirited game of ice hockey, with a crowd of others standing close by watching, placing quite a weight of bodies on a small space of ice. Consequently, on Saturday afternoon at about 3 o'clock the guards issued a louder, sterner warning to clear off the ice—at once. The children scattered, most heading over to the far side of the three-acre pond, some of the bolder ones jeering back at the "coppers," laughing, taunting them. All friendly enough. It was the usual cat-and-mouse game for children and police. The *Irish Independent* wrote:

> It was known to be very dangerous, but efforts by the Gardaí to keep local children away from it proved unsuccessful. On several occasions during Saturday the Gardaí cleared the pond of skaters—but then they came back again.[3]

The mice simply outwaited the cats. When the guards continued on their rounds, the children took to the ice once again and resumed their skating and games. Meanwhile throughout the afternoon more children were showing up, venturing out onto the ice.

————

John Byrne of Crumlin was an avid soccer fan who had been looking forward for weeks to the clash between Ireland and Spain at Dalymount Park. At breakfast on Sunday morning he invited his thirteen-year-old son Christopher—better known as Kit—to join him, telling him it would be an afternoon to remember. Kit was the third-eldest of a family of three boys and two girls and clearly one of his father's favourites, as he excelled in both hurling and football with his school teams at St Columba's CBS. His Da never tired of telling friends what a naturally talented young athlete he was, how he had won medals in both sports. What a great future lay ahead of him. Kit was not a risk-taker, especially when it came to swimming or skating at the old quarry. Many times, to family and friends, he had unabashedly expressed his fear of its deep, dark waters. His pals knew he wouldn't go near it.

He gratefully declined his father's invitation, explaining that he didn't want to sit confined on benches all afternoon and miss all the fun with his friends on the first good weekend in weeks. He had a ton of energy to burn off. His Da understood that his son didn't want to sit passively watching other athletes compete in front of him. He would let it be Kit's decision.

Close by in Crumlin lived sixteen-year-old Anthony Burke. His father, Patrick, was a widower, at present unemployed, struggling to raise his family of eight children. Anthony, the fourth-youngest of five boys and three girls, worked at Johnston, Mooney and O'Brien's flour mill to financially help his family. It was difficult to feed nine mouths and keep a bit of fire going on freezing nights. Working so hard at such a young age made Anthony more mature and responsible than most sixteen-year-olds. He hadn't got much time for boyish play. Sundays were his favourite day, time for himself to knock around with pals, forget work. He too loved hurling and was a real competitor. Always ready for a spirited contest—in a field, on the street, out on an ice pond. His father had great respect for his son, who was hard-working and had a good, sensible head on his shoulders.

Not far away lived eight-year-old Edward O'Toole, who was equally eager to get outside on Sunday afternoon in the 40-degree (4°C) air and play until he had to come home for supper. A pupil at St Agnes' Convent Schools, he was a scrappy youngster who didn't mind mixing it with the older fellas in a tough game. He also liked the cinema. Sometimes he had to make a choice between an outdoor game and a weekend matinée. He was the third-youngest of three boys and four girls.

On the afternoon of Sunday 2 March it is not known whether Christopher Byrne, Anthony Burke and Edward O'Toole knew one another. But their names were about to be linked together from that day forward.

———

At about 1:15 p.m. John Byrne decided he had better set out for Dalymount Park, as the crowd was predicted to be massive and he had heard that people could be turned away. As he pulled on his coat he half-heartedly asked Kit one more time if he'd like to come along. No, thanks. His father probably gave him an understanding smile, perhaps a pat on the shoulder when saying goodbye. He promised to tell Kit all about the match when he returned that evening.

As he waited in the long queue at Dalymount Park he was struck by the unusually large number of women, a fact about which even the newspapers would comment. He also noticed that many men had brought along their young sons to share the experience. The gathering crowd's behaviour seemed rather out of the ordinary as well. Many men in the queue were jostling those ahead of them as they anxiously edged their way forward. Some had conspicuously been drinking, acting unusually aggressively.

About half an hour after his father had departed, Kit took up his hurley, said a quick goodbye to his mother, and rushed out the door to join his pals. As newspapers would later report, "she never thought he was going to the pond, for he often spoke about the danger of it." There were plenty of streets in which they could play on a Sunday afternoon. However, someone in the group suggested a game of ice hockey—on the old quarry pond.

As they drifted towards Sundrive Road it is not known what was going through Kit's mind. But he evidently didn't protest, or part from his pals. It was close to 2:20 p.m. when he reached the Ramparts and stood at the edge of the ice, hurley in hand. He had never in his life dared to step out on the pond's frozen surface. Now he was facing the prospect of skating out on the ice, some distance from the shore. It is not known how long he stood and deliberated. There were already many children of all ages playing across the three-acre frozen pond, some as young as six and seven. His pals had found some old rags, which they tied together to place on the ice as goal markers. They were about ready to choose sides.

This time something overruled his fear. He took a step onto the ice. Then another, and another.

John Byrne was now seated in Dalymount Park, where thousands were converging to see the match. But many spectators, once inside, were becoming even more aggressive as they tried to force their way close to the field. Sometimes pushing, shoving, even knocking others down who were in their way. Officials spotted trouble brewing early in one section of spectators, as described by an *Irish Press* reporter on the scene:

> Long before the game began, the crowd on St. Peter's Road—the popular side—was swaying dangerously. Gardaí and stewards tried to push them back as, under pressure from behind, the first trickle came on to the field. Soon the trickle had become a flood and appeals for order were made.[4]

The majority of orderly spectators were by now becoming nervous about the increasingly unruly behaviour of some hundreds.

As the mayhem at Dalymount was rising, eight-year-old Eddie O'Toole, hurley in hand, was about to leave home. His exact parting words to his father were that he was "going out to play in the streets."[5] *Streets.* To be repeated in his father's mind over and over.

As he approached the pond he heard the excited shouts of other children out on the ice and saw that an ice hockey game was being organised. He was eager to join in. Just then he ran into his pal, nine-year-old Patrick Reilly, who was talking enthusiastically about a matinée film he wanted to see that afternoon. Would Eddie like to join him? He had no money in his pocket at the time. Should he return home and ask his Da for a few pence? After

28. Dublin's tenement world, such as this in Sterling Street in the Liberties, was one of broken windows, doors, stairs and roofs—little protection against freezing winds.

Young "Haulage Contractor"

29. A girl at a Dublin turf depot "for hire" to carry heavy wet sods, to help her family financially.

SUNDAY INDEPENDENT

VOL. 42. No. 8. D DUBLIN, SUNDAY, FEBRUARY 23, 1947. PRICE TWOPENCE. B

DUBLIN PARALYSED BY GREAT FREEZE-UP

A Night Of Mishaps

Forecast For To-day

AFTER A DAY OF SPASMODIC SUNSHINE AND A TEMPORARY THAW, KING WINTER RETURNED TO BATTLE WITH RENEWED VIGOUR IN DUBLIN LAST NIGHT, FROST AND SNOW COMBINING IN AN ONSLAUGHT WHICH, FOR A FEW HOURS, CAUSED GENERAL PARALYSIS OF TRAFFIC.

From 6 p.m. onwards snow fell steadily for over three hours, and by 9 p.m. the temperature had dropped several degrees below freezing point.

At this time the city had become a vast skating rink. Buses and practically all traffic on the north side of the city had virtually come to a complete standstill. The more courageous motorists, travelling at a snail's pace, found their cars executing

all sorts of weird tricks on the treacherous road surface, particularly when negotiating corners, and even amongst the most cautious pedestrians, falls were not infrequent.

Shortly after 10 p.m. a *Sunday Independent'* reporter witnessed the extraordinary sight of about 80 buses, outward and inward bound, held up between Nelson Pillar and the traffic lights at Dorset Street corner.

An incoming bus attempting to negotiate the turn from Upper Dorset St. into North Frederick St. skidded and struck the traffic lights

11 p.m. nearly all traffic was again in motion. The snow had ceased but a clear sky threatened a further freeze-up before the morning.

Cyclist Killed

Many minor accidents on the city's treacherous, slippery streets and footpaths and one tragedy were reported yesterday morning.

Percy Hughes, 6 Richmond Ave., Fairview, fell off his bicycle on North Strand Road on his way to work. He was rendered unconscious and was found to be dead when the fire brigade ambulance brought him to Jervis St. Hospital.

New Blizzard "Worst

30. The blizzard of 22–23 February created especially treacherous icy conditions, leading to a mass of pedestrian and traffic accidents. Hospitals were strained.

31. Tony Ruane (*second from left, being held*) and family of Straide, Co. Mayo. In 1947 his family took in bus and car passengers who had been marooned on local snowbound roads.

32. Workmen at a turf dump in the Phoenix Park standing around a fire during their lunch break.

"Oh, begob, it's wet all right, ma'am, but it's *HONESTLY* wet this time."

33. *Dublin Opinion* shows an "honest" man selling wet turf, as opposed to black-marketers and profiteers.

34. Dublin's farriers, such as John Boyne, worked sixteen to eighteen hours a day frost-nailing horses. The forge itself offered real fire and warmth for the favoured few allowed inside.

35. Motorists took their chances on snow-packed roads. Hundreds became stuck, with passengers marooned, many overnight.

36. In late February the Minister for Industry and Commerce, Seán Lemass, declared Ireland's fuel crisis to be the most severe in the country's history.

37. Jack Conroy (*second on right*) and his mates at Buckingham Street Fire Station were kept busy as chimney fires occurred at a record rate when people burned wet turf and wood.

38. Guinness workmates William Tinnion (*left*) and Liam Cradden (*right*). Tinnion and his fellow-stokers were forced to burn coal dust, called "duff", when coal ran out. Then they resorted to burning painters' ladders and scaffolding—"Oh, we were *desperate!*"

HOUSEHOLD FURNITURE AT *McBirney's* As Poses From O'Connell Bridge

of your hair by using **Mutesco** from Chemists

(INCORPORATING THE "EVENING TELEGRAPH")
VOL. 56, No. 49. DUBLIN, WEDNESDAY, FEBRUARY 26, 1947 PRICE THREEHALFPENCE.

GREAT DAMAGE IN WAKE OF BLIZZARD

Was Cyclist Blown Away?

ENNISKERRY-GLENCREE ROAD

SNOW PILED SIX FEET DEEP

MANY AREAS ARE STILL ISOLATED

("Herald" Staff Reporter)

FOR THE SECOND TIME THIS MONTH COMMUNICATIONS AND TRANSPORT THROUGHOUT THE COUNTRY ARE CONSIDERABLY DISRUPTED FOLLOWING THE MOST SEVERE SNOWFALL OF THE PRESENT ANTARCTIC SPELL. CONDITIONS ARE STATED TO BE "INDESCRIBABLY BAD."

Neither the Post Office authorities nor the E.S.B. are even yet aware of the extent of the damage. Areas in the Midlands and the West—which suffered the greatest effects of the storm—were to-day still isolated to a great extent.

Another Thousand

NORTH-WEST Conditions Beggar Decription

POLES DOWN

NORMAL AIR SERVICES

BREAK NEAR NENAGH

"Truman U
U.S.
OVER
ACC

39. On the day following the greatest blizzard, that of 25 February, conditions were described by the authorities as "indescribably bad" and said to "beggar description," with areas completely isolated.

40. A man at a Phoenix Park turf clamp shovelling the last remains of wet, disintegrated sods.

FERNANDO AGUS AN DRAGAN

" That's the best bit of fire I've seen for a long time. Now we know where the dry turf is going ! "

41. *Dublin Opinion* reveals the secret of "where the dry turf is going"!

42. Stonecutters like Dermot Broe were forced to work out in the elements, without gloves or fires. Conditions were primitive and painful.

43. In the first week of March a fifth major blizzard battered the south, especially Cos. Cork, Waterford and Wexford.

GRAIN SHIP LOST NEAR DUBLIN

Famous British Admiral Among The Rescued

RUNNING before a half gale, the s.s. Bolivar (5,230 tons), a model Norwegian cargo-passenger ship, on her maiden voyage from Buenos Aires to Dublin with a cargo of grain, went aground yesterday on a sandbank at the Kish Light, six miles from Dun Laoghaire, and broke her back.

The 39 members of the crew and the 12 passengers, who included Admiral Lord Mountevans ("Evans of the Broke") and his wife, were taken off by lifeboat and brought ashore, the officers and passengers going to the Royal Marine Hotel, and the remainder of the crew to the Seamen's Institute, Dublin.

The forepart of the ship, which broke away, contained a considerable part of the grain cargo (5,000 tons of maize and 600 tons of barley). It sank almost at once into the sand, and only a small portion of the bows is visible above the water.

...ebelts, arriving on the lifeboat at Dun Laoghaire.

In response to signals from the Bolivar the Dun Laoghaire lifeboat put to sea and took off all members of the crew of 39 and 12 passengers, while a Dublin Port and Docks tug, which also went to the rescue, took off six members of the crew and landed them at the North Wall.

One of the passengers Mr Trygve Andvord, a brother-in-law of Lord Mountevans, was taken to St Michael's Hospital, Dun Laoghaire, with a suspected fracture of the arm, sustained when he was clambering down the side of the broken ship to the lifeboat.

The lifeboat, with the crew and passengers, arrived at Dun Laoghaire shortly before 11 p.m., and as the crew came ashore they jumped about trying to restore circulation in their chilled limbs. Some of the women passengers had to be carried to the waiting cars obviously exhausted from their experiences.

"EVERYBODY CALM."

Smiling broadly, Lord Mountevans made light of the mishap. He told an Irish Independent representative that he had gone on the trip with his wife and son "just for the ride." They sailed from Buenos Aires and

A Model Ship

THE Bolivar, a model cargo-passenger twin-screw ship, was launched at Oslo in 1946, but this was its maiden voyage. It had special quarters for crews and most comfortable suites for passengers. A sister ship of the Bolivar, the Benghazi, is due in Dublin to-day. The master of the Bolivar is Capt. Sigurd Rasmussen.

we moved to the after part of the ship," he said. "The fo'castle and numbers one and two hatches broke away from the ship. The passengers remained huddled together under the bridge.

"When the lifeboat arrived everybody took turns scrambling down the side of the boat."

He added that they had lost all their belongings, but if the sea went down there was a chance of getting them off the broken ship. He and his wife were going to Norway for a skiing holiday. On

44. During the blizzards of 4 March the 5,230-ton *Bolivar*, carrying the famous Admiral Lord Mountevans, ran aground on a sandbank six miles off Dún Laoghaire and broke in two.

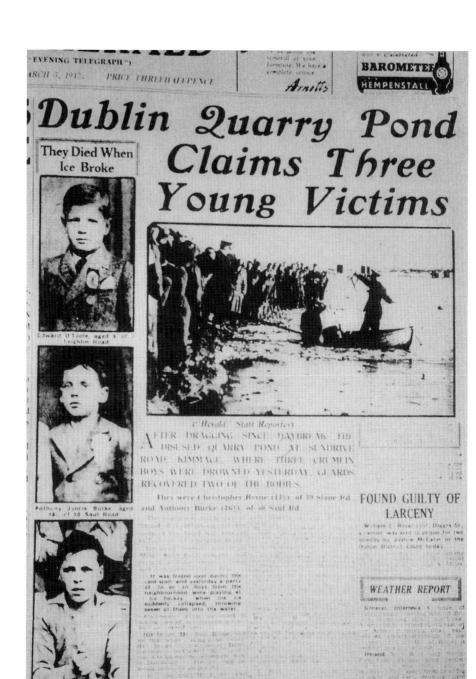

("EVENING TELEGRAPH")

ARCH 6, 1912.   PRICE THREE HALFPENCE

Arnotts

Dublin Quarry Pond Claims Three Young Victims

They Died When Ice Broke

Edward O'Toole, aged 8, of Leighlin Road

Anthony James Burke, aged 16, of 50 Saul Road

Christopher Byrne, aged 11, of 39 Slane Road

("Herald" Staff Reporter)

AFTER DRAGGING SINCE DAYBREAK THE DISUSED QUARRY POND AT SUNDRIVE ROAD, KIMMAGE, WHERE THREE CRUMLIN BOYS WERE DROWNED YESTERDAY, GUARDS RECOVERED TWO OF THE BODIES.

They were Christopher Byrne (11) of 39 Slane Rd. and Anthony Burke (16), of 50 Saul Rd.

It was frozen over during the cold spell, and yesterday a party of 20 or 30 boys from the neighbourhood were playing at ice hockey when the ice suddenly collapsed, throwing seven of them into the water.

He had four medals for playing on the senior football and hurling teams at St. Columbus Christian Brothers' School.

FOUND GUILTY OF LARCENY

William C. Boyd (39), Digges St., a carrier, was sent to prison for two months by Justice McCarthy at the Dublin District Court to-day.

WEATHER REPORT

General Inference:

Ireland

Further Outlook

46. *Dublin Opinion* devoted an entire page to a serious sketch of the herculean struggle between farmers and the weather.

THE DAY WHEN THE SHAMROCK WAS "DEAR"!

("Herald" Staff Reporter)

FROZEN UP, SNOWED ON, RAINED ON, AND FLOODED OUT, IRELAND GREETED ST. PATRICK'S DAY WITH A FERVENT HOPE THAT THE NATIONAL APOSTLE WOULD TURN THAT MUCH-TALKED-ABOUT STONE AND GIVE US THAT CHANGE OF WEATHER WE HAVE SO LONG AWAITED.

47. Arctic weather created a severe shortage of shamrock by St Patrick's Day. For the first time in history it went on the black market.

48. Eddie McGrane, eighteen years old in 1947, was hiking with pals from An Óige when a surprise blizzard struck hard in the Wicklow Mountains.

49. May Hanaphy and her workmates at Jacob's biscuit factory in Bishop Street welcomed the warmth of the big ovens but worried about losing their jobs when the factory's fuel became precariously low.

50. When the tillage crisis worsened, the *Sunday Independent* published a large shocking depiction of Famine stalking the country again, a frightening spectre to many Irish people.

mulling it over for a few seconds, he decided he would rather spend the afternoon outdoors in the sunshine than in a dark cinema. A fateful decision, Patrick Reilly remembers:

> I met Eddie O'Toole at the quarry. I had money for the pictures—but he had no money, so we spent what I had [on sweets] and then went over to the quarry and started to play on the ice.[6]

Among the players joining in was sixteen-year-old Anthony Burke, enjoying his day off from the flour mill. One of the older lads, he was a leader on his team. He knew when to mix it with a tangle of opponents and when to drop back for defence.

It is not known whether any of the ice-hockey lads talked among themselves about the danger of packing so closely together on the ice. Possibly so. But their decision was clear, as a rousing contest was under way by 2:45 or thereabouts. Surrounded by a growing crowd of onlookers.

The ice groaned.

By three o'clock some spectator sections at Dalymount Park looked more like a rugby match, with people shoving back and forth. Some groups of men had that nasty "pack mentality" look about them. As more people were admitted through the gates, the ground became jammed with humanity. Too tightly. By 3:15 some 42,000 highly charged soccer fans had been crammed inside. Others were now being turned away. Before long there were at least 5,000 displeased spectators left outside. Some in fits of protest and howls of cursing. At least fifty of them clambered over to view the match from the roof of the old tram depot that overlooked the grounds. With disruptive, physically threatening behaviour erupting both inside and outside the ground, more gardaí and stewards were being rushed to the scene to try to regain control.

———

Across the city at the old quarry pond in Kimmage, Garda Donnelan and Garda Lannin heard the cries of happy children before they arrived at the pond on their usual round. Spotting even more children out on the ice than on Saturday, they hastened to the edge of the ice and yelled the usual orders: "Clear the ice, now, clear the ice!" Some younger children immediately scampered away, while older ones reluctantly, slowly shuffled off to the far side of the pond. Especially disappointed were the ice-hockey players, caught in the middle of their highly contested game. As usual, some of the fellas jeered back at the coppers. There were some smiles on both sides. The normal cat-and-mouse routine ensued as the children simply awaited the departure of the guards. When they eventually ambled away down the road, the children filtered back onto the ice.

At 3:20, ten minutes before scheduled match time, under a bright, welcoming sun, the Spanish Minister to Ireland, Count d'Artaza, stepped into the grandstand, smiling and waving his arms. Then President Ó Ceallaigh received a cheer as he greeted the players, who were respectfully lined up. As the two countries' national anthems were played, colourful flags fluttered. For 42,000 Irishmen, cooped up in their homes during sunless, bleak weeks of sleet, snow, and blizzards, many with fireless grates and little food, the scene was gloriously colourful, lively, and exciting.

If it hadn't been for the contumacious behaviour of so many spectators it would have been a perfect setting. Unfortunately, as match time approached, their manners worsened. A good many were now acting like outright hooligans, fuelled by drink in many cases. In a few sections the gardaí had a real donnybrook on their hands, as even women and children were being shoved and knocked to the ground. Outnumbered, the gardaí fought to control the ruffians who were pushing, pushing, pushing forward onto the field, like a stampede. Those around them were fearful for their welfare, as people were being injured. At this point the Irish officials, as hosts, must have felt embarrassment, perhaps explaining to d'Artaza and his delegation that the Irish people had had a "rough winter" and were over-zealous this Sunday. A lame excuse for such unruly and uncivil behaviour.

About ten minutes past the official match time it was decided to try to get the contest under way, in the hope that the action might engage the attention of the trouble-makers and settle them down. Unfortunately it made some of the men push even harder towards the field. At 3:50 the "crowds surged down to the touch-lines while more packed themselves behind the goal posts. The guards did their best but it was impossible."[7] The situation was now completely out of hand, and the referee made the decision to halt the match, sending the Irish and Spanish players, who were even concerned for their welfare, back to their dressing-rooms for twenty-five minutes.

The young athletes at the old quarry pond were exhibiting good sportsmanship in their spirited ice hockey match. And the crowd of children around them were behaving in an orderly manner, enthusiastically cheering the play. At a glance, the happiest of scenes.

———

3:57 p.m.
It wasn't a sharp snap. More the sickening sound of a dull "crunch." The fracture raced along the ice as it would along a geological fault line. Encircling a frozen platform which broke off in pieces, creating a hole in the ice. With shocking suddenness, the boys who had been playing on that patch of ice were plunged into the freezing water.

In a split second all was pandemonium and confusion. Every person there would remember it somewhat differently. Out of fear and panic, children's minds became muddled, some as numbed as the bodies of those thrashing about in the water.

Amidst the bedlam, crying, and shrieking, children began running in every direction—*away* from the hole, *towards* it; *off* the pond, *onto* it. Racing down to the Garda station in Sundrive Road, or straight home. Some just stood in a dazed state.

Instinctively, "numbers of children who were on the pond went immediately to the aid of their playmates."[8] For a few, a near-fatal—or fatal—mistake. What they first saw was six or seven boys hysterically crying out for help, some trying to pull themselves out. Those unable to swim well, or at all, were madly dog-paddling in an effort just to stay afloat, looking desperately at those on the ice for a helping hand. Their soaked clothing and shoes weighing them down like an anchor.

Children rushing to save them reacted differently. Some foolishly ran to the very edge of the hole and leaned over to put their hand out, their weight cracking off another chunk of ice beneath their feet and toppling them in. Those more aware instantly dropped flat on the ice, spreading their body out as they crept forward. Some removed their coats, held one sleeve tightly and flung it out into the water to be grasped. Several children smartly ran in search of a rope to use as a lifeline. With would-be rescuers falling in, before long there were probably as many as ten or eleven boys struggling for their lives, and at least one girl.

Among them was Eddie O'Toole, who could have been sitting in a warm picture-house. Though younger than the others, he and his pal Patrick Reilly had been allowed to join in the hockey game. "We started to play on the ice," Patrick Reilly recalled, "and I ran after the ball—and when I came back he was in the water."

Twelve-year-old Veronica Browne and her friend Norah Kelly had been watching the game when the ice broke only a few feet from where she was standing. She acted instantly:

> I saw a little boy in the water. I ran over to help him. There was a hurley on the ice. I took it up to hand to the boy in the water. Then the ice broke and I fell in. A good few others fell into the water then.[9]

From where Patrick was standing it looked as if Eddie was about to be pulled out to safety, as "a big fella had hold of him by the hair. He was pulling him up when the ice broke and he fell in also." He was not sure of his identity, but it could well have been Anthony Burke, who had apparently not fallen into the water immediately but had gone to the rescue of those who had. A lad named

Ryan from Ferns Road saw Burke in action. "A boy of about 16 who was skating near the spot rescued at least four children—and then himself sank and disappeared."[10]

Two adults, Patrick Walsh and Thomas McMahon, saw it all happen. Out on a leisurely Sunday sunshine stroll, they happened upon the pond at the very moment of the ice split, as Walsh would later describe:

> We both ran over and saw a hole in the ice and a small boy in the water. A girl and another boy were trying to get them out—then the ice broke and *they* fell in. A boy named Burke took off his coat, held the sleeve and threw it to the youngsters in the water—but the ice broke and he also fell in.[11]

By now, thirteen-year-old Kit Byrne, who might well have been sitting beside his father at Dalymount Park, had tumbled into the water trying to pull other boys out. Walsh and McMahon quickly found themselves making every effort to save Kit Byrne and Veronica Browne. Explained Walsh:

> McMahon's feet slipped into the water and one of the lads in the water caught his foot and he was pulled in. I threw him a rope that a child had brought up and pulled him out. Then I threw the rope to young Byrne. He caught it in one hand and took hold of the girl in the water with the other hand.[12]

It looked as though both Kit Byrne and Veronica Browne, whom he was clutching by her clothing and pulling along, would be drawn to safety.

At about this same moment children who had run down to the Garda station were babbling to the guards what had happened. As Garda Steele, Garda Donnelan and Garda Lannin dashed towards the pond, Sergeant Roche was on the phone, calling for an ambulance and doctor, suggesting that he might also be needing a boat and a dragging team. Dozens of other children were now reaching their homes, crying, blurting out to parents what they had seen.

Patrick Walsh was slowly, cautiously pulling Kit Byrne by rope towards the edge of the hole, as the boy steadfastly held on to Veronica, towing her behind, somehow possessing the presence of mind to try to save her as well as himself. But Walsh saw that he was fading, beginning to lose his grip on the rope, slip away below the surface. He and the other boys who had fallen into the icy water were by now in the grip of hypothermia, and on the brink of drowning. In their frantic effort to stay afloat or reach for help they had expended great energy. Their body temperature had plummeted, limbs becoming numb, leaden. As bodily movements slowed, so did the brain. Mental grogginess made everything murky, dim. Even fear faded.

With the rope, Walsh had drawn Kit and Veronica to within only feet of being pulled safely up onto the ice. Just as he was about to grab Kit and yank him up, "he then sank, and let go of the rope. The girl sank down—but she came up again."

Beside Walsh now were two older boys, about eighteen or nineteen, who had just come on the scene, Michael Halpin and John Abbey. When Halpin saw the girl's head bob up he knew there was still a chance to save her. He grabbed the rope:

> I got out on the ice with a piece of rope, and while John Abbey held me I gave the rope to the girl in the water. She managed to catch it as she was going down, and we pulled her out.[13]

As she was trembling uncontrollably, Halpin wrapped his coat around her and was able, barely, to get out of her where she lived. He hoisted her up on his back. "I brought her home . . . She told me her name was Veronica Browne."

Meanwhile another adult, Thomas Mardy, was engaged in rescue efforts on the far side of the hole. He had been returning from the Sundrive cinema when "he saw the ice on the pond suddenly break and a number of children fell into the water."[14] He could barely believe his eyes. As he tore towards the scene he spotted a lifebuoy hanging near the pond, grabbed it, and carried it to the hole in the ice. As later recounted to a reporter from the *Irish Independent*:

> He seized the lifebuoy and going on to the ice threw it towards the hole where at least two boys were struggling. As he did so, the ice broke under his feet and he fell into the water. He tried to swim towards the boys but they disappeared . . . And he had to be assisted out of the pond.[15]

As he was nearing both of them with the lifebuoy he saw that they were succumbing to hypothermia and fatigue. It was only a matter of a few feet, he told the reporter, "I *tried* to swim towards the youths with the life-buoy . . . but I was too late, as they had gone down in the water." From his account it was not possible to identify with certainty the two boys he was trying to rescue. One was probably Anthony Burke.

Fortunately for the historical record, one fact is known. According to the later testimony of several witnesses, both Christopher Byrne and Anthony Burke were seen saving the lives of several of their friends before they themselves perished. Ryan's account of having seen "a boy of about 16 years" rescuing at least four other children certainly fits the description of Anthony Burke. Similarly, based upon other testimony, the *Evening Herald* concluded that "Christopher Byrne succeeded in saving two of his companions before he himself sank."[16]

Within ten minutes Halpin had carried Veronica Browne to her front door. She was barely coherent, suffering from the trauma of her near-death experience. She would later report that she had absolutely no recollection of being in the water and going under once, possibly twice. "I don't remember any more until a boy named Halpin was carrying me home on his back."[17] A welcome memory loss.

By this time Garda Steele, Garda Donnelan and Garda Lannin were on the scene; but there was no more splashing in the water. The surface was placid. Some children were still foolishly standing dangerously close to the hole, as if waiting for another head to emerge. Adults from all around were streaming towards the old pond, many at a trot. Amidst the growing crowd and commotion, parents were frantically searching for their own children. At that point no-one knew for certain how many children had drowned—or who they were.

———

At 4:10 p.m. John Byrne stood at Dalymount Park watching with disgust the melée that had broken out among unruly spectators. He was now surely feeling thankful that Kit had remained safely at home, not being pushed around by a mob of hooligans at the soccer match.

During the halt in the contest ordered by the referee, when players had returned to their dressing-rooms, the gardaí and stewards had to toughen their tactics to control the crowd. "In the general crushing on the unreserved side and on the sidelines," reported the *Irish Independent*, "a large number of people received minor injuries . . . as the St. John Ambulance Brigade was kept busy."[18] People were being not only shoved and knocked down but trampled upon. When some women were injured, became ill or fainted they were carried out on stretchers as the sound of ambulance bells rang out. The *Irish Press* described the chaotic scene:

> The ambulance men were busy attending to dozens of people who fainted, among them being a surprisingly high percentage of women. Like displaced persons, thousands kept wandering around the pitch. There were howls from the people who were prevented from seeing the game, as snowballs and orange peels were pelted at them.[19]

One can only imagine what President Ó Ceallaigh and his officials were thinking, watching the sordid spectacle beside his guests, the Spanish Minister and his entourage.

Finally, after many arrests and ejections, at about 4:15 the game resumed, under a cloud of ill-feeling and disgrace. Hardly a proud day for Irish sportsmanship on the international stage. For whatever it was worth, Ireland beat Spain by three goals to two.

As 42,000 spectators filed out of the ground, heading home or to pubs, many began hearing news of a far greater tragedy in another part of the city. As John Byrne was making his way home to Crumlin he was thinking how he would tell Kit all he had experienced that afternoon.

————

Besides the gardaí, some priests, doctors and newspaper reporters were showing up. Guards asked parents, "Are all your children at home?" "Do you know where they are?" Many did not know, for they hadn't seen them since they left the house earlier in the afternoon. At first the gardaí knew only that "some boys" had drowned. No verifiable names or numbers. For some parents on the scene, the reunion with their child was a visibly emotional one—"Oh, blessed be God, you're *safe* now!"

After making the necessary emergency phone calls from the station, Sergeant Roche hastily joined the three gardaí at the quarry. More began arriving to assist with rescue operations and crowd control. As word of the tragedy spread late on Sunday afternoon, people from all parts of the city were descending on the scene. Among the throng were many "gawkers," sometimes indiscreet in their behaviour. To some, the sad spectacle was exciting. Among the crowd stood local parents, a number of whom still did not know if their child was one of those who had drowned.

Reporters roamed among the crowd, seeking eye-witnesses. As children blurted out what they had seen, they scribbled away. Priests and doctors stood with gardaí beside the pond, intermittently speaking quietly.

At about 4:40, when a rescue team arrived with their rowing-boat to begin a dragging operation, the crowd grew more hushed. A particularly solemn sight for parents. For the dragging team this was not a typical lake or pond operation in shallow water. They had no way of knowing how deep the water was at the site of the hole. Nor how many children they were searching for. As the light faded, searchlights were being connected.

As the dragging process began, gardaí continued talking to parents in an effort to obtain the names of any children who had not yet been accounted for. But children were scattered among the crowd and adjacent streets, and some parents could not find them. Others told the guards that their children had gone to the cinema that afternoon—they *thought*.

When Mrs Byrne first got "word of a drowning" she wasn't worried, knowing well of her son's professed fear of the quarry pond. It couldn't *possibly* be her son. Likewise Michael O'Toole, immediately recalling Eddie's parting words that he was going out with his hurley to "play in the streets," assumed he was safe. Patrick Burke, the widower with eight children, felt confident that his son Anthony had enough good sense not to take any foolish chances on a frozen pond. John Byrne was still making his way home from Dalymount Park, as yet unaware of the tragedy. At dusk on Sunday, with the dragging operation under way, watched by an ever-growing crowd, the parents of the three boys whose bodies had by now settled on the quarry floor could not know that their sons were definitely among the missing.

At last light, all eyes were fixed on the three men in the boat carrying out dragging. It was a silent, eerie scene, as they leaned over the side trying to probe the depths. Made all the more macabre as "still lying on the ice were the bundles of rags marking the goal area where the boys had been playing . . . close to the jagged hole through which the boys fell."[20]

With darkness slowly veiling the old quarry pond, the jagged hole appeared like a sinister grin.

It was somewhere around 5:45 that "Michael O'Toole learned of the tragedy and went to the quarry."[21] Though some of the children told him that Eddie was one of those who had disappeared beneath the water, he was at first unconvinced. As he stood there he appeared to scan the crowd for his son's face—hardly possible in a sea of faces in the dark. The gardaí could not verify his son's drowning. He would remain at the pond's edge.

As John Byrne reached Crumlin he noticed the unusual hubbub in the streets but did not stop anyone to ask about it. "He first heard of the tragedy from neighbours," reported the *Evening Herald*, "as he was returning home from the match about 6.30 p.m. Then he went to the scene at once."[22] But, like his wife, he at first couldn't believe that Kit, who so feared the pond, could have been among those out on the ice playing hockey.

The whereabouts of Patrick Burke, Anthony's father, at this time is not known. As a widower with seven other children, it is likely that he was at home with his missing son's brothers and sisters. Waiting for some news to come to him.

With the assistance of local parents, the gardaí were gradually accounting for some other children at first thought to be missing, eliminating names from the list of possible victims. Other guards were interviewing those children who had been directly on the scene. Their accounts were sometimes inconsistent and confusing—hardly surprising under the circumstances. Claims varied about the number of boys who had slipped beneath the surface. It could have been five, or more. With as many as eight or ten children in the water at one time, it was impossible to tell for certain how many had disappeared.

Shortly after 7:30 p.m. the Garda authorities felt confident enough to issue a statement:

All the children who had been skating on the pond at the time have been accounted for with the exception of three boys who left their home in the afternoon and did not return.[23]

They were Edward O'Toole, Christopher Byrne, and Anthony Burke. They may not have known one another in life, but they were now together in death. As night fell over the old quarry, the temperature began slipping below freezing once again. Using lighting apparatus that cast a spooky glow over the water and ice, the dragging team continued to work. The crowd slowly dispersed, and onlookers, some of whom had stood for nearly six hours, straggled home. The gardaí in the boat dragged the pond until 10 o'clock on Sunday night, finally abandoning their efforts with a promise to return early the next morning.

By midnight the pond area was empty and silent. The temperature had dropped to 19 degrees (−7°c). Cold enough to create a new skin of ice on the hole in the pond.

———

MONDAY

Shortly before 7 a.m. the dragging resumed. Already the gardaí, reporters and a small crowd were on the site. John Byrne had arrived with the light of dawn. He had little to say to reporters about his son, though he did tell the *Irish Times* about the quarry pond. "It's a *death trap*—this quarry should be filled in."[24] Many in the crowd had been overheard muttering the same thing—but in the past tense. *Years ago* it should have been done.

Soon afterwards Mrs Byrne showed up, informing several reporters of Kit that "she *never* thought he was going to the pond, for he often spoke of the danger of it."[25] Relatives of Eddie O'Toole stood at the pond in his father's place, as he apparently remained at home with his other children. Throughout the morning hours the dragging continued, "watched by hundreds of sightseers and the grief-stricken parents of the missing boys."[26] By 10 a.m. still no bodies had been found.

Monday morning's papers published news of the tragedy, with photographs of the missing lads, accompanied by stories of the pond's diabolical history of claiming lives. How a sunny Sunday afternoon had suddenly turned deathly dark. Throughout the morning Dublin people were asking one another, "Any news yet?" But the three men in the boat still had nothing to show for their efforts, and now a diver risking his own welfare every time he probed deeper. Because of the depth of the quarry and the freezing conditions, some people were speculating that the bodies might not be recovered until the spring.

Then, at 11:10 a.m., the crowd noticed a flurry of activity within the boat. Some words were shouted to guards on the shore. Within seconds, stretcher-bearers were called forth. One boy had been found:

> Christopher Byrne's body was dragged from the pond at 11:15 . . . before the eyes of his father, who had been watching the pond since seven in the morning.[27]

Those in the crowd close to the water's edge were able to see the limp body pulled up over the side into the rowing-boat. A hush fell over the scene as a path was cleared for the stretcher-bearers. Reporters jotted notes; some rushed off to find a phone to call in their story.

About twenty minutes later the body of Anthony Burke was discovered. The two boys had apparently settled in death close to one another. He too was carried by stretcher to the waiting ambulance and taken away to the morgue. It is not known how his father was notified.

Nearing midday the crowd watched in anticipation of the recovery of the third victim, Eddie O'Toole, at eight the youngest of the three. But time passed without any further activity. Why was his body not near the other two? After all, they had all fallen into the same hole.

Throughout the afternoon the dragging operation continued. People in the crowd came and went. Michael O'Toole was not among them.

On Monday night the recovery effort was again suspended. Tuesday would follow the same routine, without success. And Wednesday. And the next day. And the next.

———

For days the newspapers kept the story alive on the front page. Stories of tragedy and of heroism made for compelling reading. Children and adults alike risking their lives to save others from drowning before their eyes. The newspaper stories were not sensationalised or even embellished, for there was no need to do so. The eye-witness accounts and recorded fact were dramatic enough. How twelve-year-old Veronica Browne, in an effort to save young O'Toole, had fallen in and nearly drowned herself. Similarly, wrote the *Irish Independent*, "heroic efforts to save the boys were made by Thomas Mardy who almost lost his life in the attempt." Saddest, and most inspiring, were the accounts of how two boys, Christopher Byrne and Anthony Burke, had given their lives to save several playmates. Between them they had possibly rescued six other boys. As the *Irish Independent* told it, "a particularly poignant feature of the tragedy was that one of the boys who eventually disappeared was seen to pull at least four children to safety."[28] The description fitted that of Anthony Burke.

While newspapers praised the heroism, they also raised troubling questions, casting criticism and blame upon those who had been negligent. Why had the local authority not erected safe, impenetrable barriers around the known "death trap" after it had already taken lives in past years?—or, better, filled in the entire quarry to remove any danger? Why had parents, instead of merely warning their children about the risks, not *forbidden* them to go on the ice? Why had the Gardaí not punished some young transgressors, as a lesson to others, to stay away? There was plenty of wisdom with hindsight. As the *Dublin Evening Mail* commented, "the tragedy is all the more poignant in that the pond is well known to be very dangerous," lives having been lost there *several* times before.[29]

Perhaps the inquest would provide some answers.

Some criticism directed against the Gardaí was particularly harsh. As if the tragedy had been their fault. Such blame struck the *Dublin Evening Mail* as quite unjust, and it rushed to their defence:

> Complaints have been heard that the guards have been remiss in not driving the children off the pond. The Guards did, in fact, clear the pond several times on Saturday and yesterday, and spoke seriously to the children of the risks they were running. But as soon as the coast was clear the skating began again.
>
> We do not think it is at all fair to blame the Guards ... It is not part of their duty to play nursemaid. If the parents cannot or will not keep the children from this perilous amusement it is difficult to see what can be done.[30]

Plenty of citizens had ideas about what could be done. Quite a number submitted their suggestions to the newspapers. Some more feasible than others. One person suggested a permanent Garda presence or cordon around the pond when frozen. Considering that the pond had already been frozen for nearly six weeks, this was hardly practicable and certainly not from the Garda point of view. Another thoughtful citizen wrote in with his idea that a man be hired to walk along the edge of the pond wherever it froze to break up the ice to a distance of several feet from the bank, thus deterring any children from walking out on it. However, considering that the pond was nearly three acres in extent, the Arctic temperature would probably have refrozen his work by the time he completed his rounds. Another person thought that local parents should "form an association, notices should be put up ... Older children could be instructed to keep the younger ones off the ice."[31] Most letter-writers agreed that the most sensible schemes were either to erect a formidable barrier or fill the quarry in.

From the press and public there was an outpouring of sympathy. It was the sort of tragedy—taking the lives of such young boys—that seemed to touch everyone. In a sense, all Dublin was mourning. Citizens sent in contributions to help the three families with burial expenses. Prayers were offered by the thousands. Peter Somers, the publican at the Turk's Head bar on Sundrive Road, near the quarry, knew almost every family in the district. A caring and practical man, he began a fund "for the relief of the stricken families . . . and the mental agony they suffered."[32] He formed a committee of local traders and residents to seek "subscriptions from sympathisers." Friends and strangers alike wanted to help out in some small way.

The *Evening Herald* had a culprit: King Winter himself. Bringing the onslaught of such prolonged, freakish weather with recurrent freezing and thawing and refreezing that had already taken hundreds of lives in various forms. In an editorial headed "Death on the ice," it warned that winter's calamities were probably not over yet:

> The shocking tragedy . . . should be held up as a dreadful warning to all parents in the city. The present furious weather seems likely to continue . . . and ponds will remain frozen and provide a temptation for children playing on the ice.[33]

King Winter remained an enemy to be feared.

Chapter 10 ❧

RESCUE ON LAND AND AT SEA

Rescue sorties were sent into the snowbound depths of Connaught . . . They stopped at a snowed-up cottage and found the family in a stupor without food or heat, unable to move.

(*Irish Times*, 4 MARCH 1947)

Shuddering from stem to stern, the Bolivar *ran aground near Kish Buoy, 9 miles from the Dublin coast. Pounded by heavy seas, the ship lay helpless in a heavy north-west gale . . . her back broken.*

(*Irish Press*, 5 MARCH 1947)

After digging for four days through a 22-foot snowdrift to reach a house . . . a rescue party found the inhabitants in an exhausted condition. The snow reached to within a foot of the top of the chimney.

(*Irish Times*, 8 MARCH 1947)

MONDAY 3 MARCH

It had been a weekend of high drama. Rare, splendorous sunshine, triumphant snow-army assaults, courageous passenger rescues, and tragic drownings. Monday's newspapers were filled with first-hand stories and graphic photographs of all the dizzying events that had occurred over the past forty-eight hours.

The great blizzard was only six days past, leaving much of the country still snowbound in its wake. Villagers and houses were isolated, people now in desperate need of food and fuel and medical attention, and marooned passengers still stuck on desolate roads. And no telling when the next blizzard might strike. Or tragedy occur.

Ships had put out to sea again, but crews seldom took their eyes off the sky.

On Monday, with fair weather holding out, a critical second phase of relief and rescue got under way. As the snow armies gradually cleared major roads they opened the way for small sorties of rescuers to dig their way through smaller, connecting roads to reach isolated villages and individual farmsteads and houses where many people had been confined now for weeks. Victims of numbing cold, hunger, and often illness. These rescue sorties normally comprised three to five men. Most were volunteers, often including a local garda, postman, shopkeeper, priest. They were often very personal rescue efforts, as the rescuers knew the blizzard victims they were trying to reach. Their own friends and neighbours.

In the hardest-struck counties some trapped inhabitants were trying to send out sos messages in the hope that they would be seen by rescue forces. They made distress flags from coloured cloth, hung a shirt or dress on a pitchfork, climbed atop their roof and waved their arms wildly. Many, however, were now too weak to make such efforts. In some instances it had been known for weeks that certain people were in urgent need of help. In Co. Wicklow it was verified that James Doyle and his sisters Elizabeth and Esther, all elderly and long ill, were now in frail and serious condition, in need of immediate transport to hospital. Similarly, in Roundwood two well-known sisters, Margaret and Elizabeth Burke—identified in the newspapers as "claimants to a share of the 'Burke millions'"—were down to the last of their food and fuel, growing weak. Under the circumstances, their money was of no value. Nature was a great leveller.

———

Over the sunny weekend several people living three miles from Roscommon noticed a small dot of bright red against the sheet-white landscape. On closer observation they determined that some inhabitants of Quaker Island in the Shannon had "hoisted a red flag as a signal of distress." The tiny island community of five families, numbering about thirty people, was described as "small farmers and fishermen . . . always self-sufficient and proud of it." Only under the most desperate conditions would they have flown a flag of distress, seeking help from the mainlanders. It was assumed by those who spotted the flag that it meant they were out of food or fuel, possibly both, or had a medical emergency.

By Monday, rescue squads that had reached the area were informed of the situation. However, there was no way to communicate with or reach the islanders. After six weeks of sub-freezing temperatures, wrote the *Irish Independent*, "the river at this point is frozen, but the ice is so dangerous that people on the mainland are unable to go out to the island with relief."[1] Approach by boat was impossible, and to walk on the ice was to risk drowning. Only an air drop of food or fuel might relieve them temporarily, but there were no means for such a plan. After all, there were now entire villages facing the same predicament.

And what if it were a medical emergency? Clearly the islanders were in some peril. Mainlanders could do nothing but look out helplessly at their red flag fluttering in the bitter east wind.

Similarly, on Gallagher's Island in Lough Gill outside Sligo lived eighty-year-old Brigid Clerkin, an uncommonly independent woman. Indeed she was the only inhabitant of the island and managed to get by through periodic contact with mainlanders. With the freezing conditions and blizzards, nothing had been heard from her for weeks. Local people had become increasingly worried about her welfare, if not survival. With the lake completely frozen it was no longer possible to reach her by boat, and it was considered extremely risky to try to walk a mile over ice of uncertain thickness and stability. At the very least she was surely low on food and fuel. And it was quite possible that she had none left. The state of her health was unknown.

On Monday, after much deliberation, several local gardaí and civilians decided to take the chance. With nervous onlookers measuring their every step, they "walked a mile over the ice-covered Lough Gill to Gallagher's Island to bring relief to Mrs. Clerkin . . . On arrival the rescue party found that she had neither food *nor* fuel."[2] She would not, they attested, have lasted much longer. They brought her back to the mainland, where she would remain until conditions were again safe.In Connacht and in Co. Wicklow especially, many other dramatic and often risky rescue sorties were being carried out. Without newspaper coverage or public praise of any sort.

Rescuers were never certain what they might find when they reached outlying dwellings nearly buried beneath snow:

> In one little thatched house we found two old men, one seventy-five and the other seventy-eight years old. They said they had had no food for a *week*—and they certainly looked like it. They were weak and cold. We supplied them from our own stocks.[3]

Such life-or-death cases were being commonly reported by rescue parties, of people on the edge of starvation or freezing. Many had been slowly "entombed"—an apt term now used in the newspapers—as snow covered doors and windows, then climbed towards the roof. Rescue parties were now spotting houses by their partially exposed rooftops or protruding chimneys, sticking up like periscopes. It could take days of shovelling and picking to reach a dwelling where it was feared a family might be perishing. In Co. Sligo a determined rescue unit, "after digging for four days through 22-foot snowdrift to reach a house," found two brothers and a sister in a weak condition through hunger, cold, and stress. "All their stock—hens, pigs, and cattle—are dead." The snow had reached to "within a foot of the top of the chimney." They were living through their own burial.

Where snow was piled so high on a house, rescuers found that they could not possibly "dig it out" but either had to walk atop hardened, crystallised layers or try to tunnel beneath it to find a door or window so as to release the inhabitants. In such cases, communication at first had to be carried out by yelling down a chimney:

> Struggling through deep snowdrifts, a Civic Guard found himself looking down a cottage chimney, the only means of communication left to the inmates. Tunnels had to be dug through the snow before the cottage could be entered.[4]

"Inmates" was a fitting description, as inhabitants were in fact imprisoned in their own dwellings. Many had been confined for weeks, watching food and fuel supplies dwindle, seeing doorways and windows blocked as outside light and airflow gradually faded. Their last turf sods leaving a haze of stale smoke. Trapped inside, they did like Dublin tenement-dwellers and relied on a "slop bucket," now emitting a sickening odour. Buried houses became putrid dungeons with barely breathable air, dark and freezing cold.

Under such deteriorating health conditions, inhabitants could lapse into a state of physical sickness and mental lethargy. Some sank into a semi-comatose state. When one rescue party reached a remote area of Connacht "they stopped at a snowed-up cottage and found the family in a stupor," without *any* food or heat, unable to move. Nor could they communicate coherently at first. Devoid of even the normal emotion for welcoming their rescuers. In a dazed, ethereal state of incomprehension about what was occurring.

Rescuers grew increasingly frustrated, angry, and openly critical that there was no sign of Government help for snowbound residents and villagers, many in critical condition. Army units, they argued, should have been scouring the countryside to find and assist blizzard victims. To make this point, a reporter from the *Sunday Independent* quoted verbatim an exasperated CIE official travelling with a rescue team in the west:

> Nobody knows what is happening in the cottages, which are small lumps in a sheet of snow. So far as the Government are concerned, "Did anybody *care* about what was happening in the cottages?"

———

While rescue squads throughout rural Ireland sought to relieve and save isolated dwellers and marooned passengers, no assistance was reaching

Dublin's needy families. They were left on their own to survive.

It was now the thirty-seventh day of the Arctic grip. No coal was coming in, and the city's turf supplies were nearly depleted. At a meeting of Dublin Corporation one member confirmed that the turf clamps in the Phoenix Park were now "nearing ground level," soggy and mixed with dirt.

It was now thought that nearly half of all Dublin's homes had a fireless grate. In both city centre and suburbs, real desperation was setting in.

Despite much talk of felling trees for logs, the schemes had never materialised. Only a few lorries laden with logs rolled into the city, and they were quickly snatched up by well-to-do householders with large fireplaces and dry garages or sheds. Ordinary Dubliners had to find their own wood to burn.

By the first week of March people were scavenging through their own homes for any wood to lift or rip out. Around Noel Hughes's part of the north side, especially the tenements along North King Street, Dominick Street, Gardiner Street, and Queen Street, every family was now burning wood in any form: doors, door-frames, sweeping-brushes, picture frames, floorboards, banisters, toys. Furniture. "It was survival!" Across the Liffey, over in the Liberties, where John Gallagher lived in the Coombe, the story was the same. "They'd try anything to get heat . . . burn furniture, and in some houses the banisters would all be gone. They'd say, 'We *have* to heat ourselves!'" He knew of many people who were putting tacks into the holes of their gas rings to bring the "glimmer up a little higher, to get extra heat." They knew it was illegal, that they could be caught, but "they'd try *anything*."

Over in North William Street, near the North Strand, Mary Dunne lived with her parents, sister Lily and baby brother Séamus in a small terrace cottage. But always cosy. Until now. Over the past six weeks of frigid temperatures she had watched her parents use up the last of their turf and then resort to burning various items of wood around the house. Each day they had to scrounge a little harder to find something that might ignite and throw off a bit of heat. It was visibly taking an emotional toll on her mother:

> It was *bitter cold*. And *no fuel*. Every family was the same. And you'd burn anything you could get. Even newspapers to try and start a little fire. And the pipes would be frozen stiff. We were very cold, and my mother cried for her children, myself, Lily and Séamus the baby . . . My sister Ann had died of diphtheria in 1944.

She can't recall the exact day it happened. Probably on one of the first days of March, when the temperature again plunged overnight to 11 degrees (−12°C). She remembers seeing her mother weepy but at fifteen didn't know its meaning. She sensed that something unusual was wrong. It seemed colder than ever before, and their grate was now completely fireless. The house felt like a crypt. Perhaps, she thought, this was why her mother softly wept. Could she have been worried about losing another child?

In the corner of the parlour stood conspicuously—now more so than ever—her mother's pride and joy, a small, lovely baby grand piano, which she loved to play on any special occasion. Or simply to please herself and her family. Over all the years it had come to feel like a member of the family. But during the last six weeks there had been no music in the house, no singing, no laughter.

Then, one morning, the decision was made:

> Oh, my mother cried! She said, "Oh, we *have* to . . . we have to, *for the kids*, they're *freezing*."
>
> It was a baby grand piano. My mother played it . . . It was *always* in the family. *Always* there. In the parlour. It was made of black ebony. *Solid* . . .
>
> Then my mother said to my father, "We'll *have* to break it up . . . We have to." So my father got a saw and some tools. Poor man, his hands were bleeding . . . My father wasn't a man who could do household chores. And I saw her crying—and that was it.
>
> We were warm for a few days at least. The fire burned bright, but Mam cried. It was a very traumatic thing. I saw her crying. I *realised* the sacrifices they were making by doing it, for the kids.
>
> In the parlour then, you'd look over and kind of expect to see it there, you know . . .

———

On Monday 3 March, Seán Moylan, Minister for Lands, made his own decision about firewood. Upon due consideration, he announced, "after a survey of available stocks of firewood in the state forests . . . as an exceptional measure about 40,000 tons" would be placed on the market soon.5 He boasted that the Forestry Department now had eighteen sawmills, compared with only four in 1940. To facilitate the effort to secure wood, the Government would also relax provisions of the Road Transport Act (1933) to allow lorry-owners, whether or not they held a merchandise licence, to carry fuel for profit. It was good news for better-off Dubliners with money and larger fireplaces to accommodate wood logs. But it was stated that the scheme would take some time to implement.

Meanwhile, during the first few days of March, Fuel Importers Ltd was allowed to begin cutting down some trees in the Phoenix Park, many of which were old or diseased and needed removal. Forty men were promptly put to work, with the promise that the number would soon be increased to a hundred. It was not, however, a very professional tree-felling operation, as "many of the implements being used—hatchets, saws, chains, wedges—are being lent to Fuel Importers by the Army." Placed in the hands of men not very adept at using them properly, or safely.

After the trees were felled they had to be transported to Alexandra Road, where they were to be cut into logs suitable for fireplace use. Many poor tenement-dwellers, still not realising that their small grates could not properly accommodate logs, were heartened to hear that trees were being cut down nearby in the Phoenix Park, spreading word and hope around the streets that "the wood is on the way!"

Throughout Monday the authorities held emergency meetings to assess their situation. CIE reported that its coal reserves were now down to 4,000 tons, a bare week's supply. The arrival of about 2,000 tons, the first of Britain's special allocation of 5,000 tons for the Irish railways, was expected by the 4th or 5th. Meanwhile it was making an all-out effort to convert its locomotives from coal to oil-burning. With the necessary equipment now available, it was estimated that at the Inchicore works about three locomotives per week could be converted—progress that seemed terribly slow when the need was so urgent.

Dublin Gas Company reported that selfish citizens continued to rob the public by siphoning off the glimmer gas, despite expanded patrolling by the glimmer men. No more warnings for the scoundrels: their gas would be cut off. The ESB too was in a bad way. Not only was it down to the last of its coal reserves at the Pigeon House but the long freeze-up of the River Shannon had significantly reduced the inflow to Ardnacrusha. On Monday it regretted having to announce that "further drastic restrictions" would go into effect in two days. It would mean another reduction of a quarter in consumption, excluding only public health and a few critical industries, such as flour-milling and newspapers. Trams would not be protected but would be cut by a quarter. When Wednesday night came, it predicted, the most visible manifestation of the new cuts would be reduced lighting along Dublin's streets.

Radio Éireann also had to tell listeners that its hours of broadcasting were to be further reduced. The midday hours were now from 1 to 2 p.m. and the evening from 6:30 to midnight.

Then came further bad news. The Vartry reservoir had been frozen over for five weeks, and "unless there is a quick thaw Dublin's water supply will be seriously affected."[6]

This revelation was followed by the announcement of "grave concern in city bakeries" over declining supplies of yeast and the poor quality of wheat. In pre-war years, it was explained, the present supply of wheat would have been "rejected as unmillable, and the resultant flour unbakable." Bakers were finding out that no matter how long they baked the bread it still came out "damp and half-baked." Little better than wet turf sods to many. To Brian Kelly "it had a doughy old taste . . . They used to say it was good for the innards, that you had no need for medicine." Many people found it barely edible.

The news about sugar production was equally dismal. At the beginning of March the Thurles sugar factory was forced to suspend operations as a result of sugarbeet not being delivered in sufficient quantities. Farmers could not get the beet out of the frozen ground, while impassable roads prevented its transport. In normal years upwards of three hundred lorryloads of beet were delivered daily to the factory at this time of year. Now, on some days fewer than half a dozen lorries passed through the factory gates.

Even potatoes were now in short supply. Most farmers, with their land frozen and covered with several feet of snow, "dared not open their pits" for fear of spoiling their store. Even those who had potatoes stored inside sheds were unable to get them into city markets, because of the condition of the roads. And there was no possibility of relieving the situation by importing potatoes, as the law prohibited the importing of tubers.

People were growing uneasy even about reading newspapers nowadays, fearful of what further bad news would topple down in their laps.

With Dubliners in need of coal, flour, tea, sugar, potatoes, candles, and cigarettes, down at the docks on Monday afternoon the *Irish Poplar* was unloading instead a cargo of nylons, typewriters, tinned salmon, cotton yarn, dates, and figs. Another ship from Antwerp brought in four tons of safety matches. To which one might have quipped, "Now if we only had some fuel, cigarettes, paraffin and candles to light!"

Another ship, the *Bolivar,* a Norwegian motor vessel on its first voyage, was expected to arrive in Dublin some time on Tuesday from Argentina, carrying maize, barley, and cotton goods. And it was revealed in the newspapers that some quite celebrated passengers were aboard.

TUESDAY 4 MARCH

The favourable weather had lasted for nearly four days. By early Tuesday morning the high pressure to the north-east of Britain was showing a slight decline, "but that to the north-west did not yield—and it was the persistence of this high pressure over Greenland and Iceland that maintained the wintry conditions."[7] At the same time a depression moving in a northerly direction across the southern coasts of Ireland was setting up a confrontational alignment of weather systems.

The seas off the south and east coasts were growing choppy, and a dense fog was forming. To seamen, there was the scent of a real storm in the making.

Captain Sigurd Rasmussen of the *Bolivar* was not bothered by a spot of nasty weather off the Irish coast. His superb ship, owned by Fred. Olsen and Company, was a twin-screw 5,230-ton vessel designed to carry both cargo and passengers. Considered a model ship, it was of superior construction, boasted luxury quarters for select passengers, and had a first-rate crew. On this, its first voyage, crew members were already praising the *Bolivar* as "the best ship I ever sailed on." Quite an accolade coming from seasoned Norwegian seamen.

Before the *Bolivar* ever set sail it was regarded as a charmed ship. Construction had begun before the war and was almost complete when the Germans entered Norway. In haste, the story goes, "she was hidden successfully and completed after the war." The successful trick of hiding the ship from the Germans gave it the reputation of being lucky, a ship destined for good fortune. Captain Rasmussen, one of the most skilled and experienced seamen in Norway, felt himself lucky to be given command.

Apart from its crew of thirty-nine the *Bolivar* carried twelve passengers, who were treated as well as, if not better than, if they were aboard a luxury liner. They enjoyed stately quarters and sumptuous meals and were fussed over by crew and captain. Paying well for such treatment. The elite passengers relished one another's company, especially on this voyage, as there was a world-renowned figure aboard. Throughout the long trip from Bergen to Rosario and onwards towards Ireland he had been the centre of attention, other passengers drawn by his unique company and conversation. Not because he sought it but because his life's achievements and honours made it inevitable.

Admiral Edward Evans, Lord Mountevans, now sixty-five, had been an Antarctic explorer and First World War hero. "His valour and distinguished service in many parts of the world" had won him more decorations than any other British admiral. He had been second in command of Scott's Antarctic expedition. While in command of the destroyer *Broke* during the 1914–18 war he engaged and defeated six German destroyers, and his "naval genius held the world's attention" on many occasions.[8] Later he commanded the Royal Australian Navy. His hobby when afloat was to swim around the entire British Home Fleet, a distance of many miles.

Accompanying Lord Mountevans on this trip was his wife, a native of Norway who had lived in Cork for a time during the First World War and made many friends in Ireland. The couple had intended to take the *Bolivar* to South America, stop off for a brief visit in Ireland, then return to Norway for a skiing holiday. As Admiral Mountevans joked with reporters, he was going along "just for a ride . . . a busman's holiday." A rare gift for other passengers, who clearly savoured his company. Despite his distinguished military record and Antarctic conquests, he was genial and gregarious, giving the "impression of gentleness, strengthened by a hearty laugh and abundant sense of humour."

His arrival in Ireland was much anticipated by the press. Exciting stories of his legendary exploits were extracted from his autobiography, *An Adventurer's Life*. In the book was the motto that, he often stated, had guided his life:

> Endeavour to meet misfortunes
> With a smile
> And success with a cheer.

"Into his sixty-five years," wrote the *Irish Independent*, "Lord Mountevans has packed enough sea adventures to last a dozen men a lifetime."[9] He had no need for more.

By mid-morning the wind had picked up and clouds were gathering aggressively. As the temperature hovered around 28 to 30 degrees (1 to 2°c), a north-easterly wind ratcheted towards half-gale force. High seas were churned up all along the east coast as intermittent squalls of sleet and snow began. Captain Rasmussen had navigated through his share of oceanic storms over his career, some with hurricane-force winds. On this morning, a mere fifteen miles or so off the Irish coast, he hardly sniffed at mounting waves rocking the *Bolivar*. However, he didn't like the fog enveloping his ship and told his crew to be vigilant. At 10:20 a.m. he had his radio officer, Kroek, send a message to Dún Laoghaire that the *Bolivar* would be arriving in a few hours and would need a pilot to guide it into the harbour. A routine request.

In the meantime Lord and Lady Mountevans, her brother, Trygve Andvord, and his wife, who were accompanying them, and the other passengers would enjoy a special lunch that was being prepared for them before they all disembarked at Dún Laoghaire for their Irish visit. All were in high spirits over arriving in Ireland.

———

Dubliners had grown nervous when the wind kicked up and sleety snow began falling. They knew by now all the trouble signs. Streets were becoming slushy but not icy. Buses, trams and cars moved slowly, cautiously. The mail boat *Princess Maud* was being tossed around, and passengers hoped they would reach shore before the weather got any worse.

At Guinness's brewery things couldn't get much worse. William Tinnion and his furnace-stoking mates were now facing the predicament they had hoped would not arrive. For weeks they had watched their "mountains" of coal dwindle to small mounds, then crumbled piles, forcing them to finally resort to using the "duff," or coal dust.

Then, recalls Tinnion, "it *ran out!*"

The men had devised an emergency plan, should this day ever come. They had scanned the brewery, the entire complex of buildings. By good fortune they found that the whole brewery was in the process of being painted, a huge job requiring a massive installation of wooden scaffolding and apparatus used by a small army of painters. Tinnion and his mates sought approval from their bosses to proceed with a radical—they thought "brilliant"—survival scheme:

> Now at that time the brewery—the *whole* place—was being painted. And there was all this scaffolding, planks, poles, ladders, wood *all* over the place. So we, the stokers, *burned* those! Burned *everything!* Oh, we were desperate. *Anything* that would burn.

The Guinness top brass put gangs of men together to tear down the wooden structures and take them to the furnaces. Before long they had piles of dry wood, to be used as sparingly as possible, stretched out till coal arrived again. Nothing was mentioned in the newspapers about this drastic measure. It is not likely that the proud Guinness company would have wanted the public to know that even the mighty brewery had nearly been brought to its knees by King Winter.

About midday on Tuesday "a c.i.e. relief bus which spent nearly a week hacking its way from Dublin to snowbound Sligo, and was once reported 'lost,'" arrived back at its base in Aston Quay. Describing their "fantastic journey" to an *Irish Press* reporter, the driver, Nicholas Scanlon, and conductor, Frank Scanlon, testified that they passed through places where "villagers were on iron rations and short of water."[10] Down to their very last.

———

As the dining-bell rang, calling the twelve passengers to lunch, the *Bolivar* was bucking wild waves, causing china, silverware and glasses to jitterbug and jangle. Everyone laughed about their last hour or so being the roughest part of their transatlantic voyage. Making it all the more memorable, everyone agreed. Lord and Lady Mountevans commented that their son, who had been with them for most of the trip, was fortunate to have disembarked during the ship's brief stopover in Liverpool to unload crates of fruit.

By the time the meal was being served, the wind had exceeded half-gale force. The *Bolivar* was now about twelve miles off the east coast of Ireland, a soupy fog severely limiting visibility. Captain Rasmussen and his chief officers, knowing of no serious storm forecasts, felt no sense of danger, merely caution. As they approached Kish No. 2 buoy, only nine miles from Dublin, Rasmussen excused himself from the convivial luncheon to attend to navigation himself.

The Kish Bank runs parallel to the coast, about nine miles from land, roughly from Dublin Bay to below Killiney. A hump-backed, narrow bank about sixteen miles in length, at places with only about six feet of water at low tide. Seamen knew well of its presence and navigated around it. But a combination of rough seas and dense fog could make it a bit tricky. Treacherous under the worst conditions.

By noon there was a blanket fog, so thick that "the Bailey lighthouse reported that the Kish lighthouse, usually visible," was virtually undetectable. Captain Rasmussen was navigating in a cloud.

Passengers were by now joking nervously about "Irish mists." Some less interested in the luncheon menu than setting foot on terra firma. However, it was ridiculous to feel any fright—after all, they had just crossed the Atlantic Ocean twice and were close enough to nearly see Dublin on a clear day. Yet when a glass or plate slipped or fell, people tensed.

Now in a porridge fog, whipped by a wind that was creating tumultuous seas, the *Bolivar* "was flung off her course by the storm," as Captain Rasmussen would later describe it. Exactly how far off course it was not possible to know at the time. Furthermore, steering the 5,230-ton vessel had become extremely difficult. As it would later be contended, perhaps the steering mechanism was not functioning properly.

At 12:22 p.m., "battered by heavy waves . . . shuddering from stem to stern," the *Irish Independent* reported, "at the mercy of a fierce north-easterly gale she ran aground." Crew and passengers were startled as the ship "sank almost at once into the sand . . . and broke her back."

In the blind fog it was impossible to assess exactly what had happened. Some passengers wondered if they had collided with another ship. If not, what could have happened so abruptly? And how serious was the peril?

Admiral Mountevans immediately assumed a dual role, that of adviser to the captain and guide to the passengers, who instantly looked to him for leadership. He had been in highly dangerous sea crises before—but never with his wife at his side. In a voice calm and confident he told fellow-passengers that there were procedures to be sensibly followed, no need for panic. Help would soon be on the way.

At 12:25 p.m. Rasmussen acted decisively, issuing orders to the radio officer, Kroek, to send a distress signal. Kroek leapt to act; "then I noticed that half the ship was gone—and my aerial with it!"[11] Rasmussen suddenly realised that when the *Bolivar* had gone aground "it seesawed, and the fore part from the bridge broke away." The only immediate action was to fire flares aloft. Amidst the storm and fog, probably a futile act.

Mountevans, meanwhile, attended to passengers, who were shaken but not panicky. His presence was their greatest comfort. His first order, issued in a manner as subdued and genteel as if he were inviting dinner guests into the drawing-room, was followed promptly, as "all passengers went quietly to the aft part of the ship and waited there until they were told to get into lifeboats." Not dressed for withstanding the wet and cold, they were shaking visibly at the prospect of having to climb down a rope ladder into lifeboats amidst the roiling seas. With Mountevans giving constant reassurance that all would be well, the "passengers huddled together under the bridge," awaiting rescue by lifeboats from the shore.

Kroek, a first-rate radio officer, was quick-thinking and resourceful. By the time the passengers were ensconced in their waiting niche he was at work trying to concoct a makeshift aerial. At best it would be a primitive device, but if it could transmit a message only nine miles or so it might save lives. It is not known whether the passengers had been told that he was endeavouring to rig up another aerial. He worked on his own, as no-one else could assist him, while other crew members watched silently. By 2 p.m. or thereabouts he had managed to "erect a temporary aerial . . . Signals were then sent to attract attention." His message—which may have struck some as an oxymoron—read:

In no immediate danger, but breaking up.[12]

On the captain's orders, he repeatedly transmitted the "mayday" signal. However, much to Kroek's dismay, his hastily devised aerial "lasted only seven minutes." Had any lifeboat stations or vessels picked up his message? There was nothing now for the thirty-nine crewmen and twelve passengers to do but wait.

It was beginning to snow.

————

They were not the only boatmen in distress. Or sending out signals for help. Along the Royal Canal and Grand Canal, bargemen had for six weeks been fighting a battle against freeze-ups, blizzards, hunger, fatigue, and mounting discouragement. Theirs could be an isolated, lonely existence. During warm summers, however, they enjoyed socialising with people along their way. Country folk and city-dwellers liked chatting to the bargemen, a real "dying breed," whose life was interesting and exotic to them. In Dublin, at Newcomen Bridge on the North Strand Road, people regularly stopped to have long chats with the bargemen at the locks, whom they saw as "fascinating fellas" and "real characters." Conversely, in inclement weather the bargemen lived a separate life, having little contact with "settled" folk.

In the winter of 1946/47 they may as well have been bargemen on one of Siberia's great rivers, for they could go for long spells without much outside contact.

Their troubles began as far back as January, around the 24th, when the Big Freeze set in and the canals began freezing over. And it had been hell for them ever since. Stuck outdoors, isolated, constantly fighting snow, ice, and a wind beyond all curses, they had become "forgotten victims." Over six weeks of Siberian weather the canals were freezing up *every* night. *Every* morning they faced the same strenuous, frustrating job of having to hack and smash their way through ice to make any slow progress. With the cut-back in service of goods trains, there was tremendous pressure on them to carry heavier loads. To make life worse, their food rations were not sufficient for men who worked so physically hard. Nor had they enough turf to keep their primitive cabins warm. They appealed to their union in Dublin for assistance with food and fuel, but to no avail.

Not until early March did their plight come to the attention of the public, when several newspapers wrote expository, sympathetic articles describing their hardship. Most readers had not known of their tribulations. On Dublin's canals, "more than sixty bargemen are suffering acutely from cold and hunger," revealed the *Irish Press,* "jammed in the ice . . . The leading boats take turns in charging the ice, reversing engines and coming back at it again."[13] As the *Irish Independent* explained, it was the interminable battle against ice that was most dispiriting. "Breaking the ice is a heartbreaking and tedious job, for as fast as they break it, it freezes up overnight—and they have their task all over again." As the paper described it, their existence had been made torturous by the Arctic winter, the men often reduced to grubbing for food and fuel to survive:

> There is a body of men whose work has literally been brought to a standstill by the frost and snow. They are the crews of over twenty Grand Canal barges, whose vessels have been jammed in the ice, within a mile of Edenderry since Tuesday of last week [nine days]. They spend their time scouring the town and district for bread . . . and they sent distress signals to their union in Dublin. Their fuel position is also pitiable.[14]

It was humbling for bargemen, with a proud tradition, to essentially have to beg for food and fuel. Some crews subsisted only through the charity of hand-outs and often went fireless on their boats during the sub-freezing nights. Along their route kind-hearted people, farmers, shopkeepers, might hand them some bread, potatoes, biscuits, turf. In one instance the skipper of a barge was "seen trudging across the fields of snow carrying a bundle of faggots on his shoulders—yet his boat was loaded with neatly-cut timber blocks."

———

Men on duty at the lifeboat stations leaned forward to listen intently to the words crackling over the radio alert system. As luck would have it, Kroek's critical seven-minute "mayday" transmissions had been picked up by Seaforth Radio in Liverpool, intercepted by Malin Head wireless station, then flashed to Dublin. Immediately Dún Laoghaire and Howth lifeboats, as well as two Dublin Port and Docks Board tugs, "raced to the scene." Fighting their way out nearly ten miles in the storm against violent wind and seas, the rescuers surely had foremost in their minds the ominous words "breaking up."

With the Dún Laoghaire lifeboat already on its way, the Howth lifeboat rushed to the position phoned to them from Dún Laoghaire, while the tug *Ben Eadar,* under M. Kinsella, "also ploughed her way to the rescue through heavy seas." Throughout the rescue operation, radio contact was maintained between the boats and shore, and information was exchanged with the Dublin Harbourmaster, Captain A. J. O'Brien-Twohig. By now snow was falling steadily as the four rescue craft lurched their way through roiling seas in search of the stricken vessel—or what might be left of it.

At 5:10 p.m. the coxswain of the Dún Laoghaire lifeboat, Sam Blackmore, caught his first faint sight of the grounded and broken *Bolivar:*

> There was a half gale blowing and coming up hard. We could see the ship cracking up. She was split in two, and the people aboard were practically at attention aft.[15]

Minutes later the tug *Coliemore,* under its skipper George Elliot, arrived at the scene. As the two boats carefully approached the crippled ship from the side with the greater lee, "standing along the rails the crew and passengers cheered." Admiral Mountevans quickly reminded them that the difficult and risky manoeuvre of being transferred by rope ladder into the rescue boats was still ahead.

Rescue conditions were now at their worst as the agitated sea rocked the lifeboats and a terrific wind blew the wet, slippery rope ladder. Even the seasoned seamen thought it a precarious manoeuvre under the unstable circumstances. If passengers slipped and fell into the water in these conditions it could be fatal. No-one knew this better than Mountevans, who had seen too many people lost at sea. Now he found himself responsible for getting several people, including his wife, to climb safely down a very slippery rope ladder. In the dark, with the wind swinging them around in all directions.

There was no time for delay. No time for indecision. As the rope ladders were tossed over the side, passengers understood that the feat would be solely up to them to execute: hold tightly, descend one foot carefully at a time. As Mountevans instructed them on how to grasp the rope and secure the best footing, they remained perfectly silent. Women would go first.

Their hands being so cold and wet made the act all the more dangerous. As the "rope ladders were flung over the side the women were lowered into the lifeboats," one by one, slowly, each assisted by crew members as they made their timid descent. With a grim determination that showed on their face, each woman gripped the ladder with all her strength and implanted one foot after the other, the wind buffeting them about. As Mountevans would describe to eager reporters some hours later:

> The women, they were very brave, although the ladders were swinging like mad . . . With the agility of athletes they clambered down the rope ladder to the lifeboat, which was being rocked violently by the heavy seas and wind.[16]

By necessity, it was a slow process. The only mishap occurred when Trygve Andvord slipped while scrambling down the ladder into the lifeboat and fractured his arm.

Sam Blackmore and his Dún Laoghaire lifeboat crew "battled for three hours" to bring most of the passengers and crew off the *Bolivar* into his boat. The *Coliemore* took the others. Kinsella stood by with *Ben Eadar* if needed, as did the Howth lifeboat. Only after everyone else had safely made the transfer did Captain Rasmussen and Admiral Mountevans finally abandon the ill-fated ship.

It was now nearly 9 p.m. and pitch-black. Now aboard the lifeboats, passengers still shivered beneath blankets, expressing great relief and gratitude at being rescued. Only then did several come to realise just how perilous their predicament had been. Blackmore told them he had "never seen passengers behave with such extraordinary courage."[17]

Then, suddenly, trouble struck again.

They had gone only a hundred yards or so from the *Bolivar* when the starboard engine of the lifeboat abruptly "conked out," as one crewman put it. With the craft partially disabled in such rough seas, anxiety arose again. It was determined that the lifeboat had hit a piece of floating debris that had jammed one of the propellers. Blackmore hastened to explain that the lifeboat would make it safely back to harbour, though the journey would take longer. Passengers exchanged wan smiles.

As their ordeal at sea was nearing its end, on shore at Dún Laoghaire preparations were under way to meet and accommodate the beleaguered passengers and crew. This meant arrangements for their transport to a hotel or shelter for the night, meals, dry clothes, medical attention if required. Finally, about 10:45 p.m., with a "northerly gale behind them they made Dún Laoghaire." Their entire harrowing adventure, which had begun at 12:22 p.m. at luncheon, had lasted for nearly eleven hours.

Upon arrival at Dún Laoghaire Harbour the twelve passengers and thirty-nine crewmen were met by Red Cross members and escorted to cars waiting to transport them to their accommodation. Andvord was taken to St Michael's Hospital for treatment of his broken arm. Several women who had had a steady resolve and courage during the rescue suddenly felt overcome by the trauma. They "became faint and had to be helped up the stairs to the pier." Reporters noted that they looked "pale and distressed and suffering from their ordeal."[18] A few of them had to be carried to the waiting cars, "obviously exhausted." By contrast, when some crew members came ashore they "jumped about trying to restore circulation to their chilled limbs," it was reported. The more reserved survivors stood shivering visibly, rubbing their hands together. All showed signs of physical and emotional fatigue.

Except, that is, Admiral Mountevans. He looked perfectly composed, stately in stature, crisp in speech. His demeanour had not varied throughout the entire episode. "Unflappable," his fellow-passengers kept calling it.

On shore, with reporters gathered around, everyone praised his leadership. He would have none of such nonsense. Indeed he was interested only in paying tribute to the stellar performance of crewmen, passengers, and their rescuers, for the "coolness with which the Irish lifeboat men went about their work." Even the three female stewards aboard the *Bolivar*, all from Oslo, were lauded for their calm and efficiency during the crisis. With reporters at his shoulders, Mountevans summed up: "They were gallant, there were no signs of panic among either passengers or crew. It seemed almost like the precision of the Royal Navy, so disciplined they were."[19] Then, in one last tribute to his wife and other women, he exulted: "The women behaved like modern Vikings!"

It was, however, a revelation by Sam Blackmore that caught the sharp attention of reporters—and stilled those passengers who heard it:

If we had been an hour later I think they would have been gone.[20]

The *Bolivar's* passengers were taken by cars to the Royal Marine Hotel, where every arrangement had been made for their comfort. First was dry, warm clothing and a hot meal. A stiff drink or two for those so inclined. About midnight, when they were having their meal, reporters were still milling about in hopes of getting a few last titbits for the next day's papers. Admiral Mountevans, wearing a guest's flannel trousers and the hall porter's overcoat, continued to cheerfully reply to every query. Joking that he felt like "a displaced subject," he gave reporters just the sort of pithy quotes and quips they were seeking.

All thirty-nine crew members were equally happy with their somewhat less plush accommodation. They were dispersed to the YMCA, the Mission to

Seamen, the Catholic Seamen's Institute, and the Rothesay Hotel on Eden Quay. Given dry clothes, a hot meal, warm bed, and some cigarettes, they were perfectly content. The next day they would be provided with a complete outfit of new clothing by the Shipwrecked Mariners' Society.

By 1 to 1:30 a.m. most survivors of the ill-fated *Bolivar* on its first voyage were finally bedded down and sinking into sleep. It would not be until the next morning that they would realise just how fortunate they had been.

WEDNESDAY 5 MARCH

Overnight the storm intensified, the temperature falling to about 24 to 26 degrees (3 to 4°c) and snowfall becoming more dense. The wind held steady at its howling pitch. From about 2 a.m. until early afternoon, twelve consecutive hours, "southern Ireland was swept by another fierce blizzard . . . a bitter north-easterly wind which at times reached gale force in most areas . . . the temperatures [remaining] below freezing." This time Cos. Cork, Waterford, Wexford, Kilkenny and Tipperary took the worst battering. With regard to snowfall, Dublin "escaped the full force of the blizzard," but winds running at 60 to 65 miles per hour along the east coast built mountainous seas. So treacherous that, after several attempts, the mail boat *Princess Maud* had to be held up for more than fifteen hours by what was classified as an extremely "violent gale," for the safety of its four hundred passengers. Ships caught out at sea found themselves in great peril.

Drivers of newspaper vans whose normal route from Dublin was via Thurles, Cashel, Mitchelstown and Mallow could get no further than Cashel. A bus that left Dublin for Waterford could not pass Arklow. The southern counties were being blanketed in feet of new snow, making roads impassable, with telephone and telegraph lines also brought down. CIE managers, having learnt hard lessons from the previous blizzards, had no hesitation in cancelling provincial bus services. They wanted no more passengers marooned on snowbound roads. Motorists, now more wary as well, used good judgement and stayed at home. People having to get to work by walking took their chances. At Dungarvan, the *Irish Independent* reported, "at the glue and gelatin factory employees had to walk two miles through waist-deep drifts."

Despite stormy conditions in Dublin, on Wednesday morning the dragging operation at the old quarry pond continued in search of the body of Edward O'Toole. There was no longer a crowd watching, only a few people pausing briefly on their way past the scene.

At the Royal Marine Hotel, when the *Bolivar's* passengers awoke and peered out the window they knew instantly how kind fate had been to them. Though Dublin had not been struck with the full force of this blizzard, the weather was nonetheless blizzardy and dangerous. No vessels dared put out to sea. Later in the morning Captain Rasmussen, anxious to check on his ship, was told that perhaps Captain Coppin might be willing to take him out on his trawler for a quick look. The fishing captain respectfully declined. As one local seafaring man said, "it would be suicide for a small boat to put out in that sea."

Following a full breakfast, Lord and Lady Mountevans and the other passengers were described by reporters, already on the early morning scene and eager for more stories, as seemingly "recovered from their ordeal," openly grateful to be alive, and in high spirits. Several talked of the fortunate timing of their shipwreck. Had it happened only a few hours later they might have been unreachable. One or two expressed some concern over their personal possessions, presumably still aboard the ship, but it was a minor worry, to be sure.

Grounded for the day by the storm, most happily remained at the hotel, sending telegrams to relatives and friends, assuring them that they had survived safely. Lord and Lady Mountevans were invited to lunch with the British Minister in Ireland, Lord Rugby, at his residence in Dundrum. Later in the afternoon, as winds subsided, several of the women ventured out to Dún Laoghaire's fashionable shops for new clothes and accessories.

All this while the *Bolivar*, now "lying exposed to the full fury of the storm," was being ripped apart. Overnight the ship had been driven further onto the Kish Bank, with the fore part, now nearly submerged, "being swept by extremely heavy seas, while the aft section, though still upright, was sinking slowly as it wedged more firmly in the sands."[21] Several hundred feet now separated the two sections.

With thrashing seas breaking over it and a strong list to starboard, the vessel was being shredded. Spars, planks and "small pieces of timber, broken to matchwood, were being eagerly salvaged for firewood all along the coast," it was reported, from Dún Laoghaire to Bray. Once word got out, scavengers made their way to the coast with sacks, hoping to fill them with pieces of wood that would fit and burn in their grates.

By late Wednesday afternoon the seas were still choppy but the snow had ceased and skies cleared partially along the central east coast. This presented an opportunity for the *Irish Press* to get a jump on the competition, all of whom were eager to get out to the *Bolivar* to cover the big story. It was hastily arranged for a reporter and photographer to be flown over the stricken ship and bring back an eye-witness account of the destruction:

> Our pilot brought the three-seater Proctor to within 50 feet of the water ... over the wave-lashed bow. What we saw of this brand new ship was not pleasant.

The bow had almost disappeared and the rest of the ship is firmly embedded in the sand. It looks like a model ship that has been sawn in half . . . A small rowing-boat attached to the stern rail bobbed crazily in an ugly, lumpy sea.[22]

No-one was more anxious for an on-site inspection than Captain Rasmussen, especially as it was being heard that "seafaring men in Dublin and Dún Laoghaire were convinced she will become a total loss." If so, Rassmussen knew that he would be known in Norway as the captain who lost his "charmed" ship on its first voyage. There seemed little hope for salvaging the valuable cargo of maize and barley in the forward hold, which was now almost under water. The action of the sea water was causing such swelling of the grain that the steel plates of the hold were bursting apart. Perhaps there was at least a chance of retrieving some personal possessions belonging to passengers and crew.

On Wednesday evening, with the storm abated, Dubliners felt thankful when reading the newspapers to learn that the blizzard that had smashed the southern counties so hard had largely spared them this time. But as nightfall came they were reminded of the ESB's announcement on Monday that "drastic restrictions" were to go into effect that night. Along many of the city's main streets, lower wattage had been substituted in the lamps, and along secondary streets only every second lamp was now lit. And the general hours of lighting were curtailed by half an hour. This dimmed cityscape had a bleak, depressing appearance. Lamenting that it had been "many years since the citizens have seen their city lighted as it should be," the Evening Herald called it "heading back to the conditions of the Seventeenth Century."[23] Describing Dublin as "left in almost Mediaeval gloom," an editorial claimed that any further diminution of street lighting would be "positively dangerous." The darkened, snow-slicked and icy streets were already treacherous enough for pedestrians at night.

———

First thing on Thursday morning, after an early breakfast, Admiral Mountevans took to the air to get a good aerial view of the shipwreck. He was piloted by Wing-Commander Johnstone, the British air attaché, who flew him directly over the dismembered Bolivar as he made rough sketches and took notes on what he saw below. He would submit these to Captain Rassmussen, as they might be useful in salvage work. He also spotted what appeared to be baggage floating nearby. This might be good news for fellow-passengers.

As Mountevans was airborne, Captain Rasmussen was arranging for the tug Coliemore to take him, his principal officers, two officials from the salvage company and a few reporters out to the site of the wreck. Shortly before 2 o'clock that afternoon they set out to inspect the vessel and search for possessions. As they "drew near the wreck," one reporter wrote, "we sighted a small vessel close to the main portion of the ship." When it quickly moved off towards Dún Laoghaire they radioed its presence back to the harbour authorities. Had they been firewood scavengers? Sightseers? *Looters*?

By the time the *Coliemore* approached the *Bolivar*, the small boat they had spotted was out of sight. All were curious to see what it had been up to. With the sea still heaving and tossing the *Coliemore* about, its skipper carefully made his way through debris-strewn waters. Rasmussen and his officers first went aboard to make certain that it was safe for the others to follow. After a quick look around they gave the go-ahead for them to begin climbing the wet, still-slippery rope ladder. Reporters felt the excitement of the moment, being the first on a shipwreck scene.

The group first headed towards the officers' quarters and passengers' accommodation. And there the story was told. Everything had been torn asunder. As one reporter would write, in something of an understatement, all "appeared to have been ransacked." The first officer promptly verified that "everything was perfectly intact as we left the ship." A locked door leading to the officers' quarters on the main deck had been crudely split open and the "cabins strewn with property of all kinds." Passengers' rooms were in similar disarray. Whoever the marauders had been, they were evidently in a big hurry.

Following the first cursory inspection, a more methodical check of the various quarters was begun. Reporters, knowing that their time aboard was short, scribbled their notes. The *Irish Times* reporter described what they observed:

> We went into the magnificent dining room and found only superficial damage. Rows of shining glassware, firmly held in a special sideboard, were undamaged. When we went into the corridor where passengers' luggage had been piled it was in a shambles. Most of their clothes were gone. Cupboards were flung open in the cabins . . . On the deck was a gramophone fitted with a jazz record, and a box of chocolates. Books and private papers were strewn in the cabins.[24]

He also described finding in the room of a Norwegian passenger an autobiography of his fellow-passenger Admiral Mountevans. Though the looters had struck fast and furiously, they showed surprising discrimination in selecting the most valuable, most portable items. While they concentrated on "jewellery, money and liquor," it would later be verified that they absconded with a wide variety of booty, including the ship's binoculars.

After about two hours they had all the evidence they needed for the moment.

As they were leaving the ship a crew member came across a fur coat. He lifted it up and, smiling slightly, told the reporters that, as they were abandoning ship, one woman suddenly wanted to go back for it. "I told her to save her life first, and not worry about the coat!" The looters had either missed it or deliberately left it behind. She would now get it back.

Before leaving the distressing scene Captain Rasmussen and his officers took one last, silent overview of the *Bolivar,* their model ship on its first voyage—broken completely in half, thrashed to pieces, looking agonised in its last throes of life. As a final act of dignity the captain left behind his first and second mates and chief engineer to remain overnight to protect against any further looting. Glad to carry out this duty, they were provided with food, water, torches, and one sound lifeboat.

On their arrival at Dún Laoghaire pier they were met with another surprise. The looters had already been nabbed! And much to their surprise it must have been, for as their smack approached the pier both gardaí and Customs officials were waiting to give them an unexpected welcome. Their confiscated booty was impressive: jewellery, men's wallets with notes, women's handbags, spirits, tobacco, typewriters, boots and shoes, radios, a piano accordion, among many other items. The goods, estimated to be worth several hundred pounds, were carted off to the Customs shed.

By pure coincidence, as all this commotion was going on, the *Bengazi,* sister-ship of the wrecked *Bolivar,* was slipping into Dublin harbour with a cargo of oranges and dates from Palestine. One can only wonder what its crew must have been thinking.

———

Throughout Thursday, as the *Bolivar* saga was still being played out, rescuers on land were engaged in what the authorities were calling an "all-out" and "last resort" effort to break through impassable Wicklow roads and reach isolated Roundwood and Glencree, as well as individual houses where the inhabitants remained at great risk. Some newspapers were calling it "D-Day." Thursday morning's headline in the *Irish Times* told the story simply enough: "Wicklow conditions desperate."

Owing to their higher altitude, Wicklow's highlands had once again drawn heavy snow from Wednesday's blizzard. A reporter for the *Sunday Independent* who probed as far as he could into the hilly country wrote: "I have seen almost indescribable conditions of the terrible ordeal of the people in the isolated districts." A Mr Condon, one of the oldest inhabitants in the county, told of his area that it had been "six weeks since the people had got any provisions, received post, or attended mass." With no bus or rail service, telephone or telegraph connections, newspapers or food deliveries, "people have been completely cut off and are short of nearly *everything*... and the sick cannot get the medical attention they need."[25] The elderly were suffering from cold, hunger, flu, pneumonia, respiratory problems, other assorted ailments. Their medical and religious needs unmet, some denied even the Last Rites. It was little wonder that some were heard to say that eternal rest would be preferable to the daily agony they faced. There were those who got their wish, as the death rate continued to climb towards double and treble the norm.

In the wake of the last blizzard, the authorities feared there would be more deaths. The *Irish Times* confirmed that "local people have been confined to their villages, some to their homes—nobody knows if [more] people have died in the snow."[26] John Flynn, aged forty-five, a farm labourer of no fixed abode, was discovered beside a stream at Vallinasillogue, about seven miles from Arklow. He was known for travelling from one farmer to another, doing odd chores for a day's wage. No-one knew much about him.

Throughout Co. Wicklow a number of people were now identified as missing or seriously ill. More deaths would surely occur if help did not reach them within the next two or three days. The three elderly Doyles were growing more ill and weak by the hour now. Before the great blizzard of the 25th a doctor had managed to hike miles through the snow to reach them and assess their deteriorating condition. However, there was little he could do for them in their dilapidated cottage. He recommended immediate removal by ambulance to hospital—which was impossible. Now, more than a week later, they were getting close to death, the roof so weighted down by snow that it was sagging just above their heads. The Rev. J. O'Beirne, aware that they were fading, determined to reach them by walking through and over the snow for miles. Telling the *Irish Press* that "it had taken him four hours" to find the half-buried cottage, he confronted the appalling sight of the three completely helpless in their misery. Only an ambulance could save their lives.

Word had somehow reached the Red Cross Society in Dublin that several of the German and Polish war orphans at Glencree were ill and now needed removal by ambulance without delay. In response it had despatched two ambulances, which made their way up a mountain road partially cleared by a snow army but were "finally halted by deep drifts two miles from Glencree." One of the children, suffering from acute appendicitis, *had* to be brought out. A small rescue team embarked on foot over the snow-packed terrain, eventually making it to Glencree, where the nuns informed them about the child's condition. There was only one solution. The "sick child was borne down the mountain . . . carried strapped to a stretcher two miles over the snow to a waiting ambulance," then rushed to a Dublin hospital.

Why had the three severely ill Doyles not been transported over the snow in some similar manner to within reach of ambulance service? After all, around the country makeshift sleighs of barn doors were being used to carry corpses miles to snow-pits for temporary burial. No explanation is recorded. One can only speculate about the matter. Were the Doyles considered "too far gone" for even an attempt at such an arduous plan? Was there the belief that an ambulance would be able to reach them "any day now"? Or did the Doyles themselves reject the suggestion of being placed on a stretcher or makeshift sleigh and being removed from their home, perhaps merely wishing to die in their own beds?

———

The continuing inability to clear a passage for ambulances, doctors and food vans was imperilling an unknown number of lives. For more than a week the Red Cross had speculated about the possibility of an airlift to isolated outposts. On Thursday morning it announced that it was definitely "now making plans to drop food and medicine from planes to those who are cut off from the outside world," most specifically Roundwood and Glencree.[27] Grocers were generously donating foodstuffs to the project. However, Red Cross officials did not reveal how the aerial relief strategy would be carried out. What aircraft would be used? The *Irish Times*, on its own, learnt some details of the proposed operation:

> Special containers were rushed by air from London to Dublin so that food could be dropped by parachute to County Wicklow villages which have been snowbound. The British Government are co-operating fully in the plan ... The containers are similar to those used by the R.A.F. to drop food to villages isolated in Britain. The Irish Red Cross have made preliminary flights over the affected areas. Aircraft of the Army Air Corps may be used.[28]

As soon as word got out that the Red Cross or the Air Corps were actually planning airlifts, people in towns around the country began to petition that they might be included as well. One of the first petitions to be submitted was from Rathdrum, where many people had been unable to leave their homes for nearly a month.

When people read about the emergency food and medicine airlifts being planned it reminded them of the newsreels they had seen of relief efforts in war-torn Europe. Images of parachuted parcels descending over the countryside only miles south of Dublin, to people suffering—even dying—from hunger, cold, isolation and illness seemed simply fantastical.

Meanwhile on the ground a new type of mechanised relief operation was under way on Thursday morning. One long overdue, it would later be argued.

In the aftermath of the great blizzard the previous week, Wicklow County Council officials began a search for heavy mechanised vehicles to try to clear roads now virtually impenetrable to men with shovels and picks. By 6 March they had secured two powerful appliances to tackle the worst snow and ice barriers. When they were unveiled on Thursday morning the men of the local snow armies and rescue parties were impressed by their size, before their engines were even fired up. As Jim Maloney recalls, many country people at that time, such as those in his Co. Galway, had never even seen a caterpillar tractor. "Oh, that was a great thing to see! A crawling tractor with two tracks and a shovel on the front, or a dozer blade, to shovel away the snow . . . It was something new to us."

Before an admiring crowd of onlookers, county council officials introduced the "trac-tractor." It had "caterpillar tracks and looks like a huge tractor . . . In front it has a big scoop and is powered by a diesel engine . . . shifting nearly a ton of snow at every push." Now that would be something to see, all right, some men said to one another. A ton of snow at a single swipe. On the front was an "angledozer," which one official boasted "can tackle any depth of snow, and where it passed, leave a clear road." *Any* depth of snow?

Standing unabashedly in awe of its imposing size and professed power, a group of men waited for the driver to climb into the seat and give a demonstration. Assuming it would be a burly fella with big arms to manipulate the brutish bulldozer, a man whose girth and strength matched that of his machine. When a slender young lad hopped up into the seat to take the controls, the men watching were visibly amused. Within minutes they were mightily impressed, shaking their heads in admiration. As the *Irish Press* described it, the huge caterpillar tractor was "driven by sixteen-year-old John Burgess who handled it as if it were a toy."[29] He had the knack of manoeuvring it smoothly and adroitly with a fast, fluid motion that was astounding to watch.

In his capable hands the bulldozer tractor team, with its convoy of shovel-and-pick men behind, set out on their expedition.

The second vehicle in the dual assault on Wicklow's roads was a gargantuan machine on loan to the county council from the hydro-electric works at Leixlip. A converted tank-transporter, it was a ponderous twelve-ton vehicle that had been fitted with a huge snow-plough, which made it appear to be not merely a snow-scraping device but a giant excavation machine. When it was rolled out for duty on Tuesday, observers seemed to have no doubts about its capability to burst through any barrier.

The two mechanised behemoths formed a "tank corps," supported by a massive infantry of men with shovels and picks to work beside them along the route. It had the feel of a small military operation, and confidence was high.

Following behind the machines and men was a convoy of lorries and vans carrying food, fuel, paraffin oil, candles. Several ambulances were ready to be called in once a passage had been cleared.

Apart from the charge towards Roundwood and Glencree, dozens of smaller gangs would try to reach other villages and houses. By mid-morning on Thursday "every available labourer in the Roundwood and Wicklow area" was being rounded up to handle shovels and picks, "concentrating on the more isolated districts to bring relief to lonely homesteads . . . from which come stories of distress and loss."[30]

The Doyles' plight had worsened, and the sagging roof was now close to falling in upon them, exposing the three elderly, ill inhabitants to the elements. It was surprising that all three were still alive. When "word came that, away up on the mountainside, the cottage had caved in on the three aged people . . . a gang of 25 men were digging their way through snowdrifts to reach them."[31] Without a doubt they would soon perish without transport to hospital. Only a cleared passage for an ambulance could give them a chance.

Thursday's weather was favourable for the "D-Day" movement. Skies were mostly clear, temperatures in the mid-thirties, the wind steady and chilling. The two-pronged assault was targeting Roundwood via the Calary Road in one direction and Ashford from another. With young Burgess at the controls, accompanied by his pick-and-shovel forces, the caterpillar tractor with its angledozer was "smashing through frozen drifts along the Calary Road to reach Roundwood from the north." Simultaneously from Ashford the 12-ton converted tank-transporter steadily charged, cracked and crunched its way forward, bullying barriers out of the way. As both machines gouged their way ahead, they sometimes became bogged down in stubborn drifts. But their shovellers and pickers were on the spot to hack their way clear within minutes. Behind them, other men would better clear the passage for the convoy of vehicles to follow.

Some time in the latter part of the afternoon—the exact hour was not recorded—the final breakthrough occurred, as mighty cheers went up along the road and throughout the village, as robust as was ever heard in Croke Park. The *Irish Press* described the triumph:

> County Council workers operating a 12-ton converted tank conveyor armed in front with a huge snow plough smashed their way through the snow and ice from Ashford to Roundwood, leaving behind a good passage for heavy vehicles, and bringing to this village the first real signs of relief in five weeks.[32]

Not long thereafter, from the other direction, the tractor-bulldozer team saw the angledozer blade clear the last few yards of packed snow as they burst into the long-isolated village to more rousing choruses of welcome. To the liberators, Roundwood appeared every bit the "snow-buried village" described by all the newspapers. Deep snow covered streets, shops, houses. People had dug trenches and tunnels to move about. Among the exultations of "thanks be to God!" one older resident, Tom Pierce, blurted, "It has been the blackest five weeks in the history of the district."

Amid the rejoicing and hoots and yells were many tears, of relief and thanks. Everyone, from youngsters to grannies, began hurrying towards the small convoy of vans to see what they were carrying. Many had run out of food and fuel. Some had subsisted on potatoes, often raw. Everyone was especially mad for bread. When they spotted Eddie Boyle, their regular bread-van driver, he was mobbed. In his younger days he had been quite a star as a Leinster Gaelic football full-back. During the past weeks he had worried about Roundwood residents surviving without his bread deliveries, feeling terrible that he was unable to get through to them. On Thursday afternoon it was a great feeling to hand out loaves to his friends with outstretched arms and huge smiles, shouting "Hiya, Eddie!" Exclaimed one joyful resident, "I could not believe my eyes when I saw Eddie's bread van!" Eddie had been accustomed to hearing cheers for his feats on the field, but never had he felt so much like a hero.

As rescuers milled about happily with residents, they found them in generally fair condition, though many were conspicuously hungry and weak. Stories were heaped upon them about their ordeal, how they had gradually run short of, or out of, food, fuel, paraffin, candles. How every time they believed the winter siege had ended, another blizzard struck, further isolating them from the outside world, confined indoors. Desperation set in when they had to start stripping their homes for wood, then burning furniture. It all left some people in the village, especially the elderly, in a somewhat confused state of mind.

When rescuers reached the home of Margaret and Elizabeth Burke, the well-to-do claimants of a fortune, it was found that they had no food left at all, their eight cattle having died of hunger. They had only the advantage of having more wood and furniture to burn than others.

With Roundwood liberated, John Burgess set out with his bulldozer to clear the secondary road leading to the Doyles' collapsed cottage before it was too late. Accompanied by his digging squad, he made good progress at first. Then they encountered massive snowdrifts that had crystallised into glaciers. Shovel blades bounced off with a reverberating "twang!" and picks broke off chips rather than chunks. With dusk descending over the landscape, it became clear that they were not going to rescue the Doyles before nightfall, as the *Irish Times* reported:

Vain efforts were made with the aid of a bulldozer to reach the three old-age pensioners who are ill in their snow-bound cottage. The bulldozer stuck in the frozen snow half a mile from the cottage. The Doyles had been waiting for weeks for aid. Their only food has been potatoes. Another attempt will be made tomorrow.[33]

Late on Thursday, in Mountplunket, Co. Roscommon, the body of Owen Brennan, age not identified, was found in the snow about a hundred yards from his house. It was believed that he had been out "relieving snowed-up cattle on his farm" when he was overtaken in the blizzard's white-out, disoriented, and driven to wander, growing weak. This may have induced a heart attack.

––––

On the morning of Friday 7 March the *Irish Independent* blared the good news: "Roundwood relieved after five weeks."

All the newspapers published the full story of the rescue operation and the residents' long ordeal. If another blizzard did not strike, their nightmare was at last really over. Later in the morning the Irish Red Cross Society made an announcement:

> The plan to drop food to Roundwood by parachute has been abandoned, as the village has been relieved.[34]

Wicklow County Council, proud of its success, promised that another, "more powerful machine of the same kind will be in operation any day now." Raising the question, why had tractor-bulldozers and converted tank-transporters not been secured by the Government and other agencies weeks earlier?

By mid-morning the Doyles, brother and two sisters, were reached, as the bulldozer broke through the last ice mounds and left a passage just wide enough for an ambulance. All three were essentially mute and motionless. Each was placed on a stretcher and carried from their crumpled cottage prison, placed in the ambulance, and driven slowly down the mountain road towards Dublin and hospital.

––––

Shortly after noon Captain Rasmussen, his officers, several salvage experts and a few reporters were again aboard the *Bolivar,* combing each chamber in search of any valuable possessions missed by the looters. Though passengers had been advised to take their jewellery with them, not all had done so, and a few pieces were found. By great good luck Captain Rasmussen himself discovered a "very valuable ring" belonging to Lady Mountevans, which her husband admitted had not been insured. He was also delighted to learn that a crewman had found "some of my decorations . . . and Norwegian War Medal given to me by King Haakon."

What had not been found was the reason why the *Bolivar*, the model ship equipped with the latest navigational and communications system, sailed by an elite crew, had run aground on the Kish Bank only a few miles off the Irish coast, and had broken completely in two.

———

That afternoon Glencree was finally reached. Every window was filled with faces as the rescuers approached the hostel, the nuns peering over the children's heads with smiles just as large. The German and Polish orphans pranced about as the nuns clasped their hands together in pure happiness. Cries of delight went up when the van with bread and other food items was seen. It was promised that a doctor and ambulance would be arriving soon. The nuns told the men that they were down to their last bare rations of food and fuel. Prayer had sustained them. They had never lost faith that help would arrive in time.

Residents of Roundwood and Glencree were starved for news of what they called the "outside world." Queries were heaped upon the rescuers. "Had all of Ireland been struck by such fierce blizzards, left isolated? Had there been any deaths? Had the animals survived? When could they expect to have bus and telephone services again?

"What was the weather forecast?"

SATURDAY 8 MARCH
King Winter tenaciously held his grip. Night temperatures dropped well below freezing. In Dublin, multitudes were still without fuel for their grates. Much of the countryside remained snowbound, many places still isolated.

Newspapers reminded readers that St Patrick's Day was only nine days away.

By Saturday most of the *Bolivar's* passengers has said their last goodbyes to one another, promised to keep in touch, and gone their own ways. The majority of crew members had returned to Norway. Wherever the survivors went, they were asked about their shipwreck experience.

Admiral Mountevans and his wife had remained in Ireland to visit friends but were now anxious to continue on their way towards their planned skiing holiday in Norway. He would also be happy to be free of reporters hounding him for further colourful quotes. Nor did he like the continuing newspaper descriptions of himself as "courageous," "heroic," "witty," and so forth. He couldn't count how many times he had been asked to repeat his favourite motto.

On Saturday morning, as he and his wife left Ireland by plane, his last words, quoted by the press, summed up his sentiments:

We want to forget the whole business.[35]

Chapter 11 ～

| INQUIRY AND INQUEST

*In an age of simpler faith it would have been said that the
wrath of God was directed against Ireland.*

(*Irish Times*, 18 MARCH 1947)

*The glorious isolation of the members of the Government
during the snowstorms . . . when people were cut away from
help and lives were lost in the snow . . . they were not roused
from their stupor, the Army was not called out. What did
the Government do? Sat snugly and smugly in Government
Buildings and did nothing. It sounds unbelievable, yet it is
true. They did nothing.*

(*Sunday Independent*, 9 MARCH 1947)

*The Coroner, expressing his deep sympathy with the
relatives of the boys, said that it was a tragic occurrence . . .
The children displayed a remarkable degree of heroism.*

(*Evening Herald*, 11 MARCH 1947)

WEEKEND OF 8/9 MARCH

As Lord and Lady Mountevans flew off to their skiing holiday in
Norway, leaving all the unpleasant "business" behind, the Irish people
remained captives of King Winter. The second Saturday in March was
the forty-second consecutive day of the Arctic spell. The prolonged Siberian
weather was both physically and mentally debilitating. By the sixth week of
the torment, Una Shaw recalls, people felt a sense of desperation, helplessness:

> The winter was horrifying in its own way, because you realised that you
> were at the mercy of nature—and there was nothing you could do about
> it!

People cursed "King Winter," the "white enemy," the "Big Freeze," the "Big
Snow." The *Sunday Independent* concluded that "the blizzards have been fierce
and malevolent . . . The whole effect and character of the weather is
implacable." Intimating an ill intent—or even evil—behind it. People were

calling it abominable, plain wicked. Blurted one fed-up country man:

> It'll kill the country, this weather. It's shockin' times . . . What's a man to
> do? It's a holy divine terror![1]

Francis McFadden of Ballymote, Co. Sligo, recalls that "some people said
Ireland was finished."

––––

For the previous six days divers at the old quarry pond at Sundrive Road had
risked their own welfare searching for the youngest of the three lads who had
drowned while skating. It looked as if they might not find the body until
spring. If ever, in such depths. Throughout the week there had been only a
scattering of onlookers, but on Saturday morning a small crowd was
gathering again. A few minutes before 11 a.m. the men in the rowing-boat
signalled to shore. Something had been found. As people along the bank
moved nearer, the body of eight-year-old Edward O'Toole was drawn to the
surface and pulled into the boat. Stretcher-bearers from the St John
Ambulance Brigade were waiting at the water's edge. A limp form was lifted
from the boat, placed gently on the stretcher, reverently covered, then taken to
the Royal City of Dublin Hospital in Baggot Street, where the inquest would
be held on Tuesday.

As the dragging team collected their gear for departing, the crowd slowly
dispersed. The rag markers used for goals were still visibly frozen in place on
the ice. Spring would come and melt the ice, and they would vanish unnoticed
into the depths of the old quarry.

––––

By the weekend of 8/9 March both public and press were posing profound
questions. What were the causes of the aberrant phenomenon?—what was
behind it all? Was it due to man, nature, God, fate? Why had the Government
failed so blatantly to act on behalf of suffering citizens? Why had the army not
been called out in force? How had weather "experts" been so consistently
wrong? When would it end? Would there be a spring tillage? If not, was
another famine looming?

With such queries came a cascade of criticism and blame.

Newspapers focused on an obvious target: de Valera's inept Fianna Fáil
Government, which well deserved blame for its inaction over six weeks of
weather crisis. The Government was not faulted, of course, for *causing* the
cold and blizzards but was held responsible for failing to *respond* vigorously
to the resulting emergencies. Newspapers alleged that the Government's

inexplicable passivity in the face of human suffering was inexcusable and unconscionable.

Building a strong case for condemnation, the press cited a litany of actions that de Valera's Government could—and *should*—have taken: promptly order the army out *en masse* to assist the ESB and Post Office in restoring communications; accompany the CIE crews in clearing roads and railways and rescuing marooned passengers; help snow armies and rescue sorties to bring relief to snowbound towns, villages, and farmsteads; haul turf and logs to the fireless; provide food and meal kitchens to the hungry; search for missing persons; help retrieve the bodies of the dead. Boost public morale and confidence by their very presence in the national recovery efforts.

Other than a few token efforts involving a paltry number of soldiers, the Government had failed abysmally to provide either leadership or substantial assistance on a national scale.

By the second week of March the press's criticism was uncharacteristically explicit and damning. One newspaper chastised the Government for focusing its attention on "grandiose schemes for 'cosmic physics,' 'luxury hotels,' 'streamlined' roads—let them get closer to the people and pay attention to their needs." The most scathing indictment of its failure appeared in the lengthy editorial in the *Sunday Independent* of 9 March:

> The glorious isolation of members of the Government in Dublin during the snowstorms is now one of the most common subjects of discussion amongst the public. People were cut away from help and lives lost. Thousands of sheep and cattle have perished in the snow. And what did the Government do? Nothing.
>
> Ministers apparently have been too occupied with receptions and lectures to think that some help might have been organised on a national scale to get relief through to families who were undergoing harrowing experiences.[2]

Most preposterous, it was argued, was the Government's failure to despatch soldiers to help citizens in distress. Some of whom would die. They were the nation's greatest resource of fit and ready manpower, outfitted with equipment and heavy-duty vehicles, trained to deal with emergencies. During the prolonged national crisis they were left by the Government to twiddle their thumbs in heated barracks while ordinary citizens went hungry, fireless, ill, snowbound, and frightened. On this point, the editorial struck hard:

> This country has an Army. The snowstorms with their resultant chaos in traffic conditions, with great isolated areas, presented a problem that soldiers would have gladly tackled. Here was a job to be done for the

people—to get food and fuel to the houses, medical aid . . . to get the travellers who were stranded. But the Army was not called upon to help. It sounds unbelievable, yet it is true. The members of the Government sat snugly and smugly in Government buildings and did nothing.

Even after it had been reported that lives had been lost, the Government were not roused from their stupor. They did nothing.[3]

The editorial was widely read and much discussed, lauded for its candour.

Other newspapers around the country were similarly accusatory towards what they saw as a feckless Government. Some towns and counties contended that they had been forgotten altogether by the Government in Dublin. Many residents of the west felt aggrieved that the Government neither physically assisted them nor gave them due attention through Radio Éireann, failing to report on their distressful conditions.

The *Western People* addressed this issue in an editorial headed "Isolation and grievance":

The entire West of Ireland has suffered the most serious dislocation of life for the past century. The blizzards left a disastrous trail of wreckage, loss of life, and untold suffering. For the terrible catastrophe . . . the people of the West entertain a sense of grievance because the Irish Radio news broadcasts conveyed no sense at all of the seriousness or isolation of our position following the blizzards.[4]

The following day de Valera, stung by the rash of criticism, issued a defensive, rather dismissive statement:

There are people who talk as if the Government is responsible for that [the weather]. We are not responsible for the sunspots or changes in the Gulf Stream, or any considerations which may be put forth in attributing the changes in the weather.[5]

No-one had suggested that. By making it sound as if the Government was being blamed for *causing* the calamitous weather he avoided responding to the real charge: that it had failed to *react* responsibly.

————

During the first days of March the amateur meteorologists at Rathfarnham Castle were conducting their own inquiries, using the best scientific techniques and weather data accumulated over the past six weeks. They sought to analyse the "big picture." How bad had the winter really been—thus far? Were there historical precedents? They had a pile of statistics on temperatures, barometric pressures, wind velocities, blizzard duration, sunshine rates, and so forth. If they could put the pieces of the puzzle together they might determine whether the winter of 1946/47 was indeed emerging as the worst not only in living memory but in history. Newspapers too were keen to get the full weather story.

In an age before satellite imagery and scientific weather-measuring technology, Ireland's small coterie of meteorologists did their best to analyse handwritten notations on daily charts. Although in 1947 the Meteorological Service, from its head office in O'Connell Street, was not yet in the business of forecasting weather, they could certainly look backwards at what had happened and make that information public.

Bare statistics told the story. The "Big Freeze," as it was now commonly called, had begun during the fourth week of January. Temperatures had plunged 25 degrees below freezing, reaching 7 degrees Fahrenheit (−14°C). A number of nights it fell to between 12 and 8 degrees (−11 to −13°C). For six consecutive weeks the night temperature had fallen below freezing, and most daytimes the mercury had remained below 32 degrees (0°C).

The bone-chilling east wind had created excruciating wind-chill. During February alone, meteorological data showed that in Dublin the "wind blew at gale force" on five of the twenty-eight days and about half-gale force on several others. It had been measured at 60–70 miles per hour. Hurricane force. The fierce winds created mountainous seas, massive snowdrifts, knocked people right off their feet. Meteorologists described these winds as "extremely violent." An uncommon term for them. When combined with temperatures below 15 degrees (−9°C), the wind-chill factor was responsible for a human comfort index of 10 to 20 degrees below zero (−23 to −29°C), at least.

Snowfall rates and accumulations had varied widely. At times snow fell at a rate of 3 to 4 inches per hour. Around the country, depths of six to ten feet of *base* snow were common; drifts were measured at twelve, fifteen, twenty feet and more. And the *Irish Times* had vouched for "at least" one fifty-foot drift. Drifts could extend hundreds of feet, even miles.

Ironically, the most astonishing statistic recorded during February may have seemed to many people the least dramatic: sunshine hours. Everyone knew that it had been uncommonly dull for weeks, but few would have imagined just how sunless it had been:

> In the first half of the month there was no sunshine.
> On February 22 there were two hours of sunshine. On the 23rd five hours; on the 24th, one hour, and on the 27th eight hours. The total sunshine for the month was 16 hours.[6]

Half of which was recorded in a single day. It was said that "sunshine was a severely-rationed commodity—not available even on the black market." It was no wonder that so many people were suffering from sunlight deprivation and associated low spirits, even depression.

———

Impressive statistics. But what about comparisons with the past? To be sure, there had been some famously harsh winters and storms over past centuries. Unfortunately, substantial descriptions of these are few. The winters of 1683/84 and 1878/79 were noted for their intense cold temperatures, with 25 degrees or more of frost. The most legendary, however, was probably that of 1740, known at the time as the "Great Frost." Considering that it occurred 207 years previously, it is not surprising that detailed accounts are missing. It was mentioned as a footnote in Lecky's *History of Ireland in the Eighteenth Century*, and there were some references to it at the time in the diaries of Charles O'Conor of Bellanagare, Co. Roscommon. Apparently, like that of 1947, it followed a pattern of hard frost first setting in, solidifying the ground, followed by heavy snows. All the lakes were said to have been "sheeted with a strong coat of ice," and the severe spell lasted for weeks.

The freeze of 1740 was an Arctic cold compounded by a severe wind-chill that was "quite outside British or Irish experience" at the time.[7] According to David Dickson, "this bizarre weather was without precedent and defied scientific explanation."[8] He concluded that it plunged Ireland into what was "in effect a mini Ice Age." However, as no barometric or temperature readings, or snowfall records, made during the "Great Frost" survive, there is no scientific basis of comparison. Furthermore, adds Timothy Cronin, "we have no description of how a people beset by cold and hunger" coped, or died, during the freeze of 1740.[9]

In March 1947 the Jesuit meteorologists at Rathfarnham Castle, analysing all the scientific data that *did* exist, determined that there was one "outstanding feature" that probably set the winter apart from its predecessors: the "continuation over such a long period" of the conditions of cold, freezing, ice, winds, and blizzards, in conjunction with one another.[10] For Ireland it was an unprecedented, mercilessly *prolonged* grip of severe weather. The Jesuits' meteorological records dated back to about 1868, some quite sketchy. Drawing on what information they possessed, in early March they compiled their data on a large table to analyse it, took a historic view, then reached their conclusion:

> There is no parallel for the weather of past February in seventy-nine years of our records; it was a freakish and phenomenal month. There was no accounting for it.[11]

Nor was it over yet.

Meanwhile newspapers were also probing deep into past Irish winters that had been written about, even if in rudimentary form. There had been some harsh winter storms, all right, with frigid temperatures, heavy snows, even *bona fide* blizzards. But in combined *severity, magnitude,* and *duration,* the winter of 1946/47 was emerging as unprecedented, indisputably the most brutal.

The *Irish Press* offered its verdict on the subject:

> These last weeks . . . it is grim; it is terrible in its urgency and misery. Nothing as bad as this has ever been seen before.[12]

———

Not everyone was so certain. Some old-timers, born in the 1870s and 80s, claimed they recalled a real "daddy" of a blizzard back in the year 1895. It was legendary, no doubt about that. But just how bad was it?

The comparison stirred some lively debate in parlours and pubs around the country. Newspapers jumped into the fray, referring to the "atrocious" blizzard of 1895. Those who had lived through it were asked for some details about snowfall, temperature, force of the wind, for the sake of comparison. Most, however, replied with general impressions: "heaps of snow!" "terrible wind blowing!" "ah, bitter cold!" Plenty of superlatives, but few facts. Nor could anyone seem to recall just how long the storm had lasted. Simply that it was "altogether awful."

People relished a good debate about which winter was the real "champion," 1895 or 1947. The *Sunday Independent* affirmed that, until the present year, the 1895 "snow story was probably the biggest ever written about in an Irish newspaper . . . The storm raged all day without intermission."[13] But there was not sufficient meteorological data from 1895 to make a valid comparison, it was concluded.

However, if the disputants had gone to the library to examine the newspaper accounts of the blizzard that struck Ireland on 12 January 1895 they would have found some interesting descriptive evidence. In particular, the *Irish Daily Independent* of 14 January had provided an uncommonly lengthy description of the famed blizzard. It ran to nearly 15,000 words in eight columns, entirely filling the main news page and providing a good picture of the storm:

> During the earlier hours of Saturday morning a stiff wind blew continuously, frequently carrying along strong gusts of sleet . . . A change ensued when the dense masses of sombre snow clouds burst. The snowfall was very heavy for the first hours of the morning after six o'clock . . . and the wind was bitterly cold, which blew the snow flakes into the faces of

pedestrians. By the time businesses should have been getting into full swing the entire city was under snow, which lay several inches deep on the ground, and covered in chimney stacks, house roofs, sign posts, public monuments and every manner of outdoor structure.

During the entire morning the snow continued . . . The snowstorm raged all day. It showed no mercy to the weak or to the strong . . . blocked up trams, delayed mails, and did not give jarveys a chance of earning their fares . . . Telephone and telegraph lines were blown down. So it continued all day until about half-past four o'clock when there was a lull.[14]

Typical of the journalistic age, the coverage was a clinical, straightforward factual account of events. It dealt almost entirely with Dublin, with scant reference to the rest of the country. (Although this omission may have been due in some part to felled telephone and telegraph lines, it was the practice of Dublin newspapers to give disproportionate coverage to the capital city.) Most attention was given to the storm's disruption of business activity, the tram service, and local communications lost because of felled poles. The blizzard's effect on ordinary people's lives was barely mentioned. Nor were there any eye-witness accounts, or photographs, that would have provided dramatic testimony to the blizzard's severity.

There is one striking point of similarity in the newspaper coverage of 1895 and 1947: that of the hardship and suffering endured by the poorest tenement-dwellers:

1895
To the poor it [the blizzard] causes, no doubt, the greatest suffering, and one shudders to think what a day the denizens of the city must have spent, crouched in their wretched hovels, a prey to snow and wet and wind." (*Irish Daily Independent*, 14 January 1895)

1947
For the poorest parts of Dublin the blizzard brought the worst day of despair. (*Dublin Evening Mail*, 28 February 1947)

The commonest sight to be seen in Dublin during the weeks of snow and frost . . . in every slum . . . shivering, ill-clad undernourished, poor Irish men, women and children. (*Sunday Independent*, 9 March 1947)

In the absence of detailed meteorological data on temperatures, wind speeds, snowfall amounts and drifting depths, it is not possible to compare accurately the two great blizzards. However, a particularly illuminating feature of the 1895 storm is what occurred forty-eight hours later when a warm air front moved across Ireland, bringing a heavy rainstorm:

A very severe rainfall took place last night [14 January] and melted a great deal of the snow. This morning very little of the heavy snowfall remains and we are glad to state that no accidents are to be chronicled. Tramcars ran freely on the different lines, while traffic of other descriptions was pretty generally resumed. On the whole, everything turned out well.[15]

No accidents or deaths. Snow largely gone, and life returning to normal. "Everything turned out well." Powerfully contrasting points of comparison.

———

With the meteorologists stymied, and the best weather experts unabashedly confessing that there was "no accounting for it," calling it a "freakish phenomenon" that apparently defied explanation, many ordinary citizens had their own ideas about what was causing the bizarre weather. Following the blizzard of 25 February and the onset of the sixth week of misery in March there was heightened controversy over the real causes behind it all. As the *Dublin Evening Mail* put it:

The abnormally long spell of hard weather is permitting theorists with fixed ideas about such matters to air their views freely.[16]

By mid-March it was *the* topic of conversation and inquiry in Dublin homes, shops, offices, and factories, on the docks and in the street markets. And particularly in pubs, where, in accordance with conversational protocol, profound thinkers as well as crackpots were entitled to their say on a subject. After all, a man could do no worse expressing his opinion than the weather "prophets" had done for the past six weeks.

Essentially, four standard hypotheses prevailed, with various twists and interpretations: sunspots, atomic bombs, changes in the Gulf Stream, and God's wrath. A new notion pertaining to the alignment of the planets was gaining in popularity as well. The difference now was that, after six weeks of misery and frustration with blundering weathermen, these hypotheses were being taken more seriously, debated more intelligently than previously.

"Sunspotters" may at first have been viewed by some merely as "lunatics" for their fanciful, far-fetched hypothesis, regarded more as amusing than scientifically sound. However, it was increasingly being pointed out by serious, well-informed sunspot proponents that in 1843 the distinguished German astronomer Samuel Heinrich Schwabe first noted that sunspots burgeon and wane over different cycles. Now newer, more powerful telescopes were showing that it was apparently "roiling magnetic fields that generate sunspot blotches." In Ireland and in Britain meteorologists and astronomers were observing definite changes in sunspots and solar flares, convinced that there might be some evidence that these could affect the earth's weather patterns. When sunspotters held forth in Dublin's pubs, more people were inclined to listen to them.

A new hypothesis, somewhat akin to that of the sun's activity, pertained to other planets. There was a certain exotic fascination about it, and intellectual regulars in pubs such as McDaid's, the Palace and the Pearl gave it a fair hearing. As Dublin's weather experts looked ever more inexpert and hapless, one devout proponent of the planets hypothesis offered them some advice:

> I suggest that students of meteorology should seriously consider the effects of the planets on the weather. Students of astro-meteorology maintain that the elevation, and the mutual configuration of the sun and the planets also condition the weather.[17]

It was his premise that Jupiter, in configuration with the sun, produced "brilliant sunshine and salubrious weather." Mars produced cold, and Saturn "cold, leaden skies and rain," while Pluto and Mercury, "possessing the greatest eccentricity, are responsible for storms and gales." Making them the villains of the Solar System.

If his hypothesis was valid, in the winter of 1946/47 it seemed as if all the planets might be out of proper alignment.

On Earth, it was well known that the Gulf Stream could be erratic and quite abnormal in course. Such misbehaviour in the North Atlantic could have serious effects on Ireland's weather, as it was responsible for bringing warm currents and mild oceanic windflows. It was nature's wonderful gift to Ireland: a temperate marine climate normally devoid of extremes of heat or cold. But it could be disrupted. As the *Dublin Evening Mail* wrote, "we have had warnings of the changing direction of the Gulf Stream and the bad effects on our climate it must bring." Disruption of the Gulf Stream, combined with the formation of the anticyclonic regime, high-pressure zone and invading east winds clearly had the potential to radically alter Ireland's pattern of normally mild winter weather. But the exact role of the Gulf Stream amidst the interaction of these other elements is complex, requiring long-term analysis. It was not a meteorological puzzle to be pieced together in a few weeks or months in 1947.

The hypothesis that aroused the greatest passion and ire was that of the effect of atomic bombs on the globe's climate. Didn't the freakish weather begin shortly after the United States tested, and then dropped, two atomic bombs towards the end of the Second World War? Hardly a coincidence in the minds of those convinced that "the bomb" was the culprit behind it all. It certainly had the *appearance* of Man meddling with nature, releasing trillions of radio-active contaminants into the upper atmosphere. With strong winds high aloft, these particles could be carried around the world.

To many people it seemed that every time a blizzard struck it was followed by another article in the newspapers about atomic bomb developments somewhere in the world. During the last week of February it was reported that the "radioactivity produced by the Bikini bombs was detected within one week in the u.s.," proving how quickly it could cover great distances. Prompting Edward Teller, the leading American atomic scientist, to admit that an enemy unleashing such a bomb far off the Pacific coast could "endanger the entire United States by radio-activity, without having to deliver a single blow on American soil." Strong winds would carry out the deed.

Close to the same time the *Evening Herald* published a particularly unsettling article revealing that "one expert gloomily forecasts a return of the Ice Age to Europe through atomic bomb efforts."[18] Similar predictions were appearing in Continental newspapers. The *Irish Press* presented a different slant on the risk of atomic bombs:

> Let off a few more Atomic bombs, loosening by the vibrations the unstable ice-fields of the Pole, and on comes the new Ice Age ... such are the speculations.[19]

Some ships' crews in the far North Atlantic were already reporting signs of glacial changes and iceberg flow.

Such widespread speculation about the effects of atomic bomb radioactivity and "vibrations" with the coming of a new Ice Age fuelled Irish suspicions about such a link. To those convinced, it was just "putting two and two together!"

———

By the fifth week of the Siberian blast, talk of a "new Ice Age" was appearing regularly in newspapers. Some of it coming from scientists. On the morning of 26 February, only hours after the "Daddy of them all" had struck, the *Irish Press* published a Doomsday scenario about a new Ice Age on the way. The article surely had to have been prepared before the blizzard. The timing of its appearance couldn't have been more unsettling to a country gripped in the chaos and fear of the moment.

The article was based on Thornton Wilder's play *The Skin of Our Teeth*, but the newspaper placed it in the context of the immediate present. The play portrayed Man facing ultimate destruction from apocalyptic events, one crisis being that of the Glacial Epoch, when "thousands of years ago ice and snow came down from the Polar regions and buried Europe." Wilder imagined the disaster occurring in the contemporary age, when newspapers, telegrams, telephones and radios were in use. Showing how newspapers and huge placards were put out, telling people that the "torrent of avalanche and ice-drifts" threatened entire regions and populations: "New York City isolated! . . . Communications with England cease!"[20] The play had great drama—and doom.

The *Irish Press* decided to place such a calamity in immediate perspective for the country's readers:

> How topical it would be if only this play were acted out in this strange and terrible winter! You could feel the cold oncoming of the tide of death. You saw humanity powerless. Eye-witness reports of the advancing white wall were arriving.
>
> Terrifying, indeed, yet not fantastic! There is no natural or obvious reason why it should not happen again in modern times . . . the northern polar cap breaking up, and a new Ice-Age spreading over the civilised world. It could happen. The end of civilisation could come with a new Glacial Epoch. Perhaps this calamity is a foretaste of the ultimate calamity—a warning, or reminder.[21]

That this Doomsday article appeared on the very heels of the worst blizzard in Ireland, when countless thousands of people were isolated, trapped in fireless homes, marooned on desolate roads, hungry and frightened, was in itself astonishing.

There were those to whom such cataclysm made sense. Apocalyptic events had occurred throughout human history. They were in the Bible: floods, plagues, famine, drought. Testimony to God's displeasure with Man? Punishment for original sin? Later sins? Merely a warning? Certainly Man in the modern age of the 1940s had fallen into some Godless ways, wallowing in materialism, greed, immorality, wars, drink, gluttony. Sins of all sorts. Even the moralistic Irish had been reprimanded by their spiritual leaders for excessive imbibing, gambling, partying, improper dancing. Even the *Irish Times* proffered: "In an age of simpler faith it would have been said that the wrath of God was directed against Ireland."[22]

Over recent weeks, from the pulpit in a number of churches, the parishioners were told that all in life is a part of "God's will," or "God's plan." There were intimations that Providence was behind it all, as science and human reason failed to explain the phenomenon of abysmal freezing and blizzards. In churches of other European countries suffering from the same winter siege similar sermons were preached.

In Ireland some priests and pastors dismissed such notions. On Sunday 9 March the Bishop of Cork, Daniel Cohalan, directed the priests in his diocese to read his Letter to the Faithful, which touched upon such thinking:

We need not suppose that the severe weather is a sign of the anger of God, but it should not surprise us when we consider what little account was taken of God at the start and during the progress of the late war. Let us pray to God to be merciful and to favour us with favourable weather for the spring work and for abundant returns in due season.[23]

Ultimately, perhaps the power of prayer would prevail.

———

By March another sort of inquiry was becoming prevalent. If it was conceded by reasonable minds that the aberrant weather could not be comprehended, or changed, by science or religion, was it possible to at least draw some intelligent, useful knowledge or lessons from it? Of a practical, philosophical or moral nature? To extract something positive from the awful ordeal? As the *Irish Times* queried:

Is there a lesson we can learn from the events of the past months? Or should we just accept that spell of weather as a freak or fate, which will never be repeated in our lifetime?[24]

There were, quite obviously, some practical lessons to be derived: how better to cope with the removal of snow, the disruption of transport and communications, rescue operations. But were there more profound meanings to be plumbed? *Human* lessons, or ponderings, pertinent to the very nature of humanity?

P. S. O'Hegarty thought so. He posed such queries in a well-reasoned and provocative article in the *Sunday Independent* headed "The blizzards have a warning." His hypothesis was that "man's conquest" in recent years of the "new sources of power, of motion, went to his head, dimmed his senses of the spiritual, and enlarged his sense of the material."[25] In essence, Man, in all his pride and vainglory, had been transformed into "an economic, mechanical and automatic animal," living a life in the "midst of buttons and levers."

Then, Ireland and Britain were struck a mighty blow by nature in January and February. Suddenly, Man saw his "mechanical contrivances" fail him: ships unable to leave ports, roads and railways blocked by snow and ice, coal pits closed, cars, buses and lorries stranded, communications crippled. O'Hegarty concluded:

The snow blizzards and the winds have shaken complacent optimism . . . They are a warning to Man, not to be too cocksure about his mastery of material forces. The button-lever devices have had to be rescued from their undignified predicaments by original Man with a shovel.[26]

Perhaps the Irish people were learning another lesson as well. Theirs was a class-stratified society, in which the poor and privileged ranks had little, if any, meaningful association or identity with one another. Dublin in particular was a city of haves and have-nots: tenement-dwellers, growing middle classes, entrenched wealthy in posh suburbs. But by the second week of March the food and fuel crisis was affecting *everyone* to some degree. More than half of all homes in the capital were out of decent fuel, facing a fireless grate, forced to strip wood and burn furniture. Even with the black market, many food items were now very difficult or impossible to obtain, as everyone felt tight rationing at home. As a result of the prolonged Arctic conditions and successive blizzards, all Dubliners were experiencing some home confinement, transport difficulties, communication problems, fear of falling and injury, disenchantment with an inert Government and inept weather forecasters. In short, as the *Dublin Evening Mail* wrote, King Winter had acted as a great leveller in Irish society:

> Citizens are now suffering many of the privations which it had been their charitable wont to relieve in others. In previous years the average citizen regarded extreme poverty with some detachment; to-day privation is the common experience of all of us.
>
> The extremely poor and ourselves have shared a common experience this year . . . We know what it is to have staple foods that we had always taken for granted to disappear from our table, to be without fuel or fire for two and three weeks . . . We may now be inclined to regard the very poor and ourselves as "all in the same boat."[27]

In principle, at least, some lessons could be learnt from shared deprivation and hardship. As the article further postulated, "our sympathy will have a deeper character . . . Fellow-feeling makes us wondrous kind." Greater Dublin society could well do with a good lesson in empathy.

The *Irish Independent* claimed that "winter, the great leveller," had at least been egalitarian in nature.

———

On Sunday 9 March a discernible change in the weather occurred. People leaving from early mass stepped outside and were pleasantly surprised by the mild feel of the air on their faces. The wind had died down, and temperatures were already well up in the 30s (2 to 4°C). They loosened their scarves. Children raced home, anxious to tear off their Sunday duds and get out to play. Adults ambled home for a change, chatting amiably along the way. Was it a sign of *real* change, they wondered.

Ireland's weather analysts were tracking some interesting developments. The anticyclonic regime and high-pressure system to the north, from Russia to Scandinavia and Greenland, seemed genuinely to be dissipating. They also identified some evidence of the resumption of the normal Gulf Stream, which could bring warmer temperatures, fresh oceanic winds, and a thaw. And possibly rain.

Dubliners flocked out of doors on Sunday afternoon as temperatures climbed into the 40s (4 to 6°C). With the thawing, streets were slushy and the earth boggy. Several hurling, football and rugby matches were scheduled. In the biggest contest, Old Belvedere met Bective Rangers on ground described as "ankle-deep in mud," causing the action to appear as if in slow motion. Around the city, youngsters were having spirited snowball fights, sometimes compacting wet snow into hard, ice-like balls that could be dangerous. Eighteen-year-old John Swift of Cootehill lost an eye when struck by one. Many others had bruises from their battles.

After forty-two consecutive days of sub-freezing temperatures, on Sunday night the mercury in Dublin did not fall below 32 degrees (0°C). It settled around 34 degrees (1°C). Heavy fog spread over the entire east coast, as most other areas of the country experienced either some fog or mist.

The Arctic spell had finally been broken.

On Monday the "first general thaw set in," reported the newspapers. Most counties enjoyed a "mild, soft day, with the thaw increasing hourly." Later in the day heavy rains began to fall in many parts, hastening the thaw. With the snow-pack of four to ten feet blanketing most of the landscape, and drifts of twenty feet and more, there was a colossal volume of water to be melted. A gradual thaw would be the ideal. Monday's forecast for the coming days was promising: "moderate to fresh south to south-west wind, with rain at times; much milder." A west wind!

The rosy prognostication, however, was quickly tempered by a despatch from Reuters reporting that "Moscow's weather report to-day forecast heavy cloud, snow, and temperatures between two and four degrees below zero."[28]

————

On Tuesday 11 March an inquest dominated the news and captured people's attention. It was nine days since the Kimmage quarry tragedy, the body of eight-year-old Edward O'Toole having been found only three days previously. With all the newspaper coverage, readers had devoured every detail of the drownings. By now they felt as if they personally knew the young lads and their grieving families. The accident, widely discussed in the city, had raised many questions. How could it have happened? Who was to blame? How could it be avoided in the future? The public were hoping the inquest might provide answers to such questions. Interest in the day's proceedings was extremely high.

Dr J. B. Brennan, county coroner, convened the jury at the Royal City of Dublin Hospital in Baggot Street to formally establish the cause of the death of Anthony Burke (16), Christopher "Kit" Byrne (13), and Edward O'Toole (8). It was still still not known whether the three boys had known one another. Because of the keen interest in the tragedy, and the controversy surrounding it, Dr Brennan felt a special responsibility to extract all pertinent facts. To get at the truth, especially for the sake of the boys' parents. He would be unfailingly professional, polite—and probing.

The room was packed to capacity with family members, witnesses, coroner's medical staff, and selected reporters. Clearly, emotions were close to the surface. It was possibly the first time that the parents of the three boys had met one another. Reporters sat with their shorthand pads, in expectation of any fresh facts to enlighten the case. Witnesses, especially children, appeared a bit nervous. They would be asked to tell it all, from the first sickening crunch of the ice to the disappearance of the three faces below the water.

First came Garda Donnelan and Garda Lannin, who were to reconstruct the events on the day before the accident, as these were extremely relevant. On duty that Saturday afternoon, they saw the welcome sunshine draw out swarms of children more rumbustious than usual from their long home confinement during the harsh weather. Making their normal rounds along Sundrive Road, they saw a number of children playing on the ice at the old quarry pond. The two guards, remembering that "a tragedy on the ice at this place happened about six years ago," proceeded to try to get them off. They first called out to the children, warning them. Then they brought a few over to personally tell them to stay off the ice, as it "might be dangerous." While some children heeded their warning, stated the guards, "those who remained went to the far side and took no notice." Unable to reach them at such a distance, the guards went on about their rounds.

On Sunday Donnelan and Lannin, with Garda Steele, were again on duty. An even warmer, sunnier day, with more children out. Again they halted in their rounds to shout out orders, personally warning several children about the dangers. With the same results:

> They treated our efforts to put them off the ice as a joke, as each time we approached, they went across the pond and started shouting at us. We continued our efforts till about 3.30, but they proved fruitless. We then left the place.[29]

This testimony placed the three guards on the spot only about thirty minutes before the ice broke.

The guards were asked, "About how many children" were on the ice at the time? The newspapers, basing their estimates apparently on the children's accounts, had given the figure at about 30 to 35. One guard, taking a few seconds to calculate in his mind, estimated that they saw "about 50 or 60 people, adults and juveniles, on the pond."[30] *Adults!*

Reporters scribbled away. The revelation instantly caught the attention of all in the inquest room. This critical fact had not been known, never mentioned in the papers. Clearly, the impression had been of a group of children playing out on the ice. The new information sent minds spinning. Wondering.

If the children had seen adults skating on the ice, would it not have sent the message to them that it must be safe? And might it explain why Christopher Byrne, who had so often professed fear of the pond, decided for the first time in his life to dare to set foot on the ice? One can only imagine his parents' feelings on hearing this news.

After the guards, there followed a small procession of participants and eye-witnesses, children and adults. Nervous youngsters were gently calmed, asked to simply tell what they remembered about that afternoon. Adults were requested to keep their testimony brief and factual. Most witnesses reiterated closely the accounts they had already given the gardaí and reporters. Thomas Mardy told how he had been returning home from the Sundrive cinema, heard cries, grabbed a lifebelt, and tossed it in the water—only to fall in himself. Another man, Patrick Walsh, recounted how he and his friend Thomas McMahon happened upon the scene at about the same moment and saw a lad named Burke throw his coat to another lad in the water and hold the sleeve trying to pull him out. Then, to their horror, watched *him* fall in, struggle, and finally disappear slowly.

Seconds later, stated McMahon, he too fell in and was pulled out with a rope by Walsh. Walsh then told, with some emotion, how he had flung the rope to a boy named Byrne, who managed to grab it with one hand, taking hold of a girl with the other. His strength then gave out and he sank slowly before his eyes.

John Halpin, about eighteen or nineteen, described how he arrived on the scene, threw a rope to the girl, Veronica Browne, pulled her out of the water, and then carried her home. Those in the room looked in her direction. So alive, sitting there.

Then Veronica told how she had fallen into the freezing, numbing water while trying to help others, and from that moment remembered nothing until she was being carried home by John Halpin. The room was silent.

Other children shared their recollections, typically brief. Some began to weep and were comforted. Nine-year-old Patrick Reilly recalled that he encountered his pal Eddie O'Toole near the quarry and the two talked of how they'd like to go to the cinema that afternoon. But Eddie hadn't got the money, so instead they shared Patrick's money to get some sweets—then headed over to the quarry pond to play. A few in the room were heard to sigh.

When the three fathers spoke about their sons there was a complete hush in the room. Each remained composed, spoke deliberately. It is not known whether they had met before. Stoically, Michael O'Toole said that his boy Eddie left home with his hurley but did not say where he was going. About 4:30 "a boy named Paddy Reilly knocked at the door and told me that Eddie was under the ice at the quarry. I went immediately to the scene."[31]

Patrick Burke affirmed that his son also left with his hurley but had said specifically that he was going to play "in the street." He recalled those words exactly—"*street.*" In concluding his brief statement he added that he "didn't know if he could swim."

Then John Byrne stepped up. He stated that he had last seen Kit some time after one o'clock as he himself was preparing to leave for the soccer match at Dalymount Park. How he had given his son several chances to decide to join him. But he understood how, after being cooped up for weeks, a lad would prefer to gallivant about, expending pent-up energy. Only when he returned home about 6:30 did he hear the news from neighbours. Explaining how his son had always "had a horror of the pond," he told the coroner that it was the "biggest surprise of my life" to learn of the tragedy.[32]

It was conspicuously difficult for some in attendance to hear the graphic re-enactments of the drownings. There was surely a feeling of relief when the last descriptive accounts of witnesses were over.

Towards the end of the proceedings Station-Sergeant D. Seery was called to give his professional opinion about the incident. What had gone so terribly awry? What could have been done to prevent it? How to make certain it never happened again? He knew the pond's dark history. He recollected that a wire fence had been erected around the three-acre pond after the last drowning, but before long, he said, it was "knocked down by children and horses." And never repaired. In any case, he did not consider it adequate to keep children out. They were too nimble and determined when they wanted to get at the pond.

At present there was no protection between Sundrive Road and the quarry pit. The deep pond, with its history of stealing young lives, stood almost tauntingly as an open death trap, awaiting its next victims. In summation, he opined forcefully that, short of filling in the quarry completely, "it would be impossible to keep children away from the pond." Throughout the room, people showed their agreement.

In conclusion, Dr Brennan thanked everyone for their co-operation. He expressed his deepest sympathy with the relatives of the three boys, stating that it was truly a great tragedy, noting that "everyone concerned with it, especially the children, displayed a marked degree of heroism." Lastly, the jury expressed their highest esteem for the bravery of all concerned in the rescue operation, with particular mention of the divers who risked their own lives for days searching to recover the bodies.

On the conclusion of the inquest, people filed out slowly, exchanging sympathies. And dwelling upon the *needlessness* of the loss of life. How easily it could—and should—have been prevented, by sensible action following previous drownings.

There were doubtless thoughts of a more philosophical nature. About the consequences of decisions made in the flash of a second. About the role of chance, luck, fate, Providence in people's lives. The testimony they had just heard revealed distressing facts about the tragedy that showed how differently things *might* have turned out.

Decisions.

What if Christopher Byrne had decided to accompany his father to the soccer match at Dalymount Park on Sunday afternoon?

What if eight-year-old Eddie O'Toole had had just a few pence in his pocket for going to the cinema?

What if Anthony Burke had simply kept his word and played in the street? Or had decided to run for help rather than rush directly to save his pals thrashing about—causing him moments later to fall in himself and drown?

What had caused Kit Byrne, who had so often expressed fear of the quarry pond, to violate his own instincts and suddenly decide to take the risk? And what if his last life decision had been different? Struggling in the water, he had grabbed a rope that could have pulled him to safety but, in his last seconds of consciousness, decided to turn slightly and take hold of the girl near him in order to pull her to safety as well. A last, selfless act that caused him to expend his last ounce of strength and to slip beneath the water as the girl was pulled out.

And what would then have happened to those *other* children—said to have been about six in number—who reportedly had been saved by Christopher Byrne and Anthony Burke?

Questions left unresolved by grieving relatives and friends.

———

By 11 March one question was beginning to loom above all others. What was to become of the country's spring tillage? Would there *be* a spring ploughing and sowing? And if not? "Famine," some farmers and newspapers were already saying.

When the first real thaw set in on Monday, ordinary citizens were elated. Then they awoke on Tuesday to read in the papers that a "tillage crisis" was being predicted. Ireland's agricultural experts agreed.

The hard facts were plain enough. Some 2½ million acres needed to be cultivated, of which 700,000 were devoted to wheat, critical for feeding the nation. Normally, ploughing began in late autumn and was usually completed by March. However, little soil had been turned over by Christmas, because of the difficulties and the lateness of the 1946 harvest. Then the cold, snow and ice locked up the land, and agricultural operations were brought to a standstill. Spring ploughing and planting were so far behind schedule that it might be impossible to produce sufficient crops to feed the country's population.

Now, in mid-March, farmers were facing the daunting challenge of trying to "squeeze into seven or eight weeks all the work that normally is spread over five or six months." Many believed it hopeless.

Everything, it seemed, was stacked against Irish farmers.

Newspapers, agricultural spokesmen and the Government called for a vigorous "tillage campaign," along the lines of the successful harvest battle of 1946. Because of the extreme urgency of the crisis there was a strong consensus that only an unprecedented national co-operative scheme could save the crops and feed the country. Demanding a herculean effort of both Man and machinery. With the use of tractors working around the clock there could be a chance of success. Only by "borrowing, lending and hiring tractors" throughout the entire country, wrote the *Irish Press*, "might the farmers be able to plough and sow" a good proportion of their land.[33] However, there were only six thousand tractors in the whole country, as compared to more than 8,000 in just the six counties of the north. No new tractors and ploughs could be manufactured or imported in time to alleviate the shortage. Tractor tyres were also in short supply. Small farmers would have to rely on their horses, most of which were poorly fed because of the fodder shortage and not at their strongest.

While de Valera enthusiastically supported the plan for a nationwide tillage campaign he also called for saving the turf just as energetically. He declared that a national "combined drive must be made at once," arguing that "we need every person who can be spared, first to sow the wheat needed, and second to cut the turf needed—other things can wait."[34] He explained that wheat was the most important crop, and that in his estimation there was probably "no community in the world in which bread played such a vital role" in the diet.

Once again city-dwellers and country folk were being called to work together side by side in the national effort. Armies of volunteers were envisaged from Dublin, Cork, Limerick, marching to farmlands to save the country from hunger. Failure in this grand challenge, contended the *Irish Press*, could result not only in hunger but in real "famine."

Despite all the daily newspaper coverage and spirited talk about a spring tillage campaign, in mid-March all that farmers could do was look fretfully at the skies with furrowed brow, and pray. They understood that a thaw of the snow-blanketed landscape would have to come gradually. Even when the snow had melted, the boggy land then had to dry out sufficiently before tractor engines could be heard turning over the earth. Everything depended upon three elements of spring weather: sunshine, warm temperatures, and drying winds. As well as the absence of heavy, soaking rains, which could create a disastrous setback—all elements of nature over which they had no control.

Never had the Irish farmer's patience been more tested.

As farmers throughout the country anxiously awaited the day when they could begin ploughing, some remarkable news was received from distant Dingle. As if it were on a different planet, the region reported having had "no heavy snow at any time as covered other parts of the country." Moreover, "much of the tillage work is now complete and there is no shortage of fodder." In fact residents told of having enjoyed a rather nice winter. Another mystery to befuddle the weather experts.

———

The second week of March had begun promisingly, with milder temperatures, no precipitation, and hopes of spring ahead. But by Wednesday the 12th the weather was again in fitful spasms, unpredictable and inequitable in behaviour. While Limerick was "bathed in sunshine," heavy rains fell in Co. Meath and a steady "24 hour snowfall in north Donegal left towns completely cut off." Motorists, if they wished to try, could drive in a matter of hours from a Mediterranean climate to a ski resort climate—if they were willing to risk getting marooned along the way.

Once again snow fell heavily throughout the Wicklow Mountains. "Just as the snow and ice of the past six weeks were beginning to thaw," wrote the *Irish Times*, "once again, heavy drifts were blocking roads and railways."[35] It no longer required the power of big machines, but frustrated gangs of men with shovels found themselves digging out the same patches of road they had cleared many times before.

Throughout Wednesday, Cos. Dublin and Wicklow experienced what was called "another major storm," but by no means a blizzard. As the sleet and snow fell in Dublin, streets became slushy and slippery. As it turned out, this time one of the "worst blizzards of the winter swept angrily across the North, barely missing the South." Enough to keep people's nerves on edge.

Nevertheless, the weather took more lives. Roads in many parts of the country were snowy and slippery, making it treacherous for motorists. On Wednesday evening in Ballinagh, Co. Cavan, 25-year-old Aidan Reilly and his friend Thomas Fitzpatrick were returning from a film show at the O'Rahilly Hall during the snowstorm. A lorry was "rounding a sharp turn at the foot of the hill" when the driver suddenly lost control, skidded, and struck the two men, killing both. Adding two more victims to winter's uncounted total.

———

Though it was hard for people to believe, St Patrick's Day, which usually heralded the arrival of spring, was only five days away. Normally, people were in high spirits. This year, however, there were rumours of a shortage of shamrock because of cold and snow. Some were predicting a real shortage. Was the dainty shamrock to be yet another victim?

The *Irish Times* was predicting that "the National Festival will be unspectacular" this year. For once, a forecast that would prove to be correct. At least socially. Weather-wise, the holiday weekend would be quite spectacular—and *most* memorable.

Chapter 12 ∾

FLOODS AND FAMINE
THREAT

Frozen up, snowed on, rained on, and flooded out, Ireland greeted St. Patrick's Day with a fervent hope that the National Apostle would give us that change of weather we have so long awaited.

(*Evening Herald*, 17 MARCH 1947)

Reports from many parts of the country tell of land lying under two to three feet of water—land that had been destined for the sowing of crops.

(*Dublin Evening Mail*, 17 MARCH 1947)

To-day the Irish nation faces a national emergency as grave as any in its history. The people face the possibility of famine. Nothing but a super-human effort can now enable the tillage to be done that will avert starvation. This is a fight for survival.

(*Irish Independent*, 17 MARCH 1947)

ST PATRICK'S DAY WEEKEND

"As a rule," the *Sunday Independent* reminded readers, "spring is definitely in the air as St. Patrick's Day approaches."[1] *Dublin Opinion*, however, quoting Swinburne's "When the hounds of spring are on winter's traces," quipped: "They must have lost the scent."[2]

Early on the morning of Saturday 15 March skies were fairly clear in Dublin. Raising hopes that the "national festival" might turn out mild and possibly sunny. Not that the Government had planned anything "festive" for Dubliners. Quite the contrary: no spirited, colourful military parade with marching bands and blaring music was to be held in O'Connell Street. In fact *nothing* had been planned for citizens in want of some lively, entertaining diversion from winter's woes.

Dubliners were therefore determined to find their own entertainment. With early morning weather looking promising, hikers and cyclists were eager to hit the roads out of the city, many carrying knapsacks for extended outings. A full range of sports events was scheduled. The Baldoyle Races were traditionally a big event, and the Railway Cup Hurling Final between Munster and Ulster was to be played before a packed Croke Park crowd, while followers of soccer were looking forward to seeing Ulster and Leinster compete at a big League of Ireland contest at Dalymount Park. A number of rugby matches were also on. After so many weekends spoiled by blizzards, sports enthusiasts were especially hopeful that the weather would co-operate for the weekend. They felt they deserved it.

By mid-morning, low clouds began gathering as the east wind picked up. At about eleven o'clock it changed from blustery to stormy-looking. At 11:40 a "storm of sleet and snow whipped the city," with temperatures hovering around the freezing mark. Soaking pedestrians, covering streets and paths with slush, and making sports fields muddy and unplayable.

On Saturday afternoon, with most outdoor activities a wash-out, people turned to indoor entertainment. Thousands flocked to the Dublin Kennel Club's 26th Annual Show at the RDS grounds in Ballsbridge, featuring more than three thousand entries this year, with a strong international character sure to expand the appeal. For the holiday weekend, cinemas were offering a good choice of films. The Adelphi was advertising *Lady in the Lake*, starring Robert Montgomery and Audrey Totter, as a real "suspense-filled mystery . . . a spine-tingling tale." With the gloomy weather many preferred the Odeon's lighter fare, Laurel and Hardy in *Bullfighters*, its very title evoking hilarious images of the twosome. The Capitol was showing *Desperate Journey*, featuring Errol Flynn and a lesser-known actor by the name of Ronald Reagan.

By the latter part of the afternoon, patrons in long cinema queues were inching their way towards the lobby as the sleety snow continued. Some slushy streets began pooling up over their kerbs. Hikers and cyclists who had left in the morning when conditions were fair now found themselves caught out in the miserable wet, windy weather, deliberating whether they should continue on or turn back.

Those who had headed to Co. Wicklow encountered the storm at its worst. With temperatures slipping below 32 degrees (0°C), sleet turned to a steady snow and the wind began blowing it into drifts across the roads. The St Kevin's bus that served Roundwood and Bray was making its first trip in six weeks, and residents who had been snowbound were thrilled to be getting back into the capital for a day of shopping and entertainment. Before long, however, the driver found himself "battling his way in a howling snowstorm," with sixteen nervous passengers aboard. At first they were concerned merely about being delayed, then worried about being marooned. When the bus became hopelessly stuck in a deep snowdrift the driver and passengers decided to set out on foot for Kilmacanogue while there was still daylight.

In Dublin the wet snow became heavier in the evening but did not deter night-goers bent on having a good time on the holiday weekend. The Metropole in O'Connell Street, showing the Dickens classic *Great Expectations,* was packed out for every showing. The building was about to undergo reconstruction at a cost of £100,000, to become a "luxury cinema on the latest American style," boasting a new restaurant, cocktail bar, and enlarged ballroom. Dubliners were looking forward to its swanky appearance and facilities. More serious theatregoers favoured the Gaiety Theatre's presentation of Shaw's *The Devil's Disciple,* getting smashing reviews. But the greatest fun seemed to be found at the city's dancehalls, which were offering a variety of St Patrick's Day specials, with Irish music, dancers, and artistes. The Four Provinces ballroom in Harcourt Street was putting on a real extravaganza, while Clery's Ballroom was hosting great musicians. Local céilithe were being held in small clubs and parish halls around the city.

The late evening weather worsened as a result of a series of deepening depressions off the south coast, with moisture-laden clouds being carried across most of the country. Driven now by strong winds of nearly half-gale force, the snow was falling heavily on most counties. By the time Dubliners left their places of entertainment to catch a bus home they had to wade through streets filled with pools of water inches deep. In some places they noticed that it had risen across the pavement to the doors of houses and shops.

By midnight, the day's total rain-snow mixture had reached 0.57 inches.

———

Overnight, as Dubliners were sleeping, the storm intensified. Many were doubtless awakened by the wind's hissing and howling. Early on Sunday morning, before first light, the temperature nudged above the freezing mark as the wet snow was turned into a steady rainstorm driven by violent winds, which now reached a force of 65 miles per hour. The storm system, generated from the south-west off the Atlantic, was to remain *in situ* for most of the day.

Dublin was being deluged. Sunday-morning mass-goers brave enough to fight their way to church were pelted in the face by rain driven horizontally. Umbrellas were useless. Once again "battling against" the weather, Dubliners held on to railings and hats, edging their way along pavements. Throughout the city, wrote the *Irish Independent,* "everywhere one could see evidence of the havoc caused by the water" and the wind. Streets inundated, sections washed out, broken branches, trees felled, crumbled stone walls. Everything not anchored down was blown asunder. Debris strewn along every street: boxes, branches, refuse, paper, slates, broken glass, ripped awnings. Some would later say it reminded them of newsreels they had seen of hurricanes in the Caribbean or the United States.

Lamented the *Sunday Independent*: "Dubliners' hopes that the bitter winter weather conditions of the past two months had finally come to an end were rudely dashed."[3]

Throughout the morning the storm continued to rage relentlessly. The city's tenement-dwellers, living in decrepit, rickety 150-year-old buildings, could feel its ferocity as their buildings shook, creaked, and leaked. Torrents of rain loosened bricks and slates that had been frozen with snow and ice, thawed and refrozen over two months. The ancient mortar had cracked and crumbled under the strain of it all. Lubricated by soaking rains, bricks came free and crashed down on pavements. With mortar and bricks destabilised, chunks of buildings toppled down:

> Tenement dwellers felt the shock during the storm . . . portions of masonry on the chimney stacks of tenements in North Cumberland Street collapsed, causing mortar to fall down the flues and onto the floors of rooms . . . rain came in through the ceilings and ran down the stairs of the houses.[4]

In some of the more dilapidated tenements of the north side and the Liberties water poured through the roof, making its way downwards through each ceiling to the ground floor. Tenement stairways became cascades. Cavernous basements turned into flooded dungeons. Even rats were seen running for higher ground.

Almost all of Ireland was being thrashed by the torrential rain, driven by hurricane-force winds. Many people were in near-disbelief that, with the land still entombed in snow and ice, such a mighty rainstorm could be unleashed upon them. As Jim Maloney of Co. Galway put it:

> The snow started melting, and *then* the rains came, and the fields and roads were flooded . . . So then we're going *from the frying pan into the fire*, if you know what I mean.

Typhoon-size downpours with destructive winds swamped the country's transport and communications systems, which, reported the *Irish Press*, "were *again* thrown into chaos on Sunday as the gale, aided by turbulent floodwaters rushing down from the hills, felled telephone poles," erased roads, caused landslides, and halted vehicles and railways.[5] The countryside and towns could not carry the water off quickly enough:

> The ten-hour rainstorm swept three-quarters of the country, heralding the most destructive flooding . . . as rivers in heavy spate from recent thaws were bursting their banks.[6]

Parts of the country were being turned into vast lakes.

––––

Some of Dublin's suburbs were especially vulnerable. Thousands of houses were built on land that was sloped or had poor drainage, many resting on recently excavated earth in new housing estates. Uneven, unstable, often hilly terrain was highly prone to quick run-off, leading to erosion, flooding, even landslides. Some of the newly built linear rows of houses were perfectly aligned for flood paths caused by sudden heavy downpours.

As the earth had been frozen for months, the rainfall could not gradually sink in deeply. Rather, as it melted the snow and ice it ran off in furious torrents. Undulating terrain in parts of the suburbs was naturally susceptible to soil erosion and destabilisation. By noon on Sunday the soil in many suburban areas was nearing its saturation point as the rains were unceasing. Topsoil became lubricated and loose, slipping, dislodging stones, creating cavities, forming larger erosional pockets. Atop this soil were houses, shops, roads, walls, railway tracks. And everywhere there were massive mounds of snow shovelled high over the past six weeks, and now melting rapidly.

Suburban Dubliners first noticed the subtle effects of the heavy rain when they looked out windows to see some of their garden soil being washed away. Then seeing a stone wall slightly shift, or shrubs and trees becoming dislodged. During the first hours of earthen decomposition, residents didn't feel threatened. People living on land with a greater gradient, or actual hills, were the most concerned, as they better understood the power of erosion if the rains persisted. In some suburbs, roads were becoming streams, carrying not only water but mud, gravel, rocks, and garden plantings. Stone walls began to crumble.

At first few householders saw the drenching rain and erosional process as serious enough to cause mudslides or property damage. And certainly not dangerous landslides.

––––

By the latter part of Sunday morning, calls were coming in to Garda stations and fire stations throughout the suburbs from residents more nervous than panicky at this point. In particular from those who lived in Bray, Greystones, Dún Laoghaire, Monkstown, Blackrock, Booterstown, Dundrum, Ballybough, Santry, Donnycarney, Howth, and Malahide. Some calls were more distressed than others. One early report verified that "water was three feet deep at Dún Laoghaire railway station and was on a level with the platform at Blackrock." The main Dublin–Belfast road at Santry was already covered by more than eighteen inches of water, and motorists were forced to abandon their cars and wade to higher ground. Another call told how "a torrent of water a foot deep rushed through the main street of Blackrock," while trams on the Dún Laoghaire side of the flood were hurriedly reversed to bring people back south. At Donnycarney on the Malahide Road people had watched with mounting worry as water all around them rose by the hour. Finally, in desperation, "residents had to open their front doors to let water have a clear run through the house when a stream at the rear overflowed."[7]

Out in hilly Howth, eyes were glued to windows throughout Sunday morning and afternoon as torrents of water rushing down streets turned them into what the *Irish Press* called "roaring mountain streams." To onlookers, the dangers were becoming all too evident. Some of the finest houses clung scenically but precariously to the sides of the steep hill. Theirs was a lovely, coveted perch but one now facing a serious threat of erosion. Some fretful residents had been braving the weather to go out into the storm to check on soil and rock being washed away on their property. At first it was perhaps just a few barrowfuls; but if the sheets of rain did not cease soon it could become lorryloads, enough to dislodge a house, possibly even carry it downwards.

One couldn't combat the force of gravity.

Daniel O'Sullivan, his wife and their 2½-year-old daughter Maureen of Balscadden Road in Howth lived in a wooden bungalow-hut built on the grass bank, tight up against the wall flanking the road. On the other side was a grass bank dropping steeply down to the sea. On Sunday morning the mother and child left for mass. During their absence Daniel watched out the window and saw a rush of water come down the road and begin to cause the wall to collapse. Realising what was happening, he dashed outside in what the *Irish Times* called "a narrow escape from death":

> He left the hut, and, to get on the road above, opened a door in the wall. Flood water from the road gushed down on him, knocking him back. Five minutes later a six-foot section of the wall, with the door and steps up to it, collapsed under the weight of the water.[8]

He could easily, he realised, have been carried down the slope into the sea. The Balscadden Road was quickly blocked off to traffic because of increasing falls of earth from the hill-bank flanking it. Local residents were promptly informed of the danger. O'Sullivan met his wife and daughter on their way home from mass and told them the whole story.

By midday, word was spreading throughout Howth that the continuing rainfall could trigger landslides in the saturated, destabilised earth. The greatest fears were for the steep cliff faces, where erosion could carve out hundreds and possibly thousands of tons of earth and rock. People would be posted outside to keep a constant watch.

Meanwhile in Monkstown a mighty "deluge struck the district" in the early afternoon when a huge rush of water down Pakenham Road and Monkstown Hill swept across the drive of Monkstown Hospital. It broke through windows and doors and flooded the kitchen, laundry, larder, cold store, cooks' rooms and maids' quarters to a depth of six feet. Hospital officers were immediately called to the scene, where they confronted an ugly sight:

> Everything was topsy turvy and in a state of ruin . . . things flung around as if some wild thing had been let loose. Crockery was strewn all over the place. In the maids' quarters beds and bedding were covered with a dark, slimy mud and personal belongings saturated with water.[9]

Food stores in the basement were spoiled and cooking equipment damaged or destroyed. A gift of drugs and medical supplies just received from the American Red Cross Society, valued at over £1,000, was damaged. Furthermore, forty pounds of precious tea was lost—just when the staff and patients could have used its calming qualities. The entire hospital staff was in distress over the ruination of their facilities. By good fortune, Dr Brennan of St Michael's Hospital in Dún Laoghaire sympathetically offered to "accommodate 18 of the 28 patients and they were quickly evacuated."

―――

The deeply snow-packed countryside was dissolving with bewildering swiftness. With temperatures now in the 30s (0 to 4°C), the torrential rains were melting the white blanket with its drifts up to twenty feet deep. The colossal volume of water it contained was inestimable.

Gravity carried the water across the terrain towards the lowest points in river basins. People living in the floodplains of rivers began watching them rise perceptibly, first measured in inches, then feet. The torrents rushing off hillsides and mountains made the landscape seem alive with movement. Rivers rose to their banks and then began overflowing, flooding their basins and gradually creating vast lakes.

Once again the Irish landscape was being dramatically—and tragically—transformed by nature. As Man looked helplessly on.

By early Sunday afternoon most rivers were on the rampage. As the *Irish Independent* described it, the country's best crop lands were being drowned:

> The most serious aspect of the weather is the heavy flooding that has followed the rains and melting of the snowdrifts . . . Rivers in many areas

have overflowed, and large areas of arable land are under many feet of water.[10]

Many rivers were now rising at the rate of a foot or more per hour. From every county came reports of crisis. At Trim the Boyne had already risen eight feet above its normal level. From Co. Carlow came stories of "bridges, cattle and sheep being carried away." Much of Co. Kilkenny was now lakeland, as the River Nore had quickly overflowed its banks and spilled out across the surrounding landscape.

A number of rivers, at certain points along their course, had become clogged with fallen trees, logs, and debris, which impeded their natural flow and abetted the flooding process. The dereliction of local farmers and townspeople had allowed much of this to occur. On Sunday 16 March many residents of Co. Kilkenny regretted their negligence:

> The unfortunate people blamed the derelict weir in the River Nore for causing extensive flooding which County Kilkenny was now experiencing. There were thousands of trees at the bottom of the river . . . They had fallen from the bank from time to time and were just left lying there.[11]

Between Kilkenny and Inistioge alone it was estimated that there were "a thousand trees in the river." A county council official, Mr Kearney, scolded that it was "disgraceful to have such valuable timber lying there" when there was such a "cry for firewood all over the country."[12]

Those parts of the midlands and south with poor drainage were the hardest hit by flooding. By Sunday afternoon almost every river had overspilled, leaving the countryside looking like a watery wasteland, dotted with islands of higher ground upon which frightened animals stood clustered and bellowing. As described by the *Irish Times,* much of Ireland's sprawling farmland had simply vanished:

> Many thousands of acres in the Midlands and South of Ireland are under water. Rivers have burst their banks, notably the Shannon, Suir, Barrow, Boyne and Nore, and over many square miles of arable land stretches of watery desolation have replaced the normal scenes of furrowed fields.[13]

Some flooded areas looked more like a sea than a lake, with the waters moving in great currents, carrying along sections of collapsed barns, sheds, fences, poles, signs, and ill-fated beasts:

> Throughout the Four Provinces arable land is lying deep in swirling waters . . . The carcases of sheep and cattle are floating down swollen rivers.[14]

Many of the country's major roads were rendered impassable within hours by the dangerous floodwaters, as towns and villages once again found themselves cut off. Meanwhile "railway services were disrupted by landslides" as embankments were eroded, and ponds formed across the rails. Throughout the afternoon CIE was sending out its weary crews with shovels to clear the tracks where landslides had blocked the route. They found themselves digging heavy shovelfuls of mud, rocks, gravel—work more back-breaking than snow clearance had been. Much of the mud was so liquid that it just flowed back across the track within minutes.

In Tony Ruane's part of Co. Mayo the roads were slowly disappearing under rising waters. Motorists, unable to determine depths ahead, took their chances on proceeding. Once a car, lorry or bus became stalled in a pool, others piled up behind. Then, he recalls, they were dependent on local farmers to pull them out:

> I remember the floods that followed in the thaw, and the roads around Ballalaghen Bridge near Foxford were covered to a depth of three feet. Cars got stuck and had to be abandoned . . . Horses were used to tow vehicles from the floods.

Drivers and passengers sometimes had no choice but to climb out of their vehicle through a window, wading towards higher ground in hopes of finding help at a farmhouse. Trying to wade through three or more feet of moving water was dangerous, and children had to be lifted and carried. Where deep water flowed in a current or swirled, a car could be slowly lifted and carried off.

On Sunday, motorists travelling along the Galway–Dublin road hoping to see the Railway Cup Hurling Final were caught in the fast-rising waters throughout the midlands. When they saw the road in front of them becoming flooded they had to decide whether to proceed and risk not coming out on the other side. Some wisely turned back, while others forged sluggishly ahead in inches, then feet, of water. Hundreds became stalled and had to abandon their cars in frigid waters, regretting their decision. It would take days for the water to recede, giving farmers' horses a chance to pull cars from the water and muck.

In some parts of rural Ireland cars and provincial buses stood trapped in pools or lakes of water, looking like hippopotami cooling themselves in a tropical lagoon.

———

Country towns often took the brunt of the rainstorms and flooding, especially those near rivers. In Cork, heavy rains lashed the city for twelve hours, melting mountains of snow that had been piled high from road clearance. Floodwaters rose and invaded houses and shops. The terrain and structural layout of some towns doomed them to serious flooding, as there was nowhere for the rising floodwaters to run off.

Throughout Co. Wicklow, which had been more abused by winter weather than any other county, the snow-pack was so immense that when it was struck simultaneously by thawing and torrential rains huge cascades of water flowed forth across both landscape and townscapes. On Sunday afternoon residents of Roundwood described their mountainy roads as "being like rivers," Niagarous, tearing downwards, gouging out earth, rocks, and rubble. Townspeople and villagers could only watch the floodwaters rise around their dwellings. In Wicklow, Church Street was soon "three feet deep in water . . . Children coming out from a cinema had to be carried across the floods on the shoulder of parents," who had difficulty keeping their own balance.[15]

Some towns and villages would see the water reach higher than a man's head.

In Kilkenny, particularly prone to flooding, along John Street the water quickly rose to more than six feet. Then seven. And climbing. Here, and in some other towns, as the water rose and pressure increased, the "windows and doors were burst open by the waters and household items, shop goods and fittings and furniture swept away."[16] Inhabitants were forced to either evacuate or scramble for their life to upper floors. This was all happening with such swiftness that there was little time for deliberation or planning: people simply reacted instinctively to the threat suddenly facing them.

Residents all over Ireland, in country and city, were putting in emergency calls to local gardaí and fire brigade to help them. But they too were caught unprepared for responding very effectively to the crisis, lacking sufficient equipment, rowing-boats and even training for rescuing people from flood danger. They did the best they could with what they had, and no doubt saved some lives.

Kilkenny was such a case. The water had reached over six feet along John Street and was still rising. Before long, "in the Black Abbey it rose to ten feet at the High Altar." As it continued to rise "confessionals and seats flooded in the water" and began floating around. By this time residents of the town realised the imminent threat of drowning and scrambled to higher storeys of their houses or shops. Many, especially the elderly, grew panicky. Local gardaí and firemen were frantically trying to improvise a plan of rescue by finding rowing-boats, ladders, and ropes. Any type of raft or floating platform was useful.

As people retreated hurriedly upstairs they could look down and see furniture and possessions floating in the flooded rooms. In many houses the water rose to ten or twelve feet within a matter of hours, higher than the ceiling of their ground floor. Then up the stairs. It was a frightening sight as they went to their windows to call out for help.

In Green Street the water poured through the top windows of houses, as fishing cots were used to rescue people. Cot-fishing crews, consisting of four men with two cots, rescued people from the upper storeys of their homes. So high was the water in the streets that people could step from the windows of their second floors into the cots.[17]

With water fifteen feet deep lapping at upper storeys, people had to be rescued by boat. Some families had to be taken through roofs. As this tense rescue work was being carried out, noted the *Irish Times*, "the rosary was recited by hundreds of onlookers."[18]

While people were being rescued, animals were left helpless. Already weakened by months of cold and hunger, many had little strength left to fight for survival against strong floodwaters. The countryside was already littered with tens of thousands of carcases of sheep, cattle, horses, donkeys, goats and pigs that had not survived the blizzards and deep freeze. Throughout Sunday, thousands more were succumbing to drowning. Ugly lumps of carcases were seen floating everywhere. Some had been entombed beneath snow and ice since early February, remarkably preserved; others were rotten and had been picked over by predators. Often clustered together in dozens, they drifted in the lakes of the midlands.

Vast herds of sheep were being lost. Many were now so weak that they could do nothing but stand helplessly as the waters rose around them, lifted them off their feet, and slowly carried them off. One group of families living in Glencoshabinnia, Co. Tipperary, near high Galtymore Mountain, would lose more than eight hundred sheep during the floods. The bounty of carcases allowed predators to satisfy their own hunger. In several areas, flocks of crows had been seen "swooping down" on dead—even dying—sheep, leaving them "devoured to the very bones."[19]

In the highlands of Co. Wicklow, Connacht and elsewhere sheep that had survived were sometimes observed acting in an unnatural manner that even the oldest of farmers had never witnessed before. What occurred on the northern slopes of the Galty Mountains in Co. Tipperary was described by the *Irish Times*:

> Sheep, sensing the dangers of snows and flooding, are fleeing down the mountain slopes, leaving their lambs to perish. Farmers say that they never in the hardest of previous years have known such "widespread panic" among sheep. On both sides of the Galtees, thousands of sheep have been lost.[20]

Late on Sunday afternoon another human body was found. It was that of Frank Duigan, a native of Co. Roscommon, discovered in a ditch near Drumree railway station. It wasn't certain whether he was a victim of the last blizzard or the present flooding, only that he had perished because of the severe weather.

Other human remains were now seen floating about. Many cemeteries had been inundated under feet of water; some coffins buried in shallow snow-pits while awaiting proper burial in spring became dislodged and were lifted by the floodwaters, shifting or floating slowly. An eerie sight. In cemeteries under deep water, tombstones obtruded like periscopes aimed in different directions. In Co. Roscommon, where people were determined to carry out one particular funeral despite the flooding, "coffin bearers had to be provided with Wellington boots to wade through water."

————

By Sunday afternoon Dubliners were coping with their own ever-worsening flood problems. Rivers in the city and surrounding areas—the Tolka, Dodder, Santry, Liffey, Blackwater, Boyne, Dargle, Glencree—had been rising ominously and had now begun spilling over their banks at various points, causing immediate flooding. People living in those areas historically prone to flooding, such as Ballybough, were very nervous. Many Dubliners were already wading around streets in water a foot deep or more. And rising fast.

Sunday's rainfall in Dublin by 3 p.m. had already exceeded Saturday's total. No-one knew how many inches of water had been added by the melting of the city's huge snow-pack, shovelled into heaps and hills as roads were cleared after the blizzards. But everyone could see that Dublin was nearing the serious flood stage. In the afternoon, fire brigade and Red Cross were preparing to carry out evacuations and provide temporary shelter for evacuees. There was no telling how many people this might be.

Parts of the suburbs began disintegrating from the flow of floodwaters and erosion. Mudslides were occurring in many places. But it was landslides that residents feared most.

For many hours, Howth's hilly terrain had been subject to destabilisation by slipping soil and rock. Some people had already abandoned their homes for fear of a sudden earth slide that could carry it off its foundations. Finally, some time about 3:30 p.m., their fears were realised when steep slopes and cliffs began to give way to the force of sodden soil, heavy rock—and gravity:

> It washed away upwards of thousands of tons of cliff face. Pines, over twenty feet, were easily uprooted and portions of the roads along the cliff have been completely washed away. The rush of water down Main Street

resembled a cataract for several hours, with muddy water following rapidly and carrying with it rubble torn from the face of the road.[21]

Landslides measured in the thousands of tons were changing the familiar face of Howth.

From Howth and Killiney were now coming reports that roads and railway track were being blocked by landslides. Meanwhile at Islandbridge twenty feet of the wall of the Phoenix Park collapsed from a height of twelve feet, smashing a telephone pole. Throughout Sunday afternoon CIE crews worked to clear the railway line between Bray and Greystones following "three landslides around Bray Head caused by the torrential rainfall." Two other landslides on the Harcourt Street line between Dublin and Bray were finally cleared after many hours of hard labour.

People heard their house foundations crack, felt a shift. As the water crept higher it seeped through cracks and crevices, then poured through windows and doors. Residents had no defence against it. By late afternoon many "suburban houses were flooded and furniture damaged," and the *Irish Press* reported that "Dundrum and Santry were hardest hit."[22] More accurately, *among* the hardest hit. At Bray, evacuations were already under way, and "tables and other furniture could be seen floating" in the rooms of houses.[23] Residents were being rescued by gardaí and fire brigade, using ladders and rowing-boats. Already more than two hundred Bray residents had been taken from their flooded houses and were being provided with shelter and assistance by the Red Cross.

Countless thousands of other residents who didn't yet need evacuation were forced to retreat to an upper floor for the night, hoping and praying that the water would have receded by morning. A traumatic experience, having to watch their ground floor being flooded, doing serious damage to possessions. Many families kept their most treasured personal mementos, photographs and "collectibles" on the ground floor, on tables or the mantelpiece, to proudly show them off. In the haste of fleeing the incoming water they had to be left behind. Some people would make the decision to go downstairs again to wade through water in an effort to salvage a few valued possessions.

As all this was going on, in Dublin's city centre people were doing their best to cope. By late afternoon word was out that "roads were blocked on both sides of the city by floods." Buses and trams were no longer running to parts of the suburbs under floods. So, thousands of suburbanites were left "unable to reach home." Many of them had previously been marooned in the city overnight by blizzards, so they took it calmly enough as they went about finding accommodation for the night.

About the time that many people were returning from the Dog Show at the RDS grounds or pouring out of the afternoon cinema showings, the temperature dropped and the weather took a nasty turn for the worse, and "at 5.00 p.m. the downpour suddenly changed to a blizzard which raged until 7.00 p.m."[24] Huge crowds in the heart of the city found themselves caught out in the open without buses or trams to take them home, not yet having secured any dry, warm refuge for the night.

"Well, make the best of it!" people were heard saying. The *Irish Press* reported that the city's "theatres and cinemas were besieged by crowds of Dubliners as the only escape" from fireless grates and miserable outdoor conditions. Restaurants quickly became packed as well.

Then, at 5:45 p.m., a black-out suddenly plunged the city into darkness. At the Adelphi, those watching the "spine-tingling tale" of *Lady in the Lake* may have been particularly unnerved by the shock of it. As soon as the electricity failure hit, the staff at cinemas, theatres and restaurants began escorting patrons by torchlight safely out of the buildings—into the blizzardy storm. At the Savoy cinema 21-year-old Herbie Donnelly did exactly as trained, leading streams of patrons calmly up the aisles, reassuring some along the way, into the lobby and out the front doors. Across the city at the small local Manor Picture House in Manor Street, Robert Hartney, who began working there when it opened in 1920 showing silent films, knew that frightened kiddies and the elderly needed special attention making their way in the darkness.

Restaurant managers faced a different predicament. Customers were in the midst of their meal when the lights, as well as cooking facilities, were cut off. Candles sufficed temporarily in some instances, and the staff waited in the hope that the power would surge on again within a few minutes. When this did not happen, customers had to be escorted out.

A multitude of patrons were "evacuated" from entertainment establishments along O'Connell Street and other streets. With street lamps out as well, they at first stood outside in semi-darkness, vehicle lights being the only illumination. In a somewhat bewildered state, most milled around waiting for the electricity to be restored so they could re-enter the cinemas, theatres, and restaurants. As minutes passed, then half an hour, then an hour, hope faded. As the crowds dispersed, people went off in search of accommodation for the night.

Through it all, thousands of pub regulars remained in place, nursing their pint, sipping whiskey, contentedly chatting away by candlelight. As many had done many a time before over the years when they had been allowed to secretly remain after hours if they stayed quiet in the dark. They were seasoned in the darkness of secrecy. This night they were quite unruffled by all the fuss elsewhere in the city.

Some time between 7:45 and 8:15 the lights popped on again. Cinemas, theatres, restaurants and dancehalls resumed business, but with smaller crowds. Then, at about 8:50, another power failure caused a black-out throughout the city's north side.

By midnight, Sunday's rainfall in Dublin measured 1.27 inches. Added to that of Saturday, the total was nearly 2 inches—in approximately 36 to 40 hours. Over this brief period the natural thaw and torrential rain had melted the country's snow-pack at an astonishing rate, causing the catastrophic flooding, in many parts of the country creating a water equivalent of 5 to 8 inches of rain.

ST PATRICK'S DAY

On the morning of Monday 17 March, "in the misty, cloudy sky the sun was no more than a pale, vaporous circle of light," reported one newspaper, "but it was good to know that it was still there."[25] People felt they had survived another winter's wallop. Never had St Patrick's Day newspapers published such abysmal headlines:

> Grave National Emergency (*Irish Independent*)
> Flooding Causes Havoc (*Irish Times*)
> National Crisis (*Dublin Evening Mail*)

And the *Irish Times* had predicted that the weekend of the national festival would be "unspectacular."

In Dublin the mood on the morning of St Patrick's Day was glum. As the *Evening Herald* put it, "frozen up, snowed on, rained on, and flooded out," Ireland greeted the day with prayer and hope that the national saint would bring relief from pitiless King Winter. Dubliners felt cheerless and luckless, facing even a shortage of shamrock. Commented the *Dublin Evening Mail*: "This morning Dublin's streets presented a bleak and desolate appearance, unusual even for a bank holiday." Everywhere there was evidence of storm damage, with debris strewn in streets still filled with foul water pools. It cast a depressive aura over the cityscape. A number of early mass-goers said they "saw a red glow in the sky." But no-one knew whether it might be a good or bad omen.

St Patrick's Day was predestined to be dull, as the Government had planned no festivities for the national festival. Lamented the *Irish Times*, the "only pageantry in the capital will be the splash of colour" provided by the President's cavalry escort as Seán T. Ó Ceallaigh and his wife drove from Áras an Uachtaráin along the North Circular Road to the Pro-Cathedral at 11:20 for high mass at noon. Hardly an event to draw cheering crowds.

At least one small group of visitors had an interesting morning when the Rev. F. R. Wilson, dean of St Patrick's Cathedral, gave them a personal tour through the historic edifice, paying tribute to his predecessor Jonathan Swift for the preservation of many important features. When the visitors came to the statue of Capt. John McNeill Boyd, who died in a shipwreck at Dún Laoghaire, the dean told them the story about Boyd's dog, which had followed his coffin to the cathedral and was years later said to haunt the cathedral, "being heard walking up and down the corridors." At least their St Patrick's Day was made memorable.

Out of public view at Collins Barracks and Portobello Barracks open-air masses were held, followed by small parades with bands for military personnel, while in the heart of Dublin all remained silent and lifeless. Only the "national flags flapped briskly" above the buildings in O'Connell Street, noted one newspaper. The *Irish Press* put it in perspective:

> Less colourful than for many years, St. Patrick's Day in Dublin was in keeping with the atmosphere . . . which has descended on the country under the iron rule of a wintry King.[26]

Dubliners were left to wonder why the Government had lacked the imagination, or motivation, to organise at least something interesting or festive for the national festival.

In Francis Street in the Liberties young Annie Gahan was feeling mopey. She had been looking forward to helping her Ma with her tea-and-cake tent at the Baldoyle Races, always a fun and profitable event for them on St Patrick's Day. But, again, all sports fixtures were drowned out. Though the rain had ceased, "there was no rush out of the city," reported the *Dublin Evening Mail*, as "even the most hardy cyclists and hikers did not go far afield." They had grown wary of weather that looked decent in the morning only to erupt into a storm by early afternoon. People were still recovering from the past forty-eight hours of drenching downpours, floods, a mini-blizzard, and black-outs. They felt little inclination to leave their homes or head out of the city, though the cinemas and restaurants did a brisk business.

A good crowd showed up at the Kennel Club to see all the foreign entries from England, Scotland and Wales this year. It was at least somewhere to go. There was rousing applause for the champion of the show, a Welsh corgi. Many visitors were intrigued by the basenjis from central Africa, only sixteen inches in size, barkless and possessing great speed. They were one of the oldest breeds in the world, dating from as far back as 3,000 BC and illustrated on the tombs of ancient Egyptians. A very exotic sight for Dubliners. It gave them something exciting to talk about when they returned home.

If a pall of boredom hung over Dublin, St Patrick's Day was celebrated with gusto in other parts of the world. While "those at home will observe the day relatively quietly, with no great military parade as was held before the war," wrote the *Irish Times*, "Irishmen in the u.s.a. and Canada will celebrate the Feast of St. Patrick to-day with pomp and show." In New York, celebrants were engaging in one of their most flamboyant parades ever. Some eighty thousand participants walked briskly in the colourful procession down Fifth Avenue. A mounted police escort opened the march, followed by a detachment of the 69th Infantry of the National Guard. Along the 2½-mile route nearly three thousand policemen—many of Irish heritage—lined the street as massive crowds cheered lustily, waving Irish flags. As a warm sun smiled down on the crowd, myriad Irish organisations passed by carrying banners and emblems, to the sound of martial music and Irish tunes. Those in the crowd sang along and danced jigs, everyone wearing some green and laughing aloud. Even the Duke of Windsor had arrived for the day, wearing a green hat and scarf. Cardinal Spellman, Archbishop of New York, watched it all with obvious delight from the steps of the cathedral.

It was noted by the *Sunday Independent* that "there is a resurgence of the Irish spirit in America this year," not only in New York but in Boston, Chicago, San Francisco, St Louis, and Denver. In Newark, New Jersey, there was an impressive "revival commemoration" with a parade of 35,000 people and bands. Similar spirited parades were held in Canada and in Britain. In Paris a "small Irish colony" celebrated the day in St Joseph's Church near the Arc de Triomphe.

Could the unusually large, exuberant foreign celebrations of St Patrick's Day have had anything to do with the awareness of, or sympathy for, the suffering of the Irish at home during their severe winter?

One of the most extraordinary and depressing features of St Patrick's Day in 1947 was the conspicuous absence of shamrock. An unprecedented sight. Weeks earlier there had been rumours that, because of the cold and snow cover, the growth of the different varieties of clover might have suffered serious damage. No-one, of course, wanted to believe it.

When the holiday weekend began on Saturday people as usual sought their sprig of shamrock green to wear. The bad news spread quickly. For, indeed, "the heavy snow prevented dealers from picking supplies during the past two weeks," revealed the *Dublin Evening Mail*. "Some women who managed to get a stock did keen business, for the shamrock went into the black market for the first time."[27] One could imagine tea, sugar, petrol, cigarettes on the black market—but shamrock!

By Saturday evening most of the shops in the city that sold shamrock had none left on their counters, and "when word spread of this unprecedented shortage the shamrock became 'very dear' indeed." Throughout Sunday and

Monday it was being sold by dealers in the streets for a shilling a sprig, "but only one in ten persons was inclined to pay this price," reporters found.

Without shamrock it just didn't feel like St Patrick's Day to people. As the *Evening Herald* opined, the weekend of wild weather and flooding would be "remembered for many things," but in years to come many people's most vivid "recollections of it will be trying to find a spray of shamrock" to wear in their button-hole.[28] It seemed like a final indignity: that King Winter had claimed even the humble shamrock as a victim.

"Irish exiles," as newspapers called them, in New York and other American cities were deprived as well. And quite unhappy about it. Normally they received boxes of the plant by air express from relatives and friends back home. This year instead they got messages saying the "shamrock is scarce here, due to snow-covered Emerald Isle." This, however, did not deter resourceful, well-to-do Americans who had planned ahead for the big day. Parcels of shamrock were ordered and flown, at considerable cost, in advance by Pan-American Airlines to the Mayor of New York, William O'Dwyer, as well as to Irish societies in New York, Boston, and Chicago. At the request of the Irish members of the Hollywood film community a large box of shamrock was sent by Pan-American from Shannon on the night of 13 March. The likes of Bing Crosby and Mickey Rooney were not about to be left without their shamrock come St Patrick's Day.

———

Throughout Monday the weather around the country was mixed. In most counties it was mild compared with past months. In the 40s (4 to 6°C), it felt rather balmy. While "spring-like weather was enjoyed for some of the day in Cork," in Dublin it rained on and off. In the afternoon the "skies were heavy and rain fell—but it was milder than it had been for weeks." The air definitely had a different feel to it, people were saying.

Though de Valera had planned nothing special for Dubliners, he had prepared his traditional messages to foreign audiences. To Birmingham United Irish Societies he sent the following words:

> The Irish Nation on this day when the unity of our race throughout the world is made so manifest, greets her exiled children, certain of their support in the effort to restore unity to the Motherland.[29]

Later, at 6:15 p.m. New York time, he broadcast to America via Radio Éireann a similar sentiment:

> Our national integrity has been destroyed by the unnatural partition of the country enacted and enforced from the outside . . . As long as this

unjust situation exists any genuine cordiality between the people of
Ireland and Britain is impossible.[30]

Some Irish people may have questioned the wisdom of such statements at a
time when Ireland was pleading with the British to send coal to relieve the fuel
crisis crippling the country.

Meanwhile in London, Cardinal Bernard Griffin, Archbishop of
Westminster, was praising the Irish people on their national holiday for their
inherent "kindness and hospitality," noting, in timely fashion, that "Irish
humour was inbred . . . This is the only way of keeping sane."

On Monday evening rain fell heavily all over the country. In Dublin, a
downpour began at 9:40, creating "another big rush from the cinemas and
theatres for late buses . . . people again drenched and some left behind." As
they climbed into bed most were probably glad that the national "festival" was
over, not having had even the small joy of wearing the traditional shamrock
on St Patrick's Day. A small deprivation, yet symbolic of the whole bloody
winter.

———

Tuesday "dawned bright and clear . . . with warm sunshine." A definite sense
of spring—no doubt about it. The air was considerably warmer and fresher.
By the hour the weather improved. Spirits rose. "Farmers in every part of
Ireland were thankful," stated the *Irish Times,* "for the strong south-east wind
which gave promise of a pick-up in the weather, and of drying land." Devout
believers were saying it was St Patrick himself who had brought a favourable
weather change. He had answered their prayers.

Not everyone was so optimistic. Those who understood agriculture knew
all too well that the threat to spring tillage was real, not to be relieved in a few
days' time by a bit of sunshine and drying winds. It had to be a prolonged
process of recovery. With the holiday over, reports began coming in from
counties all over Ireland, many with news even worse than expected.

The *Irish Times* wrote bluntly:

> From our correspondents all over the country come details of the damage
> wrought by the weather in the blackest year since the Famine.
> Agriculturalists agree that the country faces the biggest food crisis in its
> history.[31]

Farm conditions varied widely around the country. While some counties were
now mostly under water, others were still covered with snow. In some areas
the "bone" may have been taken out of the land, but elsewhere the soil
remained frozen. Depending upon many factors of local terrain and soil, the

land would drain and dry at different rates. Some farmers might have good luck, others bad. Even when a piece of land was drained of several feet of water it was far from ready for ploughing. Many farmers spoke of their good earth as having been almost "liquefied." Those like Brendan Morgan of Lusk in north Co. Dublin sounded positively despondent as he stood in one of his fields, staring down at the land, muttering, "The soil is nothing better than slop now."[32]

The *Dublin Evening Mail*, though not wanting to dim people's optimism, felt a responsibility to inform the general, non-farming population of the prevailing realities facing the country:

> The news is very grave for the people of Ireland. After months of weather of unexampled severity . . . many parts of the country are lying under two or three feet of water—land that had been destined for the sowing of crops.
>
> Even if the weather were to change to bright sunshine for a long stretch, the outlook would still be very serious. The Government and people must face the facts so that everything can be done to avoid a famine before the year has run its course.[33]

Agricultural experts laid the hard facts bare: ploughing, preparing and cultivating almost 2½ million acres of land needed now to be carried out "within the short space of five weeks." Practically no winter wheat had been planted; even drained land was like mushy porridge, "unapproachable to men or machine." There existed a critical shortage of tractors and tyres; these machines would have to be run twenty-four hours a day on a relay system.

Ultimately, all depended upon the weather. Only many consecutive days and weeks of warm temperatures, sunshine and drying winds could give farmers a decent chance of success, as they faced what the *Irish Times* was calling "their greatest task in history" to produce a harvest under such conditions.[34] One worried farmer from Co. Dublin stated: "Last year we were all anxious about saving the harvest, but at least we had a harvest to save. This year I'm worried whether there will *be* a harvest!"[35]

The president of the Agricultural Association of Ireland, D. W. Phibbs, a man not given to exaggeration, solemnly predicted: "If the weather does not improve, the grim prospect of no harvest will have to be faced."[36]

Coverage of the tillage crisis and the prospect of no harvest began filling the front pages of newspapers. People grew increasingly fearful as they read articles depicting the worst possible outcome. The *Irish Independent* published an apocalyptic-sounding editorial:

> The Irish nation faces a national emergency as grave as any in its history.

The people face the possibility of famine. Nothing but a superhuman effort can enable tillage to be done that will avert starvation. The next few weeks may well decide whether the centenary of the Famine will be marked by no less appalling catastrophe.[37]

―――

The *Dublin Evening Mail* affirmed that many impoverished Dubliners were already facing "appalling catastrophe," "perishing from want and cold in this civilised city of ours." As evidenced by the capital's death rate, which had by now nearly trebled. No food kitchens had been established to feed the desperately hungry. Thousands had no fire with which to warm themselves or even cook a potato. Their suffering was readily observable to those who visited them.

By mid-March it had reached the point where many country people, who were more self-sufficient in storing up food and dry turf for long winters, were now feeling sympathy for the cold and hungry masses of poor tenement-dwellers. In Brian Kelly's part of Co. Donegal the "country people were nearly self-sufficient: they had their own eggs, own pigs, bacon hanging in the pantry, a potato shed, a turf shed." Accustomed to feeding themselves and keeping a fire going somehow. Those who were surviving this worst of winters were feeling compassion for their city cousins. As one countrywoman, Ora Kilroe, expressed it, "few of us sit down before the glowing turf fire without saying, 'God help the poor people in cities, and the children.'"[38]

In March, as the plight of the poor worsened, newspapers published increasing numbers of letters from citizens documenting at first hand their hardship. One sympathetic person wrote to the *Dublin Evening Mail*:

Sir,—An old woman was seen to be collapsing near the Green the other day. She was given a cup of coffee and helped on her way. In response to sympathetic questioning she told a little of her story.

She is one of the old-age pensioners who live alone in a room. She had no fire and no food. She was on her way to some kind people who give her a little free milk when cold and hunger made her weak. The mute sufferings of the old folk at the end of a hard road is sad beyond words. That they should have nothing but the hideous spectre of want and despair is a thing that deserves our censure.[39]

Despite the exposure of the food crisis and the suffering of the hungry, there were still many better-off citizens who had not yet grasped the full gravity of the situation. So, in the third week of March the Minister for Agriculture, Patrick Smith, decided to address the issue forthrightly:

We fear many people have not yet fully realised the stark truth, namely, that unless we have a good harvest this year we may have a food famine.

To-day people are referring to Black 1847 and wondering are we to have a Black 1947 too. May God grant that we escape such a peril.[40]

It was the *Sunday Independent* that published the most graphic—and, to many readers, most horrifying—depiction of the spectre of famine looming over Ireland: a large drawing showing the Grim Reaper standing over the body of a woman collapsed on the ground, dead from hunger, as a girl kneels by her side in grief. The caption read:

This is what may happen—Famine and Death stalking through Ireland—unless everybody plays his or her part in the national effort to grow more food.[41]

———

The "national effort" meant country and city people working together as they had in the previous autumn's harvest campaign. As the *Irish Independent* explained:

This is a fight for survival, and the farmer cannot fight it unaided. Even if he is backed by all the people's resources it will be a grim battle.[42]

Cries went up for a national "tillage drive," to be aided by throngs of volunteers from cities, stepping forward once again to do their patriotic duty. "Every urban worker whose services can be spared," exhorted the paper, should show up at volunteer centres, adding that "school boys and girls can give a hand in the campaign, placed at the disposal of farmers." One citizen wrote to another newspaper suggesting the "abandonment of all major sporting events, particularly those of the Gaelic Athletic Association," so that the hardy athletes could devote themselves to the tillage campaign. Plans were immediately made to establish volunteer centres in Dublin, Cork, Limerick and other cities and towns. Enthusiasm among urban residents grew, as they were eager to join the fight on farms throughout the country.

Farmers themselves saw it differently. They knew what many city-dwellers did not: that ploughing and sowing were completely different from autumn harvesting. Tillage was a very specialised, highly skilled process. Cultivating, sowing, fertilising were agricultural practices requiring the handling of tools and machinery learnt by experience, not a simple act taught on the spot in a matter of minutes, or even hours. Not at all like "gathering up" harvest crops. Outsiders would only get in a farmer's way and impede his already-pressured work. The last thing they needed now was an intrusion of well-meaning but unskilled city folk—office workers, clerks, shop staff, factory hands and schoolchildren tramping on their soft land. D. W. Phibbs quickly saw the need to issue a statement on the subject for publication in the newspapers:

> Voluntary aid on the lines of last year's harvest campaign would be useless now. The only hope of saving the situation is the maximum co-operation between farmers and farm labourers—tractors, ploughs, corn drills and horses should be loaned out, and where possible, all implements should be used co-operatively.[43]

In other words, it was not a matter of manpower but of farm machines. And their shared use.

During the third week of March officials in towns and villages were organising local plans for the sharing of tractors and farm implements. Relays would be set up to run the tractors around the clock. Local mechanics and garage workers pitched in to help with installing lamps on tractors, promising to give the servicing of farm machinery their highest priority. Additional supplies of petrol and oil were obtained. Tractor tyres would be sought from every source. Those city men who had come from farm families and had experience were welcome to join the tractor relays and other operations. Everyone who had something to contribute was needed.

And what of the Government, and the army?

"It is difficult to understand," the *Dublin Evening Mail* wrote, "why the National Army has not already been organised to assist farmers with their vehicles and expertise in machinery."[44] Many soldiers were from farm families, familiar with tractors and tillage. Facing a tillage *crisis*, acknowledged by all the country's agricultural authorities, the Government had failed to assume an active role in assisting farmers. As criticism from the public and press grew, the *Irish Independent* decided to publish a direct appeal:

> We ask the Government forthwith to summon a national assembly of farmers, industrialists, trade unionists and other representatives of the community to prepare a scheme for the mobilisation of machinery and skilled farm labourers.
>
> If necessary, all but the most vital services and industries must be closed down to release horses and vehicles for the land . . . Every available government lorry, every vehicle which can be spared from commerce and industry must be placed in the hands of the farmers to transport seeds, manure . . . Provisions must be made to have every tractor work even after dark, without a moment's let up.[45]

Most city firms gladly began complying with the request to release their tractors, lorries and other equipment for emergency farm work. How would the Government respond?

————

As the national tillage scheme got under way there was news of worsening food shortages, both nationally and globally. In mid-March the Food and Agriculture Organisation of the United Nations announced that the world wheat outlook for 1947/48 was very "disquieting." Global yields were down significantly, meaning lower exports to needy countries, such as Ireland, while at home it was reported that bacon would now be in short supply. There was an "abnormally big drop" in bacon production in the country's thirty-eight bacon factories, because of the weather. In some of them, curing had been suspended because of snowbound roads that prevented the delivery of pigs. During the first week of March only 2,732 pigs were cured, as compared with nearly 7,000 in the same period the previous year.

By this time publicans around the country were receiving more bad news in the form of a circular from Guinness informing them of further drastic cut-backs on the way. By 31 March their supplies would be reduced by half. The circular stated:

> Owing to the fuel crisis, we much regret that it will not be possible to supply you with more than half your present weekly quota of extra stout and/or porter.[46]

The 30 per cent cut made on 3 February meant that supplies to publicans would now be sliced to only 35 per cent of their original supply. One prominent publican groused: "This is a bolt from the blue! I can see no way out except partial closure."[47] The news made some publicans as fretful as farmers.

Behind the scenes at Guinness's, William Tinnion and his fellow-stokers knew that the country's pubmen were lucky to be getting any drink from the brewery. Only through their extraordinary efforts of burning wood from the massive painting project was the brewery still functioning.

With serious shortages of bread, tea, sugar, butter, potatoes, bacon and Guinness—the basics of the Irish diet—some people, arguing that it was difficult enough to feed themselves, began to question why they should be feeding others. Meaning tourists. It seemed a legitimate question. But was it prudent? On 18 March, with rations tightening and spring tillage in serious jeopardy, Dr T. F. O'Higgins TD proposed the suspension of all tourist trade until the country was "able to feed her own people and have something left over for visitors."[48] Predictably, this met with a mixed reaction. The suggestion was extremely worrisome to those in the hotel, bed-and-breakfast, restaurant and general tourist business, as it threatened their very livelihood.

While some ordinary citizens thought it extreme, others favoured it. The proposal gained support when the *Dublin Evening Mail* threw its weight behind it in an editorial:

> Many of us hope that the Government will order every hotel and guesthouse and boarding house to cancel all bookings from outside the country for the coming holiday season. It would be nothing less than criminal folly to allow a repetition of last year's avalanche of tourists from Britain and other countries.[49]

"Criminal folly" for Irish people to welcome tourists? Were they now to be added to the list of winter's victims? As Una Shaw observed, after nearly two months of Siberian cold, blizzards, and flooding, the weather "affected *every aspect* of life."

———

All Ireland anxiously awaited good weather that would allow farmers to crank up their tractor engines and start turning over the soil for sowing. "Farmers must pray that nature will give them a break—then work night and day," wrote the *Irish Times*.[50] Prayers were said, in churches, homes, public meetings, in the fields. Days of high tension—"the very existence of the people of Ireland is at stake."[51] As the *Irish Times* predicted:

> The last harvest brought the farmer almost to his knees. What is needed now is a drying wind . . . and a big slice of luck as well.
>
> When the land is ready, the ploughing, harrowing and sowing of nearly 2½ million acres will become a race against time.[52]

Chapter 13 ∾

| A RACE AGAINST TIME

Never had a spring sky been more anxiously watched by those who dwell on the land.

(*Irish Independent*, 21 MARCH 1947)

Some day this terrible weather and its calamitous results will have ended.

(*Dublin Evening Mail*, 15 MARCH 1947)

That summer was one of the greatest summers we ever had. Oh, it was fabulous!

(SEÁN WHELAN, age 80)

LATE MARCH

Farmers fretfully watched the skies from sunrise till sunset—as one anxious farm wife put it, "fidgeting to get at the ploughing . . . and gloomily predicting rain."[1] Waiting for the land to dry out was torturous. All Ireland was nervous.

With all they had been through over the past two months—and now talk of possible famine ahead—there were plenty of pessimists grumbling that it was already "too late," the "crops were lost." To counter those persons spinning Doomsday scenarios and spreading pessimism, the *Irish Times* reassured readers that "the farmer's optimism is strong—he believes he can overcome the unprecedented effects of brutal weather of frost and flood."[2] The *Irish Press* was concerned about negative attitudes undermining public confidence and the national spirit:

> Serious as the position is, there is no sense in using wild words about the "wrath of God" being directed against Ireland . . . or in moaning disparagingly. Let there be an end to gloomy prognostications.
>
> The security of the country now lies where it has lain during all emergency years—in the hands of the ploughman.[3]

Immediately following St Patrick's Day the weather improved dramatically. The rain ceased, skies cleared, temperatures climbed, and drying winds swept across the flooded land. On Saturday 22 March, by 9 o'clock the mercury showed 45 degrees (7°C). At noon it had reached 65 (18°C); during the afternoon it settled in the 70s (21 to 23°C). The next day's *Sunday Independent* declared finally that "spring paid us a belated visit."

All across the country, optimism rose. Some farmers with favoured terrain and drainage were reporting that their land was drying out at a rate far faster than expected. On Saturday afternoon a reporter toured several eastern counties where he had heard that some farmers had actually begun their tillage:

> Urged by the fear of impending famine, farmers have started to plough, and I sensed the general resilience of spirit which the first day of real Spring sunshine brought. In the coming week, if fine, we will witness the greatest sowing drive in our history.[4]

In Co. Wexford it was enthusiastically boasted that "brilliant sunshine and a drying north-west wind brought ploughmen into the fields in force." Similar accounts were coming in from other counties.

By Sunday 23 March six days of consecutive fine, sunny, warm weather coming directly on the heels of St Patrick's Day prompted more people to speak of "answered prayers." Some were even saying "miracle."

Buoyed by faith and bright sunshine, some people were now becoming over-confident about King Winter's demise. The *Sunday Independent* reminded those chirruping too optimistically that "one swallow does not make a summer and one fine day does not make a spring." Only a *truly* prolonged spell of drying weather would bring out "horses, machines and men into the still-sodden fields" in full force.

——

Dubliners couldn't resist luxuriating in the sunshine and temperatures suddenly in the 60s and 70s. The capital exploded with a renewal of life.

On both sides of the Liffey, from tenement slums to Georgian mansions, windows and doors were flung open to expunge winter's stale air, accumulated over months of confinement. In the congested, squalid tenements the fetid air built up from turf smoke, body odour, slop buckets and dampness was slowly drawn out, replaced by fresh breezes blowing back the soiled lace curtains. Purging the unsanitary and sickening air, creating a feeling of healthfulness. Along Gardiner Street, Queen Street, Benburb Street, North King Street, Patrick Street, the Coombe and dozens of other tenement streets, people in stuffy, stagnant rooms spoke of feeling "disinfected" as their lungs were purified by the inflow of fresh air. It was healing to the human spirit. People once again leaned out their windows, calling across to neighbours or down to passing friends below. Bird cages were placed in windows, laundry washed and hung out on the line, and water brought up so that people could have a bath. Butter boxes and stools were dragged outside in front of doors, where people sat chatting, knitting, smiling in the warm sun.

Streets once again teemed with children running about and shrieking. Along the pavements men were seen encircled in their toss schools, as others rambled down to the docks to see what was happening. The usual clusters of "street corner men" gathered, chatting amiably, gesturing, putting on their act. At public houses, long thick with the stagnant smell of drink and smoke and men, doors were propped wide open as customers were disgorged outside onto the pavement with their pints and banter. Street dealers were out in force, their laughter and wit resonating through Moore Street and Henry Street, the Daisy Market, the Iveagh Market.

In Ballsbridge, Ranelagh and Blackrock residents ambled around outside their houses, making plans for spring gardening and tending to their window boxes, getting their front doors and railings freshly painted. The Phoenix Park, Fairview Park and St Stephen's Green were so crowded with people of all ages that they had to shuffle along the pathways. The more fortunate visitors captured a coveted bench to watch the steady parade.

One could almost see the city's suffocating "Dickensian gloom" lifting.

With the sudden spell of very warm weather, the ice on Dublin's ponds, lakes and canals—as well as rivers—was rapidly melting. Newspapers reminded people to be cautious. On 20 March the *Irish Press* warned readers that the "lands around Dublin and surrounding counties remain flooded, and the Liffey, Dodder and Tolka are in heavy flood," draining their thawing hinterland. An immense volume of water was funnelled into their flow, causing them to rage with a current stronger than ever seen before. An extreme danger to anyone caught in the torrent.

One afternoon William Tinnion, enjoying a Liffeyside ramble, was looking out over the river running fast with swirling currents. With most of the ice floes now gone or reduced in size, most ships and barges could ply the waters, but with great care. He was watching some of Guinness's lighters, or small barges, which went up and down the river carrying about three hundred barrels, when something unexpected happened:

> The river was in full flood. And we had one barge that had no engine on it, it was a barge that would just be towed. Well, it went down near the Custom House, and as it was turning around from one side of the river to

the other it was caught in the rush, the flow, of the river. Fully loaded with barrels. And the flood turned it over, and all the casks went floating off! And Guinness's just said, "Just bring the casks back—and enjoy the beer." And people had a hooley!

For the beneficiaries, winter had finally done a good deed.

Many Dubliners enjoyed standing near a swollen river, watching its waters tearing towards the sea. Carrying debris and animal carcases and all sorts of odd things along with it. Children were fascinated by the wildness of the current, sometimes drawn so close that they could toss a piece of wood or other object into the water and watch how quickly it was carried off. Despite admonitions from parents, and passers-by, many got too close.

On 24 March six-year-old Michael Keady from Rathmines was playing dangerously close to the edge of the unbridled Dodder when he fell into the rushing water and was carried off swiftly towards the waterfall by Classon's Bridge. His cries for help were heard by the Kelly sisters, living in Dartry Cottages, who first mistook the child's wriggling body in the water for a "young puppy trying to swim against the flood current." When they realised it was a child they ran to the nearby house of 24-year-old Dan O'Connor, who flew down and managed to reach the waterfall just in time to reach out and grab the child. The lucky lad was taken to Baggot Street Hospital and revived after three hours of resuscitation. By that night he was reported to be "getting on very well." When the story of his close escape appeared in the next day's newspapers it served as a lesson for other children to stay well away from the fast-running rivers.

———

As Ireland's rivers rushed towards the sea they were draining floodwaters and snow melt from the farmers' lands. The 24th marked an entire week of rainless weather, sunshine, and drying winds. An *Irish Press* journalist touring several eastern counties to report on farmers' progress wrote: "I travelled through several counties and everywhere I went tillage was in full swing." Other counties were not yet so fortunate, but there was no doubt that much spring ploughing was at least under way. The *Sunday Independent* confirmed that "an army of small plot-holders in every county . . . work night and day in order to get through the necessary tillage." Most tractors had by now been fitted with headlamps: farmers and their relay help were "not waiting for a full moon," as they worked through the entire night. Rather than disturbing country people's sleep, the sound of tractor engines grinding during the hours of darkness was a most restful, reassuring sound.

In Dublin, Cork, Limerick and other cities, firms offered their tractors, lorries and horses for work on farms. Tractors were loaned by CIE, quarries, Dublin Airport, and even golf courses. The Church did its part by granting a dispensation to farmers and farm labourers to work on Sundays to get their crops in on time.

Other work, also long overdue, was finally getting under way at a hurried pace. Every undertaker in Ireland was being pushed to the limit, with burials backlogged for two months. Coffins could now be properly placed in the earth for the eternal rest of the deceased. Some had not fared well in their snow-pits when the floodwaters and warmer temperatures came. Hearse-drivers and their horses were getting little rest. Gravediggers were slaving away to the point of exhaustion.

Bargemen could once again freely ply the canals between country and city, continuing to carry excessive loads because of the continuing cancellation of railway goods services. Dublin's plumbers and chimneysweeps were working eighteen-hour days. But making "tons" of money. The zoo staff could release pent-up animals in open-air enclosures, no longer having to keep wood-burning fires going all night to protect delicate tropical birds, reptiles, monkeys.

On the streets of Dublin, Captain A. Stanley Villeneuve of the Salvation Army could once again despatch his battalion of bell-ringers to carry out their usual spring drive for much-needed funds. During the harsh winter months they had expended their resources in assisting the poor and needy. Now their coffers needed refilling, and people were generous.

As Dublin life normalised in the bloom of spring, many individuals who had been pushed to their limits could now relax, restore their strength and sanity. Bus and tram drivers could go to work without fear of accidents or of being marooned on the road with passengers. They could return home at night and sleep peacefully. Many had suffered health problems and needed time to recuperate.

With the Arctic cold gone, icy pavements now clear, and flu epidemic subsiding, the city's hospital staffs were far less pressured. Postmen, gardaí and lamplighters could walk their beats without discomfort or risk of falling, taking time again to enjoy nature and chat with local people along their way. And everyone seemed chattier than ever. Messenger-boys zipped through traffic on their bikes without a care. Jarveys and carters plied the streets without worrying about their horses slipping and collapsing on the cobblestones.

Dublin seemed a relaxed city again, going about life at its famous leisurely pace.

Motorists took their cars out on the roads again. Many, however, found that the ravages of winter weather had taken a toll on their vehicle.

Automobile associations advised them to have a thorough check of suspension and steering linkage. Because of the freezing cold and bad roads, steering joints and shock-absorbers suffered damage, and much harm was done from the corrosive effect of salt on roads. On most cars service needed to be carried out on all greasing and oiling points. Owners found that their cars had taken a beating, some quite costly to have serviced and repaired. But most were simply happy to again have the freedom to take a drive on a fine spring day.

———

Although city life bustled and fields were being ploughed, Ireland's fuel crisis remained critical. Despite the warmer days, nights were still chilly to cold. Frosts still occurred in many areas.

Just after St Patrick's Day the 4,000 tons of British coal approved for emergency purposes arrived, and the 9,400 tons of American coal was unloaded in the nick of time to keep CIE and the Gas Company going for a few more days. But these did not help to keep people warm or cook food. So, on 21 March, Seán Lemass flew to London for a conference with British ministers on "supply matters," where he discussed in the most candid terms the "gravity of the fuel and food situation in this country." He met Emanuel Shinwell, Minister of Fuel and Power, and John Strachey, Minister of Food, laying conditions on the table. His premise for negotiations was that "barter is the basis of much present-day diplomacy." Lemass's objective was to arrange a favourable "coal-cattle pact" with the British. "We are in desperate need of coal, but we can send the British as much beef as they want in return," he promised.[5]

By 28 March, after a week of intense negotiations, the *Irish Times* hailed Lemass's trip as successful, noting, however, that it was "long overdue." And it would do nothing in the immediate days ahead to relieve the fuel crisis. Later that day, in an effort to do something positive in the present, Lemass asserted that, "no matter how scanty our timber reserves, trees must be cut down almost ruthlessly."[6] For those fortunate enough to have fireplaces large enough to accommodate logs, this was welcome news. Tenement-dwellers' grates would remain fireless.

The 28th was the eleventh consecutive day of near-perfect weather for ploughing and sowing. The "race against time" was furiously under way, newspapers proclaimed. "The most favourable weather since October," reported the *Irish Press*, "with brilliant sunshine."

The tide was turning.

On the morning of Saturday 29 March farmers rose early to set out on their twelfth day of the tillage drive. The tapping sound of rain against their windows immediately drew them to peer outside. Angry storm clouds were gathering over the land as the winds were picking up. They ate breakfast with their vision fixed out the window on their fields as a steady rain began. Some hurriedly mounted their tractors and began work. But most were soon driven back inside again by downpours. By midday, farmers in most counties were housebound, watching their fields getting a good soaking. "Farmers had their hopes crushed by torrential rain," wrote one paper, "having to leave their fields after turning a few sods." For the first time in nearly two weeks the humming of tractor engines across the land was not heard. It was a reminder, stated the *Irish Press*, that "weather is still the governing factor in the spring tillage drive."[7]

As March ended, the Jesuit meteorologists at Rathfarnham Castle looked over their statistics and found that, despite the late eleven-day spell of fine, rainless weather, March, which is normally a dry month, was the wettest one ever recorded at the Castle, with a total of 6.42 inches of rainfall. It went down in the record books as "the wettest, sludgiest March in almost 300 years."[8]

APRIL

On All Fools' Day the weather played no tricks. It began splendidly. Skies were clear, temperatures in the 50s and 60s, with "high, warm drying winds." Fields dried quickly, and tractor engines were again heard grinding across the fields. Declared the *Irish Independent*: "The fate of the vital spring crops of 1947 is now hanging precariously in the balance."[9] No-one doubted this declaration. Indeed April was being called the "last lap in the grim race against time." Farmers would find it a frustrating roller-coaster ride of days fine and foul.

April began happily. Perhaps a good omen was the presentation at the Olympia Theatre of *While the Sun Shines*, called by one critic a "hilariously funny" play. Pedestrians in the streets were conspicuously more spirited: smiling, taking time to chat and banter. The famous Irish sense of humour seemed to be in revival. Weather forecasters felt safe again. If they predicted the day to be 65 degrees (18°C) with bright sunshine and it turned out to reach only 58 (14°C) and "partially sunny," no-one was after their hide. The *Irish Times* even quipped, "After jeering for so long at the forecasters, let us take no notice of newspaper weather forecasts."[10]

With spirits on the rise, the *Irish Press*, reflecting seriously, sought to draw positive meaning from winter's ordeal in an editorial headed "The bad weather made us good neighbours":

> Weather, if it is bad enough, brings out the best in people . . . A blizzard or a flood . . . and lo and behold, the most self-centred and morose will develop a most kindly and neighbourly attitude . . . The bad weather made

us good neighbours.

It is amazing that, when real discomfort and danger descend upon us we behave better ... The feeling of good will and unselfish desire to share was inspiring and exhilarating.[11]

It was, upon reflection, "a time of extraordinary collaboration and resourcefulness."[12] People helped one another. With a few notable exceptions, such as the mercenary black-market profiteers, who thrived upon others' misery.

In all Ireland nothing more gaily heralded the arrival of the season than the appearance of spring fashions at Dublin's most fashionable department stores. By good fortune, when Clery's, Brown Thomas and Switzer's introduced this spring's collection—straight from New York and Paris, even Hollywood—the attire was unusually colourful, exotic, a bit daring. With some whimsical outfits. Just what Dubliners needed to see after their long winter blues. As described by the *Irish Times*, they were a mixed collection of elegance, gaiety, and frivolity:

Playsuits featuring the midriff and bare back, elaborate negligées and sleek evening dresses ... The clothes have bright colours and trimming, and the entire trend is towards a more leisurely, frivolous way of life.[13]

Irish people would surely welcome a more leisurely, frivolous way of life!

The large window displays of spring fashions were a great tonic for people long afflicted with the bleak greyness of winter. Men, women and children stood in front of the shops ogling the "playsuits," chic gowns and Jean Harlow-style negligées in good cheer. A dazzling variety of spring outfits, high-stylish, a bit quirky in design and slightly risqué, caught the eye and raised a few eyebrows. But it was all *colourful, lively, entertaining* ... "great gas" even for the poorest tenement women standing in awe. Far more *festive* than the "national festival" of St Patrick's Day. How could one not smile at the display of hats featuring "an especially care-free note," decorated with bunches of flowers and fruit, and "feather head-dresses"! After months of sunless gloom, their brightness and "humour" were wonderfully therapeutic for onlookers.

As all the springtime fun was being enjoyed, along Sundrive Road the last of the ice on the quarry pond finally melted. The rags that had marked the goals for the hockey game slowly sank to the bottom of the pit. No-one noticed. Local children were scampering around, laughing in the warm sunshine. Some adults walking past were pensive, a few pausing to peer into the dark waters. Then moving on with their lives.

The site of the tragedy is now marked by a memorial bench bearing the boys' names on a plaque, dedicated in 2007.

———

The first five days of April were blessed with warm temperatures and winds that caressed and dried the soft earth. Ploughing was proceeding at an intense pace in all counties. By Saturday 5 April many farmers claimed they were now at full throttle, actually "catching up" in the tillage race.

On Sunday the roller-coaster ride was on again, as "heavy rains, driven by a fierce wind," fell over a wide area of the country, bringing "almost all tillage to a standstill."[14] The very next day "boisterous winds and brilliant sunshine did a great deal to remedy the damage" caused by the rainstorm twenty-four hours earlier.[15]

For the most part the three weeks following St Patrick's Day had brought farmers splendid weather, exactly the prolonged period they so needed. As they were working around the clock with the help of farm workers, the 24-hour relay system using tractors through the night meant that in a single day's cycle a farmer was really accomplishing nearly three days' work. As one week of ploughing now meant three weeks of real progress, Ireland's farmers seemed to be racing successfully against time.

But the weather remained fickle, and there was no assurance of ultimate success. In the end, every tilled plot, regardless of size, would count.

During the first week of April, with farmers working to their physical capacity, the *Sunday Independent* raised a pointed question. "Are the townsmen and city men to play a part, or remain idle? The answer must be an emphatic 'no'."[16] As volunteers from cities were not needed in the farmers' fields, urban residents had been content to stand on the sidelines and passively cheer them on, merely following their daily progress in the newspapers. The papers' argument was that they too had a responsibility to assume an active, productive role in producing the country's food. It was contended that every arable piece of ground in Dublin and other cities "must be tilled." Every family must be obliged to grow the "maximum possible of potatoes and other vegetables." It was practical, patriotic—and necessary.

City food gardens were not a new concept. Many people naturally enjoyed growing a few items beside their home, as city-dwellers had done during the Second World War. With newspapers and agricultural experts still talking of the possibility of famine—or, at the very least, a diminished harvest—the need for supplemental small city plots was perfectly logical. Most citizens agreed that it was a good idea. The *Sunday Independent,* however, carried it to an extreme that many found disquieting:

It should be a crime this year for anybody to have a garden untilled. If the law does not impose a penalty, PUBLIC OPINION should brand the owner of an uncultivated plot or garden an enemy of the people, as a person who will not work to feed himself, and therefore has no right to expect others to feed him.

If necessary, every town and city should have a BLACK LIST of such offenders.[17]

Plain common sense and civil responsibility—or excessive, reactionary zeal?

Whether motivated by patriotism or coercion, Dubliners responded in great numbers during April. Certainly no-one wanted to be branded an "enemy of the people," or have their name on a black list. So they dug up the earth in the heart of the capital to plant potatoes, cabbage, carrots and other vegetables. Apart from cultivating their own home gardens, people could acquire plots from Dublin Corporation. Not only ordinary householders but "civil servants, businessmen, gardaí and soldiers," reported the newspapers, all enthusiastically tending to their plots when free time allowed.

Competition was keen for good plots convenient to one's home. "The most worried people in Dublin at the moment," wrote the *Sunday Independent*, "are those in search of suitable plots."[18] People found great satisfaction in their food gardening and pride in their contribution to the national tillage drive.

In early April the Red Cross Society had a happy announcement to make. As a result of the abundant press coverage of their ordeal, the German and Polish orphans at Glencree had received great public sympathy. As a consequence, Irish families had been eager to adopt them. Of the 313 children they had brought to Ireland since the end of the war, the society reported that 285 had now been "placed with families." Placement was going so well, in fact, that the Red Cross announced that it had "offered to take another 100 German refugee children." So, for them, the Glencree experience had ultimately turned out to be a positive one.

———

The days of 12 and 13 April were so glorious that the *Irish Independent* gushed that it was "a week-end stolen from June." With a radiantly sunny sky and temperatures well into the 70s (21 to 25°C), there was an exodus of Dubliners: "by bus, tram, car and bicycle, they flocked out of the city with picnic parcels, buckets and spades."[19] The huge crowds swarming to the seaside were overjoyed to get out of their long-stuffy dwellings and inhale fresh sea air once again. But it was the penetrating warmth of the sun they found most therapeutic, as the *Irish Times* reported:

Dublin people, sun-starved, made their biggest pilgrimage of the year to the seaside and near country districts over the weekend, when the first real touch of summer came to Dublin.[20]

By early afternoon every seaside resort had large crowds. Mothers brought their whole flock of children—some as many as twelve—from the tenements for the entire day, running, chasing, building sand castles, pleading for ice cream, happily settling for milk and a sandwich or biscuit. Women sat contentedly in small clusters, chatting, knitting, dozing in the sun. Sunshine, the scent of sea and sand, the sound of children laughing—the best tonic for a beleaguered mother after her prolonged winter struggle. Some seaside visitors overindulged, returning to the city as red as lobsters, a misery for days to come.

In praising the weekend of perfection, the *Irish Independent* may have carried hyperbole a bit too far:

> It carried away the memory of the bitter winter and filled every heart with hope of sunny days to come.[21]

The weekend was marred only by the rude behaviour of some sports fans. Having had racing, rugby, football, hurling and other matches cancelled weekend after weekend, some over-zealous men heading for the big match at Milltown between Shamrock Rovers and Shelbourne became unruly when boarding buses to get there. With all the buses crowded, they began pushing and shoving. Some men "surged on the bus so violently," it was reported, "that many found it difficult to keep on their feet."[22]

Just the opposite was occurring over the weekend at Dublin Zoo, where a "steady stream of people young and old" passed politely through the turnstiles. Many were anxious to see two llamas that had just arrived. On both Saturday and Sunday more than fifteen thousand visitors entered the zoo grounds, smiling at strangers in simple shared appreciation for the grand day they were sharing.

Meanwhile the country's farmers were more grateful than anyone for the ideal weather as they continued their round-the-clock relay of ploughing and sowing. There was no let-up, no relaxation. Over the weekend they got in a full forty-eight hours of work, comparable to nearly six normal farming days. In mid-April, after nearly a month of excellent weather, blemished only by a few intermittent rains, the *Irish Independent*'s headline, if slightly exaggerated, summed up the farmers' race against time: "Most of the grain crop now sown."[23]

Within days of the good tillage report came welcome news about the country's fuel crisis. As Britain was experiencing the same prolonged spell of fine weather as Ireland, it was announced that its coal industry was returning to capacity output. By the third week of April, with the coal ban lifted, Britain was shipping 11,000 tons weekly to Ireland, with the hope that it would be increased to 30,000 tons a week "fairly soon." Only days before, CIE, the ESB, Dublin Gas Company and many industries had been literally down to their last lumps of coal.

Finally, William Tinnion and his furnace-stoking mates at Guinness's could cease stripping wood and begin shovelling coal again. The nation would have its pints.

MAY

Weather-wise, May turned out to be an even better month than April. On 2 May the country's last frost occurred. Nailing King Winter's coffin shut.

However, he had left behind shocking evidence of his destructive reign. With the snow blanket largely gone, country people now surveyed their surroundings and saw the widespread ruination wrought by two months of freezing, snow, ice, blizzards, and floods. A landscape ravaged beyond anything seen before:

> When at last the green fields of Ireland reappeared, the countryside looked as if it had been pummelled by a twister—it was a veritable ocean of mangled bicycles, broken poles, fallen trees and the corpses of dead animals.[24]

Some likened the destruction to that left by a hurricane or typhoon. Roads washed out, trees toppled, stone walls crumbled, barns and sheds drooping, signposts missing, telephone and electricity cables dangling and tangled into impossible puzzles. Countless animal carcasses, sometimes in bunches, others alone, gave off fetid odours. The sight of their bloated, rotting remains sickened adults and frightened children. Predators picked at them as if at a banquet.

The sight of live foxes, deer, rabbits and birds was heartening. Across the tormented landscape the emergence of green fields, leafing trees, budding flowers and bushes told of natural rebirth. As Ora Kilroe exulted, "the land is once again coming to life."[25]

People walked the roads, fields, boreens just to become reacquainted with the earth, sky, soil. A *gentle* nature.

Despite a few brief, intermittent spells of rain and chilly weather, May proved to be an excellent month, with generous sunshine and warm temperatures mostly in the 60s and 70s. As farmers all over the country were completing their tillage, looking forward to a good summer and decent harvest, the *Irish Independent* exclaimed:

> Once again, the farmers, under Providence, saved the country.[26]

SUMMER

"Oh!" Sixty years later that is the exultation of those who lived through the winter of 1946/47 when asked about the summer that followed. Superlatives abound.

Indeed the very first day of June was one long to be remembered. Scorching sunshine and a temperature of 84 degrees (29°C) brought every living soul outdoors. Even invalids and recluses showed their faces. Soaking in the healing solar rays, remembering the bone-chilling days of January and February. As the *Irish Times* portrayed it:

> Flaming June burst forth in all its fullness, giving promise of colourful gardens, burgeoning crops and delightful holidays.[27]

The coast roads out of Dublin "took on a pre-war appearance with motor traffic achieving processional volume."[28] Queues for buses, trams and trains stretched the length of streets, the most lengthy being that for the southbound trams from Nelson's Pillar, reaching well past Parnell Street. Sandymount, Blackrock, Dalkey, Dún Laoghaire, as well as Malahide and Skerries, were invaded by happy throngs

And so summer went. Day after day. As Garda Brian Kelly tells it:

> The weather took up real good around June, and there was a marvellous summer after that—oh, a beautiful summer! I think the lovely summer sort of blocked out the onslaught of this bad winter . . . in their minds, for some people.

Only quite temporarily, they found.

Strangely, all through the summer months there were still vestiges of winter to be seen here and there. "There were still big blocks of snow and the water dripping out of it, on the road," he recalls. "In *June*! It lasted." As one story goes, in Co. Wicklow the boys at Sunbeam Orphanage, outside Bray, had made a giant snowman during the winter months. Johnny Golden, "one of the architects, swears that the snowman was still standing in June."[29] Similarly, Tony Ruane and his young pals in Straide, Co. Mayo, could still play in the remnants of huge snowdrifts in early summer.

Another unexpected sight was the unusually excellent corn crop towering in the fields. As it turned out, the "Big Snow appears to have done the arable farmers a favour," for when summer came the "yields of corn and potatoes were lush and beautiful," beyond all expectation.[30] This lent credence to the old belief that frost and snow during a hard winter were good for ridding the soil of pests and diseases. The evidence seemed to be abundant.

Throughout summer's splendid months, streams of holidaymakers and foreign tourists visited the lovely mountains and lake country of Co. Wicklow.

The landscape had never appeared more enchanting, lush and green, with fragrant grasses and forests, the streams fresher than ever. Wild flowers on the rampage across valleys and slopes, extravagantly colourful and bright. The majesty of Wicklow's scenery awed visitors. Naturally many were drawn to the Roundwood and Glencree areas, about which they had read so much during the winter months. By late summer local residents had grown tired of telling their tale over and over again, having been polite to well-meaning, inquisitive visitors. While many graciously repeated accounts of their hardship, others now had few words to say. Let history stand as history.

———

Two-thirds of a century later, people still rave about how extraordinarily warm and beautiful that summer was, always relying upon grandiose descriptions: "heavenly," "gorgeous," "exquisite." The absolute "best ever," they swear. "That summer was the *greatest* summer we *ever had!*" vouches Seán Whelan. "It was fabulous!" Bar none. A clear consensus.

Just as the brutal winter had so often been characterised as "freakish" by the press and even meteorologists, people talked of the summer as being "freakishly" glorious. Unnatural. An aberration. Week after week after week of clear, sunny, *hot* weather. Utterly, untypically Irish.

It turned out not to be exaggeration, as meteorological records confirmed the spectacular claims. According to the records of the National Botanic Gardens, Ireland's summer of 1947 was characterised by "a memorable heat wave in the summer, and a month of August which was the best in 80 years of record keeping . . . The month had record sunshine."[31]

In short, 1947's entire weather record was phenomenally bizarre. The worst winter in Irish history—followed by the best summer in living memory.What are the odds of that?

———

Back in mid-February 1947 the *Irish Press* had made a prediction:

> That white insidious sheet has wrapped up this place good and proper— and won't be unravelled till June. If you travel high enough next summer you can have a tablecloth of snow to picnic on.[32]

It was, of course, taken as pure hyperbole.

In August's last simmering days, hikers, cyclists and picnickers were relishing summer's swansong, seeking to explore less travelled roads and paths in Wicklow's highlands. Hardy hikers like Eddie McGrane and his pals from An Óige always sought the roughest, most remote terrain. About midday, highland adventurers looked for a shady spot to rest, have lunch.

Occasionally, in a deep shadowed forest nook or rocky niche, they spotted a curious white patch. Going over to inspect it more closely, they might let out an exclamation, or laugh. Their friends a short distance away looked over, wondering what their discovery might be.

Suddenly, the answer came flying their way as a snowball whizzed past them. Snowballing in August! In Ireland! Now that was a great story to tell their grandchildren.

Chapter 14 ❧

A COLD-HEARTED
EPITAPH

*Christmas is a time for memories. We in this country have,
through the mercy of Providence, escaped the worst disasters
of the times—hunger, freezing, real famine—and our
Christmas will be correspondingly brighter.*
(*Irish Times*, 24 DECEMBER 1947)

The year which dies to-night will have few mourners.
(*Irish Press*, 31 DECEMBER 1947)

AUTUMN

Splendorous weather prevailed through autumn. Dry, warm days of August and September "made the saving of the harvest, smaller though it was, an easy matter."[1] Followed by an October with an "extraordinarily low rainfall of 1.08 inches, which set a record for dryness."

Fears of famine vanished.

During the autumn Ireland negotiated a new trade agreement with Britain, with the exchange of cattle for coal. British colliers were already arriving in such numbers at the Dublin docks that dockers could hardly unload them fast enough. With such favourable summer and autumn weather, turf-cutting in the boglands produced huge supplies to be stored for the winter ahead.

Fears of fuel shortages dissipated.

DECEMBER

By December, Ireland's food and fuel crises seemed but a bitter memory. Beneficent weather had graced Ireland for eight months—since St Patrick's Day, as many would reverentially remember. Through the "mercy of Providence," in the words of the *Irish Times*, the country had survived Arctic freezing, blizzards, hunger, floods and threat of famine. "That's what it was," affirms Noel Hughes: "survival, *survival!*" King Winter's cruel reign had been endured, the "white enemy" finally defeated. The *Irish Press* lauded the ultimate victory of Man over nature, citing the unheralded acts of courage and sacrifice:

There are heroes in this winter saga.[2]

With 1947 nearing its end, it was time to give thanks, count one's blessings, celebrate the season spiritually and socially. With the arrival of December, people's Christmas spirits were conspicuously more ebullient than usual. In Dublin, unprecedented crowds filled the streets and the shops, listening to carollers, packing Bewley's, delighting in the lavish window displays at Brown Thomas, Switzer's, Clery's and Arnott's with their elaborate animated Christmas scenes of Santa, his reindeer and elves working industriously in the toy shop.

Along Grafton Street, bright green, red, gold and silver garlands and wreaths embroidered the setting. Henry Street's women dealers were never in better form as they sold toys, holly, and decorations. Shops were reporting record sales. "Toys were unusually plentiful this year," wrote one newspaper, "as Dublin went over the top!"[3] Cinemas and theatres were all doing smashing business. Especially popular were the Gaiety Theatre's presentation of *Hansel and Gretel*, starring Jimmy O'Dea, and the Carlton's showing of the hilarious *Jailbirds*, with Laurel and Hardy. People were in the mood for fun.

Some were even overheard to say that they were hoping for some snow by Christmas.

To further bolster holiday spirits, on Christmas Eve the Government sprang what it called a "surprise announcement," as neither public nor coal merchants had any inkling of it. With a stock now of nearly half a million tons of British and American coal, and larger imports of British coal to "commence forthwith," the Government declared that, from New Year's Day, coal was "off the ration." Meaning that customers could purchase any quantity they desired, or could afford. The *Evening Herald* hailed it as an "unexpected Christmas box."[4] There was even speculation that in cities and towns turf "as a domestic fuel may largely disappear."

NEW YEAR'S EVE
Following Christmas, people's thoughts turned to New Year's Eve. A time for reflection. A year to remember, all right. Regarded as the worst hardship and human suffering since the Great Famine. As the *Irish Independent* wrote at year's end, "with a winter and early spring of unprecedented severity, 1947 will have few pleasant memories."[5] Particularly for the "weather experts," for whom it had been their most humiliating year ever. As the paper summed it up:

With one day left to run, 1947 will go down in weather history with a number of records . . . the story of weather contradictions which for Ireland must be unique . . . for which meteorologists will remember it.[6]

As well as every other living soul who had experienced it.

On 31 December throngs gathered outside Christ Church Cathedral for the traditional New Year's celebration. Exuberant Dubliners anxiously awaited the clanging of the mighty bells, sounds of horns and sirens from ships and factories, and a sweeping chorus of "Auld Lang Syne." Most had experienced it many times before. This year, however, it felt different.

Ordinarily, most people held warm sentiments for the year passing away. This New Year's Eve there was a pervasive mood of happiness that the year was finally ending. A shared feeling that they had "made it through" the awful ordeal. Tinged with a natural wariness about the new year ahead. As the *Irish Times* proffered, "when Éire peeps around the corner into 1948 to-night, it will need a crystal ball to indicate what the New Year may bring."[7]

One thing was certain, commented the *Irish Press*, the old year in its last gasps would have "few mourners." With a cold eye and cold heart, on 31 December the newspaper bade a fitting farewell to the year 1947:

When you die to-night, nobody will regret you, and there will be a general sigh of relief.[8]

*   *   *   *   *

NOTES

Prologue (p. 1–17)

1. "Action Stations", *Irish Times*, 18 March 1947, p. 5.
2. "Supplies," *Irish Press*, 14 January 1947, p. 4.
3. C. K. M. Douglas, "The Severe Winter of 1946 to 1947," *Meteorological Magazine*, vol. 76, no. 897 (March 1947), p. 51–6.
4. "The Snows of 1947," unpublished document on file at Met Éireann.
5. "Peculiar weather," *Time*, 31 March 1947. Copy on file at Met Éireann, no page cited.
6. "Blizzard sweeps Ireland," *Irish Independent*, 3 February 1947, p. 1.
7. Jim Nolan, "The big snow of '48," Archives, *Carlow Nationalist*, 24 April 2003.
8. "Snow menace," *Evening Herald*, 3 February 1947, p. 4.
9. "Country is facing 'first class' fuel crisis," *Irish Press*, 13 February 1947, p. 1.
10. "Oil fuel may keep industries open," *Irish Times*, 15 February 1947, p. 1.
11. "Days of gloom for house keepers," *Sunday Independent*, 12 January 1947, p. 7.
12. "Cold said to have doubled death-rate," *Irish Times*, 19 February 1947, p. 3.
13. "A plea for the old," *Irish Independent*, 14 February 1947, p. 7.
14. "Dublin paralysed by great freeze-up," *Sunday Independent*, 23 February 1947, p. 1.
15. "King Frost still reigns," *Irish Independent*, 22 February 1947, p.3.
16. "Fuel shortage may lead to closing of c.i.e. rail system," *Irish Times*, 21 February 1947, p. 1.
17. "National crisis," *Dublin Evening Mail*, 25 February 1947, p. 2.
18. "Cold comfort from Government," *Irish Independent*, 25 February 1947, p. 4.
19. "Where science fails," *Dublin Evening Mail*, 21 February 1947, p. 4.
20. Christy Wynne, "The greatest snowfall of the century," at homepage.eircom.net/~greenst/blizzardof47.html.
21. Thomas Crosby, "Memories of 1947 big snow live on," *Sligo Weekender*, 27 January 2004.
22. "Blizzard," *Cuisle na Tíre*, April 1947, p. 32.
23. "Blizzard," *Cuisle na Tíre*, April 1947, p. 34.
24. "Blizzard," *Cuisle na Tíre*, April 1947, p. 35.
25. "Bid to save starving livestock," *Irish Times*, 4 March 1947, p. 1.
26. "On nothing," *Irish Press*, 26 February 1947, p. 4.
27. "The blizzard has a warning," *Sunday Independent*, 9 March 1947, p. 7.
28. "Isolated in Dublin," *Sunday Independent*, 9 March 1947, p. 4.
29. "Ireland is threatened by worst floods in many years," *Irish Times*, 17 March 1947, p. 1.
30. "Grave national emergency," *Irish Independent*, 17 March 1947, p. 4.
31. "Fate of tillage drive still in the balance," *Irish Independent*, 3 April 1947, p. 2.
32. "A year of disappointments," *Irish Independent*, 31 December 1947, p. 1.
33. "Christmas," *Irish Press*, 24 December 1947, p. 4.
34. G. Manley, *Climate and the British Scene*, Fontana New Naturalist Series, February 1947, p. 270.
35. "After the storm," *Irish Press*, 22 March 1947, p. 3
36. "People lost in their hills," *Irish Press*, 14 February 1947, p. 6.
37. "An Irishman's Diary," *Irish Times*, 13 March 1947, p. 5.

Chapter 1 (p. 18–35)

1. "Weather frowned on fashions," *Irish Independent*, 9 August 1946, p. 5.
2. "Weather frowned on fashions," *Irish Independent*, 9 August 1946, p. 5.
3. "Rain storm causes wide havoc," *Irish Independent*, 13 August 1946, p. 5.
4. "Rain storm causes wide havoc," *Irish Independent*, 13 August 1946, p. 5.
5. "Rain storm causes wide havoc," *Irish Independent*, 13 August 1946, p. 5.
6. *Irish Independent*, 13 August 1946, p. 5.
7. *Irish Independent*, 13 August 1946, p. 5.
8. *Irish Independent*, 13 August 1946, p. 5.
9. "Wettest august in 16 years," *Irish Independent*, 2 September 1946, p. 5.
10. "Wheat crop may still give good yield," *Irish Independent*, 14 August 1946, p. 5.
11. "Cork wins another title," *Irish Independent*, 2 September 1946, p.
12. "Big harvest losses in many areas," *Irish Independent*, 5 September 1946, p. 5.
13. "Midlands suffer badly," *Irish Independent*, 6 September 1946, p. 5.
14. "Widespread floods menace harvest—Appeal for volunteers," *Irish Independent*, 6 September 1946, p. 5.
15. *Irish Independent*, 6 September 1946, p. 5.
16. "No ordinary crisis," *Irish Independent*, 16 September 1946, p. 7.
17. "No time to be lost," *Irish Independent*, 9 September 1946, p. 7.
18. "Father Flanagan tells of his Irish visit," *Irish Independent*, 6 September 1946, p. 3.
19. *Irish Independent*, 13 August 1946, p. 7.
20. "Week-end spurt to save harvest," *Irish Independent*, 14 September 1946, p. 5.
21. "Critical days for Ireland," *Irish Independent*, 14 September 1946, 1946, p. 5.
22. "Harvest army is winning battle," *Irish Independent*, 16 September 1946, p. 5.
23. Thomas Crosby, "Memories of the 1947 Big Snow live on," *Sligo Weekender*, 27 January 2004.
24. "End of year disillusions," *Irish Independent*, 1 January 1947, p. 3.
25. "Welcome to the new year," *Irish Press*, 1 January 1947, p. 1.
26. *Irish Independent*, 1 January 1947, p. 3.
27. Thomas Crosby, "Memories of the 1947 Big Snow live on," *Sligo Weekender*, 27 January 2004.

Chapter 2 (p. 36–57)

1. "A happy new year," *Irish Press*, 1 January 1947, p. 3.
2. "Irish astronomer's 1946 observations," *Irish Press*, 24 January 1947, p. 5.
3. "Ships held up by ice," *Irish Independent*, 1 January 1947, p. 5.
4. "Bread and flour to be rationed from January 18," *Irish Press*, 4 January 1947, p. 1.
5. "Weather report," *Evening Herald*, 8 January 1947, p. 1.
6. "Lightning hits public house; Snowstorms," *Irish Press*, 13 January 1947, p. 1.
7. "Lightning hits public house; Snowstorms," *Irish Press*, 13 January 1947, p. 1.
8. "Supplies," *Irish Press*, 14 January 1947, p. 4.
9. "Supplies," *Irish Press*, 14 January 1947, p. 4.
10. "Fuel crisis developing," *Irish Independent*, 14 January 1947, p. 5.
11. "Eire expected to eke out ration with maize," *Irish Independent*, 14 January 1947, p. 5.
12. "1847–1947," *Irish Press*, 14 January 1947, p. 4
13. "Flu sweeps city," *Irish Press*, 22 January 1947, p. 1.
14. "The first snow," *Irish Times*, 27 January 1947, p. 5.
15. "Drove up mountain with camera to get snow pictures," *Irish Press*, 28 January 1947, p. 1.

16. "Lifeboat's dash in swirling snow," *Irish Press*, 29 January 1947, p. 1.

17. "Thaw follows another night of frost," *Evening Herald*, 31 January 1947, p. 1.

18. C. K. M. Douglas, "The severe winter of 1946 to 1947," *Meteorological Magazine*, vol. 76, no. 897 (March 1947), p. 51–6.

19. "Widespread snow and frost—Blizzards slow up traffic," *Irish Independent*, 30 January 1947, p. 3.

20. "Widespread snow and frost—Blizzards slow up traffic," *Irish Independent*, 30 January 1947, p. 3.

21. "Frost takes over, but snow keeps turf 'marooned'," *Irish Press*, 30 January 1947, p. 1.

22. *Evening Herald*, 31 January 1947, p. 1.

23. "Coldest night for several years," *Evening Herald*, 29 January 1947, p. 1.

24. "Output is greatest need," *Irish Press*, 31 January 1947, p. 1.

25. "The snows of 1947," unpublished document on file at Met Éireann, no date or pagination.

26. "Death of James Larkin," *Irish Press*, 31 January 1947, p. 1.

27. "'Jim' Larkin dies—Seán O'Casey tribute," *Irish Times*, 31 January 1947, p. 1.

28. "For whom the bell tolls," *Evening Herald*, 23 January 1947, p. 4.

29. "City thaws as country freezes," *Irish Times*, 1 February 1947, p. 1.

30. "Winter tightens grip," *Evening Herald*, 29 January 1947, p. 1.

31. "Peculiar weather," *Time*, 31 March 1947.

32. "Peculiar weather," *Time*, 31 March 1947.

33. "Peculiar weather," *Time*, 31 March 1947.

Chapter 3 (p. 58–89)

1. "City thaws as country freezes," *Irish Times*, 1 February 1947, p. 1.

2. D. E. Foster, "Climate not changing, but we are now more vulnerable," *Irish Independent*, 13 February 1947, p. 5.

3. C. K. M. Douglas, "The severe winter of 1946 to 1947," *Meteorological Magazine*, vol. 76, no. 897 (March 1947), p. 51–6.

4. Gordon Manley, "Looking back at last winter: February 1947: Its place in meteorological history," *Weather*, vol. 2 (1947), p. 267.

5. "Eye-witness story," *Irish Times*, 3 February 1947, p. 1.

6. "Irish ship aground in gale," *Irish Independent*, 3 February 1947, p. 1.

7. *Irish Times*, 3 February 1947, p. 1.

8. "7,250-ton Irish ship runs aground off Co. Cork," *Irish Times*, 3 February 1947, p. 1.

9. *Irish Independent*, 3 February 1947, p. 1.

10. *Irish Times*, 3 February 1947, p. 1.

11. *Irish Times*, 3 February 1947, p. 1.

12. "Blizzard sweeps ireland," *Irish Independent*, 3 February 1947, p. 1.

13. "Tons of snow," *Dublin Evening Mail*, 3 February 1947, p. 2.

14. Jim Nolan, "The Big Snow of '47," Archives, *Carlow Nationalist*, 24 April 2003.

15. "Plight of County Wicklow residents," *Irish Independent*, 7 February 1947, p. 5.

16. "Zoo monkeys down with pneumonia," *Irish Press*, 1 February, 1947 p. 1

17. "Zoo monkeys down with pneumonia," *Irish Press*, 1 February, 1947 p. 1.

18. "Snow menace," *Evening Herald*, 3 February 1947, p. 4.

19. "Influenza epidemic threatened," *Irish Times*, 14 April 1947, p. 1.

20. "Rheumatic fever a heart crippler," *Sunday Independent*, 12 January 1947, p. 7.

21. "'Quickfire' flu epidemic," *Irish Press*, 4 February 1947, p. 7.
22. "Big Jim crosses the city," *Irish Press*, 4 February 1947, p. 1.
23. "Big Jim crosses the city," *Irish Press*, 4 February 1947, p. 1.
24. "Big Jim crosses the city," *Irish Press*, 4 February 1947, p. 1.
25. "Cut off by snow," *Irish Times*, 6 February 1947, p. 4.
26. "Cut off by snow," *Irish Times*, 6 February 1947, p. 4.
27. "The Taoiseach 30 years a Dáil member," *Irish Press*, 4 February 1947, p. 7.
28. *Irish Times*, 6 February 1947 p. 4.
29. "Britain stops coal exports from N.W. ports," *Irish Times*, 7 February 1947, p. 1.
30. "Shortage of fuel starts crisis in Irish industry," *Irish Times*, 6 February 1947, p. 1.
31. "Shortage of fuel starts crisis in Irish industry," *Irish Times*, 6 February 1947, p. 1.
32. *Irish Times*, 6 February 1947, p. 1.
33. "Hunger," *Evening Herald*, 6 February 1947, p. 2.
34. "County Wicklow hills trek," *Irish Independent*, 8 February 1947, p. 7.
35. "Warmer to-day but more snow likely," *Evening Herald*, 5 February 1947, p. 1.

Chapter 4 (p. 90–123)
1. George Booth, "Winter 1947 in the British Isles," *Weather*, vol. 62, no. 3 (March 2007), p. 61–7.
2. "Pole tells of loss of collier," *Irish Times*, 15 February 1947, p. 1.
3. Laskin, *The Children's Blizzard*, p. 184.
4. Laskin, *The Children's Blizzard*, p. 186.
5. Laskin, *The Children's Blizzard*, p. 184.
6. Laskin, *The Children's Blizzard*, p. 186.
7. "Keep the home fires burning," *Evening Herald*, 8 February 1947, p. 4.
8. "People 'lost' in their hills," *Irish Press*, 14 February 1947, p. 6.
9. "People 'lost' in their hills," *Irish Press*, 14 February 1947, p. 6.
10. "News from the zoo," *Irish Times*, 13 February 1947, p. 3.
11. "80, and bathed yesterday," *Irish Press*, 10 February 1947, p. 1.
12. "Week-end of wild weather," *Irish Independent*, 10 February 1947, p. 5.
13. "Success at third attempt," *Irish Independent*, 11 February 1947, p. 5.
14. "Success at third attempt," *Irish Independent*, 11 February 1947, p. 5.
15. "British moves on coal crux," *Irish Press*, 13 February 1947, p. 1.
16. "Shaw's solution for fuel crisis," *Irish Times*, 15 February 1947, p. 1.
17. "Second seaman from collier washed ashore," *Irish Times*, 14 February 1947, p. 1.
18. "Waterford bound ship overdue," *Irish Press*, 13 February 1947, p. 9.
19. *Irish Times*, 14 February 1947, p. 1.
20. "Country is facing 'first-class' fuel crisis," *Irish Press*, 13 February 1947, p. 1.
21. "Country is facing 'first-class' fuel crisis," *Irish Press*, 13 February 1947, p. 1.
22. *Irish Press*, 13 February 1947, p. 1.
23. "Country shocked by fuel statement," *Irish Independent*, 14 February 1947, p. 5.
24. "Country shocked by fuel statement," *Irish Independent*, 14 February 1947, p. 5.
25. *Evening Herald*, 8 February 1947, p. 4.
26. Margaret Lee, "Do not let wet turf get you down: It can be burned," *Irish Press*, 14 February 1947, p. 3.
27. "Dublin firemen's busy year," *Irish Times*, 5 February 1947, p. 7.
28. "Oil fuel may keep industries going," *Irish Times*, 15 February 1947, p. 1.

29. "Dublin again 'dimmed-out'," *Irish Independent,* 15 February 1947, p.7.

30. "City's poor hit hard by fuel crisis," *Irish Times,* 15 February, 1947, p. 3.

31. "Battening on the poor," *Evening Herald,* 14 March 1947, p. 4.

32. "Gas hours reduced again," *Sunday Independent,* 9 February 1947, p. 1.

33. "Deputies were up in stars," *Irish Independent,* 14 February 1947, p. 5.

34. Mary Frances Keating, "Days of gloom for housekeepers," *Sunday Independent,* 12 January 1947, p. 7.

35. *Irish Times,* 15 February 1947, p. 1.

36. "Letters to the editor," *Dublin Evening Mail,* 15 February 1947, p. 3.

37. "Letters to the editor," *Dublin Evening Mail,* 15 February 1947, p. 3.

38. "Letters to the editor," *Dublin Evening Mail,* 15 February 1947, p. 3.

39. D. E. Foster, "Climate not changing, but we are now more vulnerable," *Irish Independent,* 13 February 1947, p. 5.

Chapter 5 (p. 124–53)

1. John D. Sheridan, "An article on the weather," *Irish Independent,* 22 March 1947, p. 6.

2. *Dublin Opinion,* April 1947, p. 48.

3. "An Irishman's Diary," *Irish Times,* 18 March 1947, p. 5.

4. "A new form of frostbite," *Evening Herald,* 17 February 1947, p. 4.

5. "The importance of optimism," *Sunday Independent,* 16 February 1947, p. 4.

6. G. M. Hawksley, "February 1947," *Weather,* vol. 2 (1947), p. 101.

7. O'Flaherty, Ken, "Looking back: Dr Ken O'Flaherty MB Bch BAO '52 recalls the blizzard of '47," *UCD Connections,* 7 (autumn–winter 2001).

8. "The fuel crisis," *Irish Press,* 18 February 1947, p. 4.

9. "Dublin had a blizzard—and some sun," *Evening Herald,* 19 February 1947, p. 1.

10. "King Frost still reigns," *Irish Independent,* 22 February 1947, p. 2.

11. "Fuel shortages may lead to closing of c.i.e. rail system," *Irish Times,* 21 February 1947, p. 1.

12. "Cold said to have doubled death-rate," *Irish Times,* 19 February 1947, p. 3.

13. Turtle Bunbury, "So you think it's freezing?" *Irish Daily Mail,* 9 January 2010, p. 46.

14. "A plea for the old," *Irish Independent,* 14 February 1947, p. 7.

15. "Royal Meteorological Society News—The severe winter," *Weather,* vol. 2 (1947), p. 89.

16. "Experts say snow has gone," *Irish Times,* 20 February 1947, p. 4.

17. "Experts say snow has gone," *Irish Times,* 20 February 1947, p. 4.

18. George Booth, "Winter 1947 in the British Isles," *Weather,* vol. 62, no. 3 (March 2007), p. 61–7.

19. "Worst blizzard for 25 years hits Ireland," *Irish Times,* 26 February 1947, p. 1.

20. "Sun actually shone in Dublin to-day," *Evening Herald,* 22 February 1947, p. 1.

21. "King Frost still reigns," *Irish Independent,* 22 February 1947, p. 2.

22. "Main roads dangerous after heavy snowfalls," *Irish Times,* 22 February 1947, p. 1.

23. "Many street fall casualties," *Irish Times,* 22 February 1947, p. 1.

24. "Week-end of many weathers," *Irish Independent,* 24 February 1947, p. 5.

25. *Evening Herald,* 22 February 1947, p. 1.

26. *Evening Herald,* 14 February 1947, p. 1.

27. *Irish Independent,* 22 February 1947, p. 1.

28. "Dublin paralysed by great freeze-up," *Sunday Independent,* 23 February 1947, p. 1.

29. "Dublin paralysed by great freeze-up," *Sunday Independent,* 23 February 1947, p. 1.

30. "Dublin experiences a welcome thaw," *Evening Herald,* 24 February 1947, p. 1.

31. Ora E. Kilroe, "After the storm," *Irish Press*, 22 March 1947, p. 3.
32. "Tribute to bus drivers," *Irish Independent*, 25 February 1947, p. 4.
33. "Tribute to the roundsmen," *Dublin Evening Mail*, 15 March 1947, p. 2.
34. *Irish Times*, 20 February 1947, p. 4.
35. Keith J. Collie, "1947: The Year of the Big Snow," *Irish Mountain Log*, winter 2007, p. 28–9.
36. *Irish Independent*, 22 February 1947, p. 2.
37. "Country is again in grip of frost and snow," *Irish Press*, 21 February 1947, p. 1.
38. *Irish Times*, 19 February 1947, p. 3.
39. "Sheep still lost in mountains," *Irish Press*, 21 February 1947, p. 1.
40. *Evening Herald*, 24 February 1947, p. 1.
41. "Grey crows have picked out the eyes of helpless animals caught in the snow," *Irish Times*, 13 March 1947, p. 1.
42. "Rail restrictions hit trade at Dublin cattle market," *Irish Independent*, 20 February 1947, p. 5.
43. Ora E. Kilroe, "After the storm," *Irish Press*, 22 March 1947, p. 3.
44. "Hungry deer," *Irish Press*, 10 March 1947, p. 1.
45. Ora E. Kilroe, "After the storm," *Irish Press*, 22 March 1947, p. 3.
46. "Sunshine follows night of snow," *Irish Times*, 24 February 1947, p. 1.

Chapter 6 (p. 154–70)

1. "Bleak fuel prospect for capital," *Evening Herald*, 24 February 1947, p. 1.
2. "Letters to the editor," *Irish Times*, 16 April 1947, p. 5.
3. "Battening on the poor," *Evening Herald*, 14 March 1947, p. 4.
4. "Traffic obstructing thoughtlessness," *Irish Times*, 17 March 1947, p. 3.
5. "Good grooming," *Irish Independent*, 25 February 1947, p. 3.
6. "A tenement scene," *Dublin Evening Mail*, 24 February 1947, p. 2.
7. "Appalling scenes of want in Dublin," *Dublin Evening Mail*, 25 February 1947, p. 2.
8. "An appeal for the poor of Dublin," *Sunday Independent*, 9 March, 1947 p. 6.
9. Anna Kelly, "I join the fuel queue," *Irish Press*, 27 February 1947, p. 3.
10. "Letters to the editor," *Dublin Evening Mail*, 24 February 1947, p. 2
11. "Cold comfort from Government," *Irish Independent*, 25 February 1947, p. 4.
12. "National crisis," *Dublin Evening Mail*, 25 February 1947, p. 2.
13. "Fine Gael to move condemnation of Government," *Irish Times*, 25 February 1947, p. 1.
14. "The lesson," *Irish Press*, 25 February 1947, p. 4.
15. *Dublin Evening Mail*, 25 February 1947, p. 2.
16. *Irish Independent*, 25 February 1947, p. 4.
17. "E.S.B. and the fuel crisis," *Dublin Evening Mail*, 25 February 1947, p. 3.
18. J. F. Hoey, "Gas from turf," *Dublin Evening Mail*, 21 February, 1947, p. 4.
19. "Map shows Ireland to be rich in large coal fields," *Irish Times*, 11 March, 1947, p. 7.
20. John D. Sheridan, "An article on the weather," *Irish Independent*, 22 March 1947, p. 6.
21. "Prophets and the weather," *Evening Herald*, 21 February 1947, p. 4.
22. "Where science fails," *Dublin Evening Mail*, 21 February 1947, p. 4.
23. "Weather experts differ," *Irish Independent*, 21 February 1947, p. 4.
24. "Weather experts differ," *Irish Independent*, 21 February 1947, p. 4.
25. "Cable sets the weather experts buzzing," *Evening Herald*, 24 February 1947, p. 1.
26. "Weather report," *Evening Herald*, 24 February 1947, p. 1.

Chapter 7 (p. 171–213)

1. "Four-foot drifts block roads," *Irish Times*, 26 February 1947, p. 1.
2. George Booth, "Winter 1947 in the British Isles," *Weather*, vol. 62, no. 2 (March 2007), p. 61–7.
3. Canon Martin Halloran, "People had to be dug from houses," *Sligo Weekender*, 26 October 2004.
4. Christy Wynne, "The greatest snowfall of the century," at homepage.eircom.net/ ~greenst/ blizzardof47.html.
5. Miriam Sweetman, "30 men had to dig path to grave," *Sligo Weekender*, 11 April 2006,.
6. Keith J. Collie, "1947: The Year of the Big Snow," *Irish Mountain Log*, winter 2007, p. 28–9.
7. "Blizzard's big damage," *Irish Press*, 27 February 1947, p. 5.
8. "Large areas are still isolated," *Irish Independent*, 27 February 1947, p. 5.
9. Turtle Bunbury, "So you think it's freezing?" *Irish Daily Mail*, 9 January 2010, p. 46.
10. Keith J. Collie, "1947: The Year of the Big Snow," *Irish Mountain Log*, winter 2007, p. 29.
11. "Snowed-up families dig their way out," *Irish Times*, 27 February 1947, p. 1.
12. "Snowed-up families dig their way out," *Irish Times*, 27 February 1947, p. 1.
13. "Conditions beggar description," *Evening Herald*, 26 February 1947, p. 1.
14. *Irish Independent*, 27 February 1947, p. 5.
15. Keith J. Collie, "1947: The Year of the Big Snow," *Irish Mountain Log*, winter 2007, p. 29.
16. "Weather hits the Dáil," *Evening Herald*, 26 February 1947, p. 4.
17. *Irish Times*, 26 February 1947, p. 1.
18. "Long hill drifts beat jeep," *Irish Press*, 26 February 1947, p. 1.
19. "Long hill drifts beat jeep," *Irish Press*, 26 February 1947, p. 1.
20. "Long hill drifts beat jeep," *Irish Press*, 26 February 1947, p. 1.
21. "Long hill drifts beat jeep," *Irish Press*, 26 February 1947, p. 1.
22. *Evening Herald*, 26 February 1947, p. 4.
23. *Irish Press*, 26 February 1947, p. 1.
24. Miriam Sweetman, "30 men had to dig path to grave," *Sligo Weekender*, 11 April 2006.
25. "Blizzard," *Cuisle na Tíre*, April 1947, p. 31–6.
26. "Blizzard," *Cuisle na Tíre*, April 1947, p. 34.
27. "Blizzard," *Cuisle na Tíre*, April 1947, p. 34.
28. "Blizzard," *Cuisle na Tíre*, April 1947, p. 35.
29. "Blizzard," *Cuisle na Tíre*, April 1947, p. 36
30. "Blizzard," *Cuisle na Tíre*, April 1947, p. 36
31. "All-out drive to repair blizzard havoc," *Irish Press*, 27 February 1947, p. 1.
32. "Worst blizzard in 25 years hits Ireland," *Irish Times*, 26 February 1947, p. 1.
33. *Cuisle na Tíre*, April 1947, p. 36.
34. "Country hit by fierce blizzard," *Irish Independent*, 26 February 1947, p. 5.
35. "Transport, electricity and phones disorganised," *Irish Times*, 27 February, 1947, p. 1.
36. "On nothing," *Irish Press*, 26 February, 1947, p. 4.
37. Turtle Bunbury, "So you think it's freezing?" *Irish Daily Mail*, 9 January 2010, p. 46.
38. Jim Nolan, "The Big Snow of '47," Archives, *Carlow Nationalist*, 24 April 2003.
39. *Irish Times*, 26 February 1947, p. 1.
40. "The daddy of them all: The '47 Snow," *Glens of Antrim Historical Project*.
41. Keith J. Collie, "1947: The Year of the Big Snow," *Irish Mountain Log*, winter 2007, p. 29.
42. Thomas Crosby, "Memories of 1947 Big Snow live on," *Sligo Weekender*, 27 January 2004.
43. "The daddy of them all: The '47 Snow," *Glens of Antrim Historical Project*.

44. Bunbury, Turtle, "The big snows of 1947, 1963 and 1982," at turtlebunbury.com/history /history_irish/history_irish_big_snow.htm.

45. Bunbury, Turtle, "The big snows of 1947, 1963 and 1982," at turtlebunbury.com/history/ history_irish/history_irish_big_snow.htm.

46. *Cuisle na Tíre*, April 1947, p. 33.

47. *Cuisle na Tíre*, April 1947, p. 36.

48. *Irish Independent*, 27 February 1947, p. 5.

49. "Bid to relieve Roundwood fails again," *Irish Press*, 27 February 1947, p. 1.

50. "The hopes of Dubliners are now dashed," *Evening Herald*, 25 February 1947, p. 1.

51. "State urged to free army for tree cutting," *Irish Times*, 27 February 1947, p. 5.

52. "State urged to free army for tree cutting," *Irish Times*, 27 February 1947, p. 5.

53. "State urged to free army for tree cutting," *Irish Times*, 27 February 1947, p. 5.

54. Keith J. Collie, "1947: The Year of the Big Snow," *Irish Mountain Log*, winter 2007, p. 28–9.

55. *Irish Press*, 27 February 1947, p. 1.

56. *Irish Times*, 26 February 1947, p. 1.

57. *Irish Times*, 27 February 1947, p. 5.

58. *Irish Press*, 27 February 1947, p. 5.

59. "Corporation move in fuel crisis," *Irish Press*, 27 February 1947, p. 5.

60. *Irish Times*, 27 February 1947, p. 5.

61. *Irish Press*, 27 February 1947, p. 1.

62. "Snowbound buses and motorists released," *Dublin Evening Mail*, 28 February 1947, p. 6.

63. "An Irishman's Diary," *Irish Times*, 13 March 1947, p. 5.

64. "Fuel reserves filling gap," *Irish Press*, 28 February 1947, p. 1.

65. "Phoenix Park trees to be cut," *Irish Times*, 28 February 1947, p. 1.

66. "Sunshine brings problems in blizzard's wake,"*Irish Times*, 28 February 1947, p. 1.

67. "Search for 'lost' lorries," *Irish Press*, 1 March 1947, p. 7.

68. "Wind change may improve the weather," *Irish Press*, 27 February 1947, p. 1.

69. "Ireland lashed by sleet and snow to-day," *Evening Herald*, 25 February 1947, p. 1.

Chapter 8 (p. 214–35)

1. *Carlow Nationalist*, 19 November 1999.

2. Turtle Bunbury, "So you think it's freezing?" *Irish Daily Mail*, 9 January 2010, p. 46.

3. Keith J. Collie, "1947: The Year of The Big Snow," *Irish Mountain Log*, winter 2007, p. 28–29.

4. "Like Steppes of Siberia," *Irish Independent*, 4 March 1947, p. 5.

5. "Blizzard," *Cuisle na Tíre*, April 1947, p. 31–6.

6. "Breaking through to ice-bound west," *Irish Independent*, 3 March 1947, p. 5.

7. "Breaking through to ice-bound west," *Irish Independent*, 3 March 1947, p. 5.

8. "Blizzard," *Cuisle na Tíre*, April 1947, p. 33.

9. "Blizzard," *Cuisle na Tíre*, April 1947, p. 34.

10. "Blizzard," *Cuisle na Tíre*, April 1947, p. 35.

11. "Blizzard," *Cuisle na Tíre*, April 1947, p. 36.

12. "Air effort to relieve 'lost' mountain hamlets fails," *Irish Press*, 1 March 1947, p. 1.

13. "Wicklow men are beating the snow," *Irish Press*, 10 March 1947, p. 1.

14. "Blizzard," *Cuisle na Tíre*, April 1947, p. 34.

15. "Snowed-up convoy enters Sligo," *Irish Independent*, 4 March 1947, p.5.

16. "Passengers dug for eight hours on road to Sligo," *Sunday Independent*, 2 March 1947, p. 1.

17. *Irish Press,* 1 March 1947, p. 1.
18. "Tatler," *Ballina Herald,* March 1947.
19. "Blizzard," *Cuisle na Tíre,* April 1947, p. 33.
20. Jill Uris, *Ireland Revisited,* p. 73.
21. "More snow sweeps southern counties," *Irish Press,* 5 March 1947, p. 1.
22. *Irish Press,* 1 March 1947, p. 1.
23. "Blizzard," *Cuisle na Tíre,* April 1947, p. 35.
24. Miriam Sweetman, "30 men had to dig path to grave," *Sligo Weekender,* 11 April 2006, no page.
25. Miriam Sweetman, "30 men had to dig path to grave," *Sligo Weekender,* 11 April 2006, no page.
26. Canon Martin Halloran, "People had to be dug from houses," *Sligo Weekender,* 26 October 2004.
27. *Irish Press,* 1 March 1947, p. 1.
28. "Wicklow villagers mob breadvan," *Dublin Evening Mail,* 28 February 1947, p. 6.
29. "Blizzard," *Cuisle na Tíre,* April 1947, p. p. 35.
30. *Irish Independent,* 3 March 1947, p. 5.
31. "Blizzard," *Cuisle na Tíre,* April 1947, p. 36.
32. "Blizzard," *Cuisle na Tíre,* April 1947, p. 36.
33. "Blizzard," *Cuisle na Tíre,* April 1947, p. 35.
34. "Stock starve in Dublin Mountains," *Irish Press,* 3 March 1947, p. 1.
35. "'Food relief for the isolated," *Irish Press,* 5 March 1947, p. 5.
36. "Cattle and sheep die of starvation," *Irish Press,* 6 March 1947, p.1
37. Ora E. Kilroe, "After the storm," *Irish Press,* 22 March 1947, p. 3.
38. *Irish Independent,* 3 March 1947, p. 5.
39. "Move to aid stock dying in snow belt," *Irish Press,* 4 March 1947, p. 5.

Chapter 9 (p. 236–54)

1.   "Skater drowned in River Erne," *Irish Press,* 6 March 1947, p. 1.
2.   "Sunshine beating snow," *Irish Times,* 3 March 1947, p. 1.
3.   "Dublin boys lost in quarry hole," *Irish Independent,* 3 March 1947, p. 5.
4.   "Spain game stopped as intruders rush pitch," *Irish Press,* 3 March 1947, p. 1.
5.   "Bodies of two victims found," *Irish Independent,* 4 March 1947, p. 2.
6.   "Quarry pond tragedy," *Evening Herald,* 11 March 1947, p. 3.
7.   "Big crowd sees Irish victory," *Irish Independent,* 3 March 1947, p.5
8.   *Irish Independent,* 3 March 1947, p. 5.
9.   *Evening Herald,* 11 March 1947, p. 3.
10. *Irish Independent,* 3 March 1947, p. 5.
11. *Evening Herald,* 11 March 1947, p. 3.
12. *Evening Herald,* 11 March 1947, p. 3.
13. *Evening Herald,* 11 March 1947, p. 3.
14. "3 boys feared drowned in quarry pond," *Irish Times,* 3 March 1947, p. 1.
15. *Irish Independent,* 4 March 1947, p. 5.
16. "Dublin quarry pond claims three young victims," *Evening Herald,* 3 March 1947, p. 1.
17. *Evening Herald,* 11 March 1947, p. 3.
18. *Irish Independent,* 3 March 1947, p. 5.
19. *Irish Press,* 3 March 1947, p. 1.
20. *Evening Herald,* 11 March 1947, p. 3.

21. *Irish Independent,* 4 March 1947, p. 2.
22. *Evening Herald,* 11 March 1947, p. 3.
23. *Irish Independent,* 3 March 1947, p. 5.
24. "Dangerous quarry pool may be filled in," *Irish Times,* 4 March 1947, p. 1.
25. *Irish Independent,* 4 March 1947, p. 2.
26. *Irish Times,* 3 March 1947, p. 1.
27. *Irish Times,* 3 March 1947, p. 1.
28. *Irish Independent,* 3 March 1947, p. 5.
29. "Death on the ice," *Dublin Evening Mail,* 3 March 1947, p. 2.
30. "Death on the ice," *Dublin Evening Mail,* 3 March 1947, p. 2.
31. "Death on the ice," *Dublin Evening Mail,* 3 March 1947, p. 2.
32. "Letters to the Editor," *Dublin Evening Mail,* 11 March 1947, p. 2.
33. *Dublin Evening Mail,* 11 March 1947, p. 2.

Chapter 10 (p. 255–84)
1. "Warm sunshine brings thaw," *Irish Independent,* 7 March 1947, p. 3.
2. "Bid to save starving livestock," *Irish Times,* 4 March 1947, p. 1.
3. "Blizzard," *Cuisle na Tíre,* April 1947, p. 31–6.
4. "Bus service returning to normal," *Irish Times,* 8 March 1947, p. 1.
5. "40,000 tons of firewood logs," *Irish Press,* 1 March 1947, p. 1.
6. "Rescuers fighting snow in bid to reach sick family," *Irish Times,* 8 March 1947, p. 1.
7. George Booth, "Winter 1947 in the British Isles," *Weather,* vol. 62, no. 3 (March 2007), p. 61–7.
8. "Hero of many sea adventures," *Irish Independent,* 7 March 1947, p. 5.
9. "Hero of many sea adventures," *Irish Independent,* 7 March 1947, p. 5.
10. "Weather reports," *Irish Press,* 5 March 1947, p. 5.
11. "Ship runs aground off Dublin," *Irish Press,* 5 March 1947, p. 1.
12. "Grain ship wrecked off Dublin coast," *Irish Times,* 5 March 1947, p. 1.
13. "Ice holds canal boats," *Irish Press,* 28 February 1947, p. 1.
14. "Plight of barge crews at Edenderry," *Irish Independent,* 28 February 1947, p. 2.
15. *Irish Press,* 5 March 1947, p. 1.
16. *Irish Press,* 5 March 1947, p. 1.
17. *Irish Press,* 5 March 1947, p. 1.
18. *Irish Times,* 5 March 1947, p. 1.
19. *Irish Times,* 5 March 1947, p. 1.
20. *Irish Press,* 5 March 1947, p. 1.
21. "Hopes of saving grain gone," *Irish Press,* 6 March 1947, p. 1.
22. "The broken Bolivar lies on Kish Bank," *Irish Press,* 6 March 1947, p. 1.
23. "Lights of Dublin," *Evening Herald,* 6 March 1947, p. 4.
24. "Captain boards wrecked Bolivar," *Irish Press,* 7 March 1947, p. 1.
25. "Roundwood kept its lights on," *Irish Press,* 7 March 1947, p. 5.
26. *Irish Times,* 8 March 1947, p. 1.
27. *Irish Independent,* 7 March 1947, p. 1.
28. "Britain aids 'parachute food' plan," *Irish Times,* 7 March 1947, p. 1.

29. "Wicklow men are beating the snow," *Irish Press*, 10 March 1947, p. 1.
30. "Roundwood relieved after five weeks," *Irish Independent*, 7 March 1947, p. 5.
31. "People's ordeal in frozen Wicklow," *Sunday Independent*, 9 March 1947, p. 1.
32. *Irish Independent*, 7 March 1947, p. 3.
33. *Irish Times*, 8 March 1947, p. 1.
34. *Irish Times*, 8 March 1947, p. 1.
35. "Lord Mountevans lost every suit in the Bolivar," *Irish Times*, 10 March 1947, p. 1.

Chapter 11 (p. 285–306)

1. Michael J. Murphy, "Bog road gossip on a wintry day," *Irish Press*, 25 February 1947, p. 5.
2. "Isolated in Dublin!" *Sunday Independent*, 9 March 1947, p. 4.
3. "Isolated in Dublin!" *Sunday Independent*, 9 March 1947, p. 4.
4. "Isolation and grievance," *Western People*, 8 March 1947, p. 1.
5. "Wheat drive to avoid hunger, call by Taoiseach," *Irish Press*, 10 March 1947, p. 1.
6. "February's freakish weather," *Irish Independent*, 3 March 1947, p. 3.
7. Dickson, *Arctic Ireland*, p. 12.
8. Dickson, *Arctic Ireland*, p. 12.
9. Timothy Cronin, "It was far worse in 1740," *Irish Press*, 7 February 1963, p. 9.
10. *Irish Independent*, 3 March 1947, p. 3.
11. *Irish Independent*, 3 March 1947, p. 3.
12. "I join the fuel queue," *Irish Press*, 27 February 1947, p. 3.
13. "Fifty-two years ago Dublin had its 'Night of the Big Snow,'" *Sunday Independent*, 16 March 1947, p. 2.
14. *Irish Daily Independent*, 14 January 1895, p. 5.
15. "The Blizzard," *Irish Daily Independent*, 15 January 1895, p. 5.
16. "Gulf Stream or atom bomb blamed," *Dublin Evening Mail*, 24 February 1947, p. 3.
17. "The stars and the weather," *Dublin Evening Mail*, 25 February 1947, p. 2.
18. "Cable sets the weather experts buzzing," *Evening Herald*, 24 February 1947, p. 1.
19. "A playboy and a prophecy?" *Irish Press*, 26 February 1947, p. 4.
20. "A playboy and a prophecy?" *Irish Press*, 26 February 1947, p. 4.
21. "A playboy and a prophecy?" *Irish Press*, 26 February 1947, p. 4.
22. "Action stations," *Irish Times*, 18 March 1947, p. 5.
23. "Crazy weather at the week-end," *Irish Press*, 10 March 1947, p. 1.
24. "An Irishman's Diary," *Irish Times*, 13 March 1947, p. 5.
25. P. S. O'Hegarty, "The blizzard had a warning," *Sunday Independent*, 9 March 1947, p. 4.
26. P. S. O'Hegarty, "The blizzard had a warning," *Sunday Independent*, 9 March 1947, p. 4.
27. "Dublin's oldest charity," *Dublin Evening Mail*, 15 March 1947, p. 2.
28. "Heavy weather for Moscow," *Dublin Evening Mail*, 10 March 1947, p. 3.
29. "Quarry pond tragedy," *Evening Herald*, 11 March 1947, p. 3.
30. "Quarry pond tragedy," *Evening Herald*, 11 March 1947, p. 3.
31. "Quarry pond tragedy," *Evening Herald*, 11 March 1947, p. 3.
32. "Quarry pond tragedy," *Evening Herald*, 11 March 1947, p. 3.
33. "Only united effort can get crops in," *Irish Press*, 7 March 1947, p. 1.
34. *Irish Press*, 10 March 1947, p. 1.
35. "Blizzard sweeps the North," *Irish Times*, 13 March 1947, p. 1.

Chapter 12 (p. 307–31)

1. "The calendar says spring—but the weather says winter," *Sunday Independent*, 16 March 1947, p. 1.
2. *Dublin Opinion*, March 1947, p. 7.
3. *Sunday Independent*, 16 March 1947, p. 1.
4. "Big tillage hold-up by floods," *Irish Press*, 17 March 1947, p. 1.
5. "Big tillage hold-up by floods," *Irish Press*, 17 March 1947, p. 1.
6. "Ireland is threatened by worst flooding in many years," *Irish Times*, 17 March 1947, p. 1.
7. *Irish Press*, 17 March 1947, p. 1.
8. *Irish Times*, 17 March 1947, p. 1.
9. "Serious loss of stores," *Irish Independent*, 18 March 1947, p. 6.
10. "Another blizzard in south and east," *Irish Independent*, 17 March 1947, p. 5.
11. "Heavy rains check tillage work in many counties," *Irish Times*, 31 March 1947, p. 1.
12. "Heavy rains check tillage work in many counties," *Irish Times*, 31 March 1947, p. 1.
13. "Outlook for farmers is worst yet," *Irish Times*, 15 March 1947, p.1.
14. *Irish Times*, 17 March 1947, p. 1.
15. *Irish Times*, 17 March 1947, p. 1.
16. "Landslides disrupt rail services," *Irish Times*, 18 March 1947, p. 1.
17. "Landslides disrupt rail services," *Irish Times*, 18 March 1947, p. 1.
18. "Landslides disrupt rail services," *Irish Times*, 18 March 1947, p. 1.
19. "Our duty to the birds," *Irish Independent*, 17 March 1947, p. 4.
20. *Irish Times*, 1 March 1947, p. 1.
21. "Subsiding floods show trail of damage," *Irish Press*, 18 March 1947, p. 5.
22. "Subsiding floods show trail of damage," *Irish Press*, 18 March 1947, p. 5.
23. *Irish Times*, 17 March 1947, p. 1.
24. *Irish Independent*, 17 March 1947, p. 5.
25. "The day when the shamrock was 'dear'," *Evening Herald*, 17 March 1947, p. 1.
26. "How Dubliners and visitors spent the day," *Irish Press*, 18 March 1947, p. 5.
27. "Shamrock enters black market," *Dublin Evening Mail*, 17 March 1947, p. 3.
28. *Evening Herald*, 17 March 1947, p. 1.
29. "Mr. de Valera's message to Birmingham," *Irish Press*, 17 March 1947, p. 1.
30. "Mr. de Valera asks for help to end partition," *Irish Times*, 18 March 1947, p. 1.
31. *Irish Times*, 17 March 1947, p. 1.
32. "Fine weather soon—or no harvest," *Sunday Independent*, 16 March 1947, p. 1.
33. "National crisis," *Dublin Evening Mail*, 17 March 1947, p. 2.
34. "Farmers plan 24-hour day to ensure harvest," *Irish Times*, 18 March 1947, p. 1.
35. *Sunday Independent*, 16 March 1947, p. 1.
36. *Irish Times*, 18 March 1947, p. 1.
37. "Grave national emergency," *Irish Independent*, 17 March 1947, p.4
38. Ora E. Kilroe, "After the storm," *Irish Press*, 22 March 1947, p. 3.
39. "Sufferings of old folk," *Dublin Evening Mail*, 17 March 1947, p. 2.
40. "Grow food to avoid famine," *Sunday Independent*, 23 March 1947, p. 4.
41. "Grow food to avoid famine," *Sunday Independent*, 23 March 1947, p. 4.

42. *Irish Independent,* 17 March 1947, p. 4.
43. *Irish Times,* 18 March 1947, p. 1.
44. *Dublin Evening Mail,* 17 March 1947, p. 2.
45. *Irish Independent,* 17 March 1947, p. 4.
46. "Guinness cut supplies," *Irish Press,* 25 March 1947, p. 1.
47. "Guinness cut supplies," *Irish Press,* 25 March 1947, p. 1.
48. "Suspend tourist trade called for by Dr. O'Higgins," *Irish Times,* 22 March 1947, p. 7.
49. *Dublin Evening Mail,* 17 March 1947, p. 2.
50. *Irish Times,* 15 March 1947, p. 1.
51. *Dublin Evening Mail,* 17 March 1947, p. 2.
52. "A Government plan to help farmers in present crisis," *Irish Times,* 19 March 1947, p. 1.

Chapter 13 (p. 332–46)

1. Ora E. Kilroe, "After the storm," *Irish Press,* 22 March 1947, p. 3.
2. "Outlook for farmers is worst yet," *Irish Times,* 15 March 1947, p. 1.
3. "Sowing the crops," *Irish Press,* 20 March 1947, p. 4.
4. "Five weeks to till 2,000,000 acres," *Sunday Independent,* 23 March 1947, p. 1.
5. "In the same boat," *Irish Times,* 22 March 1947, p. 7.
6. "Tillage drive now under way," *Irish Independent,* 28 March 1947, p.4
7. "March ends in tillage set-back," *Irish Press,* 31 March 1947, p. 1.
8. Turtle Bunbury, "So you think it's freezing?" *Irish Daily Mail,* 9 January 2010, p. 46.
9. "Fate of tillage drive still in the balance," *Irish Independent,* 3 April 1947, p. 2.
10. "An Irishman's Diary," *Irish Times,* 28 March 1947, p. 5.
11. "The bad weather made us good neighbours," *Irish Press,* 29 March 1947, p. 3.
12. *Irish Daily Mail,* 9 January 2010, p. 46.
13. "Attractive city fashion show," *Irish Times,* 19 March 1947, p. 4.
14. "Rainstorm again halts attack on tillage arrears," *Irish Times,* 7 April 1947, p. 1.
15. "Most of grain crop now sown," *Irish Independent,* 7 April 1947, p. 7.
16. "Grow food to avoid famine," *Sunday Independent,* 23 March 1947, p. 4.
17. "Grow food to avoid famine," *Sunday Independent,* 23 March 1947, p. 4.
18. "Dublin is in need of more plots," *Sunday Independent,* 13 April 1947, p. 1.
19. "Sunshine brought Dubliners to sea and hillside," *Irish Times,* 14 April 1947, p. 1.
20. "Sunshine brought Dubliners to sea and hillside," *Irish Times,* 14 April 1947, p. 1.
21. "Week-end stolen from June," *Irish Independent,* 14 April 1947, p. 5.
22. *Irish Times,* 14 April 1947, p. 1.
23. *Irish Independent,* 7 April 1947, p. 7.
24. Turtle Bunbury, "So you think it's freezing?" *Irish Daily Mail,* 9 January 2010, p. 46.
25. Ora E. Kilroe, "After the storm," *Irish Press,* 22 March 1947, p. 3.
26. "A year of disappointments," *Irish Independent,* 31 December 1947, p. 4.
27. "Sun takes citizens to seaside," *Irish Times,* 2 June 1947, p. 1.
28. "Sun takes citizens to seaside," *Irish Times,* 2 June 1947, p. 1.
29. Turtle Bunbury, "So you think it's freezing?" *Irish Daily Mail,* 9 January 2010, p. 46.
30. Turtle Bunbury, "So you think it's freezing?" *Irish Daily Mail,* 9 January 2010, p. 46.
31. "1947 a year of weather extremes," *Irish Independent,* 31 December 1947, p. 6.
32. "People 'lost' in their hills," *Irish Press,* 14 February 1947, p. 6.

Chapter 14 (p. 347–9)

1. "1947," *Irish Press*, 31 December 1947, p. 4.
2. "People 'lost' in their hills," *Irish Press*, 14 February 1947, p. 6.
3. "Dublin went over the top," *Evening Herald*, 24 December 1947, p. 1.
4. "Gas situation may be eased," *Evening Herald*, 24 December 1947, p. 1.
5. "A year of disappointments," *Irish Independent*, 31 December 1947, p. 4.
6. "1947 a year of weather extremes," *Irish Independent*, 31 December 1947, p. 6.
7. "An Irishman's Diary," *Irish Times*, 31 December 1947, p. 3.
8. "Open letter to an old friend," *Irish Press*, 31 December 1947, p. 4.

BIBLIOGRAPHY

Newspapers and periodicals
Cuisle na Tíre (monthly publication of Córas Iompair Éireann, Dublin)
Carlow Nationalist
Dublin Evening Mail
Evening Herald
Irish Daily Mail
Irish Independent
Irish Mountain Log
Irish Press
Irish Times
Meteorological Magazine
Sligo Weekender
Sunday Independent
Weather
Time Magazine

Books
Bracken, Pauline, *Light of Other Days: A Dublin Childhood*, Dublin: Mercier Press, 1992.
Cameron, Sir Charles A., *How the Poor Live*, Dublin: privately printed, 1904.
Chart, D. A., *The Story of Dublin*, London: Dent, 1932.
Citizens' Housing Council, *Report on Slum Clearance, 1938*, Dublin: Citizens' Housing Council, 1938.
Clarke, Desmond, *Dublin*, London: Batsford, 1977.
Cosgrove, Dillon, *North Dublin City and Environs*, Dublin: M. H. Gill and Sons, 1909.
Cronin, Anthony, *Dead As Doornails: Chronicle of Life*, Dublin: Poolbeg Press, 1976.
Crosbie, Paddy, *"Your Dinner's Poured Out!": Boyhood in the Twenties in a Dublin That Has Disappeared*, Dublin: O'Brien Press, 1982.
Cullen, Bill, *It's a Long Way from Penny Apples*, Cork: Mercier Press, 2001.
Daly, Mary, *Dublin: The Deposed Capital*, Cork: Cork University Press, 1984.
Dickinson, Page L., *The Dublin of Yesterday*, London: Methuen, 1929.
Dickson, David, *Arctic Ireland*, Belfast: White Row Press, 1997.
Fagan, Terry, and Savage, Ben, *All Around the Diamond*, Dublin: North Inner City Folklore Project [1994].
Johnston, Máirín, *Around the Banks of Pimlico*, Dublin: Attic Press, 1973.
Kearns, Kevin C., *The Bombing of Dublin's North Strand, 1941*, Dublin: Gill & Macmillan, 2009.
Kearns, Kevin C., *Dublin's Lost Heroines*, Dublin: Gill & Macmillan, 2004.
Kearns, Kevin C., *Dublin Tenement Life: An Oral History*, Dublin: Gill & Macmillan, 1994.
Kearns Blain, Angeline, *Stealing Sunlight: Growing Up in Irishtown*, Dublin: A. and A. Farmar, 2000.
Laskin, David, *The Children's Blizzard*, New York: Harper-Collins, 2004.

Lewis, G. C., *Observations on the Habits of the Labouring Classes in Dublin*, Dublin: Miliken and Sons, 1936.

Longford, Christine, *A Biography of Dublin*, London: Methuen, 1936.

Mac Thomáis, Éamonn, *Gur Cakes and Coal Blocks*, Dublin: O'Brien Press, 1976.

Manley, Gordon, *Climate and the British Scene* (New Naturalist, No. 22), London: Collins, 1952; reprinted London: Fontana, 1971.

Neary, Bernard, *North of the Liffey: A Character Sketchbook*, Dublin: Lenhar Publications, 1984.

Newman Devin, Edith, *Speaking Volumes: A Dublin Childhood*, Belfast: Blackstaff Press, 2000.

O'Brien, Joseph V., *Dear, Dirty Dublin: A City in Distress, 1899–1916*, Berkeley: University of California Press, 1982.

O'Donovan, John, *Life by the Liffey: A Kaleidoscope of Dubliners*, Dublin: Gill & Macmillan, 1986.

O'Keefe, Phil, *Down Cobbled Streets: A Liberties Childhood*, Dingle: Brandon Publishers, 1978.

Peter, Ada, *Dublin Fragments: Social and Historic*, Dublin: Hodges, Figgis, 1925.

Redmond, Lar, *Show Us the Moon: The Dublin Days of Lar Redmond*, Dingle: Brandon Books, 1988.

Rutty, John, *An Essay towards a Natural History of the County of Dublin . . .*, Dublin: printed for the author, 1772.

Uris, Jill, *Ireland Revisited*, New York: Doubleday, 1982.

Articles

"Action stations!" *Irish Times*, 18 March 1947, p. 5.

"After the storm," *Irish Press*, 22 March 1947, p. 3.

"Air effort to relieve 'lost' mountain hamlets fails," *Irish Press*, 1 March 1947, p. 1.

"All-out drive to repair blizzard havoc," *Irish Press*, 27 February 1947, p. 1.

"Another blizzard in south and east," *Irish Independent*, 17 March 1947, p. 5.

"Appalling scenes of want in Dublin," *Dublin Evening Mail*, 25 February 1947, p. 2.

"An appeal for the poor," *Sunday Independent*, 9 March 1947, p. 6.

"Attractive city fashion show," *Irish Times*, 19 March 1947, p. 4.

"The bad weather made us good neighbours," *Irish Press*, 29 March 1947, p. 3.

"Battening on the poor," *Evening Herald*, 14 March 1947, p. 4.

"Bid to relieve Roundwood fails again," *Irish Press*, 27 February 1947, p. 1.

"Bid to save starving livestock," *Irish Times*, 4 March 1947, p. 1.

"Big harvest losses in many areas," *Irish Independent*, 5 September 1947, p. 5.

"Big Jim crosses the city," *Irish Press*, 4 February 1947, p. 1.

"Big tillage hold-up by floods," *Irish Press*, 17 March 1947, p. 1.

"Bleak fuel prospect," *Evening Herald*, 24 February 1947, p. 1.

"Blizzard," *Cuisle na Tíre*, April 1947, p. 31–6.

"The blizzard," *Irish Daily Independent*, 15 January 1895, p. 5.

"Blizzard's big damage," *Irish Press*, 27 February 1947, p. 5.

"Blizzard sweeps Ireland," *Irish Independent*, 3 February 1947, p. 1.

"Blizzard sweeps the North," *Irish Times*, 13 March 1947, p. 1.

"Bodies of two victims found," *Irish Independent*, 4 March 1947, p. 2.

Booth, George, "Winter 1947 in the British Isles," *Weather*, vol. 62, no. 2 (March 2007), p. 61–7.

"Bread and flour to be rationed from January 18," *Irish Press*, 4 January 1947, p. 1.

"Breaking through to ice-bound west," *Irish Independent*, 3 March 1947, p. 5.

"Britain aids 'parachute food' plan," *Irish Times*, 7 March 1947, p. 1.

"Britain stops coal exports from N.W. ports," *Irish Times*, 7 February 1947, p. 1.

"British moves on coal crux," *Irish Press*, 13 February 1947, p. 1.

"The broken Bolivar lies on Kish Bank," *Irish Press*, 6 March 1947, p. 1.

Bunbury, Turtle, "So you think it's freezing?" *Irish Daily Mail*, 9 January 2010, p. 46.

"Bus service returning to normal," *Irish Times*, 8 March 1947, p. 1.

"Cable sets the weather experts buzzing," *Evening Herald*, 24 February 1947, p. 1.

"The calender says spring—but the weather says winter," *Sunday Independent*, 16 March 1947, p. 1.

"Captain boards wrecked Bolivar," *Irish Press*, 7 March 1947, p. 1.

Carlow Nationalist, 19 November 1999.

"Cattle and sheep die of starvation," *Irish Press*, 6 March 1947, p. 1.

"Christmas," *Irish Press*, 24 December 1947, p. 4.

"City's poor hit hard by fuel crisis," *Irish Times*, 15 February 1947, p. 3.

"City thaws as country freezes," *Irish Times*, 1 February 1947, p. 1.

"Cold comfort from Government," *Irish Independent*, 25 February 1947, p. 4.

"Coldest night for several years," *Evening Herald*, 29 January 1947, p. 1.

"Cold said to have doubled death-rate," *Irish Times*, 19 February 1947, p. 3.

Collie, Keith J., "1947: The Year of the Big Snow," *Irish Mountain Log*, winter 2007, p. 28–9.

"Conditions beggar description," *Evening Herald*, 26 February 1947, p. 1.

"Cork wins another title," *Irish Independent*, 2 September 1946, p. 5.

"Corporation move in fuel crisis," *Irish Press*, 27 February 1947, p. 5.

"Country hit by fierce blizzard," *Irish Independent*, 26 February 1947, p. 5.

"Country is again in grip of frost and snow," *Irish Press*, 21 February 1947, p. 1.

"Country is facing 'first class' fuel crisis," *Irish Press*, 13 February 1947, p. 1.

"Country shocked by fuel statement," *Irish Independent*, 14 February 1947, p. 5.

"County Wicklow hills trek," *Irish Independent*, 8 February 1947, p. 7.

"Crazy weather at the week-end," *Irish Press*, 10 March 1947, p. 1.

"Critical days for Ireland," *Irish Independent*, 14 September 1946, p. 5.

Cronin, Timothy, "It was far worse in 1740," *Irish Press*, 7 February 1963, p. 9.

Crosby, Thomas, "Memories of the 1947 Big Snow live on," *Sligo Weekender*, 27 January 2004.

"Cut off by snow," *Irish Times*, 6 February 1947, p. 4.

"The daddy of them all: The '47 Snow," *Glens of Antrim Historical Project*.

"Dangerous quarry pool may be filled in," *Irish Times*, 4 March 1947, p. 1.

"Days of gloom for house keepers," *Sunday Independent*, 12 January 1947, p. 7

"The day when the shamrock was 'dear'," *Evening Herald*, 17 March 1947, p. 1.

"Death of James Larkin," *Irish Press*, 31 January 1947, p. 1.

"Death on the ice," *Dublin Evening Mail*, 3 March 1947, p. 2.

de Búrca, Séamus, "Growing up in Dublin," *Dublin Historical Record*, vol. 29, no. 3 (1976), p. 82–97.

"Deputies were up in stars," *Irish Independent*, 14 February 1947, p. 5.

Douglas, C. K. M., "The severe winter of 1946 to 1947," *Meteorological Magazine*, vol. 76, no. 897 (March 1947), p. 51–6.

"Drove up the mountain with camera to get some snow pictures," *Irish Press*, 28 January 1947, p. 1.

"Dublin again 'dimmed-out'," *Irish Independent*, 15, 1947, p. 7.

"Dublin boys lost in quarry hole," *Irish Independent*, 3 March 1947, p. 5.

"Dublin experiences a welcome thaw," *Evening Herald*, 24 February 1947, p. 1.

"Dublin firemen's busy year," *Irish Times*, 5 February 1947, p. 7.

"Dublin had a blizzard—and some sun," *Evening Herald*, 19 February 1947, p. 1.

"Dublin is in need of more plots," *Sunday Independent*, 13 April 1947, p.1

Dublin Opinion, March 1947, p. 7.

Dublin Opinion, April 1947, p. 48.

"Dublin paralysed by great freeze-up," *Sunday Independent*, 23 February 1947, p. 1.

"Dublin quarry pond claims three young victims," *Evening Herald*, 3 March 1947, p. 1.

"Dublin's oldest charity," *Dublin Evening Mail*, 15 March, p. 2.

"Dublin went over the top," *Evening Herald*, 24 December 1947, p. 1.

"1847–1947," *Irish Press*, 27 January 1947, p. 1.

"80, and bathed yesterday," *Irish Press*, 10 February 1947, p. 1.

"Eire expected to eke out ration with maize," *Irish Independent*, 14 January 1947, p. 5.

"End of year disillusions," *Irish Independent*, 1 January 1947, p. 3.

"E.S.B. and the fuel crisis," *Dublin Evening Mail*, 25 February 1947, p. 3.

"Experts say snow has gone," *Irish Times*, 20 February 1947, p. 4.

"Eye-witness story," *Irish Times*, 3 February 1947, p. 1.

"Farmers plan 24-hour day to ensure harvest," *Irish Times*, 18 March 1947, p. 1.

"Fate of tillage drive still in the balance," *Irish Independent*, 3 April 1947, p. 2.

"February's freakish weather," *Irish Independent*, 3 March 1947, p. 3.

"Fifty-two years ago Dublin had its 'Night of the Big Snow,'" *Sunday Independent*, 16 March 1947, p. 2.

"Fine Gael to move condemnation of Government," *Irish Times*, 25 February 1947, p. 1.

"Fine weather soon—or no harvest," *Sunday Independent*, 16 March 1947, p. 1.

"The first snow," *Irish Times*, 27 January 1947, p. 5.

"Five weeks to till 2,000,000 acres," *Sunday Independent*, 23 March 1947, p. 1.

Flood, Donal T., "The decay of Georgian Dublin," *Dublin Historical Record*, vol. 28, no. 3 (1974), p. 78–100.

"Flu sweeps city," *Irish Press*, 22 January 1947, p. 1.

"Food relief for the isolated," *Irish Press*, 5 March 1947, p. 5.

"40,000 tons of firewood logs," *Irish Press*, 1 March 1947, p. 1.

"For whom the bell tolls," *Evening Herald*, 23 January 1947, p. 4.

Foster, D. E., "Climate not changing, but we are now more vulnerable," *Irish Independent*, 13 February 1947, p. 5.

"Four-foot drifts block roads," *Irish Times*, 26 February 1947, p. 1.

"Frost takes over but snow keeps turf 'marooned,'" *Irish Press*, 30 January 1947, p. 1.

"The fuel crisis," *Irish Press*, 18 February 1947, p. 4.

"Fuel crisis developing," *Irish Independent*, 14 January 1947, p. 5.

"Fuel reserves filling gap," *Irish Press*, 28 February 1947, p. 1.

"Fuel shortages may lead to closing of C.I.E. rail system," *Irish Times*, 21 February 1947, p. 1.

"Gas situation may be eased," *Evening Herald*, 25 December 1947, p. 1.

"Good grooming," *Irish Independent*, 25 February 1947, p. 3.

"A Government plan to help farmers in present crisis," *Irish Times*, 19 March 1947, p. 1.

"Grain ship wrecked off Dublin coast," *Irish Times*, 5 March 1947, p. 1.

"Grave national emergency," *Irish Independent*, 17 March 1947, p. 4.

"Grey crows have picked out the eyes of helpless animals caught in the snow," *Irish Times*, 13 March 1947, p. 1.

"Grow more food to avoid famine," *Sunday Independent*, 23 March 1947, p. 4.

"Guinness cut supplies," *Irish Press*, 25 March 1947, p. 1.

"Gulf Stream or atom bomb blamed," *Dublin Evening Mail*, 24 February 1947, p. 3.

Halloran, Canon Martin, "People had to be dug from houses," *Sligo Weekender*, 26 October 2004.

"A happy new year," *Irish Press*, 1 January 1947, p. 3.

"Harvest army is winning battle," *Irish Independent*, 16 September 1946, p. 5.

Hawksley, G. M., "February 1947," *Weather*, vol. 2 (1947), p. 101.

"Heavy rains check tillage work in many counties," *Irish Times*, 31 March 1947, p. 1.

"Heavy weather for Moscow," *Dublin Evening Mail*, 10 March 1947, p. 3.

"Hero of many sea adventures," *Irish Independent*, 7 March 1947, p. 5.

Hoey, J. F., "Gas from turf," *Dublin Evening Mail*, 21 February 1947, p. 4.

"The hopes of Dubliners are now dashed," *Evening Herald*, 25 February 1947, p. 1.

"Hopes of saving grain gone," *Irish Press*, 6 March 1947, p. 1.

"How Dubliners and visitors spent the day," *Irish Press*, 18 March 1947, p. 5.

"How the poor are housed in Dublin," *Irish Builder*, 1 February 1899, p. 16.

"Hunger," *Evening Herald*, 6 February 1947, p. 2.

"Hungry deer," *Irish Press*, 10 March 1947, p. 1.

"Ice holds canal boats," *Irish Press*, 28 February 1947, p. 1.

"The importance of optimism," *Sunday Independent*, 16 February 1947, p. 4.

"Influenza epidemic threatened," *Irish Times*, 14 April 1947, p. 1.

"In the same boat," *Irish Times*, 22 March 1947, p. 7.

"Ireland is threatened by worst flooding in many years," *Irish Times*, 17 March 1947, p. 1.

"Ireland lashed by sleet and snow to-day," *Evening Herald*, 25 February 1947, p. 1.

"Irish astronomer's 1946 observations," *Irish Press*, 24 January 1947, p. 5.

"An Irishman's Diary," *Irish Times*, 13 March 1947, p. 5.

"An Irishman's Diary," *Irish Times*, 28 March 1947, p. 5.

"An Irishman's Diary," *Irish Times*, 31 December 1947, p. 3.

"Irish ship aground in gale," *Irish Independent*, 3 February 1947, p. 1.

"Isolated in Dublin," *Sunday Independent*, 9 March 1947, p. 4.

"Isolation and grievance," *Western People*, 8 March 1947, p. 1.

"'Jim' Larkin dies—Seán O'Casey tribute," *Irish Times*, 31 January 1947, p. 1.

Keating, Mary Frances, "Days of gloom for housekeepers," *Sunday Independent*, 12 January 1947, p. 7.

"Keep the home fires burning," *Evening Herald*, 8 February 1947, p. 4.

Kelly, Anna, "I join the fuel queue," *Irish Press*, 27 February 1947, p. 3.

Kilroe, Ora E., "After the storm," *Irish Press*, 22 March 1947, p. 3.

"King Frost still reigns," *Irish Independent*, 22 February 1947, p. 2.

"Landslides disrupt rail services," *Irish Times*, 18 March 1947, p. 1.

"Large areas are still isolated," *Irish Independent*, 27 February 1947, p. 5.

Lee, Margaret, "Do not let wet turf get you down—it can be burned," *Irish Press*, 14 February 1947, p. 3.

"The lesson," *Irish Press*, 25 February 1947, p. 4.

Letters to the Editor, *Dublin Evening Mail*, 24 February 1947, p. 2.

Letters to the Editor, *Dublin Evening Mail*, 11 March 1947, p. 2.

Letters to the Editor, *Irish Times*, 16 April 1947, p. 5.

"Lifeboats dash in swirling snow," *Irish Press*, 29 January 1947, p. 1.

"Lightning hits public house; snowstorms," *Irish Press*, 13 January 1947, p. 1.

"Lights of Dublin," *Evening Herald*, 6 March 1947, p. 4.

"Like Steppes of Siberia," *Irish Independent*, 4 March 1947, p. 5.

"Long hill drifts beat jeep," *Irish Press*, 26 February 1947, p. 1.

"Lord Mountevans lost every suit in the Bolivar," *Irish Times*, 10 March 1947, p. 1.

Lysaght, Moira, "My Dublin," *Dublin Historical Record*, vol. 30, no. 4 (1977), p. 122–35.

"Main roads dangerous after heavy snowfalls," *Irish Times*, 22 February 1947, p. 1.

McGrath, Fergal, "Houses for the people," *Studies*, June 1932, p. 269–82.

Manley, Gordon, "Looking back at last winter: February 1947: Its place in meteorological history," *Weather*, vol. 2 (1947), p. 267.

"Many street fall casualties," *Irish Times*, 22 February 1947, p. 1.

"March ends in tillage set-back," *Irish Press*, 31 March 1947, p. 1.

"Midlands Suffer Badly," *Irish Independent*, 6 September 1946, p. 5.

"More snow sweeps southern counties," *Irish Press*, 5 March 1947, p. 1.

"Most of grain crop now sown," *Irish Independent*, 7 April 1947, p. 7.

"Move to aid stock dying in snow belt," *Irish Press*, 4 March 1947, p. 5.

"Mr. de Valera asks for help to end partition," *Irish Times*, 18 March 1947, p. 1.

"Mr. de Valera's message to Birmingham," *Irish Press*, 17 March 1947, p. 1.

"National crisis," *Dublin Evening Mail*, 25 February 1947, p. 2.

"A new form of frostbite," *Evening Herald*, 17 February 1947, p. 4.

"News from the zoo," *Irish Times*, 13 February 1947, p. 3.

"1947," *Irish Press*, 31 December 1947, p. 4.

"1947 a year of weather extremes," *Irish Independent*, 31 December 1947, p. 6.

Nolan, Jim, "The Big Snow of '47," Archives, *Carlow Nationalist*, 24 April 2003.

"No ordinary crisis," *Irish Independent*, 16 September 1946, p. 7.

"No time to be lost," *Irish Independent*, 9 September 1946, p. 7.

O'Flaherty, Ken, "Looking back: Dr Ken O'Flaherty MB Bch BAO '52 recalls the blizzard of '47," *UCD Connections*, 7 (autumn–winter 2001), p. 39–41.

O'Hegarty, P. S., "The blizzard had a warning," *Sunday Independent*, 9 March 1947, p. 4.

"Oil fuel may keep industries going," *Irish Times*, 15 February 1947, p. 1.

"Only united effort can get crops in," *Irish Press*, 7 March 1947, p. 1.

"On nothing," *Irish Press*, 26 February 1947, p. 4.

"Open letter to an old friend," *Irish Press*, 31 December 1947, p. 4.

"Our duty to the birds," *Irish Independent*, 17 March 1947, p. 4.

"Outlook for farmers is worst yet," *Irish Times*, 15 March 1947, p. 1.

"Output is greatest need," *Irish Press*, 31 January 1947, p. 1.

"Passengers dug for eight hours on road to Sligo," *Sunday Independent*, 2 March 1947, p. 1.

"Peculiar weather," *Time*, 31 March 1947.

"People lost in their hills," *Irish Press*, 14 February 1947, p. 6.

"People's ordeal in frozen Wicklow," *Sunday Independent*, 9 March 1947, p. 1.

"Phoenix Park trees to be cut," *Irish Times*, 28 February 1947, p. 1.

"A playboy and a prophecy," *Irish Press*, 26 February 1947, p. 4.

"A plea for the old," *Irish Independent*, 14 February 1947, p. 7.

"Plight for barge crews at Edenderry," *Irish Independent*, 28 February 1947, p. 2.

"Plight of County Wicklow residents," *Irish Independent*, 7 February 1947, p. 5.

"Pole tells of loss of collier," *Irish Times*, 15 February 1947, p. 1.

"Prophets and the weather," *Evening Herald*, 21 February 1947, p. 4.

"Quarry pond tragedy," *Evening Herald*, 11 March 1947, p. 3.

"'Quickfire 'flu epidemic," *Irish Press*, 4 February 1947, p. 7.

"Rail restrictions hit trade at Dublin cattle market," *Irish Independent*, 20 February 1947, p. 5.

"Rainstorm again halts attack on tillage areas," *Irish Times*, 7 April 1947, p. 1.

"Rain storm causes wide havoc," *Irish Independent*, 13 August 1946, p. 5.

"Rescuers fighting snow in bid to reach sick family," *Irish Times*, 8 March 1947, p. 1.

"Rheumatic fever a heart crippler," *Sunday Independent*, 12 January 1947, p. 7.

"Roundwood kept its lights on," *Irish Press*, 7 March 1947, p. 5.

"Roundwood relieved after five weeks," *Irish Independent*, 7 March 1947, p. 5.

"Royal Meteorological Society News: The Severe Winter," *Weather*, vol. 2 (1947), p. 89.

"Search for 'lost' lorries," *Irish Press*, 1 March 1947, p. 7.

"Second seaman from collier washed ashore," *Irish Times*, 14 February 1947, p. 1.

"Serious loss of stores," *Irish Independent*, 18 March 1947, p. 6.

"7,250-ton Irish ship runs aground off Co. Cork," *Irish Times*, 3 February 1947, p. 1.

"Shamrock enters black market," *Dublin Evening Mail*, 17 March 1947, p. 3.

"Shaw's solution for fuel crisis," *Irish Times*, 15 February 1947, p. 1.

"Sheep still lost in mountains," *Irish Press*, 21 February 1947, p. 1.

Sheridan, John D., "An article on the weather," *Irish Independent*, 22 March 1947, p. 6.

"Ship runs aground off Dublin," *Irish Press*, 5 March 1947, p. 1.

"Ships held up by ice," *Irish Independent*, 1 January 1947, p. 5.

"Shortage of fuel starts crisis in Irish industry," *Irish Times*, 6 February 1947, p. 1.

"Skater drowned in River Erne," *Irish Press*, 6 March 1947, p. 1.

"The slum peril," *Daily Nation*, 8 September 1898, p. 5.

"Snowbound buses and motorists released," *Dublin Evening Mail*, 28 February 1947, p. 6.

"Snowed-up convoy enters Sligo," *Irish Independent*, 4 March 1947, p. 5.

"Snowed-up families dig their way out," *Irish Times*, 27 February 1947, p.1.

"Snow menace," *Evening Herald*, 3 February 1947, p. 4.

"Sowing the crops," *Irish Press*, 20 March 1947, p. 4.

"Spain game stopped as intruders rush pitch," *Irish Press*, 3 March 1947, p. 1.

"The stars and the weather," *Dublin Evening Mail*, 25 February 1947, p. 2.

"State urged to free army for tree cutting," *Irish Times*, 27 February 1947, p. 5.

"Stock starve in Dublin Mountains," *Irish Press*, 3 March 1947, p. 1.

"Subsiding floods show trail of damage," *Irish Press*, 18 March 1947, p. 5.

"Success at third attempt," *Irish Independent*, 11 February 1947, p. 5.

"Sufferings of the old folk," *Dublin Evening Mail*, 17 March 1947, p. 2.

"Sun actually shown to-day," *Evening Herald*, 22 February 1947, p. 1.

"Sunshine beating snow," *Irish Times*, 3 March 1947, p. 1.

"Sunshine brings problems in blizzard's wake," *Irish Times*, 28 February 1947, p. 1.

"Sunshine brought Dubliners to sea and hillside," *Irish Times*, 14 April 1947, p. 1.

"Sunshine follows night of snow," *Irish Times*, 24 February 1947, p. 1.

"Sun takes citizens to seaside," *Irish Times*, 2 June 1947, p. 1.

"Supplies," *Irish Press*, 14 January, 1947, p. 5.

"Suspend tourist trade called for by Dr. O'Higgins," *Irish Times*, 22 March 1947, p. 7.

Sweetman, Miriam, "30 men had to dig path to grave," *Sligo Weekender*, 11 April 2006.

"Take us out of this horrible place," *Irish Press*, 2 October 1936, p. 9.

"The Taoiseach 30 years a Dáil member," *Irish Press*, 4 February 1947, p. 7.

"Tatler," *Ballina Herald*, March 1947.

"Tenement fire hazards," *Irish Press*, 7 October 1936, p. 9.

"A tenement scene," *Dublin Evening Mail*, 24 February 1947, p. 2.

"Thaw follows another night of frost," *Evening Herald*, 31 January 1947, p. 1.

"3 boys feared drowned in quarry pond," *Irish Times*, 3 March 1947, p. 1.

"Tillage drive now under way," *Irish Independent*, 28 March 1947, p. 4.

"Tons of snow," *Dublin Evening Mail*, 3 February 1947, p. 2.

"Traffic obstructing thoughtlessness," *Irish Times*, 17 March 1947, p. 3.

"Transport, electricity and phones disorganised," *Irish Times*, 27 February 1947, p. 1.

"Tribute to the bus drivers," *Irish Independent*, 28 February 1947, p. 4.

"Tribute to the roundsmen," *Dublin Evening Mail*, 15 March 1947, p. 2.

"Warmer to-day but more snow likely," *Evening Herald*, 5 February 1947, p.1.

"Warm sunshine brings thaw," *Irish Independent*, 7 March 1947, p. 3.

"Waterford-bound ship overdue," *Irish Press*, 13 February 1947, p. 9.

"Weather experts differ," *Irish Independent*, 221 February 1947, p. 4.

"Weather frowned on fashions," *Irish Independent*, 9 August 1946, p. 5.

"Weather hits the Dáil," *Evening Herald*, 26 February 1947, p. 4.

"Weather report," *Evening Herald*, 8 January 1947, p. 1.

"Weather report," *Evening Herald*, 24 February 1947, p. 1.

"Weather reports," *Irish Press*, 5 March 1947, p. 5.

"Week-end of many weathers," *Irish Independent*, 24 February, p. 1.

"Week-end of wild weather," *Irish Independent*, 10 February 1947, p. 5.

"Week-end spurt to save harvest," *Irish Independent*, 14 September 1946, p. 5.

"Week-end stolen from June," *Irish Independent*, 14 April 1947, p. 5.

"Welcome to the New Year," *Irish Press*, 1 January 1947, p. 1.

"Wettest August in 16 years," *Irish Independent*, 2 September 1946, p. 5.

"Wheat crop may still give good yield," *Irish Independent*, 14 August 1946, p. 5.

"Where science fails," *Dublin Evening Mail*, 21 February 1947, p. 4.

"Wicklow men are beating the snow," *Irish Press*, 10 March 1947, p. 1.

"Wicklow villagers mob breadvan," *Dublin Evening Mail*, 28 February, 1947, p. 6.

"Widespread floods menace harvest—Appeal for volunteers," *Irish Independent*, 6 September 1946, p. 5.

"Widespread snow and frost—Blizzards slow up traffic," *Irish Independent*, 30 January 1947, p. 3.

"Wind change may improve the weather," *Irish Press*, 27 February 1947, p. 1.

"Winter tightens grip," *Evening Herald*, 29 January 1947, p. 1.

"Worst blizzard for 25 years hits Ireland," *Irish Times*, 26 February 1947, p. 1.

"A year of disappointments," *Irish Independent*, 31 December 1947, p. 4.

"Zoo monkeys down with pneumonia," *Irish Press*, 1 February 1947, p. 1.

Other documents

"The Snows of 1947," unpublished document on file at Met Éireann, no date or page cited.

Web pages

Bunbury, Turtle, "The big snows of 1947, 1963 and 1982," at turtlebunbury.com/history/history_irish/history_irish_big_snow.htm.

Wynne, Christy, "The greatest snowfall of the century," at homepage.eircom.net/~greenst/blizzardof47.html

INDEX

*Photograph numbers are indicated by the use of **bold**.*